Grand Blue Dreaming 6

PRESENTED BY KENJI INOUE & KIMITAKE YOSHIOKA

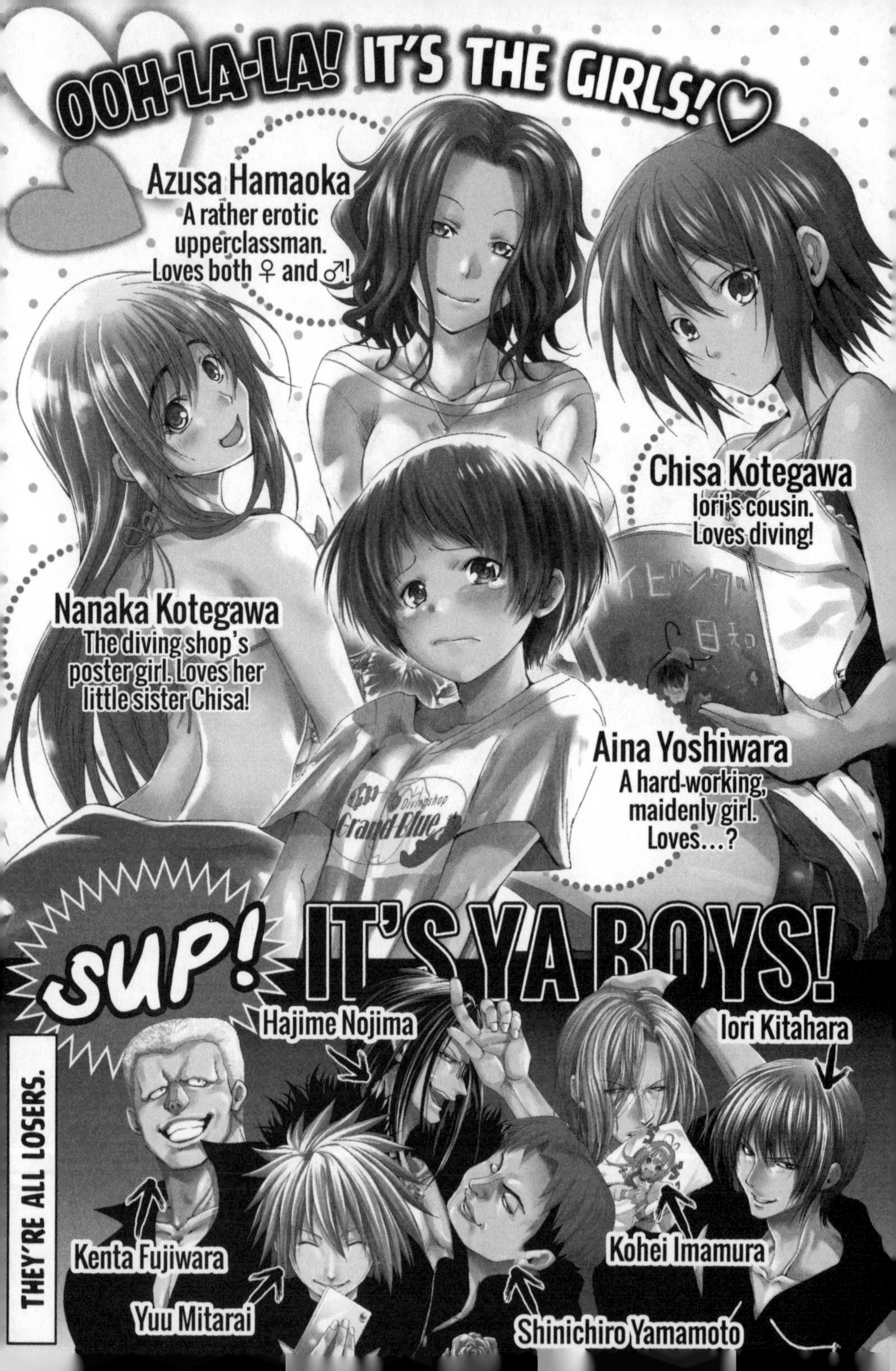
OOH-LA-LA! IT'S THE GIRLS! ♡
Azusa Hamaoka
A rather erotic upperclassman. Loves both ♀ and ♂!
Chisa Kotegawa
Iori's cousin. Loves diving!
Nanaka Kotegawa
The diving shop's poster girl. Loves her little sister Chisa!
Aina Yoshiwara
A hard-working, maidenly girl. Loves…?
Divingshop Grand Blue
SUP! IT'S YA BOYS!
THEY'RE ALL LOSERS.
Hajime Nojima
Iori Kitahara
Kenta Fujiwara
Kohei Imamura
Yuu Mitarai
Shinichiro Yamamoto

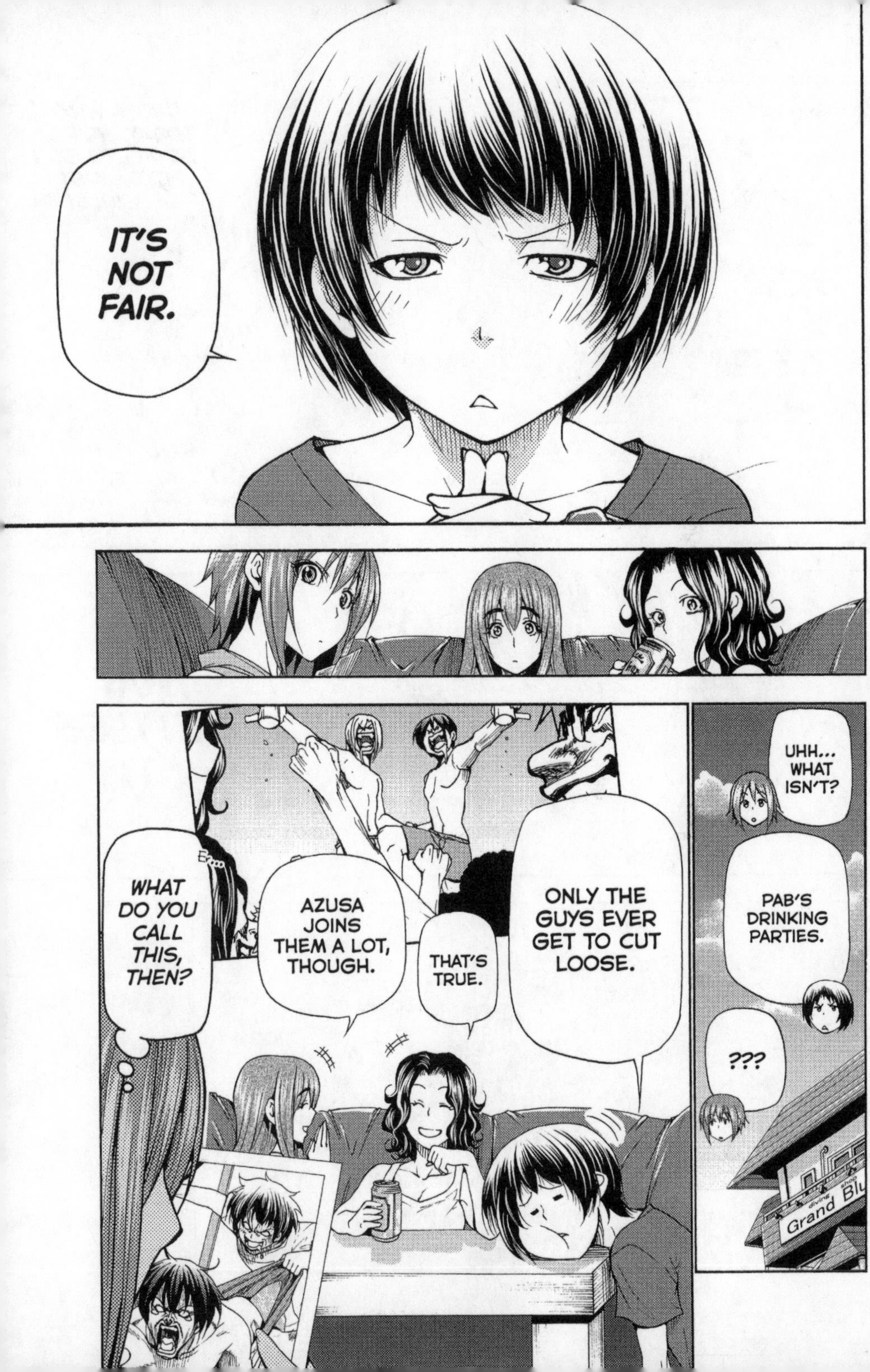
IT'S NOT FAIR.
UHH... WHAT ISN'T?
PAB'S DRINKING PARTIES.
???
Grand Blu
ONLY THE GUYS EVER GET TO CUT LOOSE.
THAT'S TRUE.
AZUSA JOINS THEM A LOT, THOUGH.
WHAT DO YOU CALL THIS, THEN?

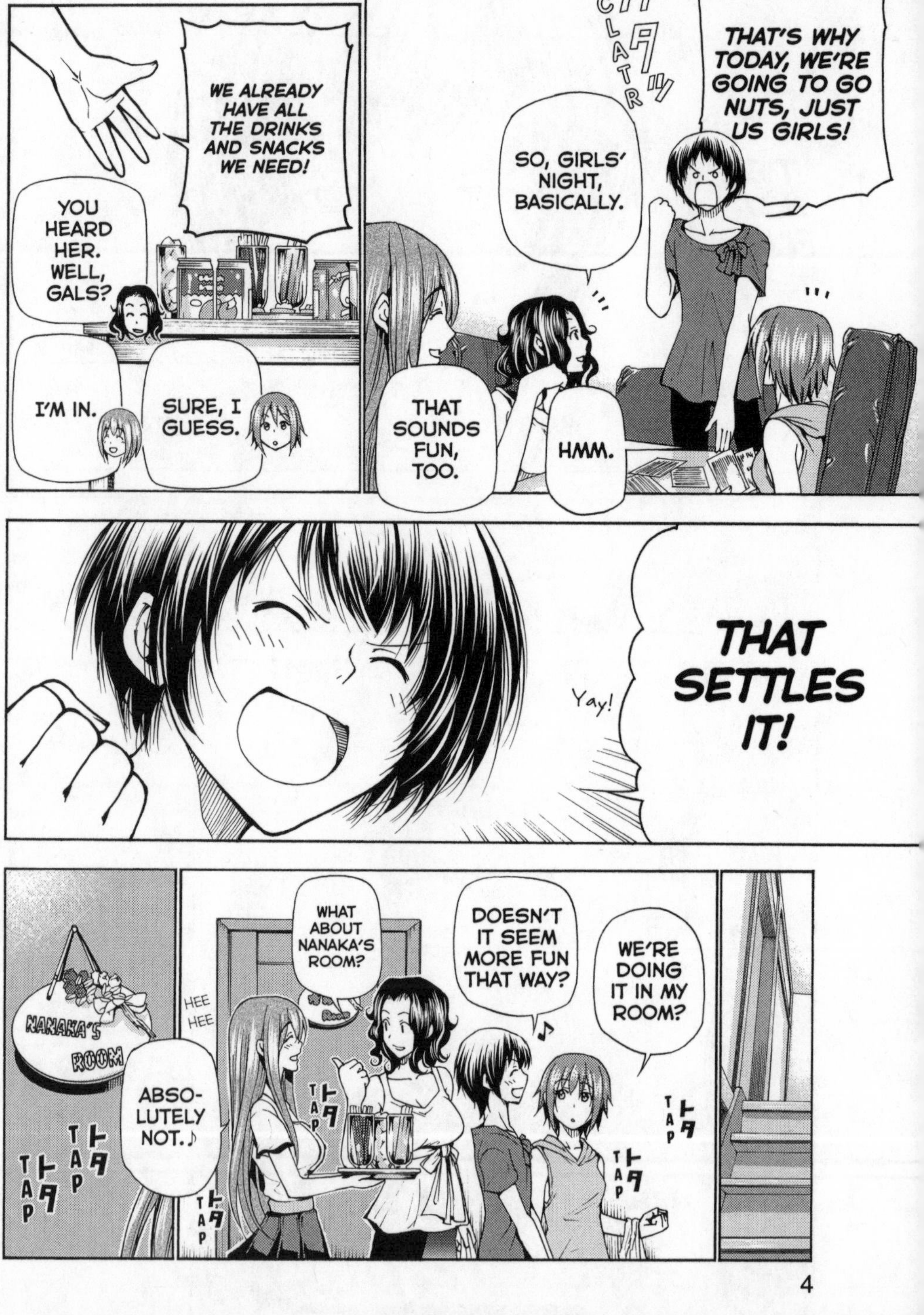

THAT'S WHY TODAY, WE'RE GOING TO GO NUTS, JUST US GIRLS!
CLATTR
SO, GIRLS' NIGHT, BASICALLY.
HMM.
THAT SOUNDS FUN, TOO.
WE ALREADY HAVE ALL THE DRINKS AND SNACKS WE NEED!
YOU HEARD HER. WELL, GALS?
SURE, I GUESS.
I'M IN.
THAT SETTLES IT!
Yay!
WE'RE DOING IT IN MY ROOM?
DOESN'T IT SEEM MORE FUN THAT WAY?
♪
WHAT ABOUT NANAKA'S ROOM?
HEE HEE
ABSO-LUTELY NOT.♪
TAP
TAP
TAP
TAP
TAP
TAP
NANAKA'S ROOM

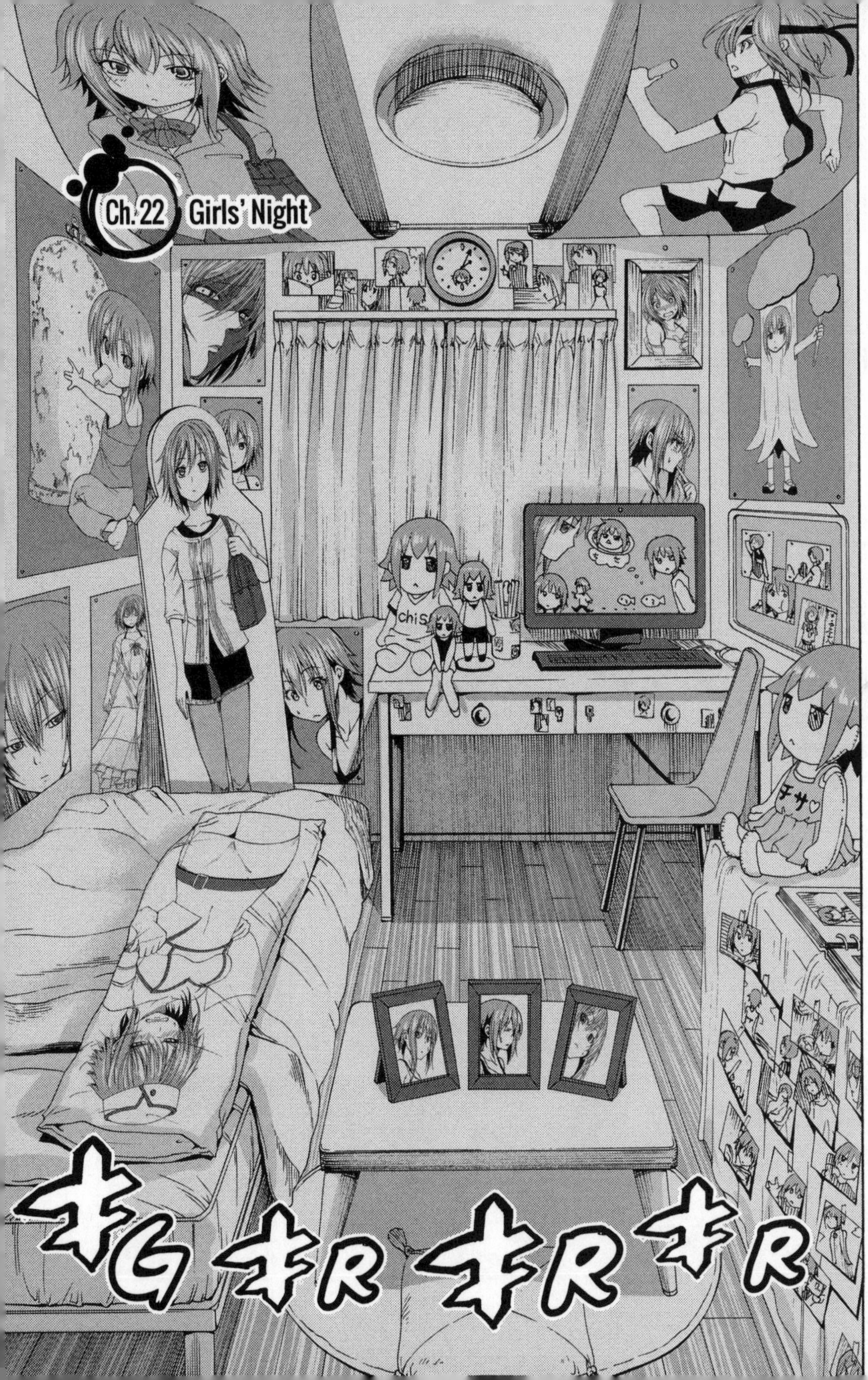
Ch. 22 Girls' Night
チサ♡

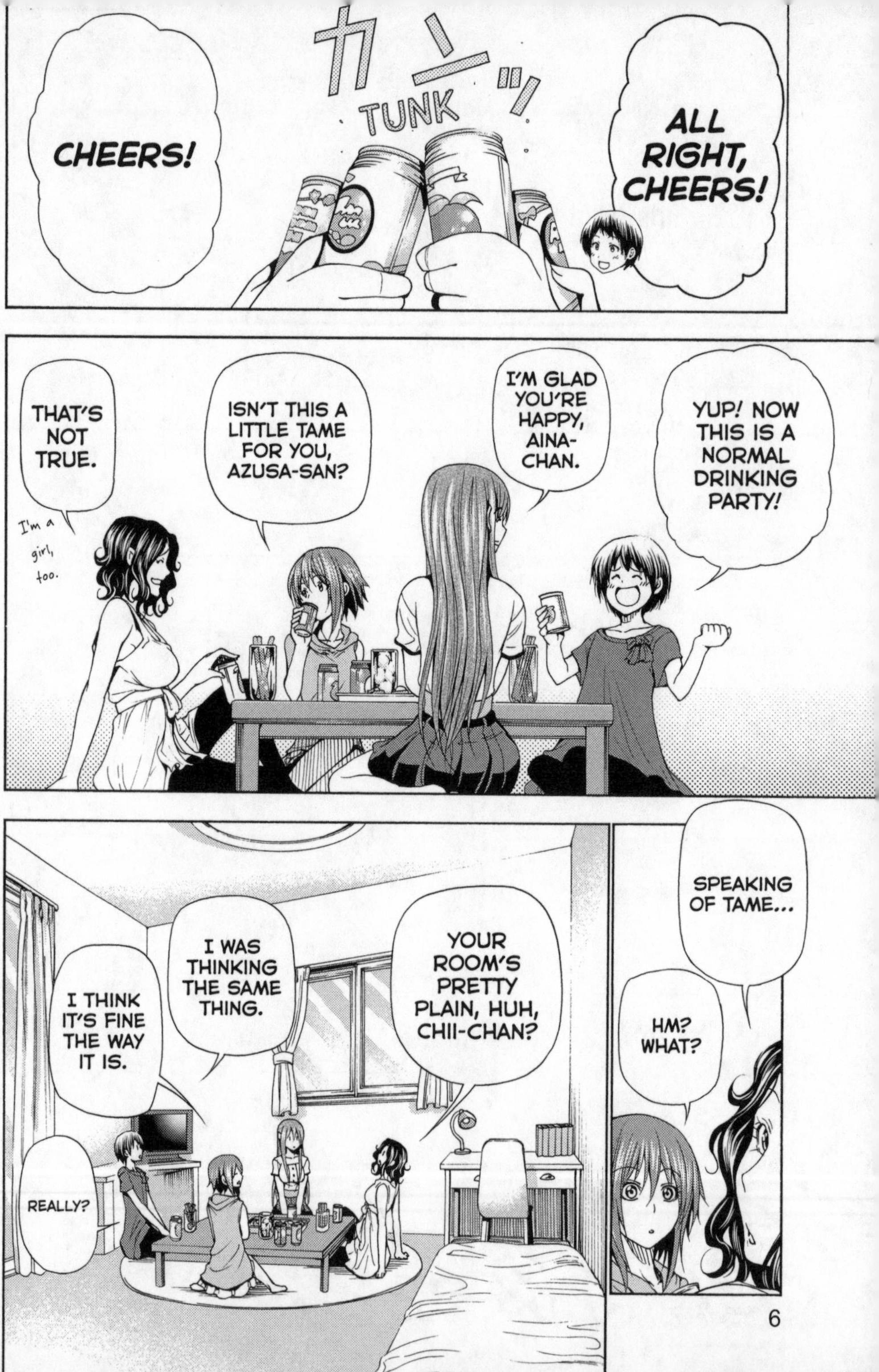
ALL RIGHT, CHEERS!
TUNK
CHEERS!
YUP! NOW THIS IS A NORMAL DRINKING PARTY!
I'M GLAD YOU'RE HAPPY, AINA-CHAN.
ISN'T THIS A LITTLE TAME FOR YOU, AZUSA-SAN?
THAT'S NOT TRUE.
I'm a girl, too.
SPEAKING OF TAME...
HM? WHAT?
YOUR ROOM'S PRETTY PLAIN, HUH, CHII-CHAN?
I WAS THINKING THE SAME THING.
I THINK IT'S FINE THE WAY IT IS.
REALLY?

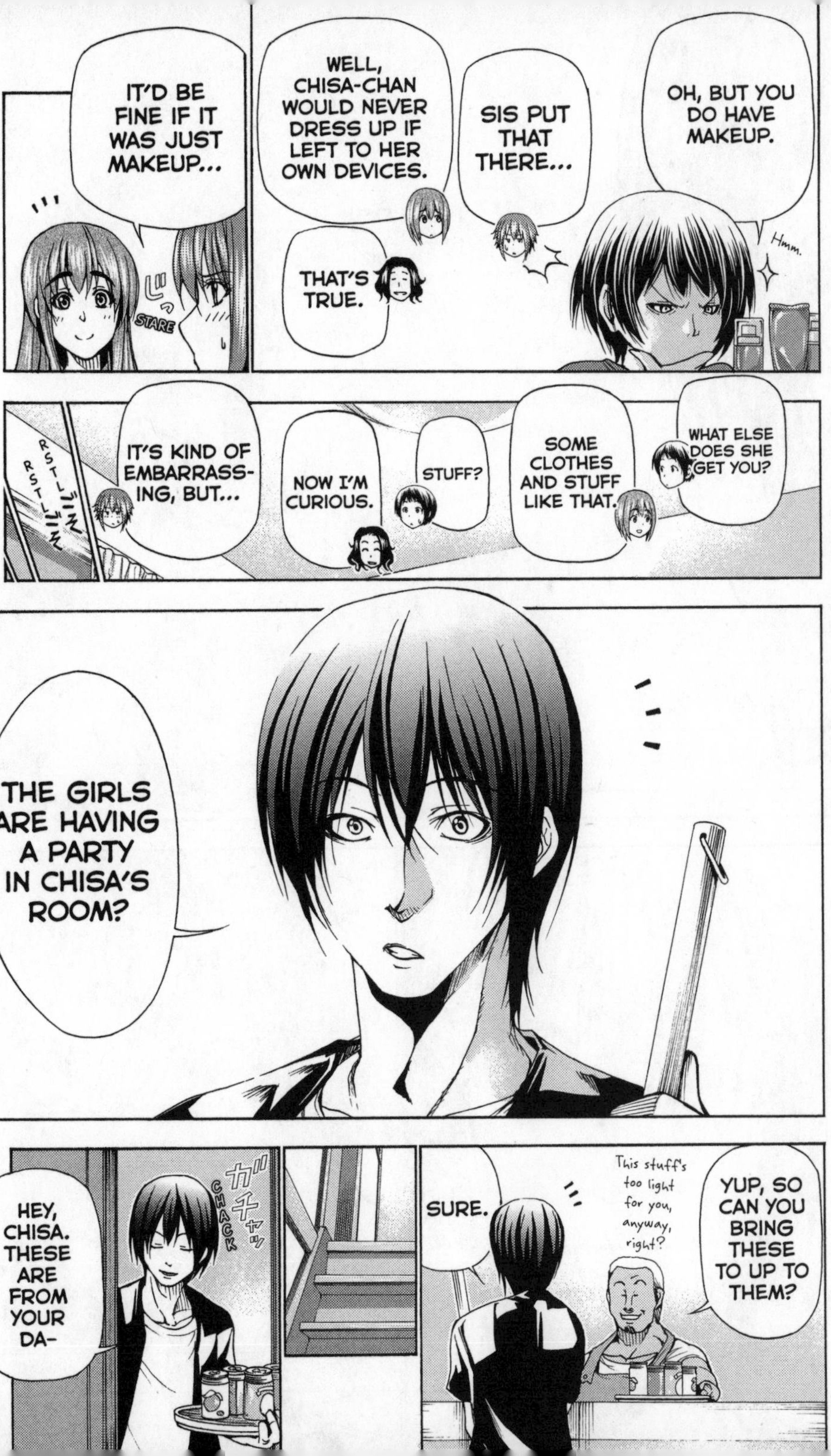
OH, BUT YOU DO HAVE MAKEUP.
Hmm.
SIS PUT THAT THERE...
WELL, CHISA-CHAN WOULD NEVER DRESS UP IF LEFT TO HER OWN DEVICES.
THAT'S TRUE.
IT'D BE FINE IF IT WAS JUST MAKEUP...
STARE
WHAT ELSE DOES SHE GET YOU?
SOME CLOTHES AND STUFF LIKE THAT.
STUFF?
NOW I'M CURIOUS.
IT'S KIND OF EMBARRASSING, BUT...
RSTL
RSTL
THE GIRLS ARE HAVING A PARTY IN CHISA'S ROOM?
YUP, SO CAN YOU BRING THESE TO UP TO THEM?
This stuff's too light for you, anyway, right?
SURE.
CHACK
HEY, CHISA. THESE ARE FROM YOUR DA-

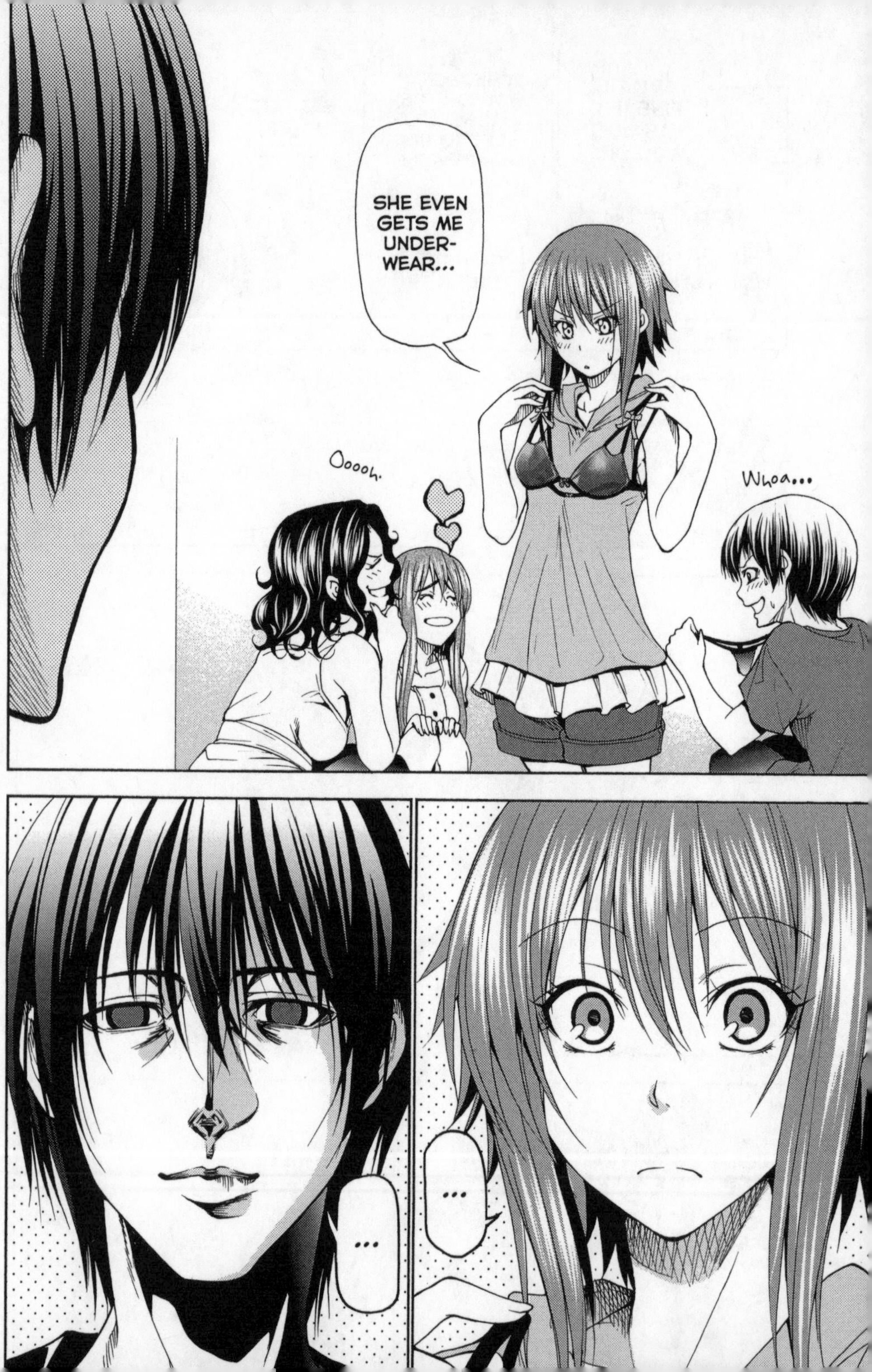
SHE EVEN GETS ME UNDER-WEAR...
Whoa...
Ooooh.
...
...

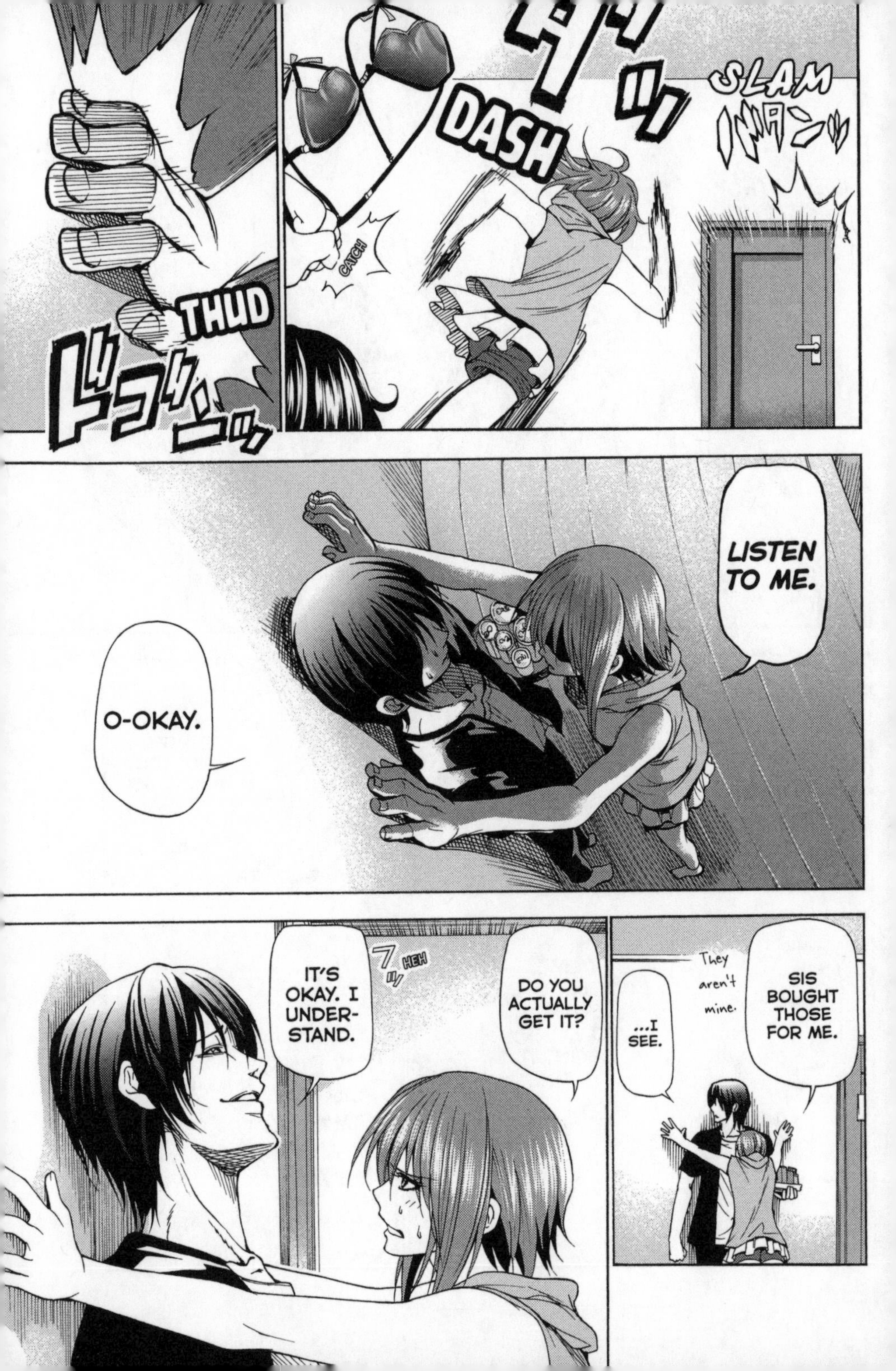
SLAM
DASH
CATCH
THUD
LISTEN TO ME.
O-OKAY.
SIS BOUGHT THOSE FOR ME.
They aren't mine.
...I SEE.
DO YOU ACTUALLY GET IT?
HEH
IT'S OKAY. I UNDERSTAND.

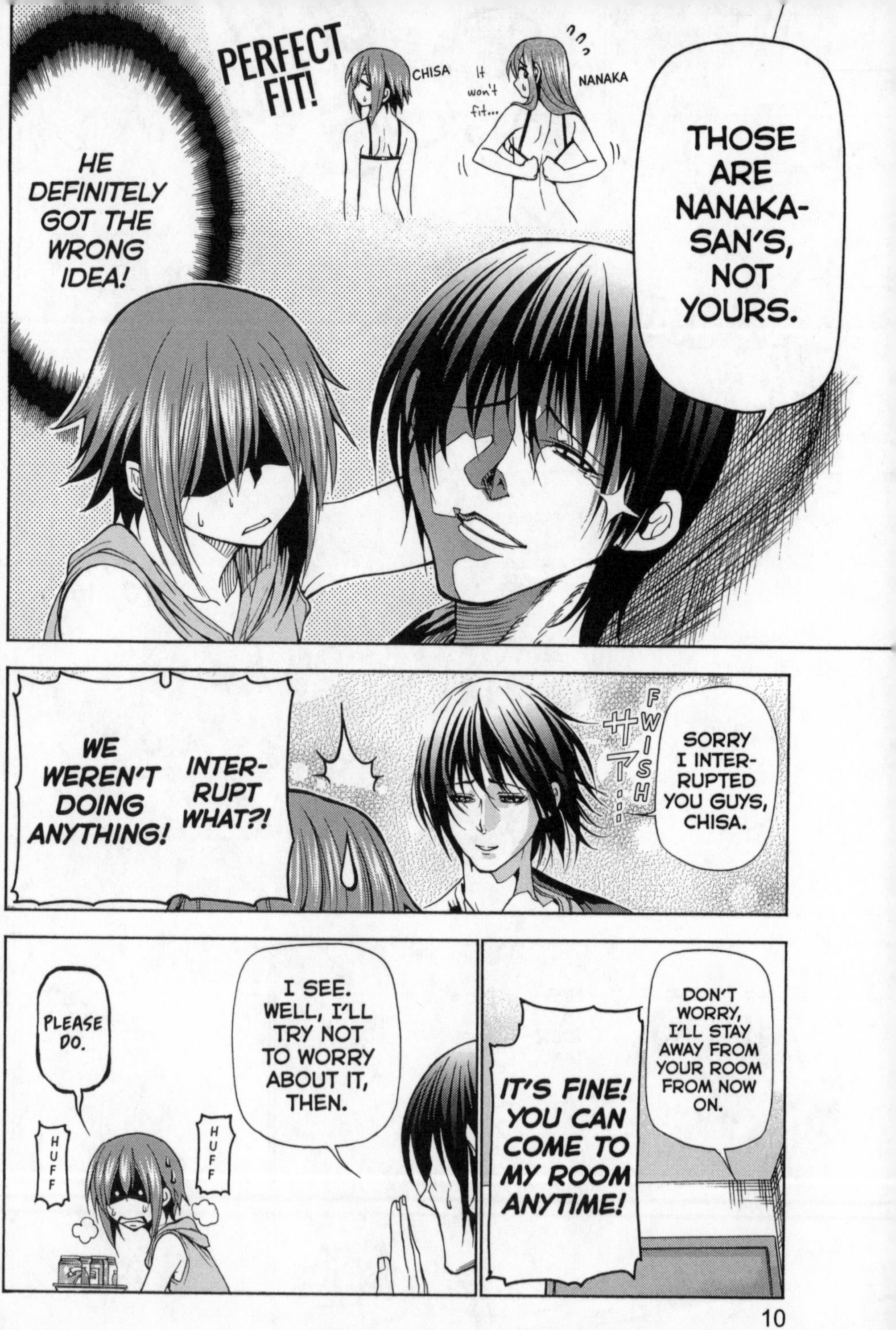
THOSE ARE NANAKA-SAN'S, NOT YOURS.
NANAKA
It won't fit...
CHISA
PERFECT FIT!
HE DEFINITELY GOT THE WRONG IDEA!
SORRY I INTER-RUPTED YOU GUYS, CHISA.
FWISH
INTER-RUPT WHAT?!
WE WEREN'T DOING ANYTHING!
DON'T WORRY, I'LL STAY AWAY FROM YOUR ROOM FROM NOW ON.
IT'S FINE! YOU CAN COME TO MY ROOM ANYTIME!
I SEE. WELL, I'LL TRY NOT TO WORRY ABOUT IT, THEN.
HUFF
HUFF
PLEASE DO.

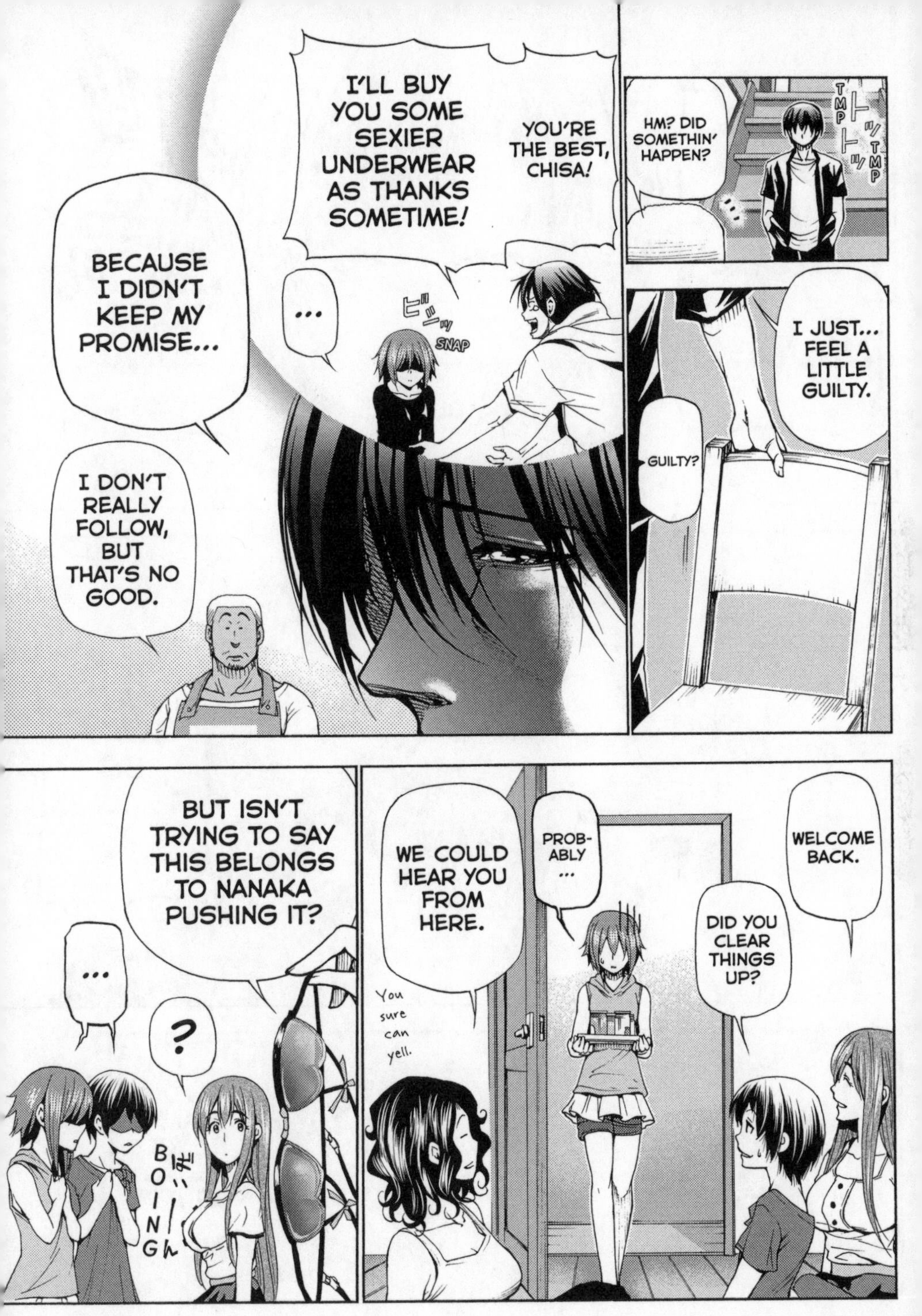
TMP TMP
HM? DID SOMETHIN' HAPPEN?
...
I JUST... FEEL A LITTLE GUILTY.
GUILTY?
I'LL BUY YOU SOME SEXIER UNDERWEAR AS THANKS SOMETIME!
YOU'RE THE BEST, CHISA!
...
SNAP
BECAUSE I DIDN'T KEEP MY PROMISE...
I DON'T REALLY FOLLOW, BUT THAT'S NO GOOD.
WELCOME BACK.
DID YOU CLEAR THINGS UP?
PROBABLY...
WE COULD HEAR YOU FROM HERE.
You sure can yell.
BUT ISN'T TRYING TO SAY THIS BELONGS TO NANAKA PUSHING IT?
?
...
BOING

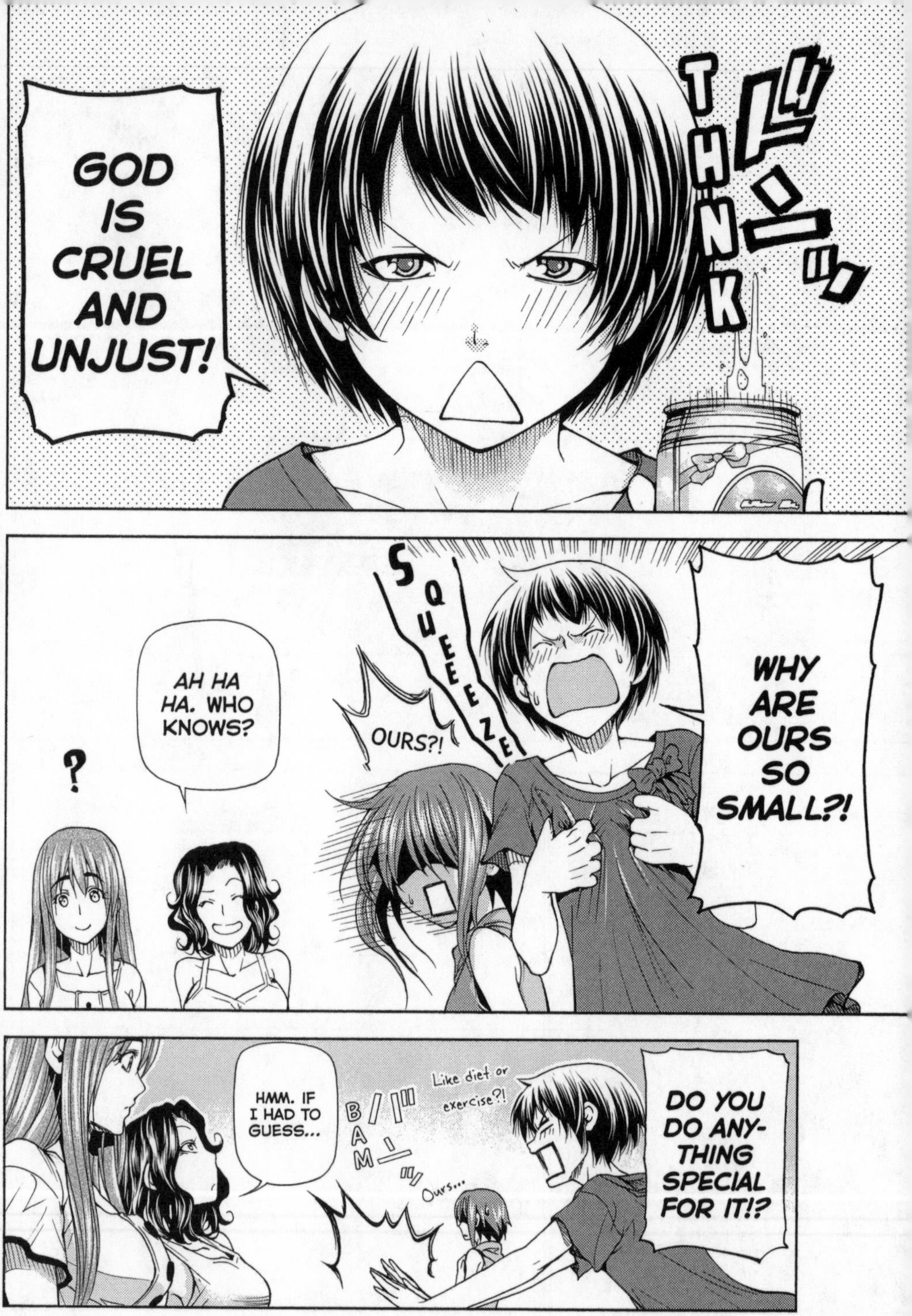
THUNK
GOD IS CRUEL AND UNJUST!
WHY ARE OURS SO SMALL?!
SQUEEEEZE
OURS?!
AH HA HA. WHO KNOWS?
?
DO YOU DO ANY-THING SPECIAL FOR IT!?
Like diet or exercise?!
BAM
Ours...
HMM. IF I HAD TO GUESS...

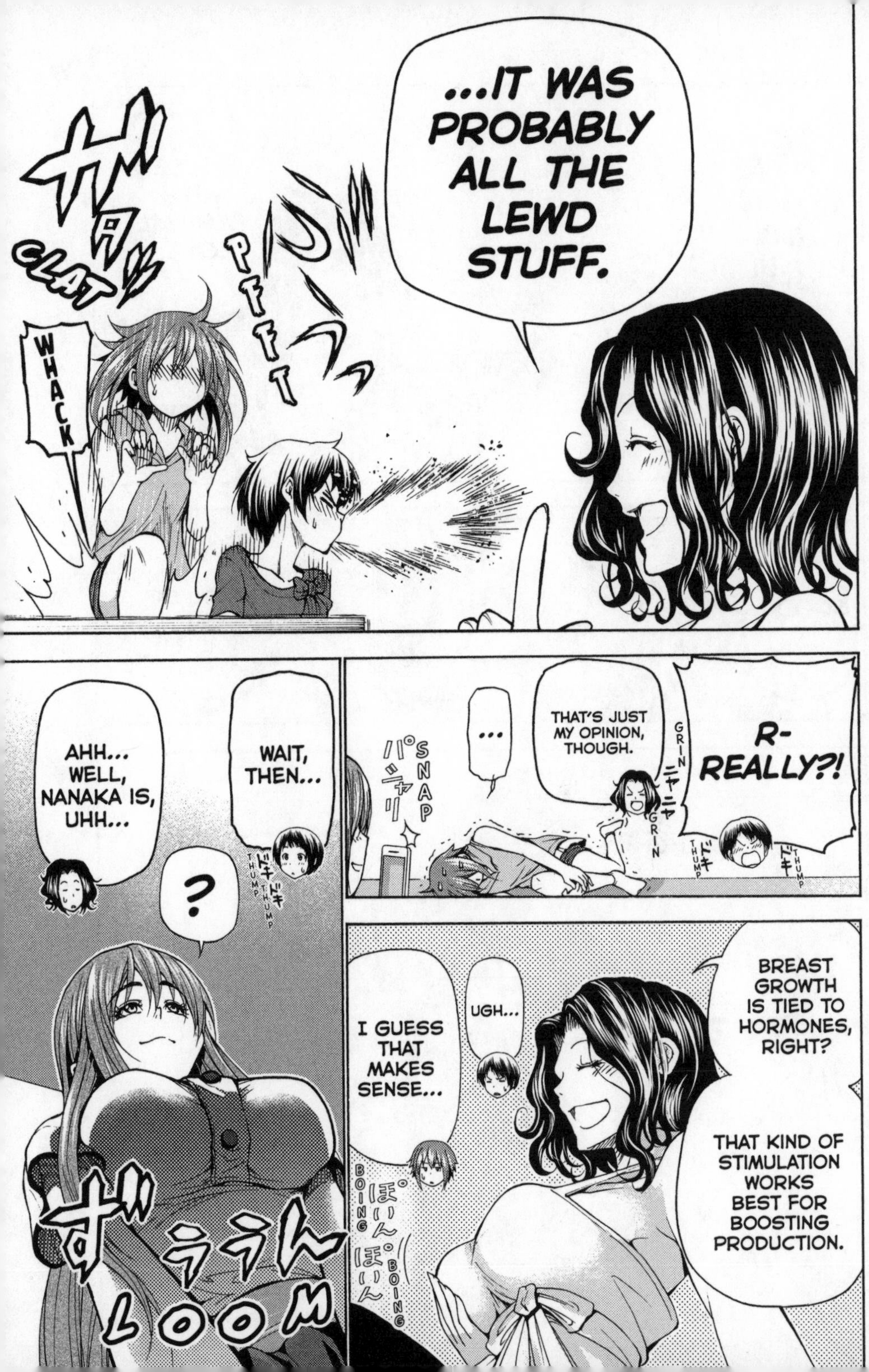
...IT WAS PROBABLY ALL THE LEWD STUFF.
PFFT
CLAT
WHACK
R- REALLY?!
THUMP
THUMP
THAT'S JUST MY OPINION, THOUGH.
GRIN GRIN
...
SNAP
BREAST GROWTH IS TIED TO HORMONES, RIGHT?
THAT KIND OF STIMULATION WORKS BEST FOR BOOSTING PRODUCTION.
UGH...
I GUESS THAT MAKES SENSE...
BOING
BOING
WAIT, THEN...
THUMP THUMP
AHH... WELL, NANAKA IS, UHH...
?
LOOM

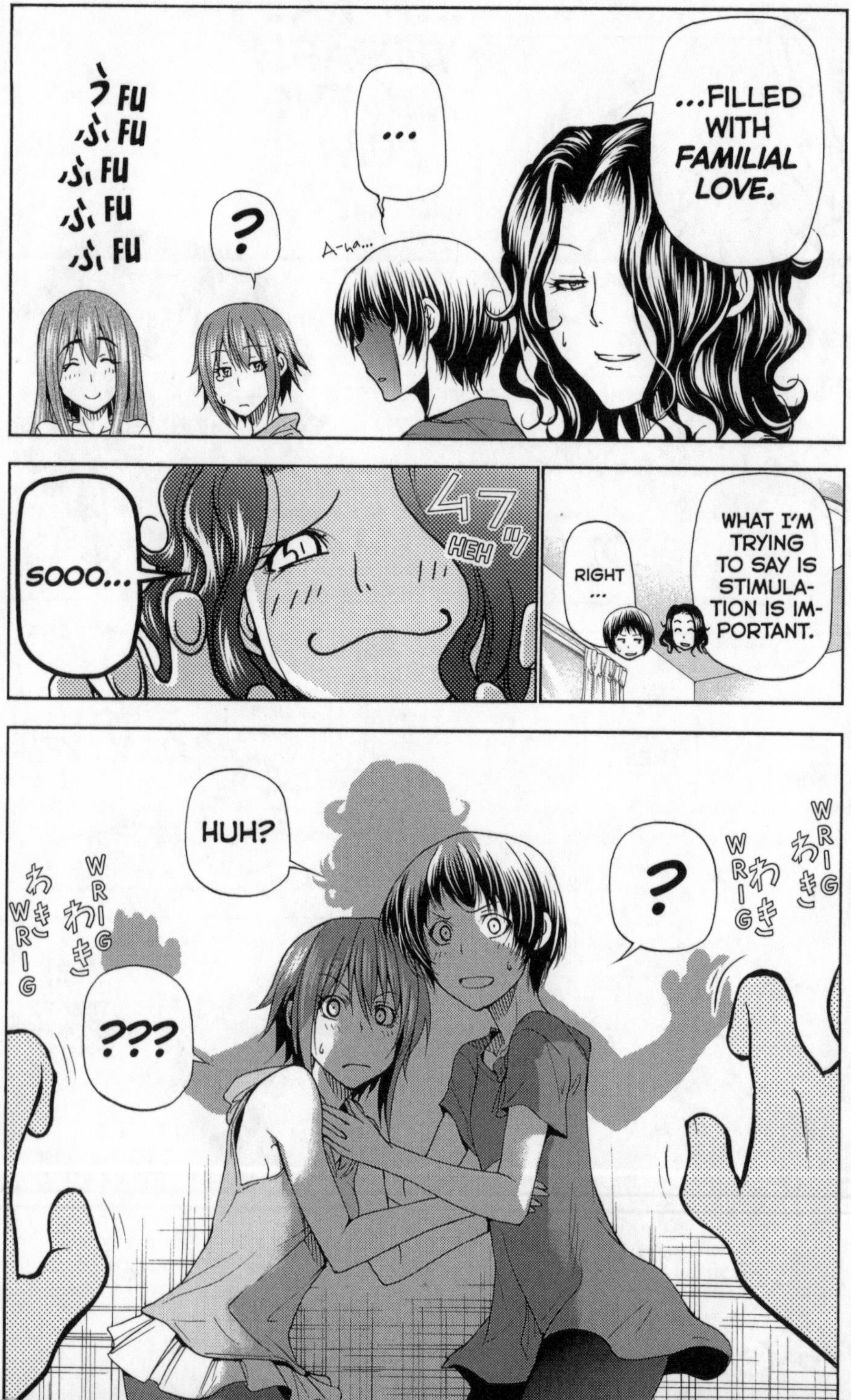
...FILLED WITH FAMILIAL LOVE.
A-ha...
...
?
う FU ふ FU ふ FU ふ FU ふ FU
WHAT I'M TRYING TO SAY IS STIMULATION IS IMPORTANT.
RIGHT ...
ムフッ HEH
SOOO...
わき WRIG わき WRIG
?
HUH?
わき WRIG わき WRIG
???

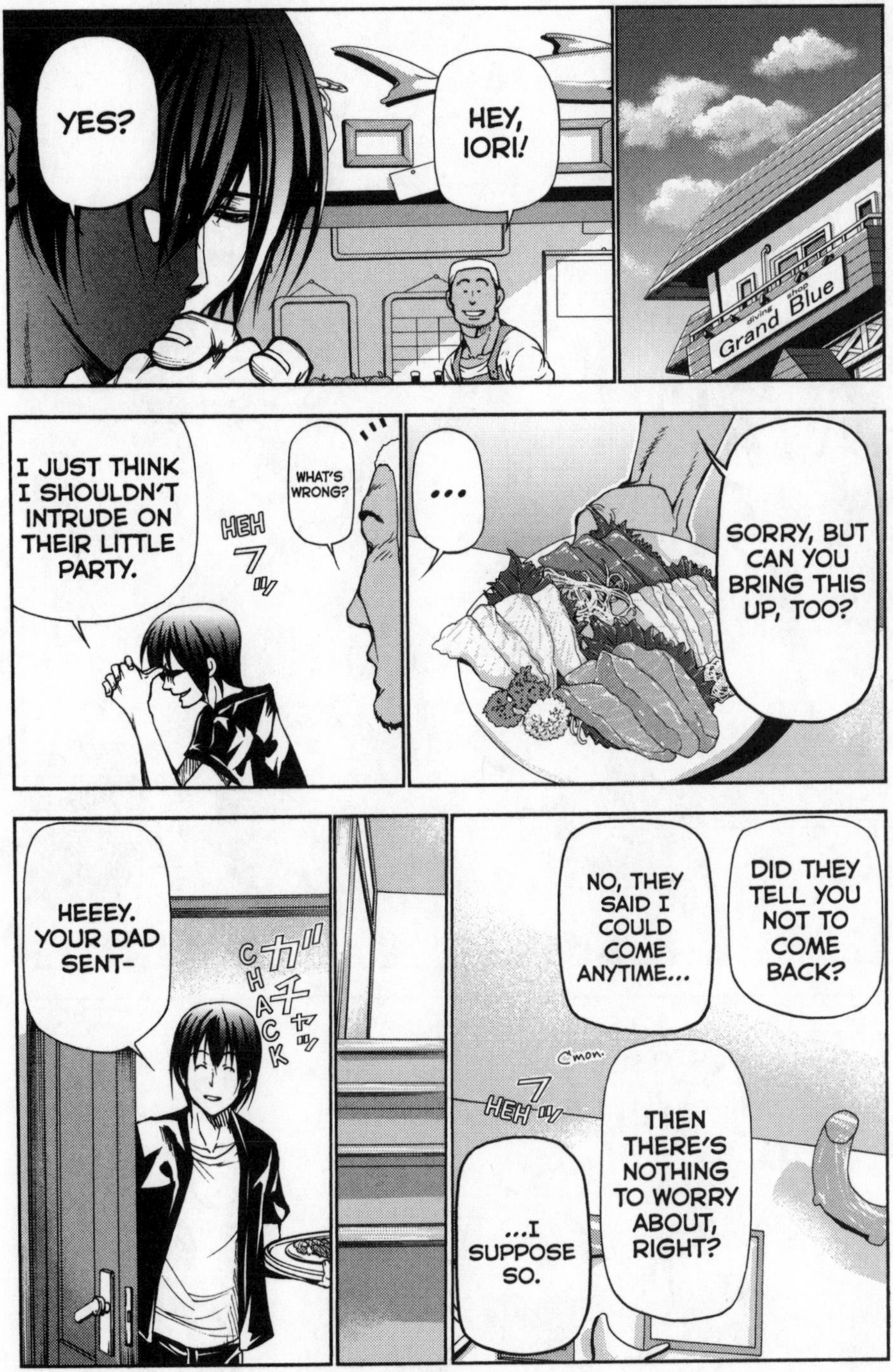
diving shop Grand Blue
HEY, IORI!
YES?
SORRY, BUT CAN YOU BRING THIS UP, TOO?
...
WHAT'S WRONG?
HEH フッ
I JUST THINK I SHOULDN'T INTRUDE ON THEIR LITTLE PARTY.
DID THEY TELL YOU NOT TO COME BACK?
NO, THEY SAID I COULD COME ANYTIME...
C'mon.
HEH フッ
THEN THERE'S NOTHING TO WORRY ABOUT, RIGHT?
...I SUPPOSE SO.
CHACK ガチャッ
HEEEY. YOUR DAD SENT-

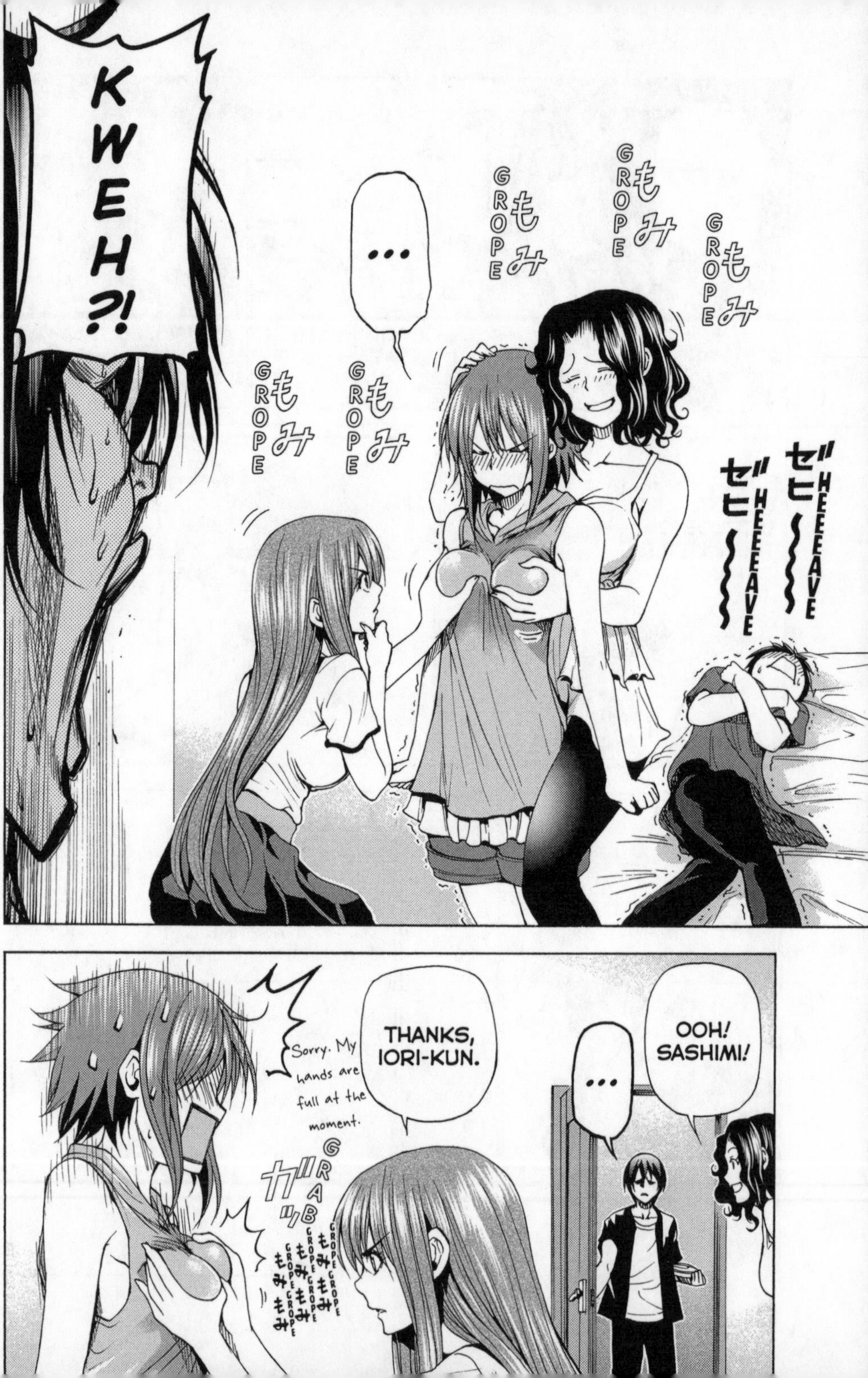
GROPE もみ
GROPE もみ
GROPE もみ
...
GROPE もみ
GROPE もみ
HEEEAVE ゼヒ~
HEEEAVE ゼヒ~
KWEH?!
OOH! SASHIMI!
...
THANKS, IORI-KUN.
Sorry. My hands are full at the moment.
GRAB ガバッ
GROPE GROPE GROPE GROPE もみもみもみもみ

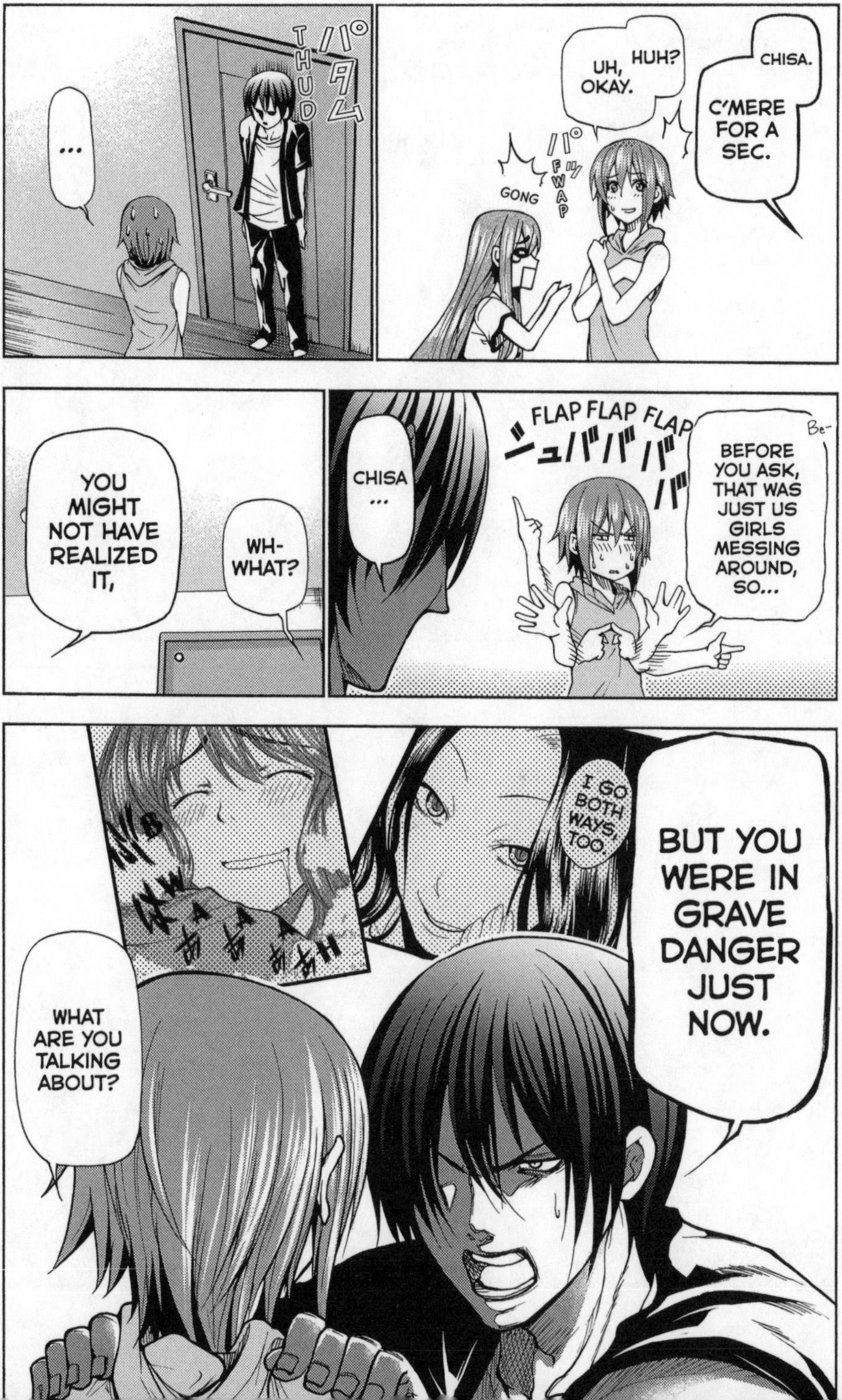
CHISA.
C'MERE FOR A SEC.
HUH?
UH, OKAY.
FWAP
GONG
THUD
...
Be-
BEFORE YOU ASK, THAT WAS JUST US GIRLS MESSING AROUND, SO...
FLAP FLAP FLAP
CHISA ...
WH-WHAT?
YOU MIGHT NOT HAVE REALIZED IT,
BUT YOU WERE IN GRAVE DANGER JUST NOW.
I GO BOTH WAYS, TOO.
BWAAAAH
WHAT ARE YOU TALKING ABOUT?

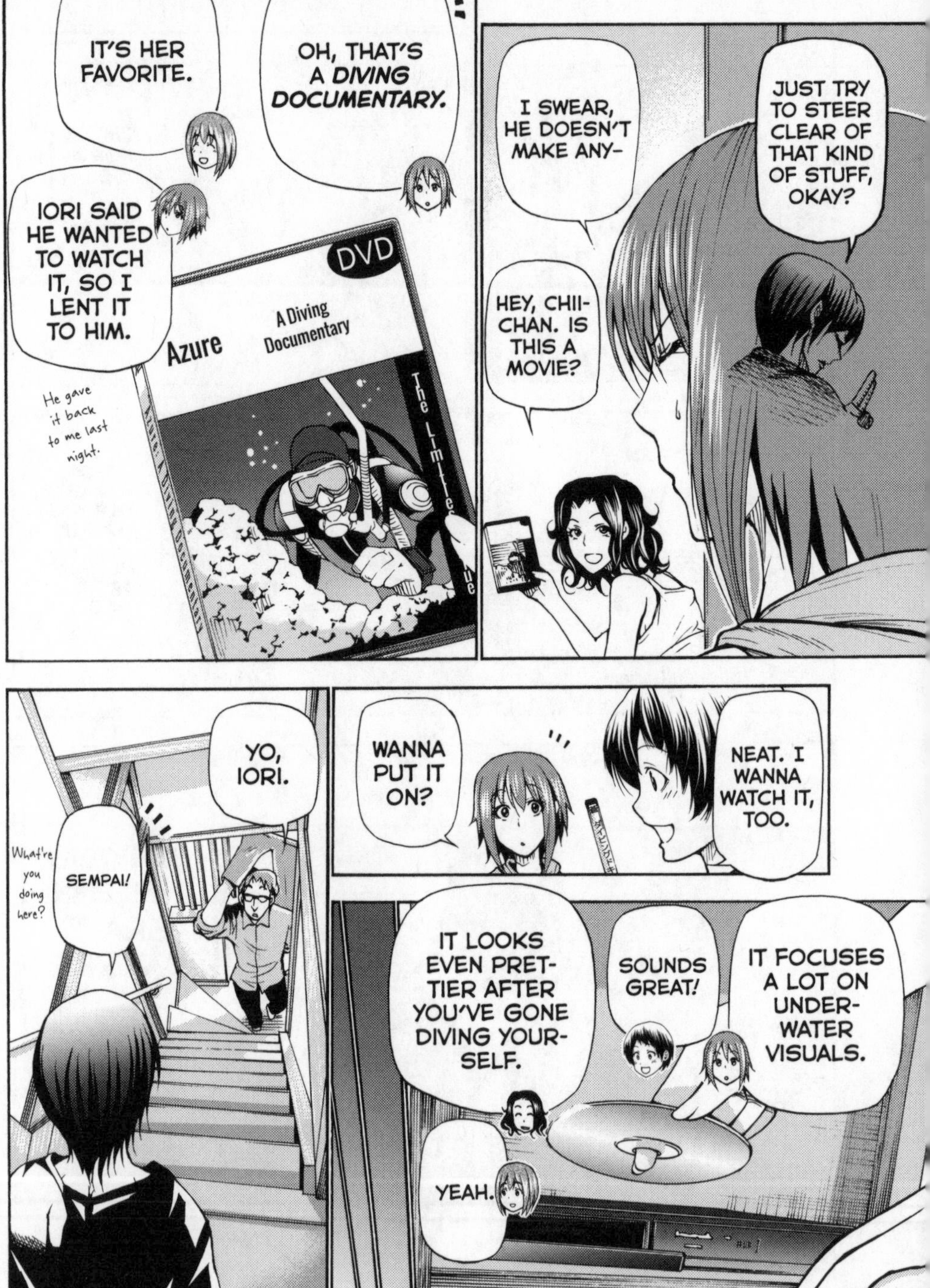
JUST TRY TO STEER CLEAR OF THAT KIND OF STUFF, OKAY?
I SWEAR, HE DOESN'T MAKE ANY-
HEY, CHII-CHAN. IS THIS A MOVIE?
OH, THAT'S A *DIVING DOCUMENTARY.*
IT'S HER FAVORITE.
IORI SAID HE WANTED TO WATCH IT, SO I LENT IT TO HIM.
He gave it back to me last night.
DVD
Azure
A Diving Documentary
NEAT. I WANNA WATCH IT, TOO.
WANNA PUT IT ON?
IT FOCUSES A LOT ON UNDER-WATER VISUALS.
SOUNDS GREAT!
IT LOOKS EVEN PRET-TIER AFTER YOU'VE GONE DIVING YOUR-SELF.
YEAH.
YO, IORI.
SEMPAI!
What're you doing here?

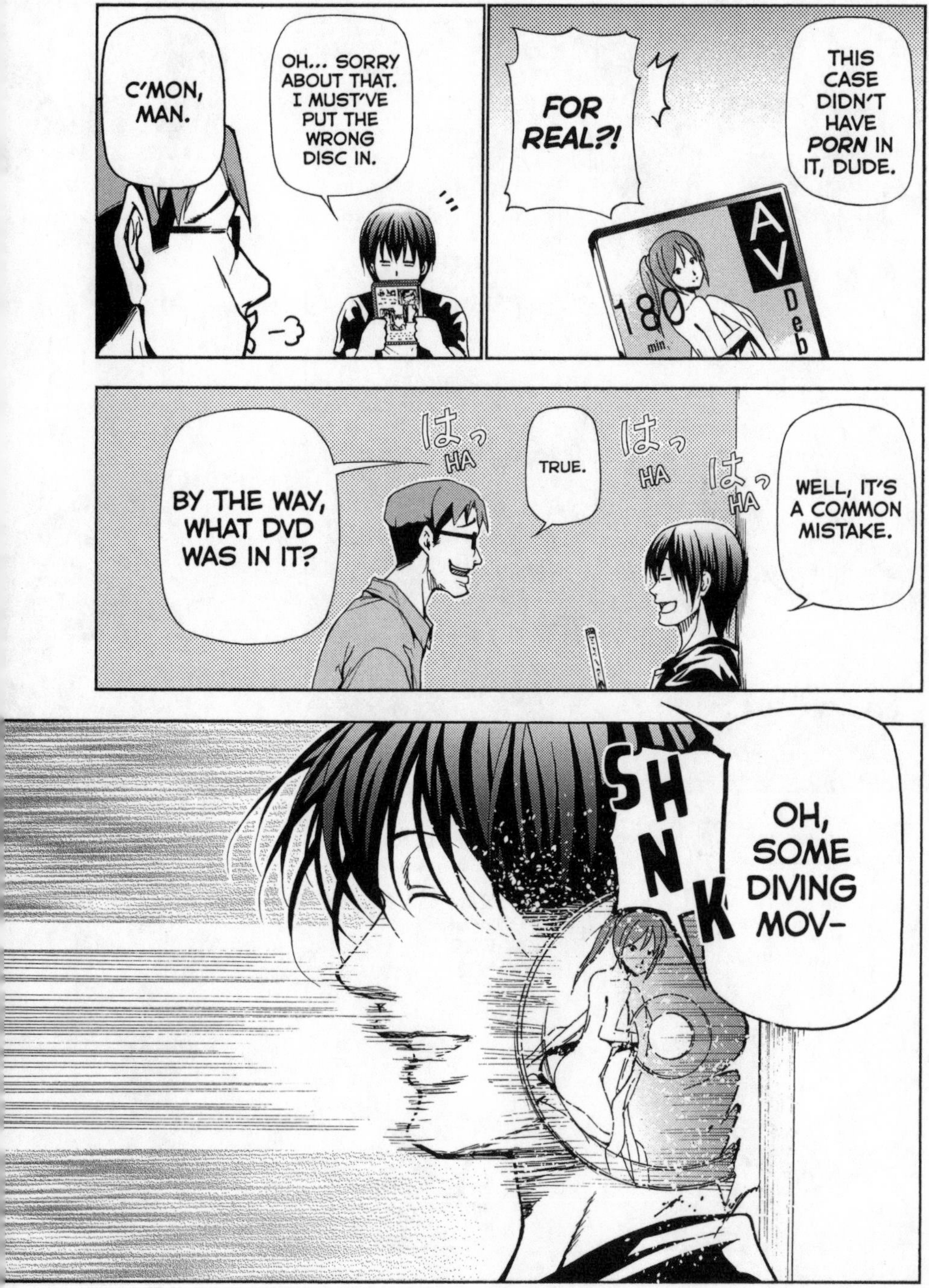
THIS CASE DIDN'T HAVE *PORN* IN IT, DUDE.
FOR REAL?!
AV
180 min.
Deb
OH... SORRY ABOUT THAT. I MUST'VE PUT THE WRONG DISC IN.
C'MON, MAN.
WELL, IT'S A COMMON MISTAKE.
はっ HA
TRUE.
はっ HA
はっ HA
BY THE WAY, WHAT DVD WAS IN IT?
OH, SOME DIVING MOV–
SHNK

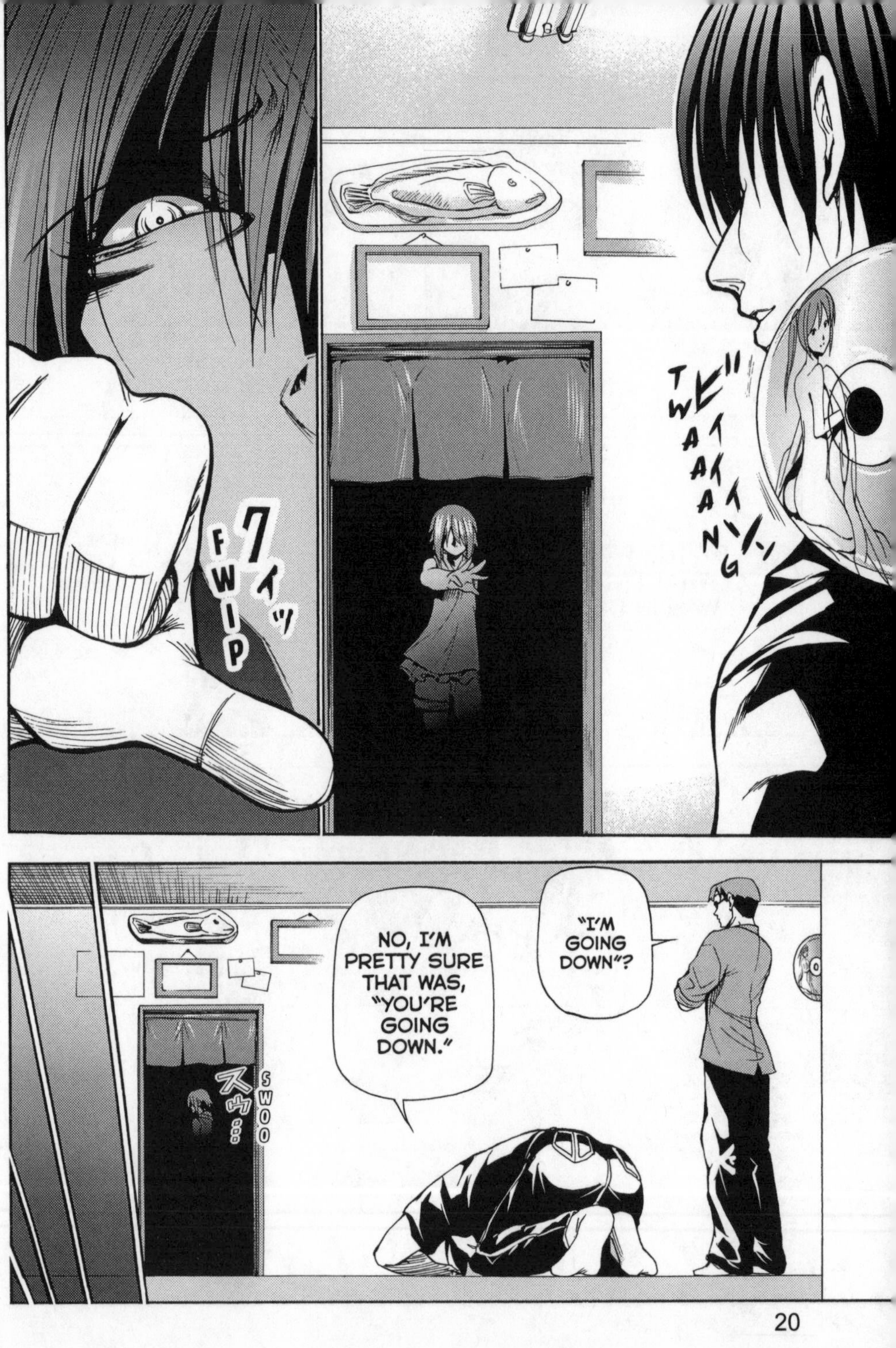
TWAAAANG
FWIP
クイッ
"I'M GOING DOWN"?
NO, I'M PRETTY SURE THAT WAS, "YOU'RE GOING DOWN."
スゥ…
SWOO

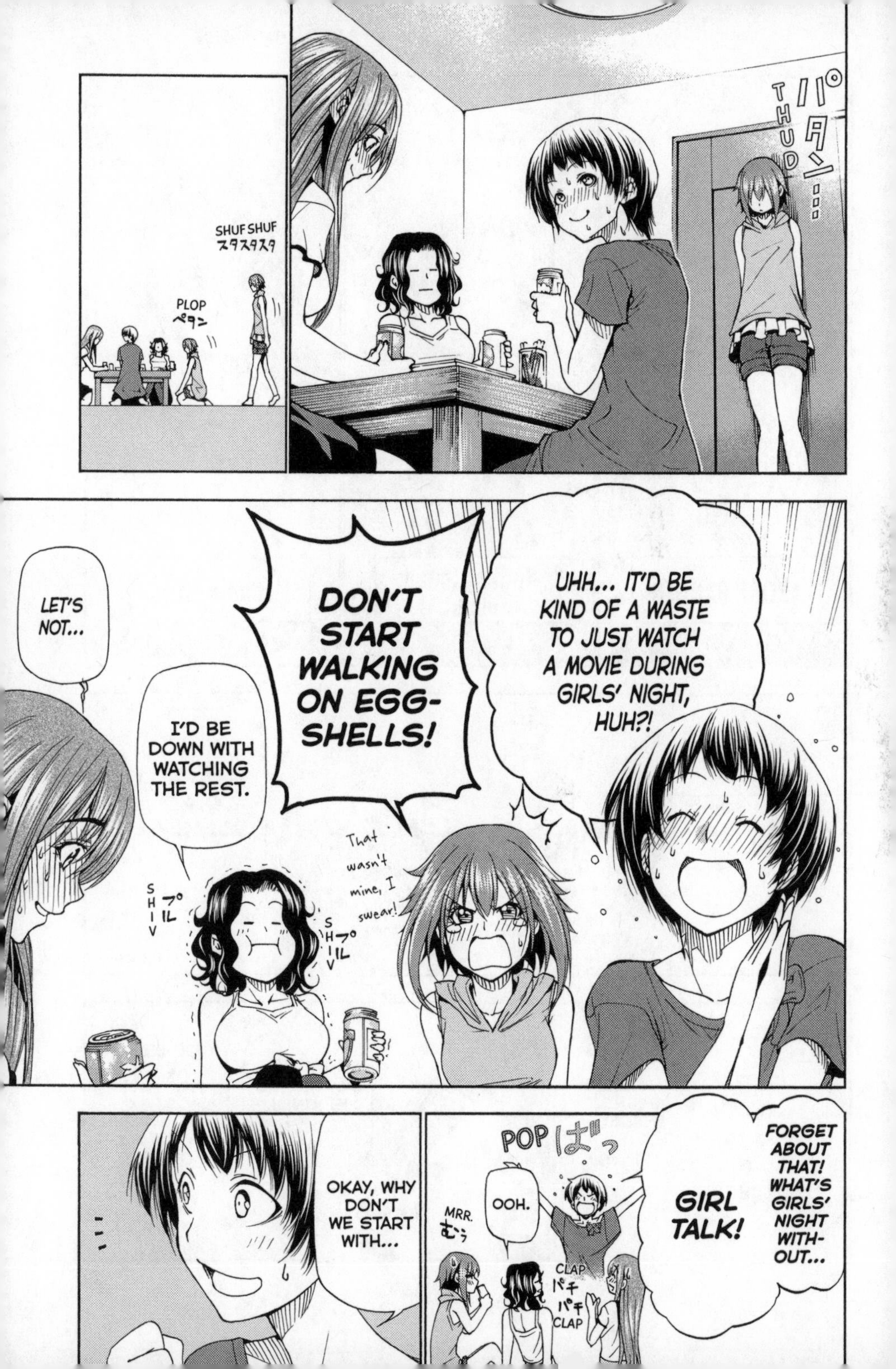
THUD
パタン…
SHUF SHUF
スタスタスタ
PLOP
ペタン
UHH... IT'D BE KIND OF A WASTE TO JUST WATCH A MOVIE DURING GIRLS' NIGHT, HUH?!
DON'T START WALKING ON EGG-SHELLS!
That wasn't mine, I swear!
SHIV
ブル
SHIV
ブル
I'D BE DOWN WITH WATCHING THE REST.
LET'S NOT...
FORGET ABOUT THAT! WHAT'S GIRLS' NIGHT WITH-OUT...
GIRL TALK!
POP
ぱっ
OOH.
MRR.
むぅ
CLAP
パチ
パチ
CLAP
OKAY, WHY DON'T WE START WITH...

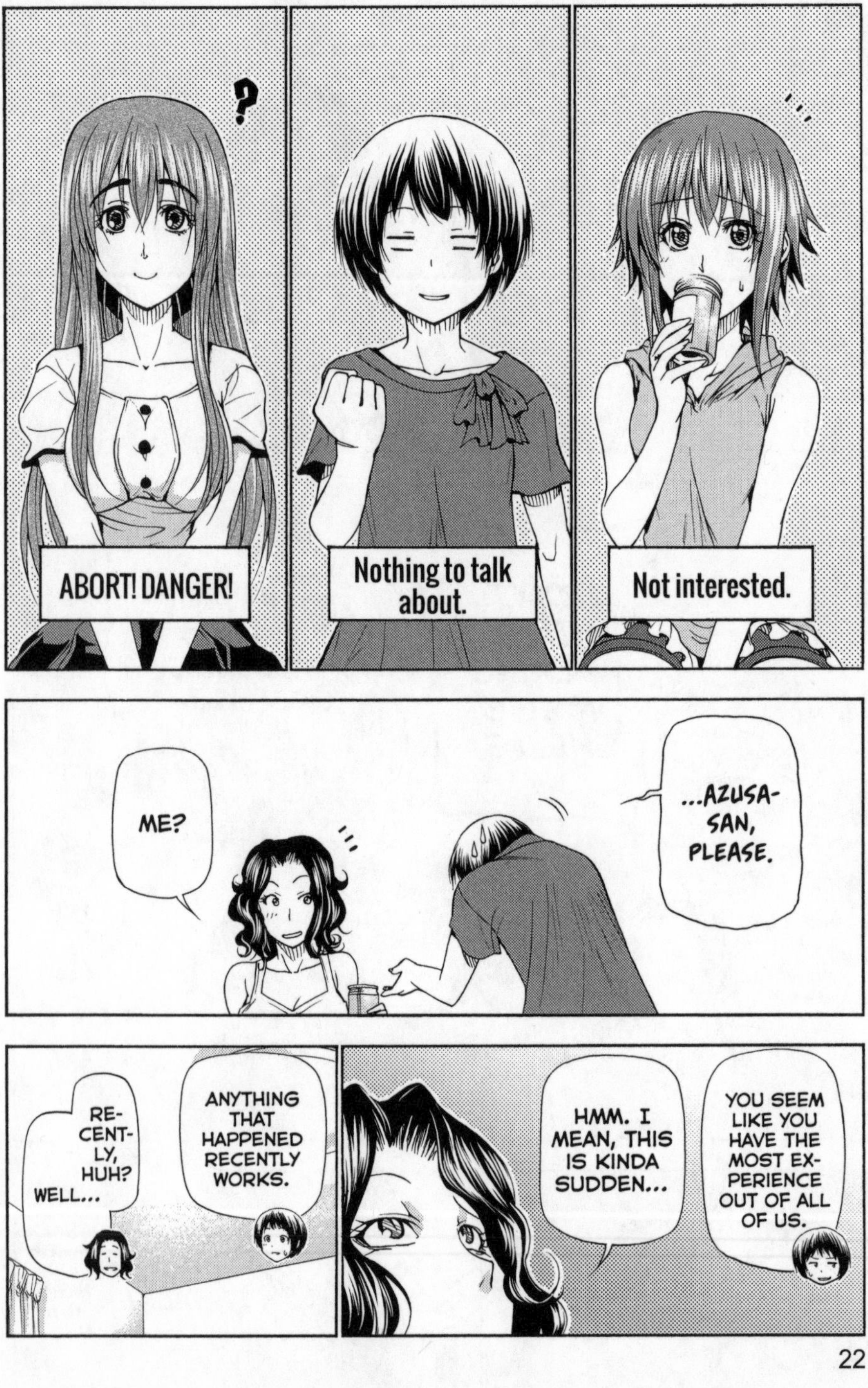
Not interested.
Nothing to talk about.
ABORT! DANGER!
...AZUSA-SAN, PLEASE.
ME?
YOU SEEM LIKE YOU HAVE THE MOST EXPERIENCE OUT OF ALL OF US.
HMM. I MEAN, THIS IS KINDA SUDDEN...
ANYTHING THAT HAPPENED RECENTLY WORKS.
RECENTLY, HUH? WELL...

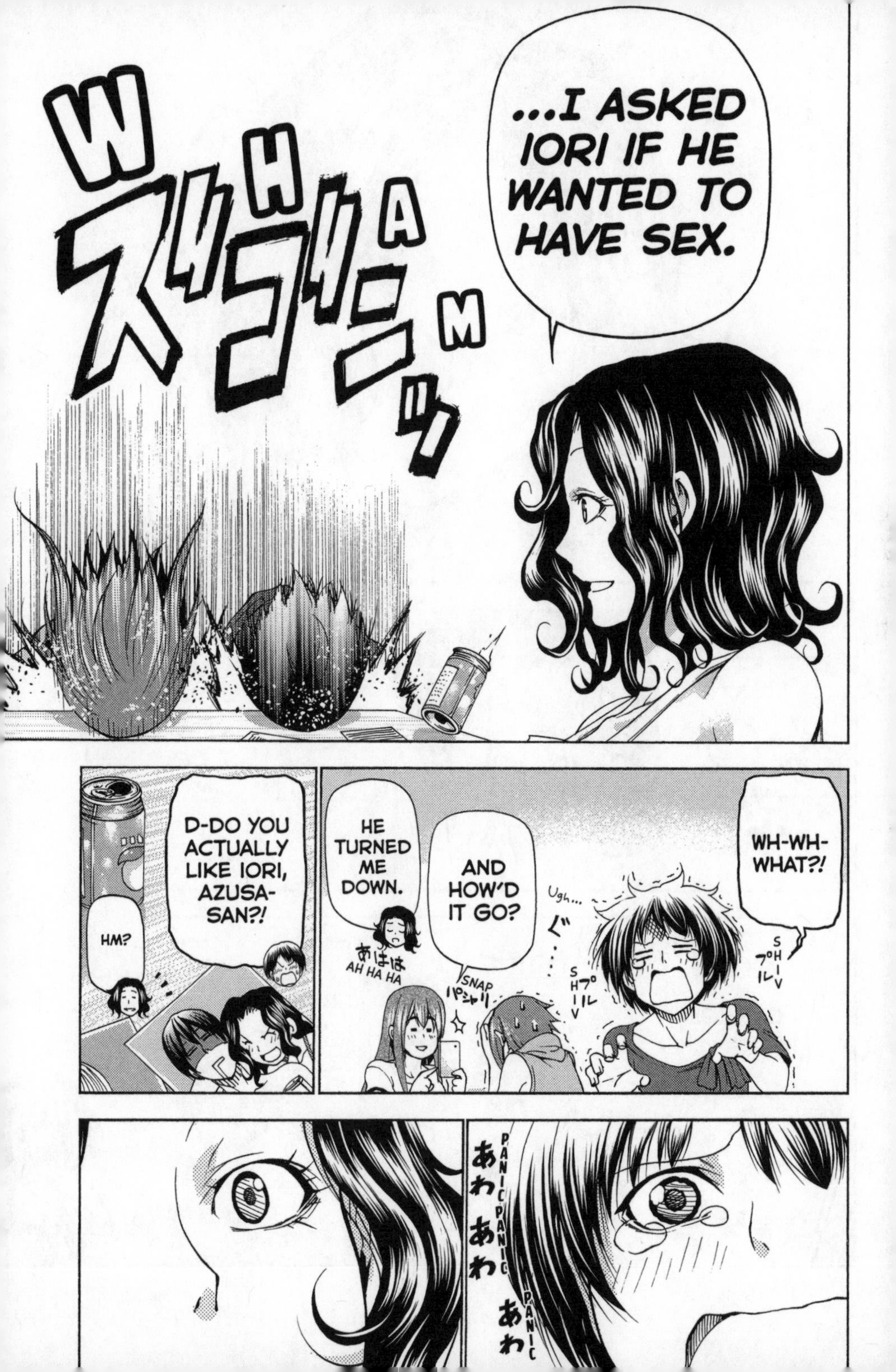
...I ASKED IORI IF HE WANTED TO HAVE SEX.
WHAM
WH-WH-WHAT?!
SHIV
Ugh...
AND HOW'D IT GO?
SNAP
HE TURNED ME DOWN.
AH HA HA
D-DO YOU ACTUALLY LIKE IORI, AZUSA-SAN?!
HM?
PANIC PANIC PANIC

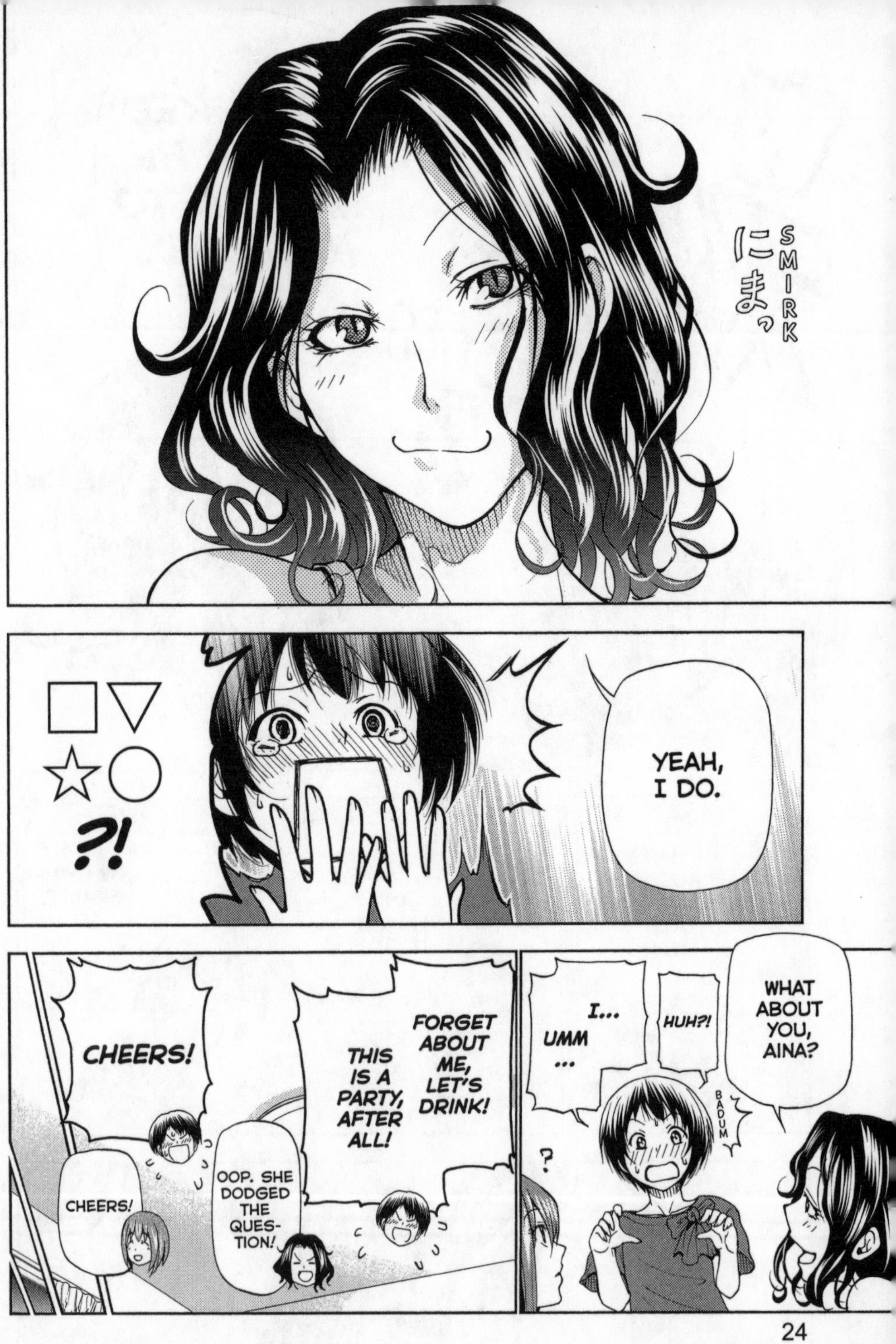
SMIRK
にまっ
YEAH, I DO.
□▽☆○
?!
WHAT ABOUT YOU, AINA?
BADUM
HUH?!
I... UMM ...
?
FORGET ABOUT ME, LET'S DRINK!
THIS IS A PARTY, AFTER ALL!
CHEERS!
OOP. SHE DODGED THE QUES-TION!
CHEERS!

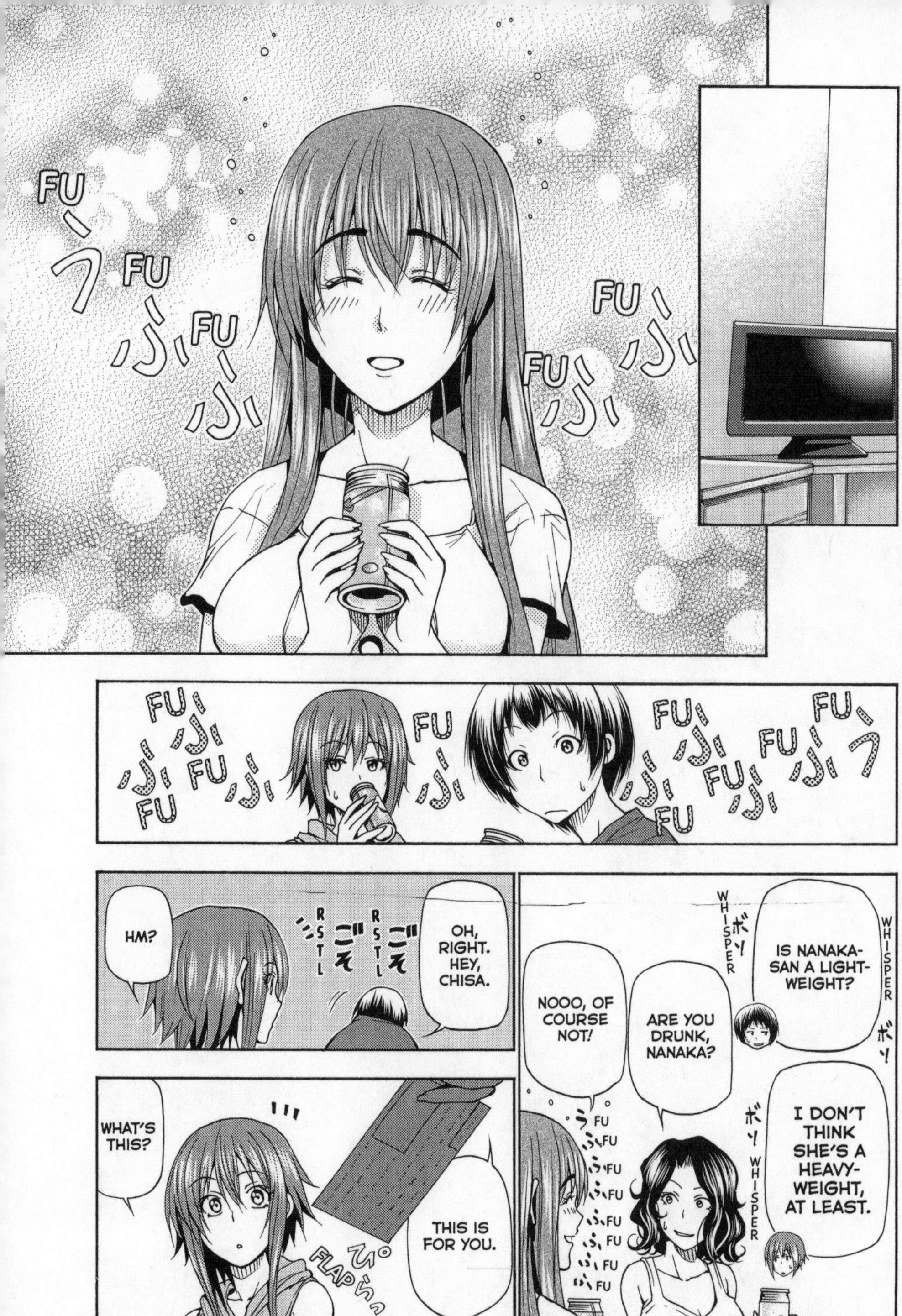
FU FU FU FU FU
FU FU FU FU FU FU FU FU FU FU FU
WHISPER
IS NANAKA-SAN A LIGHT-WEIGHT?
WHISPER
ARE YOU DRUNK, NANAKA?
NOOO, OF COURSE NOT!
FU FU FU FU FU FU FU
WHISPER
I DON'T THINK SHE'S A HEAVY-WEIGHT, AT LEAST.
OH, RIGHT. HEY, CHISA.
RSTL RSTL
HM?
THIS IS FOR YOU.
FLAP
WHAT'S THIS?

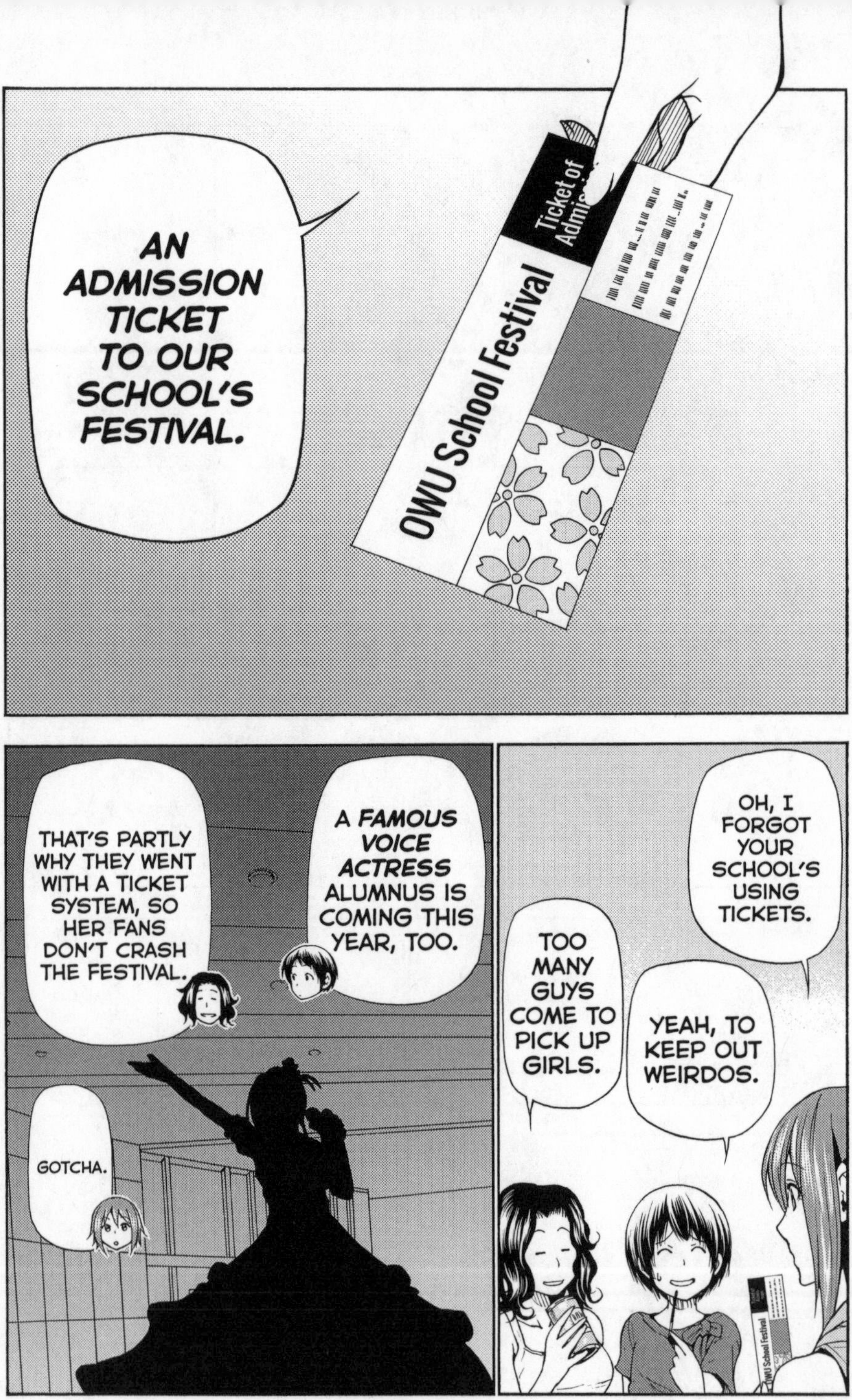
AN ADMISSION TICKET TO OUR SCHOOL'S FESTIVAL.
OWU School Festival
OH, I FORGOT YOUR SCHOOL'S USING TICKETS.
YEAH, TO KEEP OUT WEIRDOS.
TOO MANY GUYS COME TO PICK UP GIRLS.
A *FAMOUS VOICE ACTRESS* ALUMNUS IS COMING THIS YEAR, TOO.
THAT'S PARTLY WHY THEY WENT WITH A TICKET SYSTEM, SO HER FANS DON'T CRASH THE FESTIVAL.
GOTCHA.

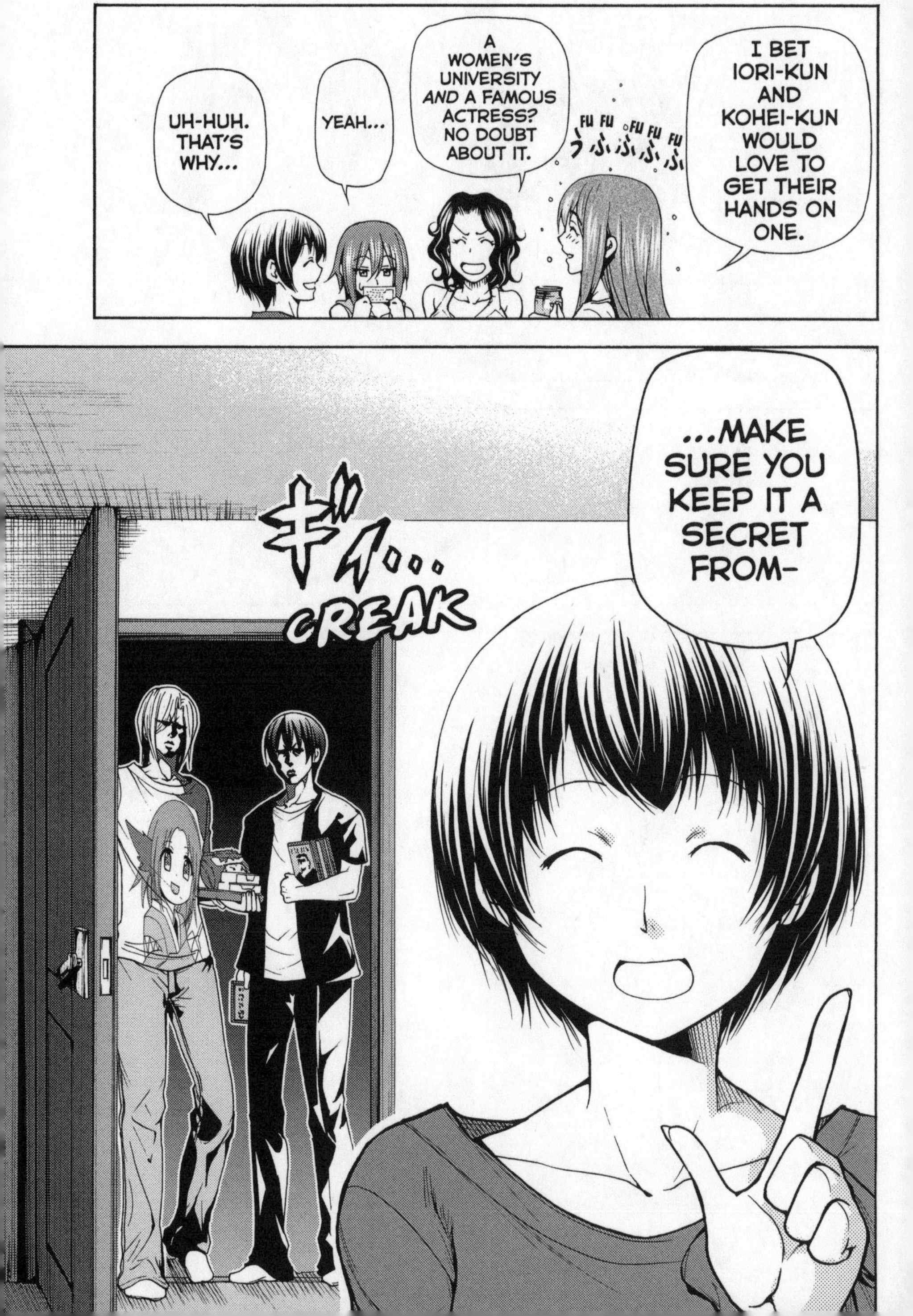
I BET IORI-KUN AND KOHEI-KUN WOULD LOVE TO GET THEIR HANDS ON ONE.
FU FU FU FU FU
うふふふふ
A WOMEN'S UNIVERSITY *AND* A FAMOUS ACTRESS? NO DOUBT ABOUT IT.
YEAH...
UH-HUH. THAT'S WHY...
...MAKE SURE YOU KEEP IT A SECRET FROM-
ギイ...
CREAK

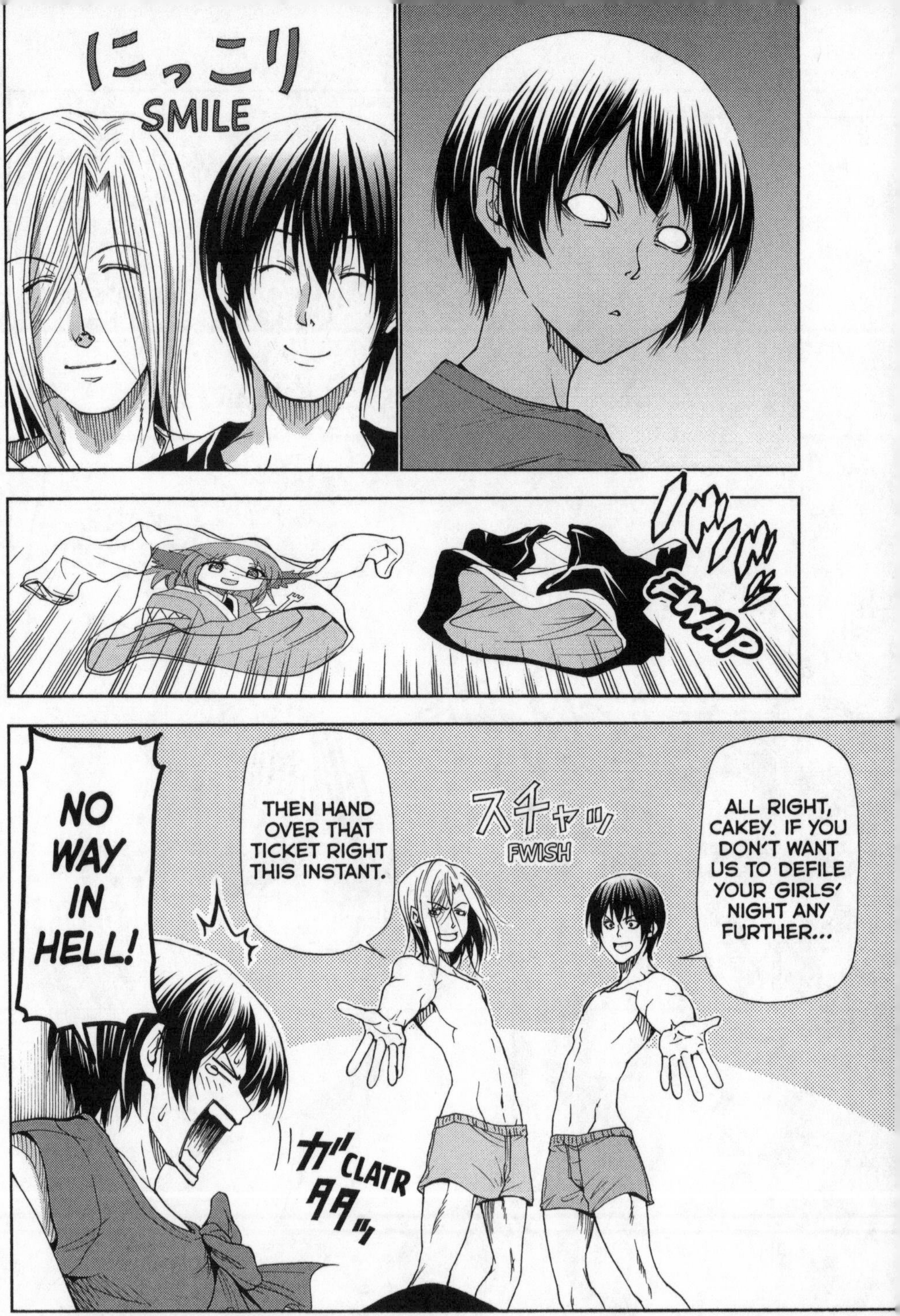

にっこり
SMILE
FWAP
ALL RIGHT, CAKEY. IF YOU DON'T WANT US TO DEFILE YOUR GIRLS' NIGHT ANY FURTHER...
スチャッ
FWISH
THEN HAND OVER THAT TICKET RIGHT THIS INSTANT.
NO WAY IN HELL!
ガタタッ
CLATR

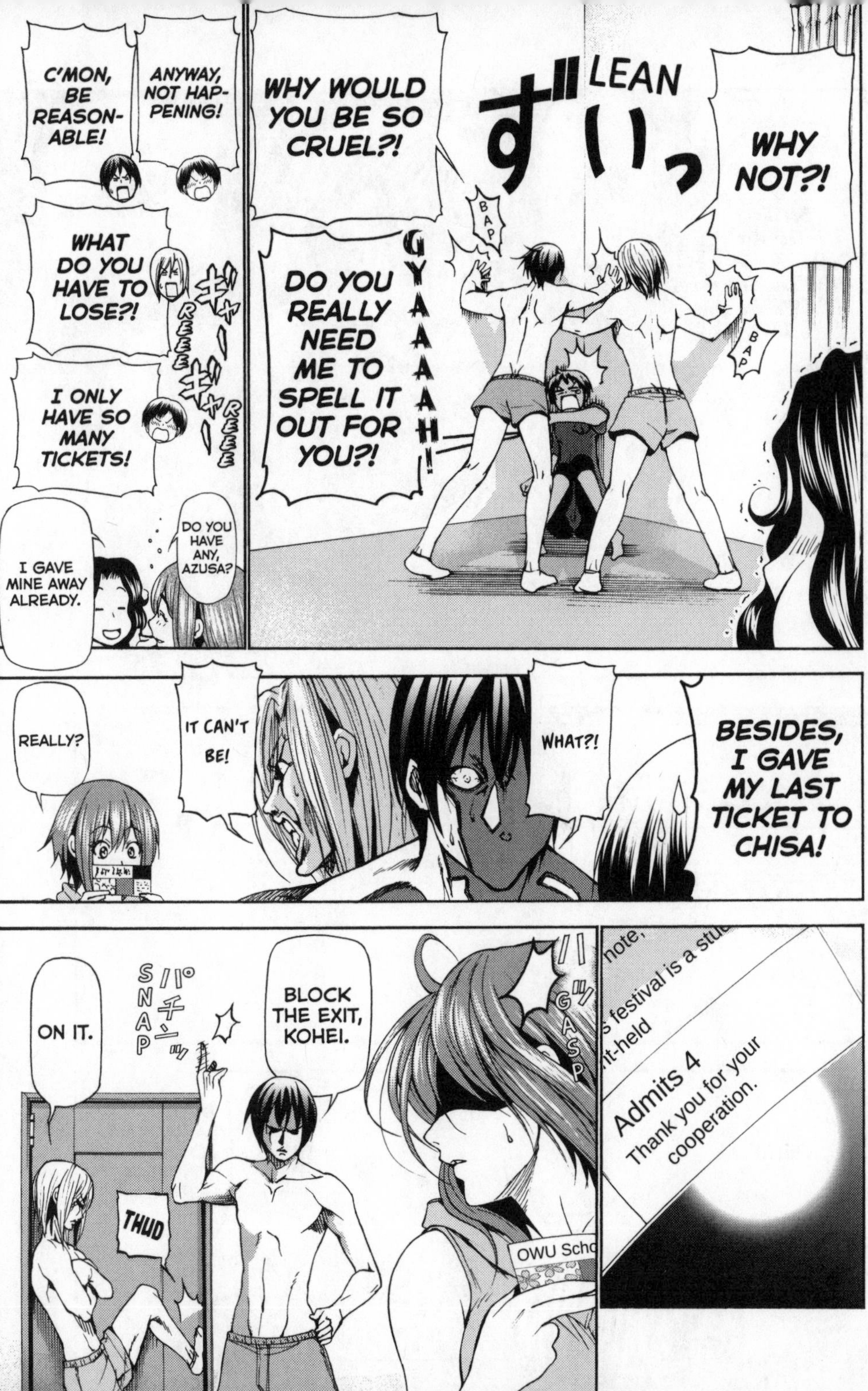

LEAN
WHY NOT?!
BAP
BAP
WHY WOULD YOU BE SO CRUEL?!
DO YOU REALLY NEED ME TO SPELL IT OUT FOR YOU?!
GYAAAAAH!
ANYWAY, NOT HAP-PENING!
C'MON, BE REASONABLE!
WHAT DO YOU HAVE TO LOSE?!
REEE
REEE
I ONLY HAVE SO MANY TICKETS!
DO YOU HAVE ANY, AZUSA?
I GAVE MINE AWAY ALREADY.
BESIDES, I GAVE MY LAST TICKET TO CHISA!
WHAT?!
IT CAN'T BE!
REALLY?
GASP
note,
s festival is a stu
it-held
Admits 4
Thank you for your cooperation.
OWU Scho
BLOCK THE EXIT, KOHEI.
SNAP
ON IT.
THUD

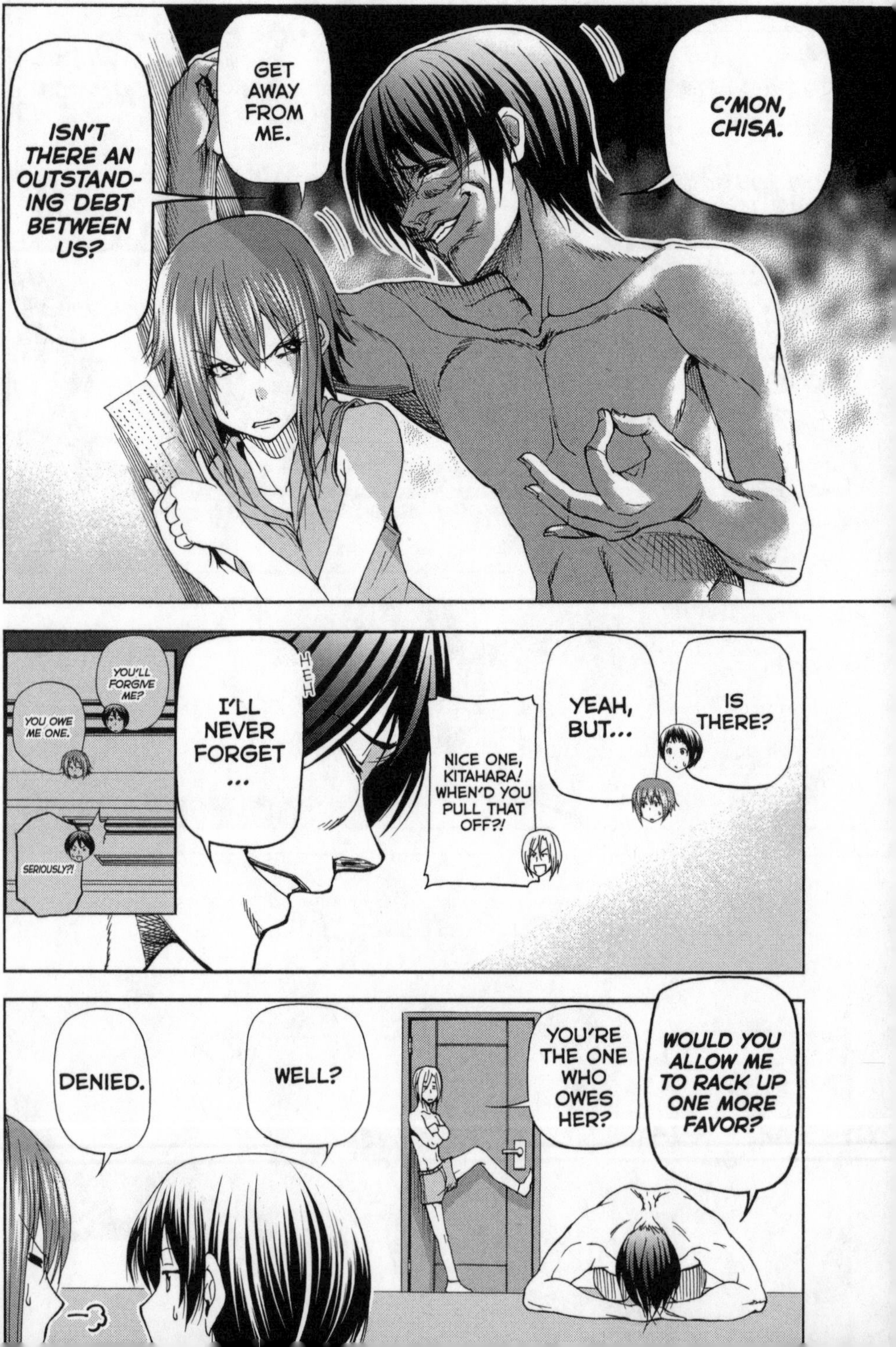
C'MON, CHISA.
GET AWAY FROM ME.
ISN'T THERE AN OUTSTANDING DEBT BETWEEN US?
IS THERE?
YEAH, BUT...
NICE ONE, KITAHARA! WHEN'D YOU PULL THAT OFF?!
HEH
I'LL NEVER FORGET...
YOU'LL FORGIVE ME?
YOU OWE ME ONE.
SERIOUSLY?!
WOULD YOU ALLOW ME TO RACK UP ONE MORE FAVOR?
YOU'RE THE ONE WHO OWES HER?
WELL?
DENIED.

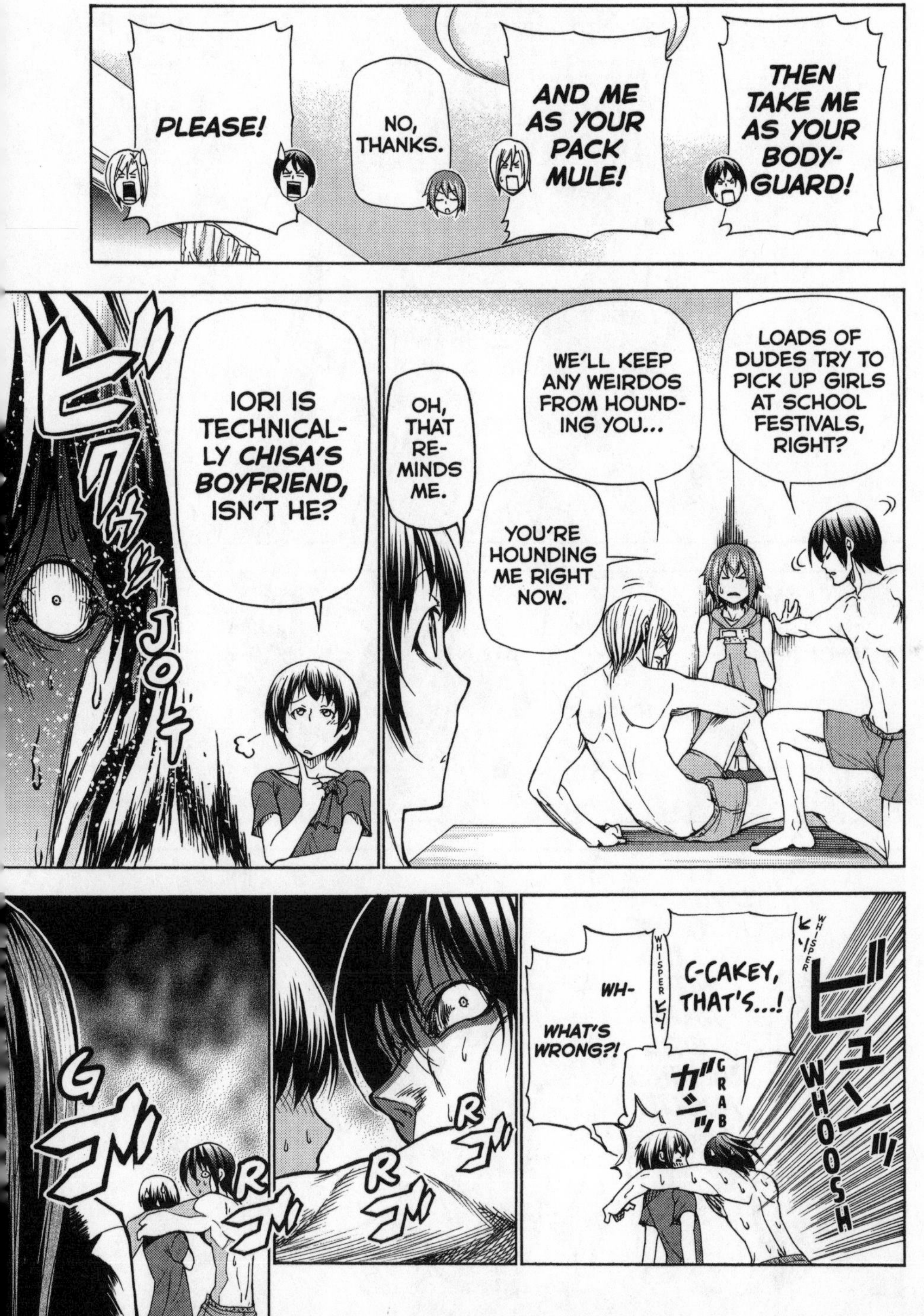
THEN TAKE ME AS YOUR BODY-GUARD!
AND ME AS YOUR PACK MULE!
NO, THANKS.
PLEASE!
LOADS OF DUDES TRY TO PICK UP GIRLS AT SCHOOL FESTIVALS, RIGHT?
WE'LL KEEP ANY WEIRDOS FROM HOUNDING YOU...
YOU'RE HOUNDING ME RIGHT NOW.
OH, THAT REMINDS ME.
IORI IS TECHNICAL-LY CHISA'S BOYFRIEND, ISN'T HE?
JOLT
WHISPER
WHOOSH
C-CAKEY, THAT'S...!
WHISPER
WH-
WHAT'S WRONG?!
GRAB
R
R
R
G

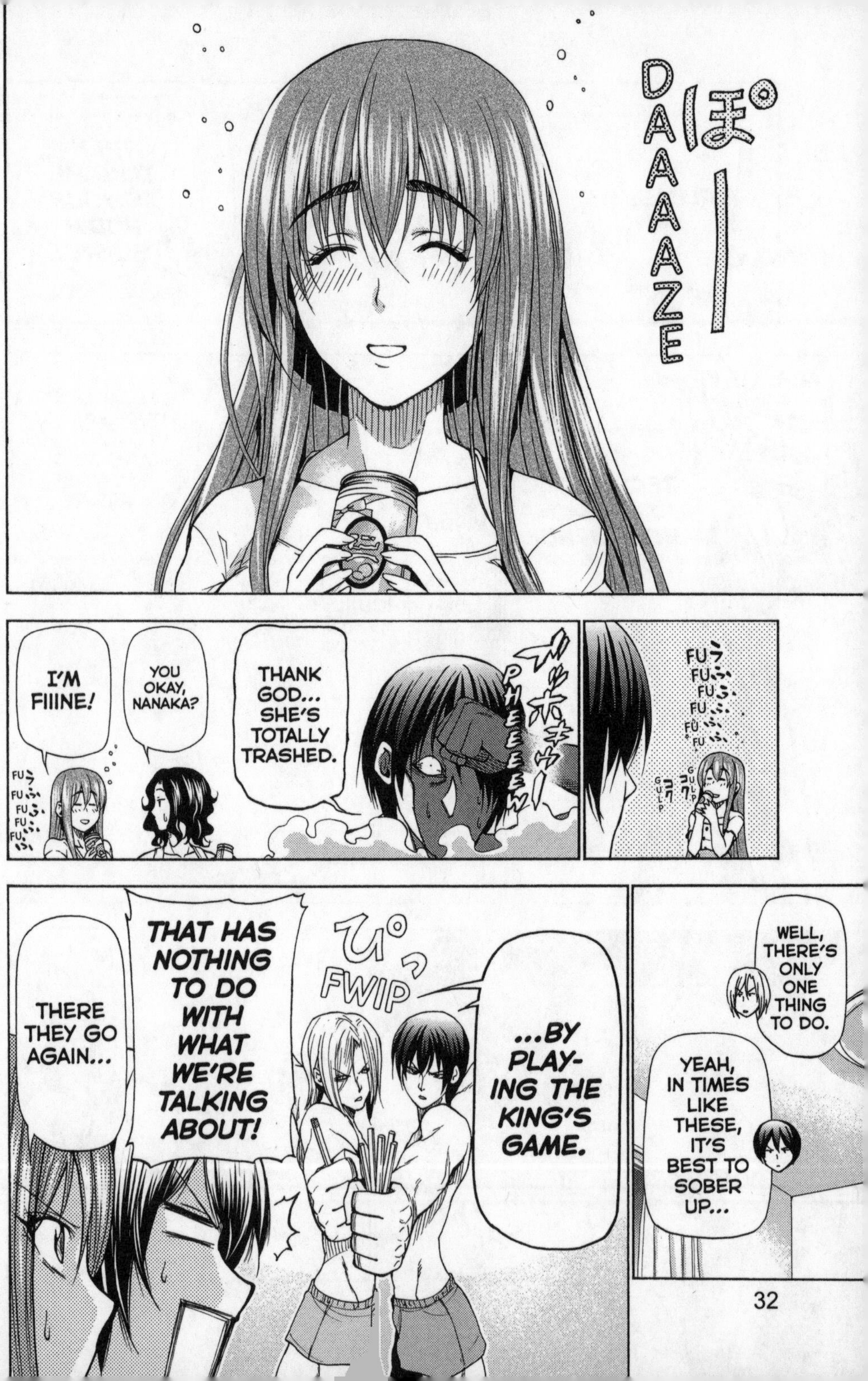
ぽー
DAAAAZE
FU ふ FU ふ FU ふ FU ふ FU ふ FU ふ
ゴク ゴク
GULP GULP
プッホキュー
PHEEEEW
THANK GOD... SHE'S TOTALLY TRASHED.
YOU OKAY, NANAKA?
I'M FIIINE!
FU ふ FU ふ FU ふ FU ふ FU ふ
WELL, THERE'S ONLY ONE THING TO DO.
YEAH, IN TIMES LIKE THESE, IT'S BEST TO SOBER UP...
...BY PLAY-ING THE KING'S GAME.
ぴっ
FWIP
THAT HAS NOTHING TO DO WITH WHAT WE'RE TALKING ABOUT!
THERE THEY GO AGAIN...

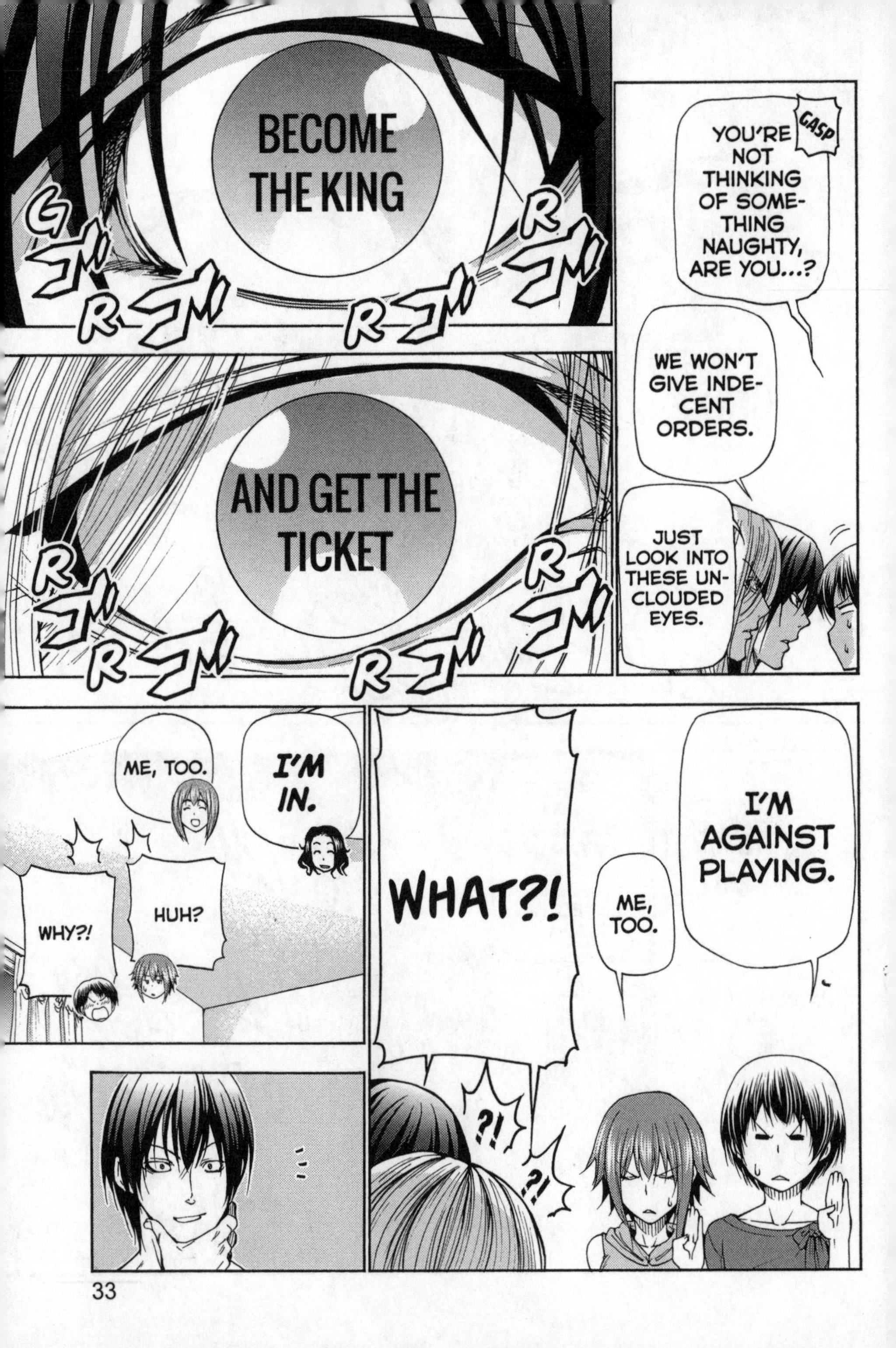
GASP
YOU'RE NOT THINKING OF SOME-THING NAUGHTY, ARE YOU...?
WE WON'T GIVE INDE-CENT ORDERS.
JUST LOOK INTO THESE UN-CLOUDED EYES.
BECOME THE KING
G R R R R
AND GET THE TICKET
R R R R R
I'M AGAINST PLAYING.
ME, TOO.
WHAT?!
I'M IN.
ME, TOO.
HUH?
WHY?!
?!
?!

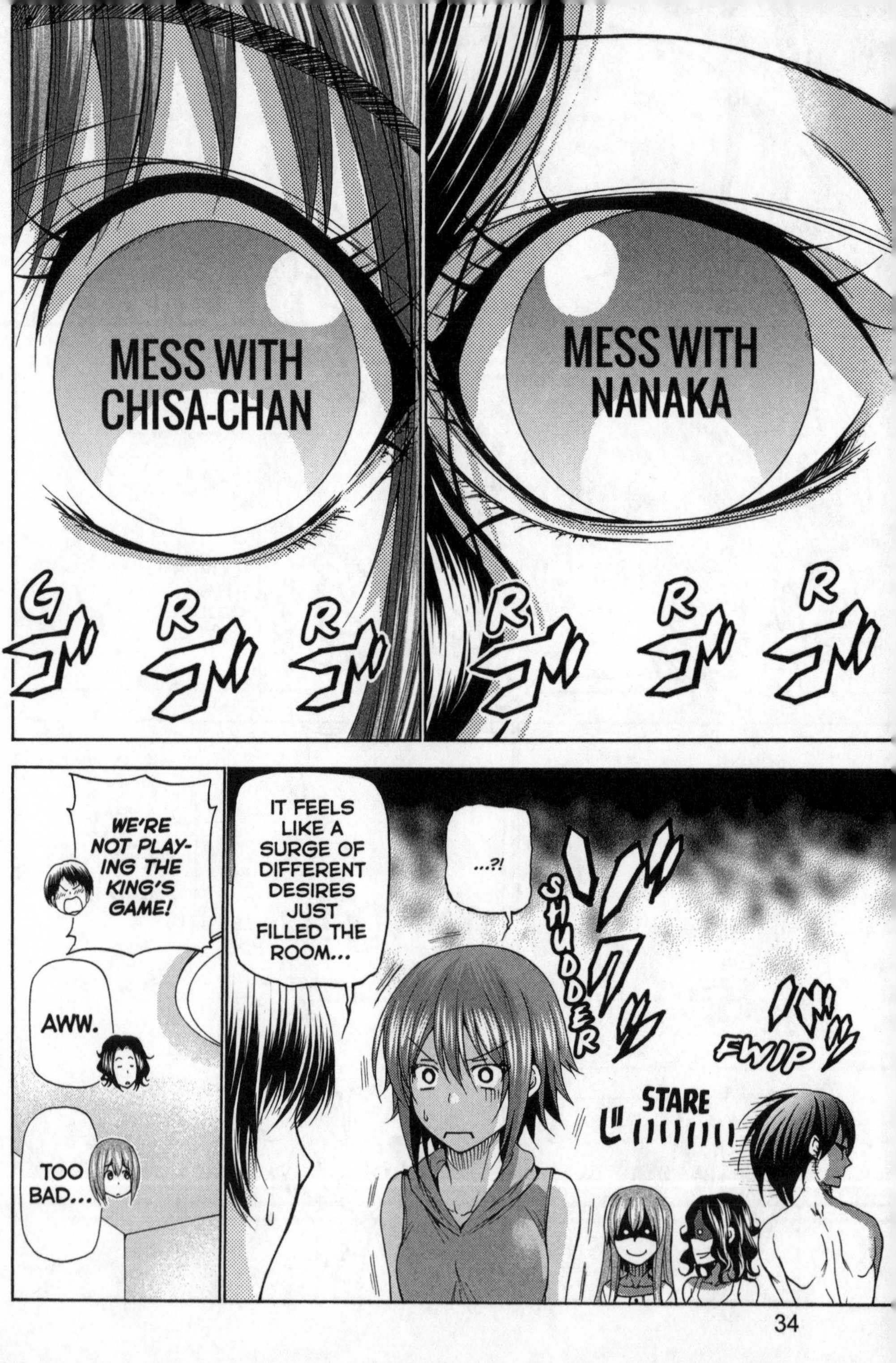
MESS WITH NANAKA
MESS WITH CHISA-CHAN
GRRRRR
...?!
IT FEELS LIKE A SURGE OF DIFFERENT DESIRES JUST FILLED THE ROOM...
SHUDDER
FWIP
STARE
WE'RE NOT PLAY-ING THE KING'S GAME!
AWW.
TOO BAD...

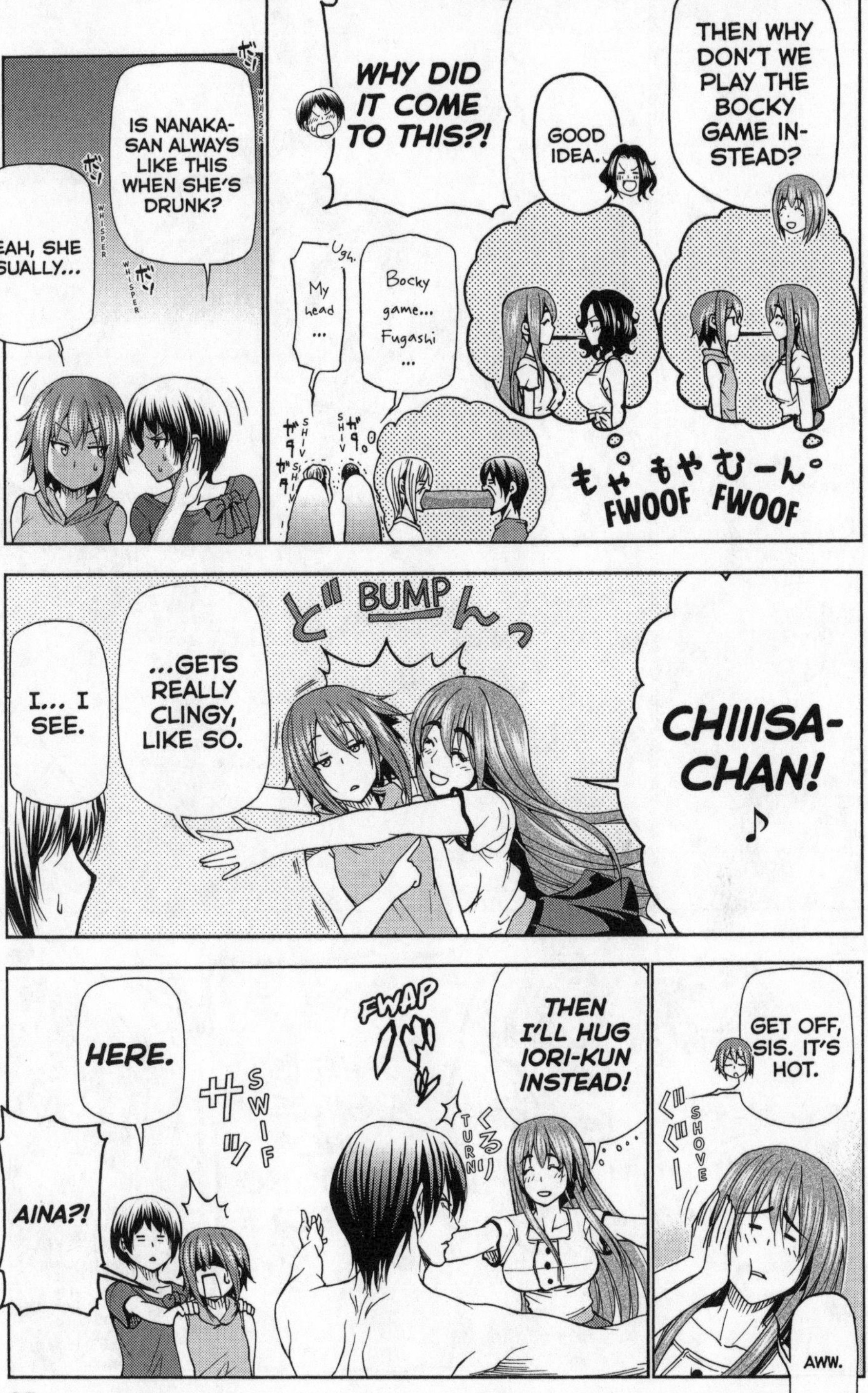
THEN WHY DON'T WE PLAY THE BOCKY GAME IN-STEAD?
GOOD IDEA.
WHY DID IT COME TO THIS?!
Bocky game... Fugashi...
Ugh. My head...
SHIV
SHIV
FWOOF FWOOF
IS NANAKA-SAN ALWAYS LIKE THIS WHEN SHE'S DRUNK?
WHISPER
WHISPER
WHISPER
YEAH, SHE USUALLY...
WHISPER
CHIIISA-CHAN! ♪
BUMP
...GETS REALLY CLINGY, LIKE SO.
I... I SEE.
GET OFF, SIS. IT'S HOT.
SHOVE
AWW.
THEN I'LL HUG IORI-KUN INSTEAD!
TURN
FWAP
SWIF
HERE.
AINA?!

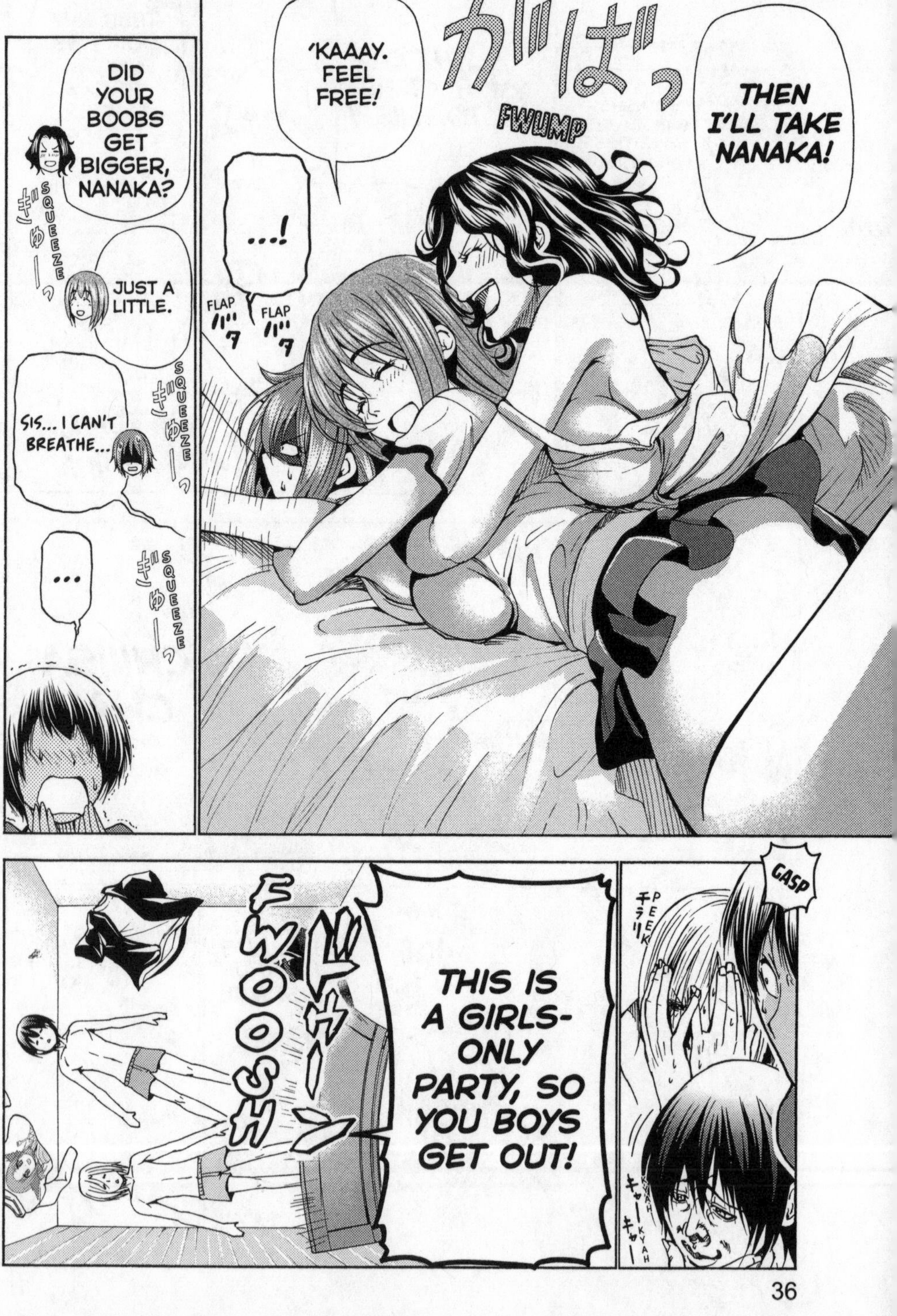
THEN I'LL TAKE NANAKA!
がばっ
FWUMP
'KAAAY. FEEL FREE!
...!
FLAP バタ
FLAP バタ
DID YOUR BOOBS GET BIGGER, NANAKA?
ぎゅーっ SQUEEZE
JUST A LITTLE.
ぎゅーっ SQUEEZE
SIS... I CAN'T BREATHE...
ぎゅーっ SQUEEZE
...
GASP
チラリ PEEK
キャーキャー KYAH KYAH
THIS IS A GIRLS-ONLY PARTY, SO YOU BOYS GET OUT!
ドサー
FWOOSH

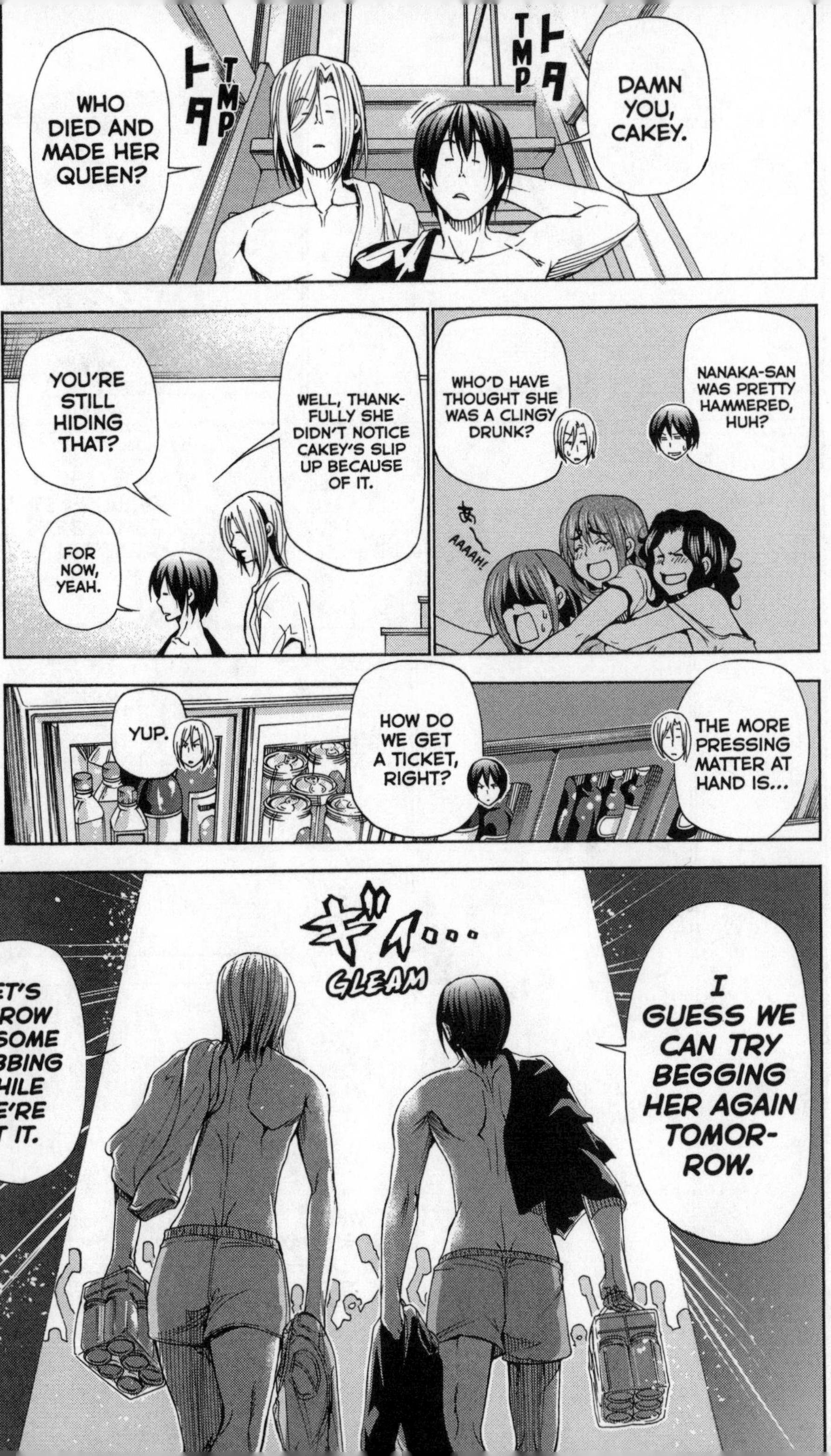

DAMN YOU, CAKEY.
トタ
TMP
トタ
TMP
WHO DIED AND MADE HER QUEEN?
NANAKA-SAN WAS PRETTY HAMMERED, HUH?
WHO'D HAVE THOUGHT SHE WAS A CLINGY DRUNK?
あ~
AAAAH!
WELL, THANK-FULLY SHE DIDN'T NOTICE CAKEY'S SLIP UP BECAUSE OF IT.
YOU'RE STILL HIDING THAT?
FOR NOW, YEAH.
THE MORE PRESSING MATTER AT HAND IS...
HOW DO WE GET A TICKET, RIGHT?
YUP.
I GUESS WE CAN TRY BEGGING HER AGAIN TOMOR-ROW.
GLEAM
LET'S THROW IN SOME SOBBING WHILE WE'RE AT IT.

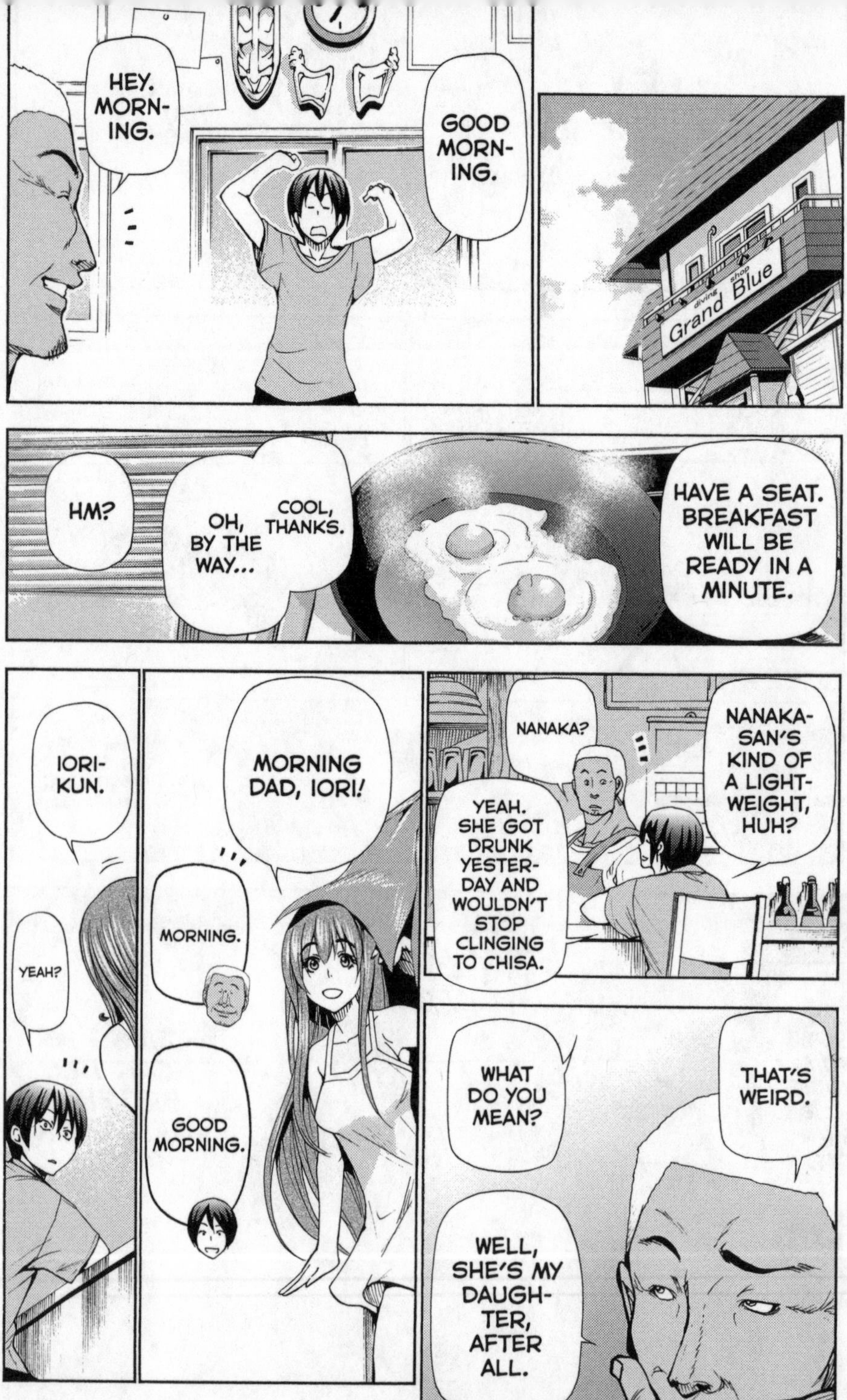
diving shop
Grand Blue
GOOD MORNING.
HEY. MORNING.
HAVE A SEAT. BREAKFAST WILL BE READY IN A MINUTE.
COOL, THANKS.
OH, BY THE WAY...
HM?
NANAKA-SAN'S KIND OF A LIGHTWEIGHT, HUH?
NANAKA?
YEAH. SHE GOT DRUNK YESTERDAY AND WOULDN'T STOP CLINGING TO CHISA.
THAT'S WEIRD.
WHAT DO YOU MEAN?
WELL, SHE'S MY DAUGHTER, AFTER ALL.
MORNING DAD, IORI!
MORNING.
GOOD MORNING.
IORI-KUN.
YEAH?

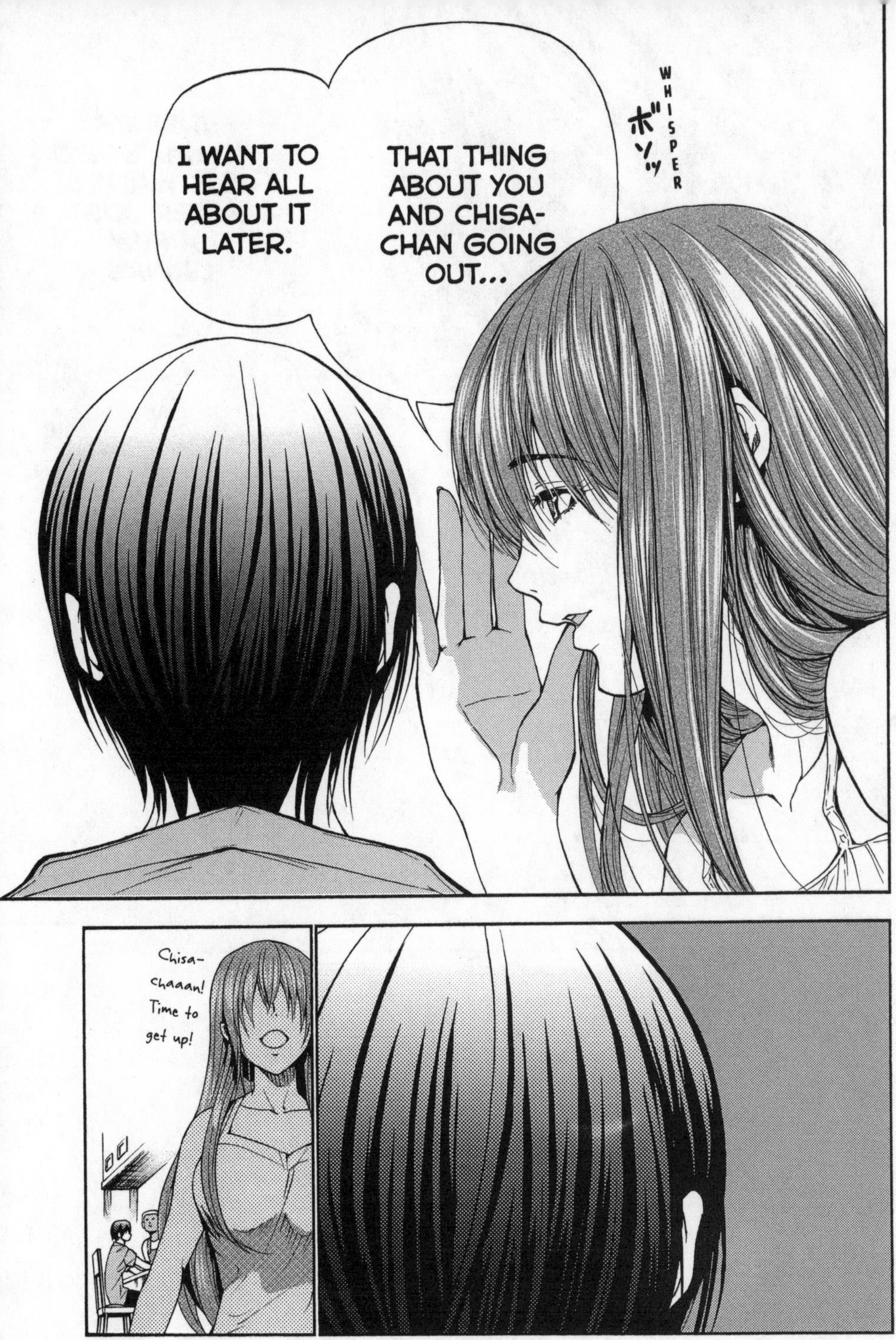
ボソッ WHISPER
THAT THING ABOUT YOU AND CHISA-CHAN GOING OUT...
I WANT TO HEAR ALL ABOUT IT LATER.
Chisa-chaaan! Time to get up!

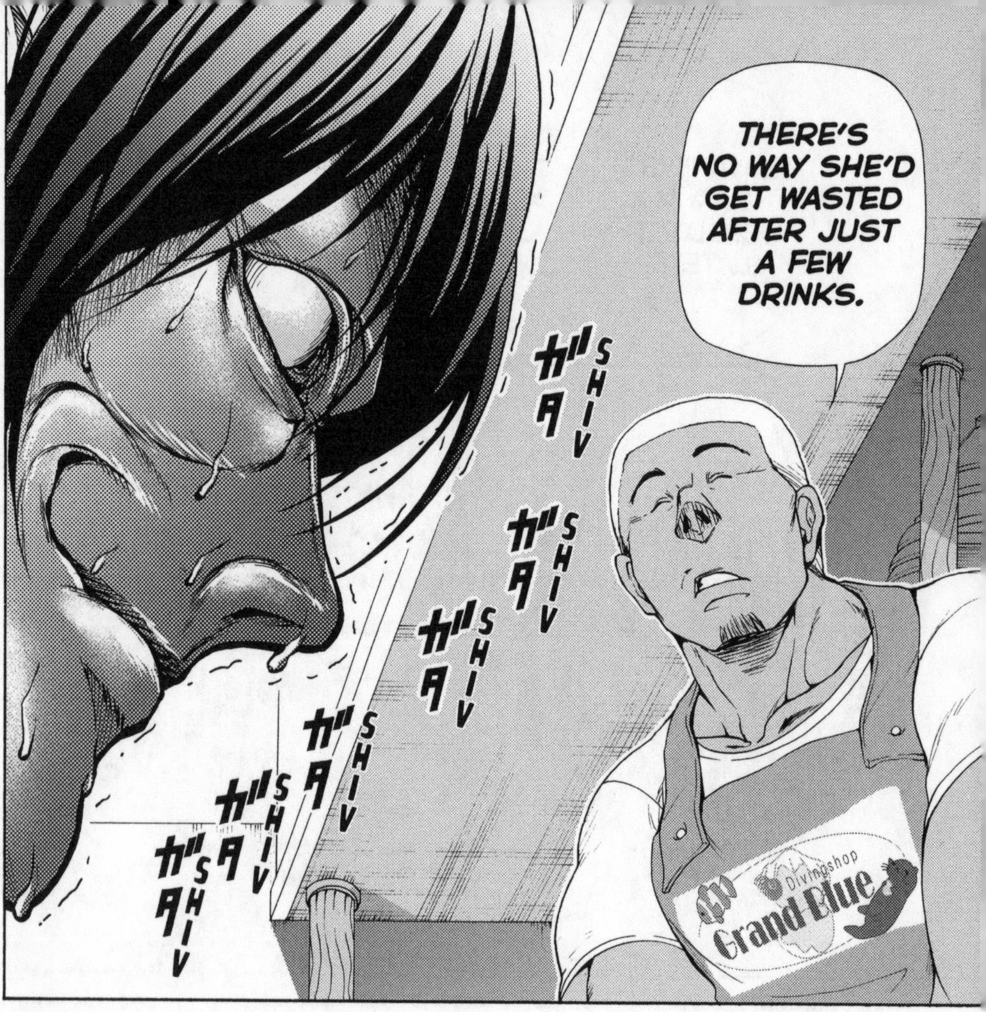
THERE'S NO WAY SHE'D GET WASTED AFTER JUST A FEW DRINKS.
ガタ SHIV
ガタ SHIV
ガタ SHIV
ガタ SHIV
ガタ SHIV
ガタ SHIV

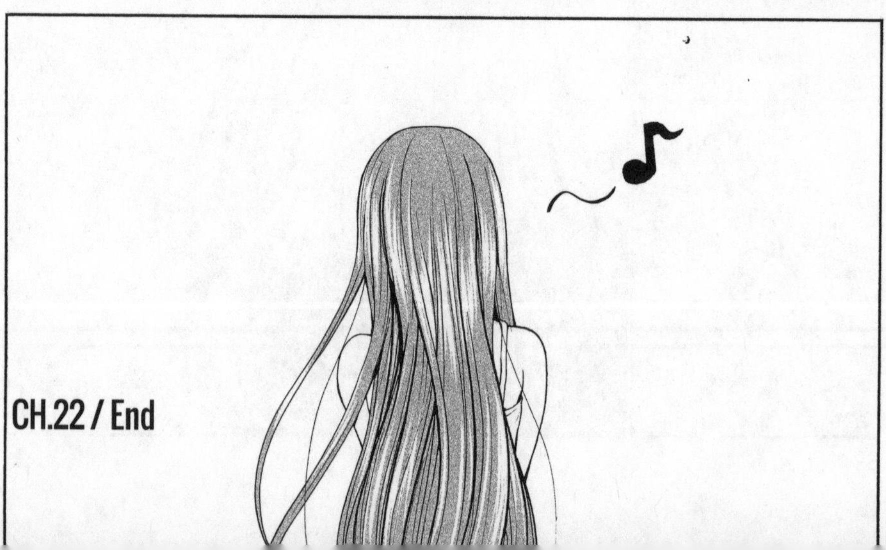
CH.22 / End

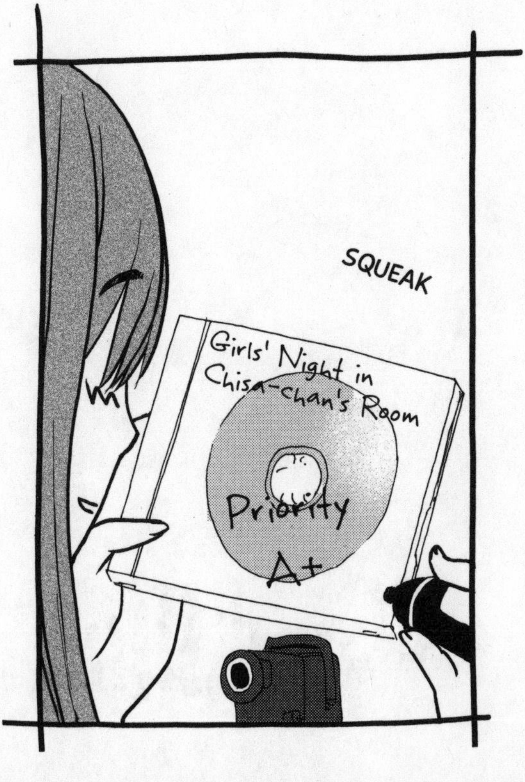
SQUEAK
Girls' Night in Chisa-chan's Room
Priority A+

Grand Blue Dreaming

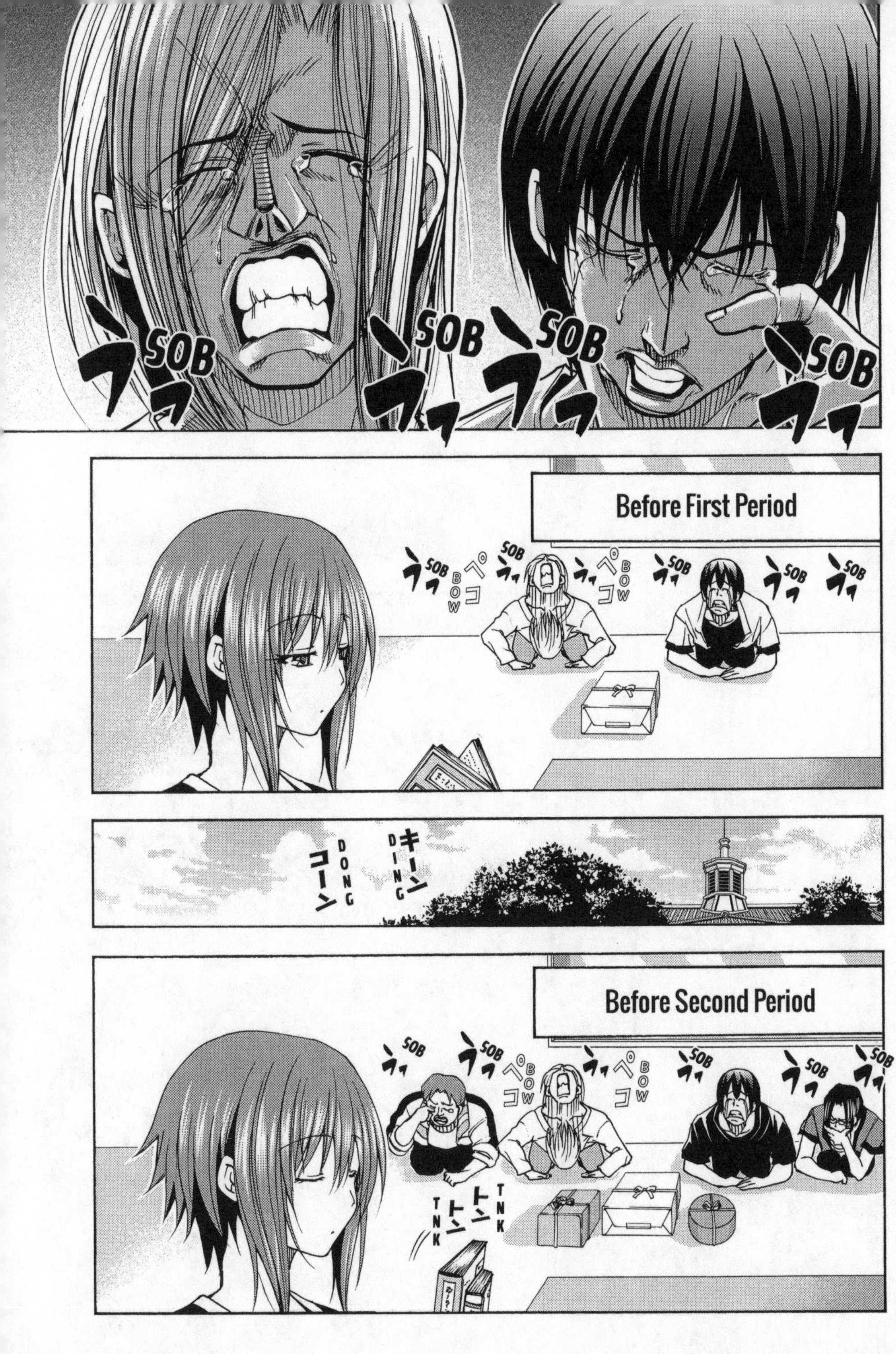
SOB
SOB
SOB
SOB
Before First Period
SOB
SOB
ペコ BOW
ペコ BOW
SOB
SOB
SOB
キーン DING
コーン DONG
Before Second Period
SOB
SOB
SOB
SOB
ペコ BOW
ペコ BOW
SOB
SOB
トン TNK
トン TNK

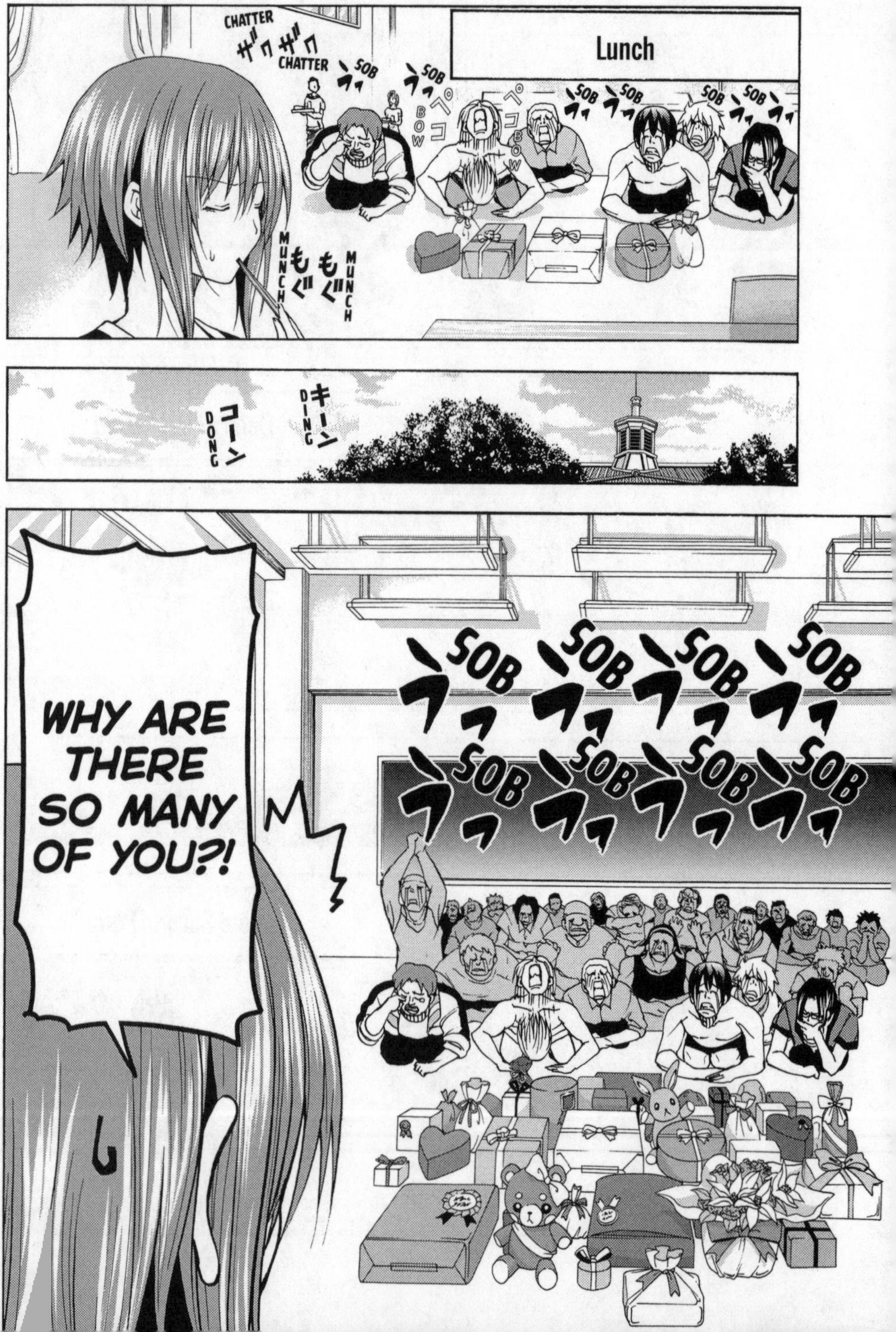

Lunch
SOB SOB SOB SOB
SOB SOB
ペコ BOW
ペコ BOW
SOB
SOB
ザワザワ
CHATTER
CHATTER
もぐもぐ
MUNCH
MUNCH
キーン DING
コーン DONG
SOB SOB SOB SOB
SOB SOB SOB SOB
WHY ARE THERE SO MANY OF YOU?!

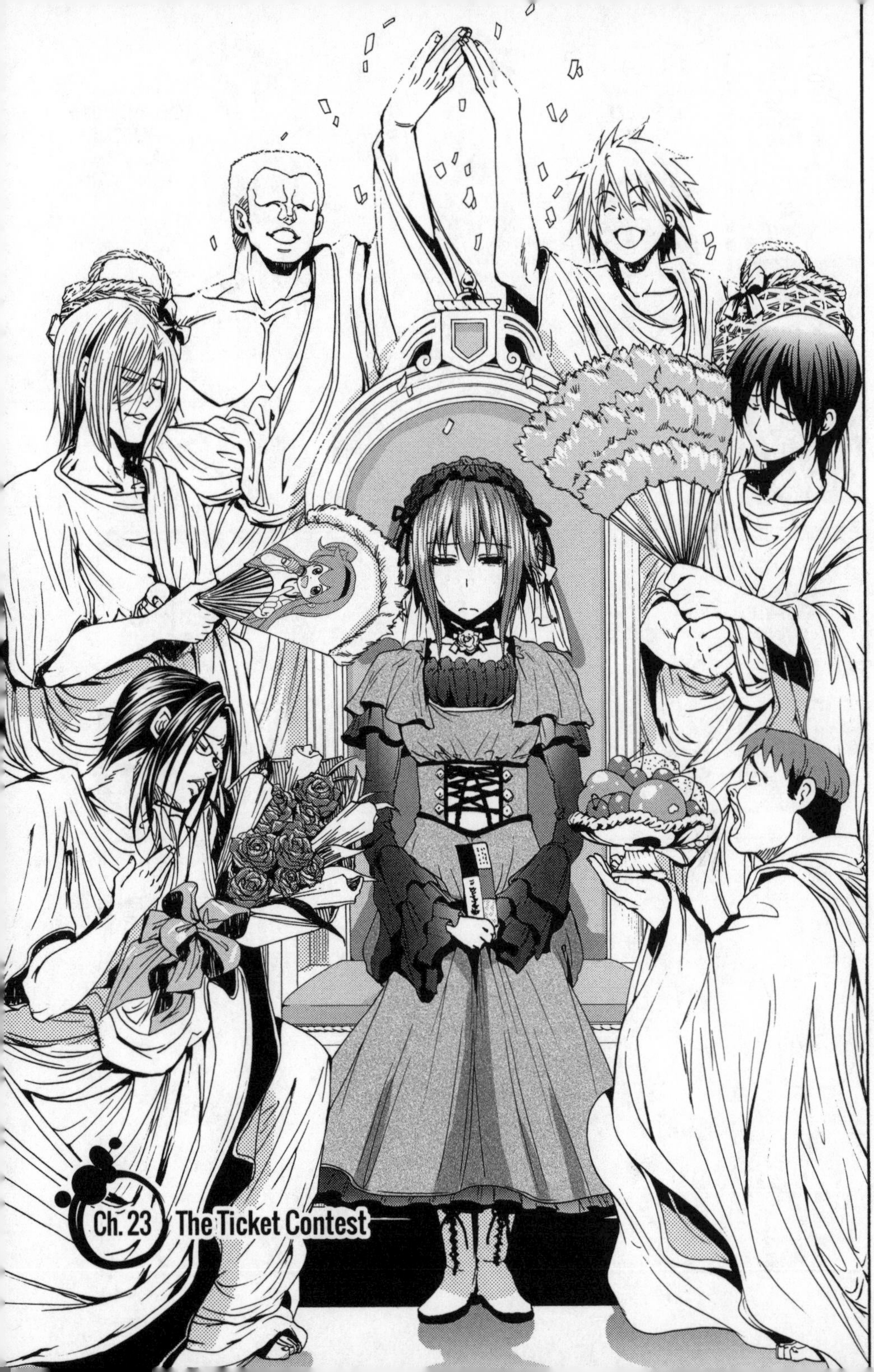
Ch. 23 The Ticket Contest

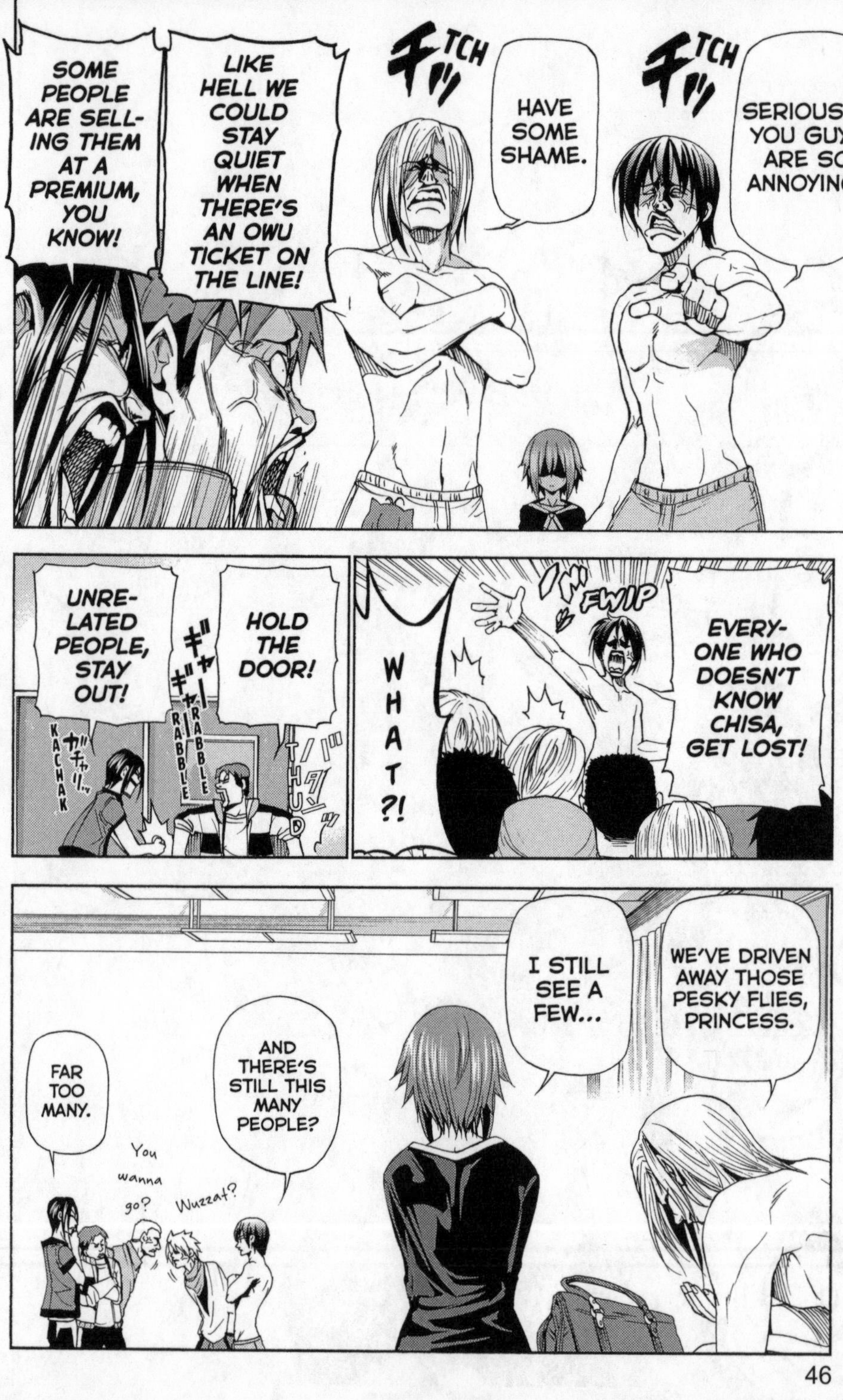
TCH
SERIOUSLY. YOU GUYS ARE SO ANNOYING.
TCH
HAVE SOME SHAME.
LIKE HELL WE COULD STAY QUIET WHEN THERE'S AN OWU TICKET ON THE LINE!
SOME PEOPLE ARE SELL-ING THEM AT A PREMIUM, YOU KNOW!
FWIP
EVERY-ONE WHO DOESN'T KNOW CHISA, GET LOST!
WHAT?!
HOLD THE DOOR!
THUD
RABBLE RABBLE
UNRELATED PEOPLE, STAY OUT!
KACHAK
WE'VE DRIVEN AWAY THOSE PESKY FLIES, PRINCESS.
I STILL SEE A FEW...
AND THERE'S STILL THIS MANY PEOPLE?
FAR TOO MANY.
Wuzzat?
You wanna go?

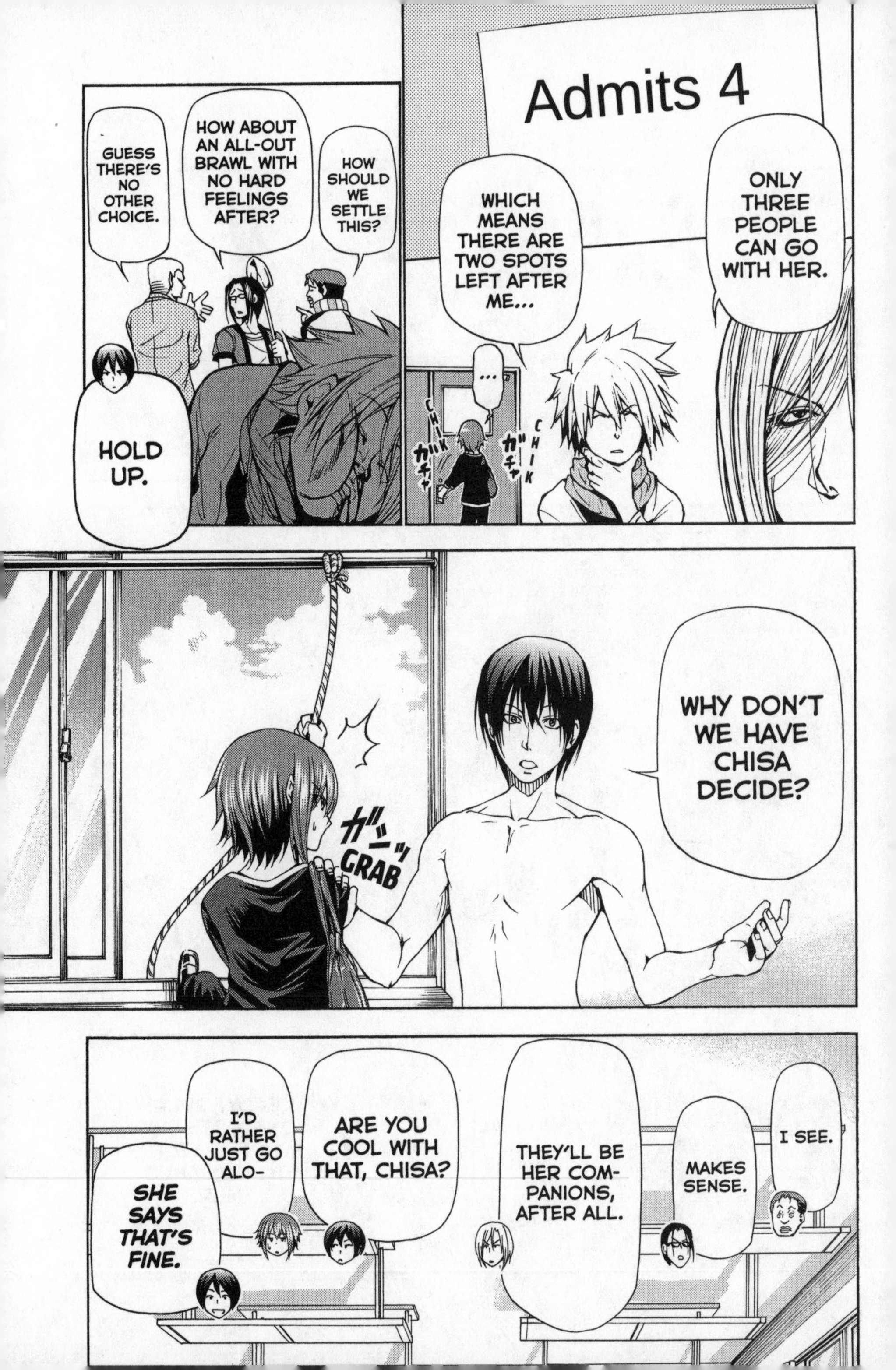
Admits 4
ONLY THREE PEOPLE CAN GO WITH HER.
WHICH MEANS THERE ARE TWO SPOTS LEFT AFTER ME...
...
ガチャ CHIK
ガチャ CHIK
HOW SHOULD WE SETTLE THIS?
HOW ABOUT AN ALL-OUT BRAWL WITH NO HARD FEELINGS AFTER?
GUESS THERE'S NO OTHER CHOICE.
HOLD UP.
WHY DON'T WE HAVE CHISA DECIDE?
ガッ GRAB
I SEE.
MAKES SENSE.
THEY'LL BE HER COMPANIONS, AFTER ALL.
ARE YOU COOL WITH THAT, CHISA?
I'D RATHER JUST GO ALO-
SHE SAYS THAT'S FINE.

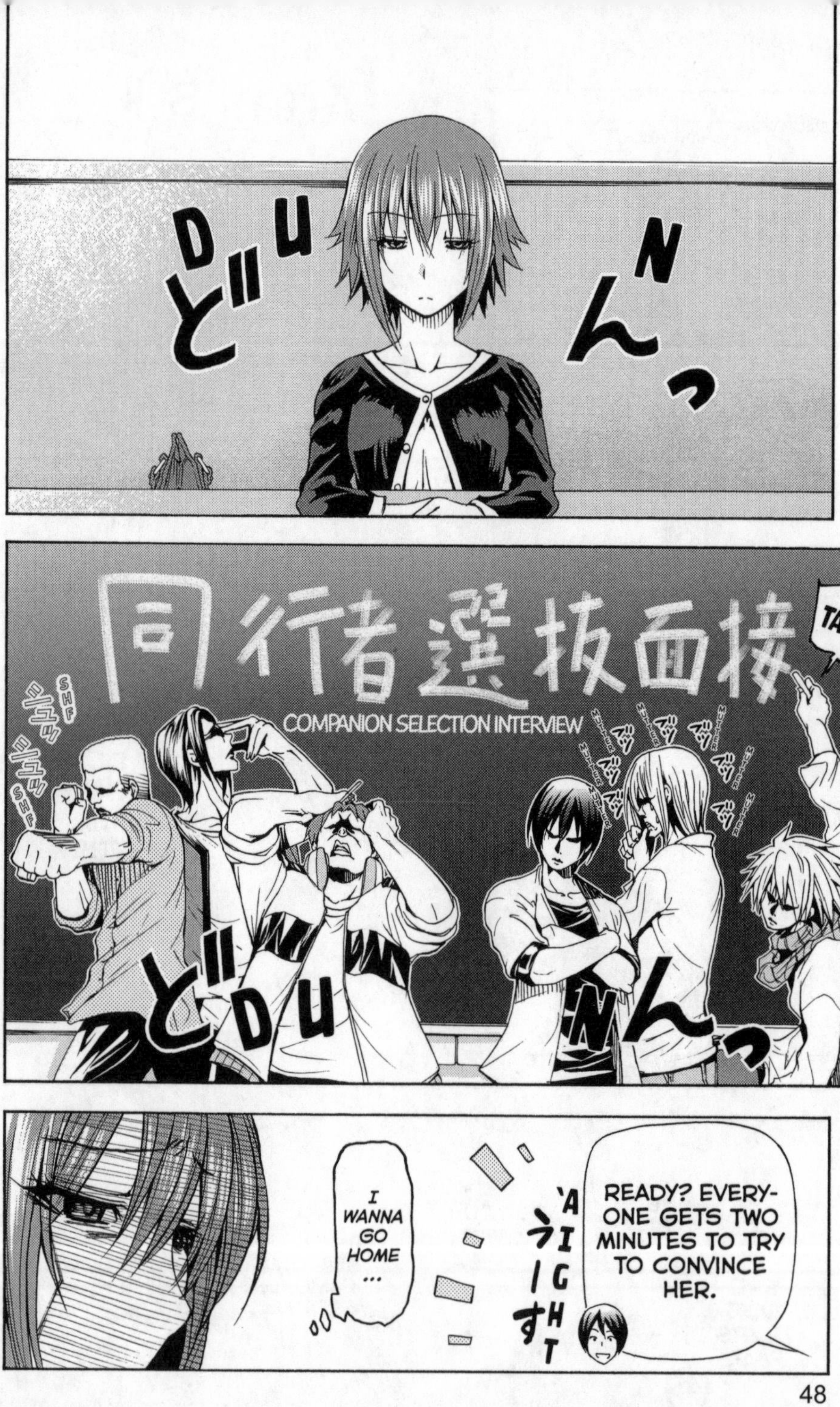

どん DUN
TAK
同行者選抜面接
COMPANION SELECTION INTERVIEW
MUTTER MUTTER
SHF SHF
どん DUN
READY? EVERY-ONE GETS TWO MINUTES TO TRY TO CONVINCE HER.
'AIGHT
I WANNA GO HOME ...

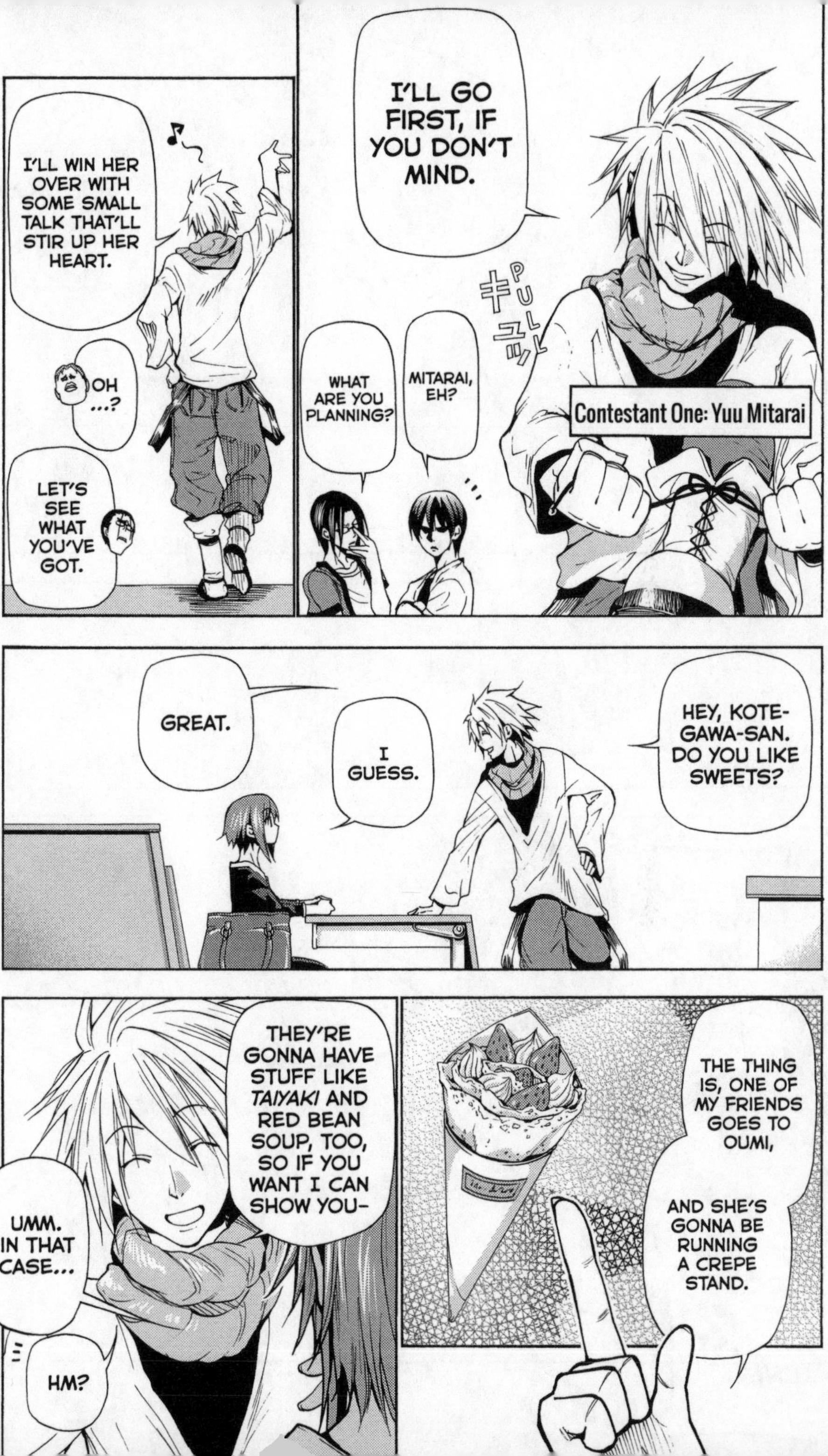
I'LL GO FIRST, IF YOU DON'T MIND.
PULL
Contestant One: Yuu Mitarai
MITARAI, EH?
WHAT ARE YOU PLANNING?
I'LL WIN HER OVER WITH SOME SMALL TALK THAT'LL STIR UP HER HEART.
OH ...?
LET'S SEE WHAT YOU'VE GOT.
HEY, KOTE-GAWA-SAN. DO YOU LIKE SWEETS?
I GUESS.
GREAT.
THE THING IS, ONE OF MY FRIENDS GOES TO OUMI,
AND SHE'S GONNA BE RUNNING A CREPE STAND.
THEY'RE GONNA HAVE STUFF LIKE *TAIYAKI* AND RED BEAN SOUP, TOO, SO IF YOU WANT I CAN SHOW YOU-
UMM. IN THAT CASE...
HM?

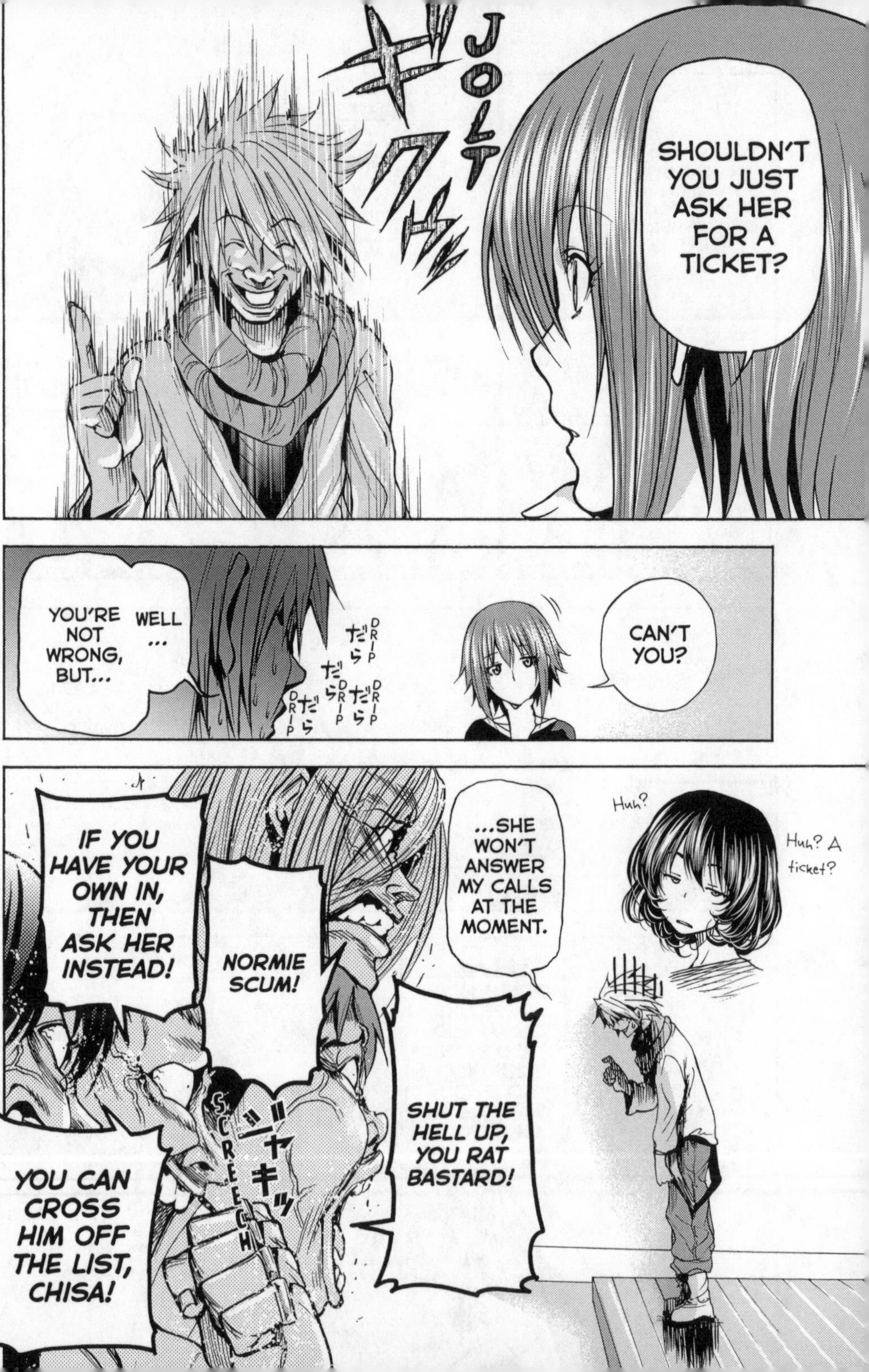
SHOULDN'T YOU JUST ASK HER FOR A TICKET?
JOLT
CAN'T YOU?
DRIP DRIP DRIP DRIP
WELL ...
YOU'RE NOT WRONG, BUT...
Huh?
Huh? A ticket?
...SHE WON'T ANSWER MY CALLS AT THE MOMENT.
NORMIE SCUM!
IF YOU HAVE YOUR OWN IN, THEN ASK HER INSTEAD!
SHUT THE HELL UP, YOU RAT BASTARD!
SCREEECH
YOU CAN CROSS HIM OFF THE LIST, CHISA!

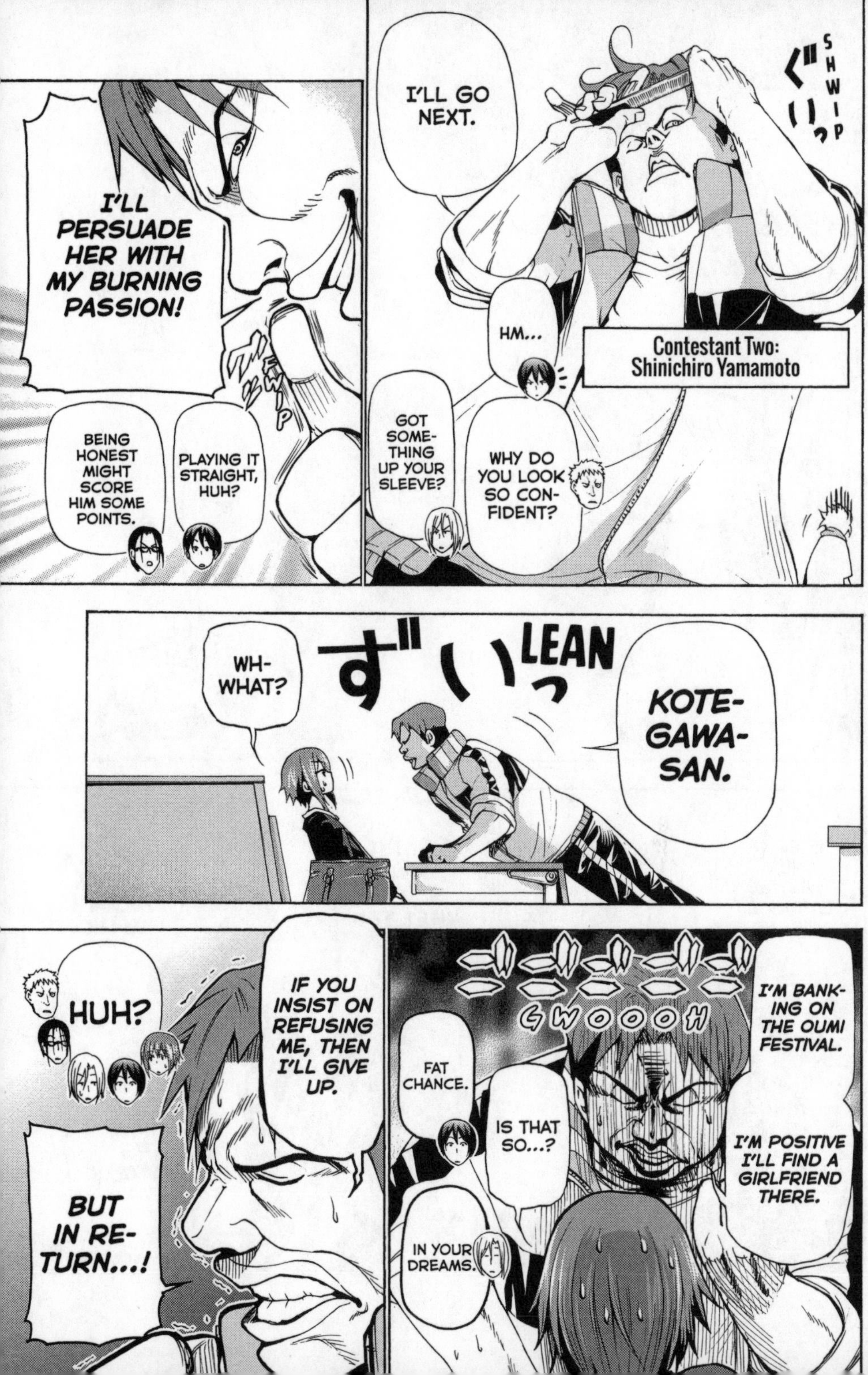
I'LL GO NEXT.
SHWIP
Contestant Two: Shinichiro Yamamoto
HM...
WHY DO YOU LOOK SO CON-FIDENT?
GOT SOME-THING UP YOUR SLEEVE?
I'LL PERSUADE HER WITH MY BURNING PASSION!
FWIP
PLAYING IT STRAIGHT, HUH?
BEING HONEST MIGHT SCORE HIM SOME POINTS.
KOTE-GAWA-SAN.
LEAN
WH-WHAT?
I'M BANK-ING ON THE OUMI FESTIVAL.
GWOOOH
I'M POSITIVE I'LL FIND A GIRLFRIEND THERE.
IS THAT SO...?
FAT CHANCE.
IN YOUR DREAMS.
IF YOU INSIST ON REFUSING ME, THEN I'LL GIVE UP.
HUH?
BUT IN RE-TURN...!

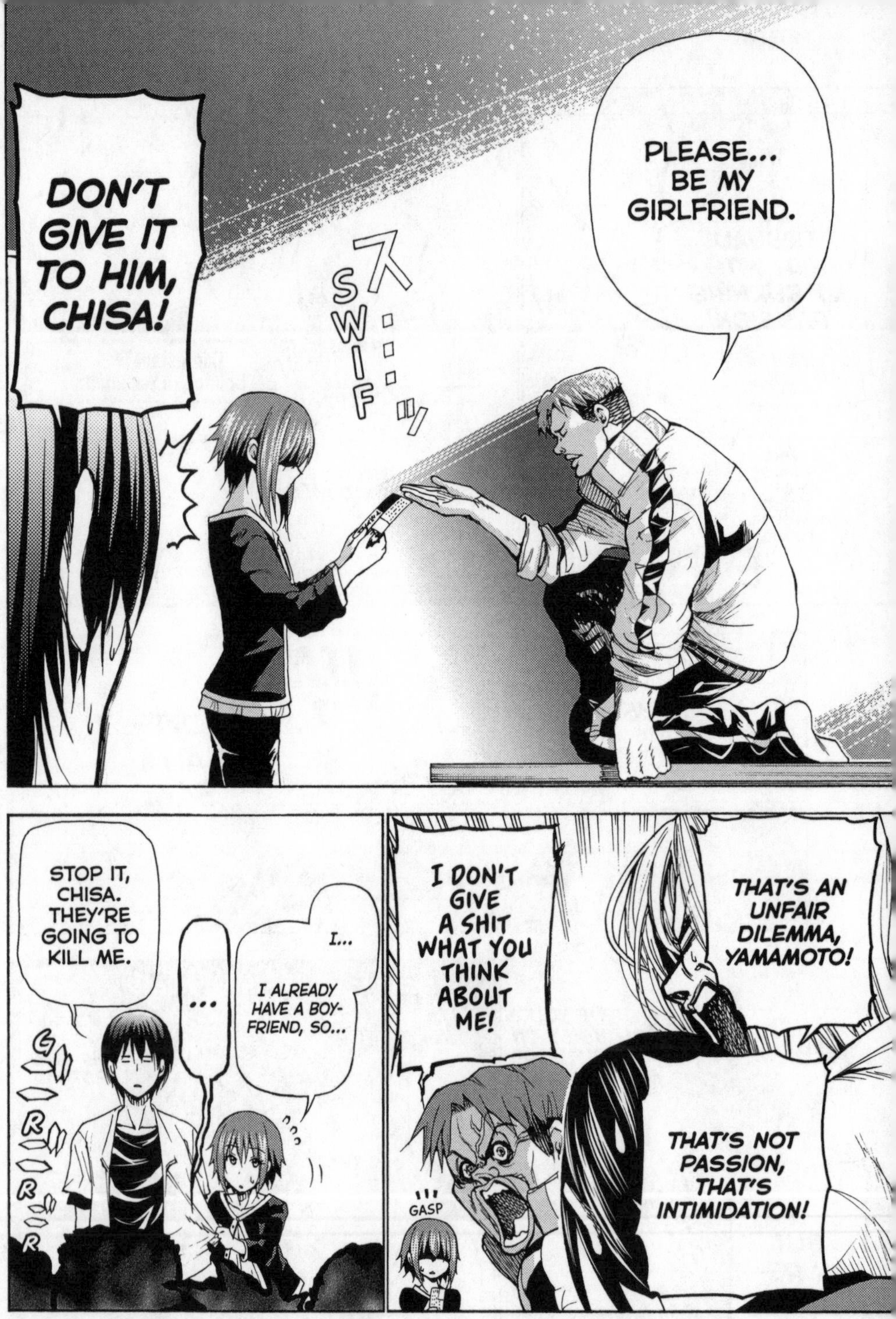
PLEASE... BE MY GIRLFRIEND.
SWIF
DON'T GIVE IT TO HIM, CHISA!
THAT'S AN UNFAIR DILEMMA, YAMAMOTO!
I DON'T GIVE A SHIT WHAT YOU THINK ABOUT ME!
THAT'S NOT PASSION, THAT'S INTIMIDATION!
GASP
I...
I ALREADY HAVE A BOY-FRIEND, SO...
...
STOP IT, CHISA. THEY'RE GOING TO KILL ME.
GRRRR

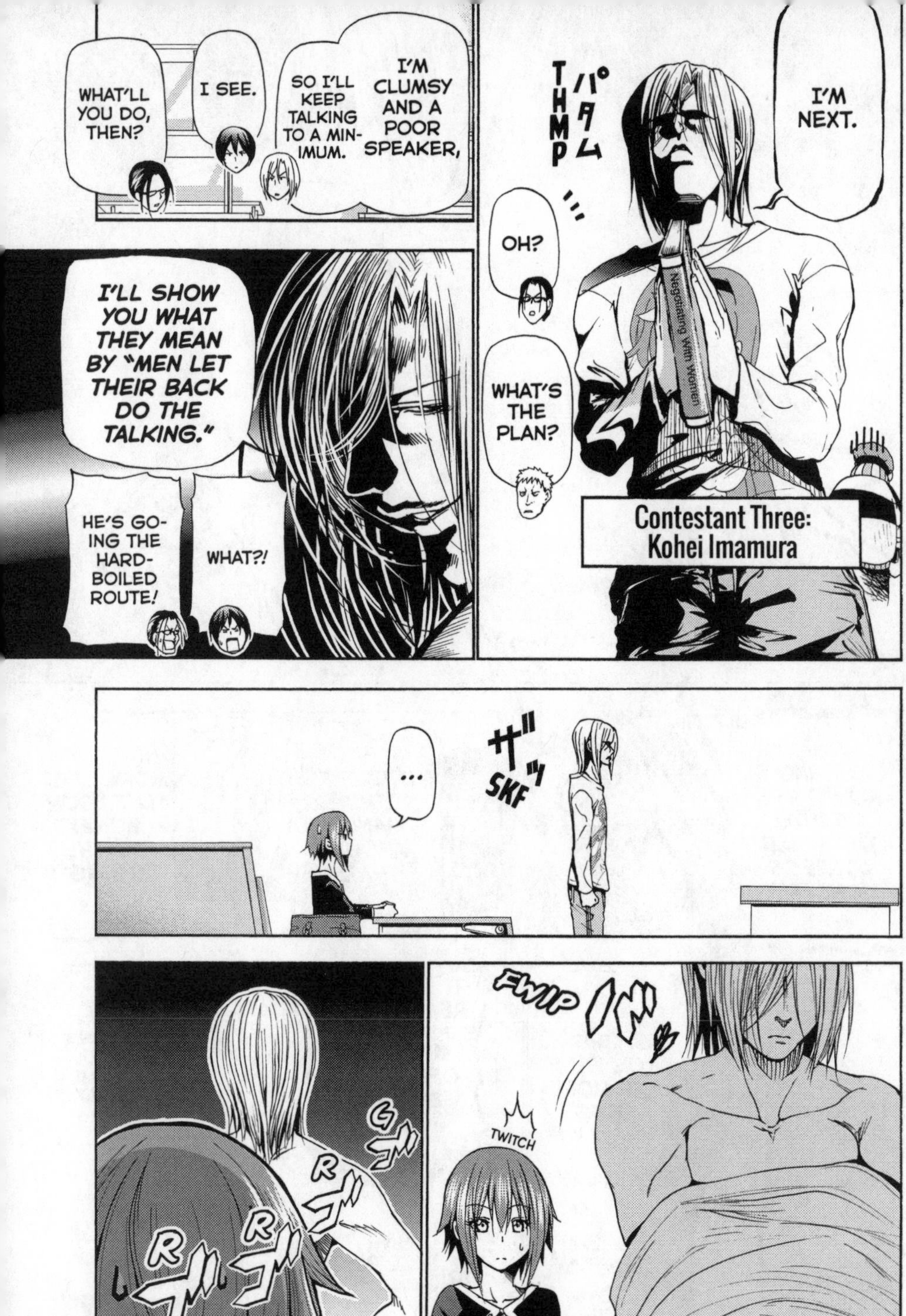
I'M NEXT.
THMP
パタム
Negotiating With Women
OH?
WHAT'S THE PLAN?
Contestant Three: Kohei Imamura
I'M CLUMSY AND A POOR SPEAKER,
SO I'LL KEEP TALKING TO A MIN-IMUM.
I SEE.
WHAT'LL YOU DO, THEN?
I'LL SHOW YOU WHAT THEY MEAN BY "MEN LET THEIR BACK DO THE TALKING."
WHAT?!
HE'S GO-ING THE HARD-BOILED ROUTE!
ザッ
SKF
...
FWIP
TWITCH
G
R
R
R

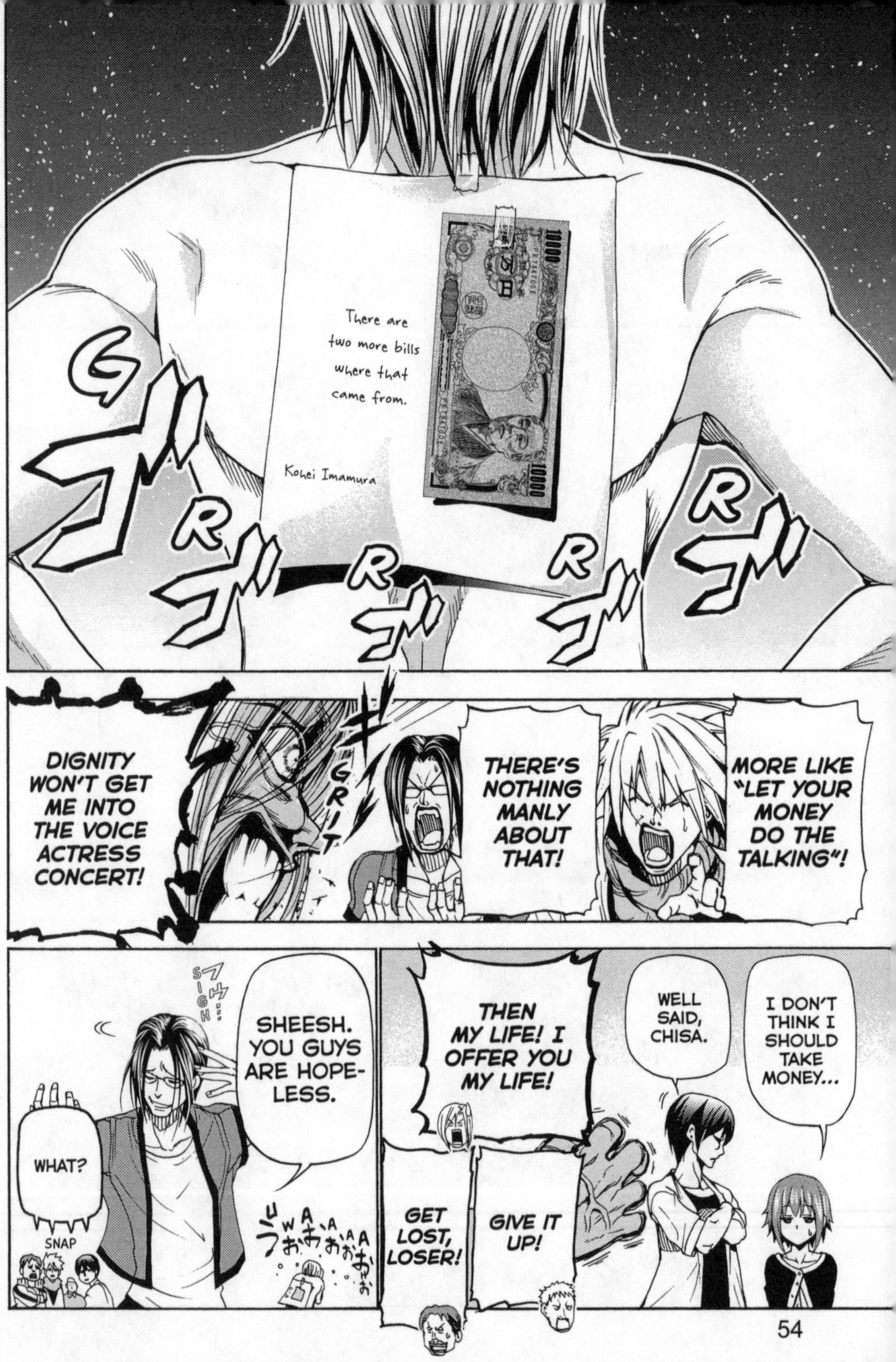
There are two more bills where that came from.
Kohei Imamura
GRRRR
MORE LIKE "LET YOUR MONEY DO THE TALKING"!
THERE'S NOTHING MANLY ABOUT THAT!
GRIT
DIGNITY WON'T GET ME INTO THE VOICE ACTRESS CONCERT!
I DON'T THINK I SHOULD TAKE MONEY...
WELL SAID, CHISA.
THEN MY LIFE! I OFFER YOU MY LIFE!
GIVE IT UP!
GET LOST, LOSER!
WAAAA
SIGH
SHEESH. YOU GUYS ARE HOPELESS.
WHAT?
SNAP

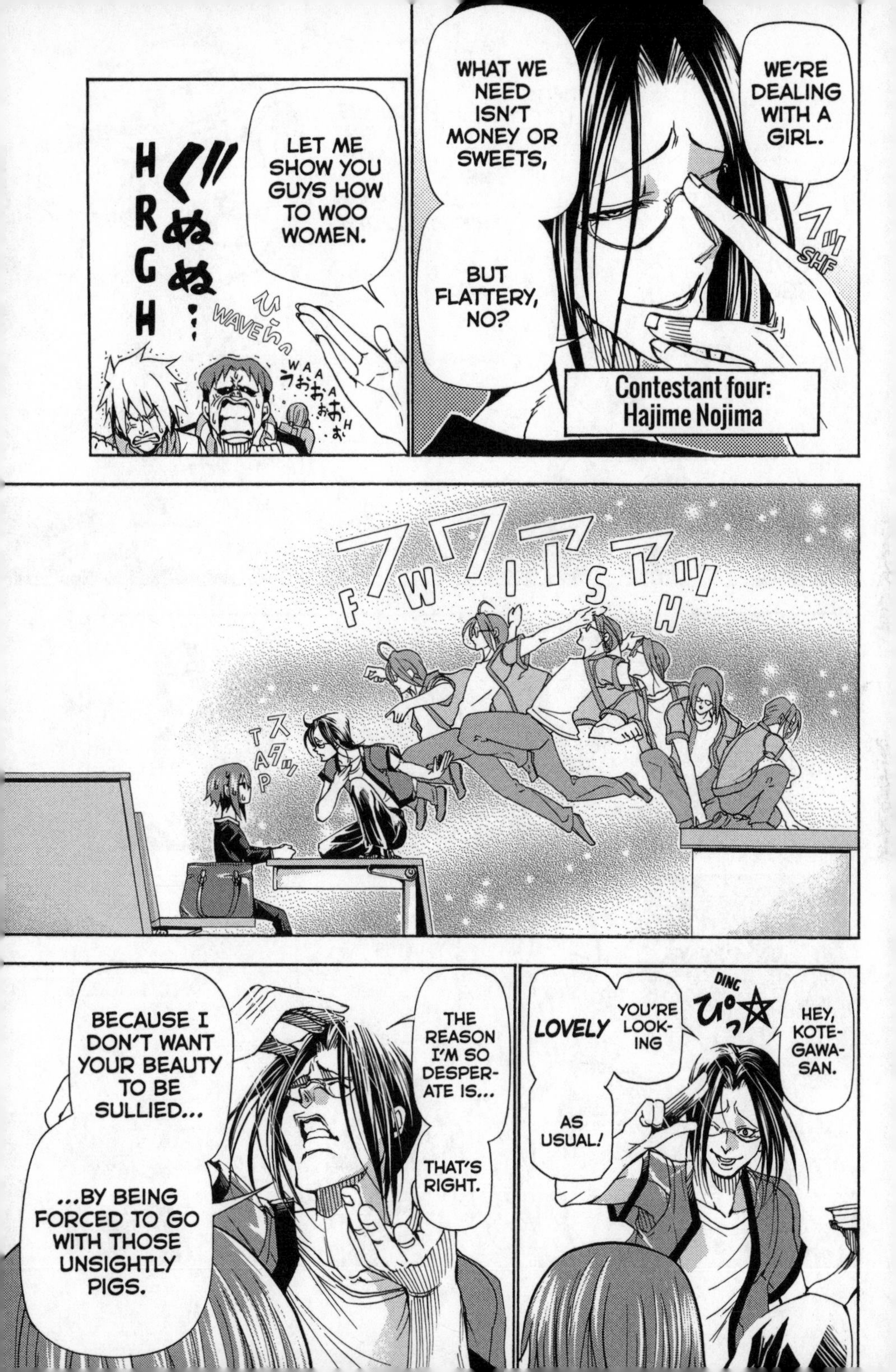
WE'RE DEALING WITH A GIRL.
WHAT WE NEED ISN'T MONEY OR SWEETS,
BUT FLATTERY, NO?
フッ SHF
Contestant four: Hajime Nojima
LET ME SHOW YOU GUYS HOW TO WOO WOMEN.
ぐぬぬ… HRGH
ひらっ WAVE
うおおおお WAAAH
フワァッ FWISH
スタッ TAP
HEY, KOTEGAWA-SAN.
ぴっ☆ DING
YOU'RE LOOKING LOVELY
AS USUAL!
THE REASON I'M SO DESPERATE IS...
THAT'S RIGHT.
BECAUSE I DON'T WANT YOUR BEAUTY TO BE SULLIED...
...BY BEING FORCED TO GO WITH THOSE UNSIGHTLY PIGS.

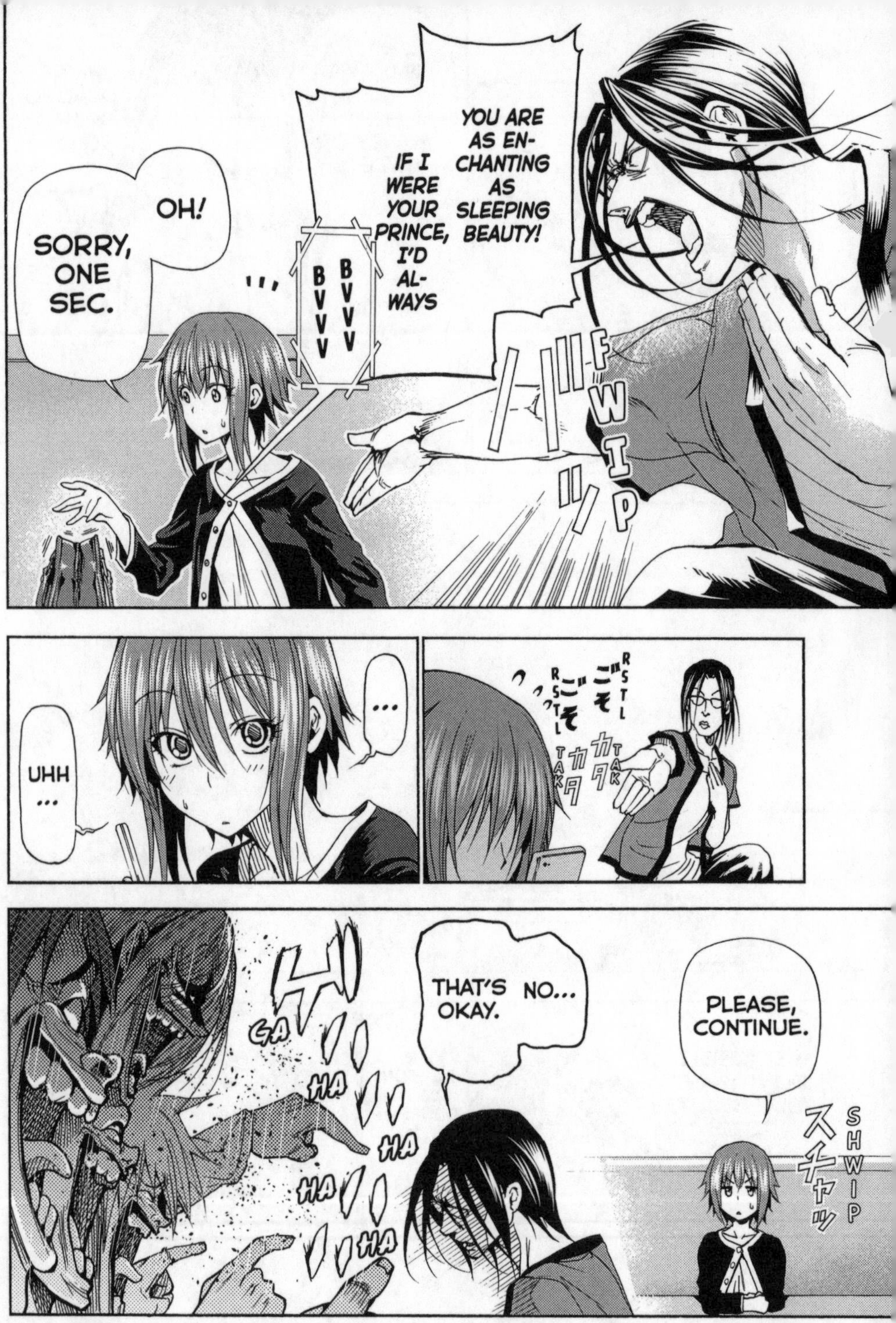
YOU ARE AS ENCHANTING AS SLEEPING BEAUTY!
IF I WERE YOUR PRINCE, I'D ALWAYS
BVVV BVVV
FWIP
OH! SORRY, ONE SEC.
RSTL ごそ RSTL ごそ
TAK カタ TAK カタ
...
UHH ...
PLEASE, CONTINUE.
SHWIP スチャッ
NO... THAT'S OKAY.
GA HA HA HA HA

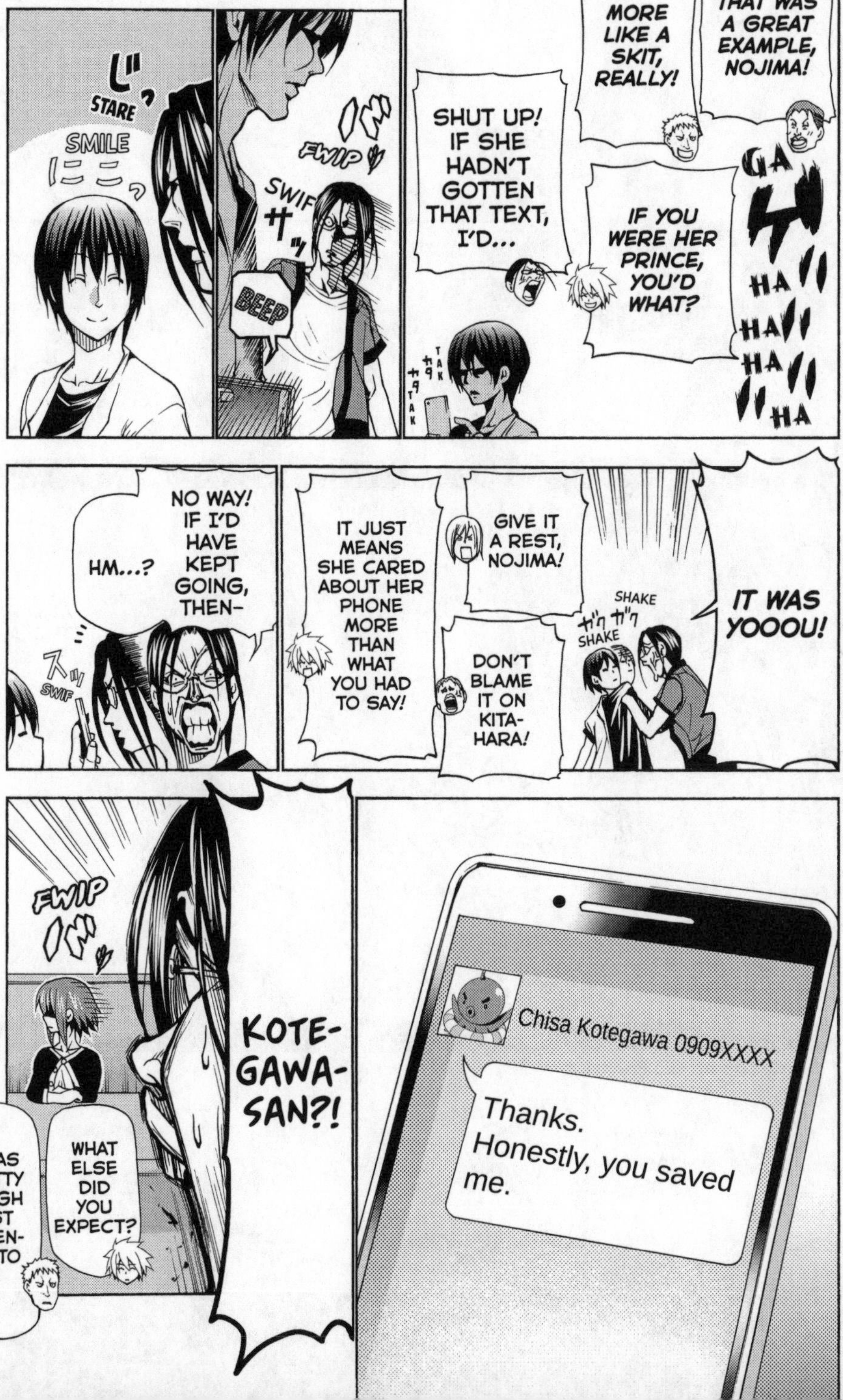
THAT WAS A GREAT EXAMPLE, NOJIMA!
MORE LIKE A SKIT, REALLY!
GA HA HA HA HA
SHUT UP! IF SHE HADN'T GOTTEN THAT TEXT, I'D...
IF YOU WERE HER PRINCE, YOU'D WHAT?
TAK TAK
FWIP
SWIF
BEEP
STARE
SMILE
IT WAS YOOOU!
SHAKE SHAKE
GIVE IT A REST, NOJIMA!
DON'T BLAME IT ON KITA-HARA!
IT JUST MEANS SHE CARED ABOUT HER PHONE MORE THAN WHAT YOU HAD TO SAY!
NO WAY! IF I'D HAVE KEPT GOING, THEN-
HM...?
SWIF
Chisa Kotegawa 0909XXXX
Thanks. Honestly, you saved me.
FWIP
KOTE-GAWA-SAN?!
WHAT ELSE DID YOU EXPECT?
IT WAS PRETTY ROUGH JUST LISTENING TO IT.

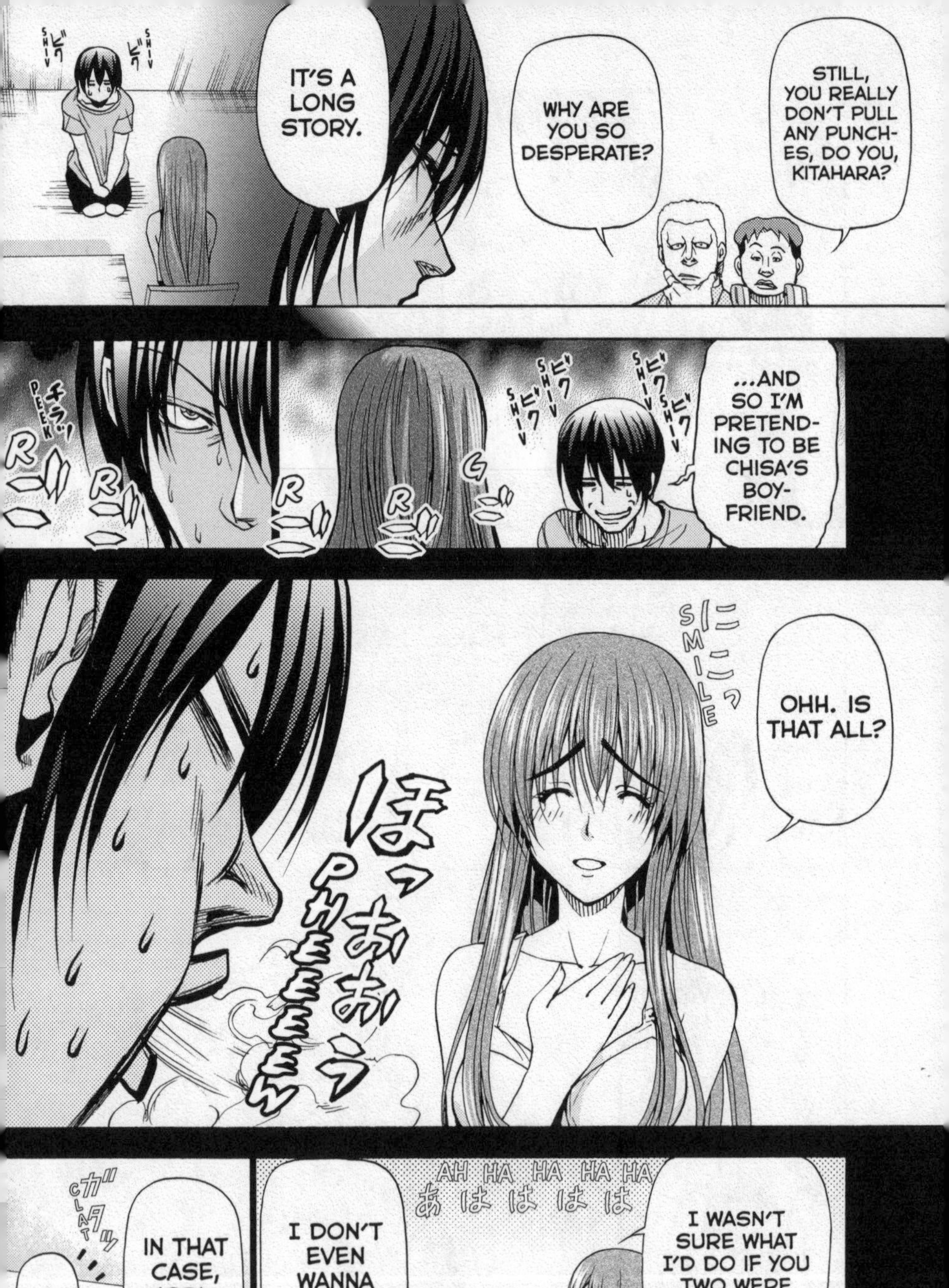
STILL, YOU REALLY DON'T PULL ANY PUNCHES, DO YOU, KITAHARA?
WHY ARE YOU SO DESPERATE?
IT'S A LONG STORY.
SHIV SHIV
...AND SO I'M PRETENDING TO BE CHISA'S BOYFRIEND.
SHIV SHIV SHIV SHIV
G
R R R R
PEEK
SMILE
OHH. IS THAT ALL?
PHEEEEW
I WASN'T SURE WHAT I'D DO IF YOU TWO WERE ACTUALLY GOING OUT.
AH HA HA HA HA
I DON'T EVEN WANNA ASK.
CLAT
IN THAT CASE, IORI-KUN.
YEAH?

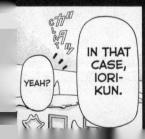

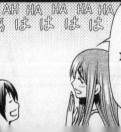

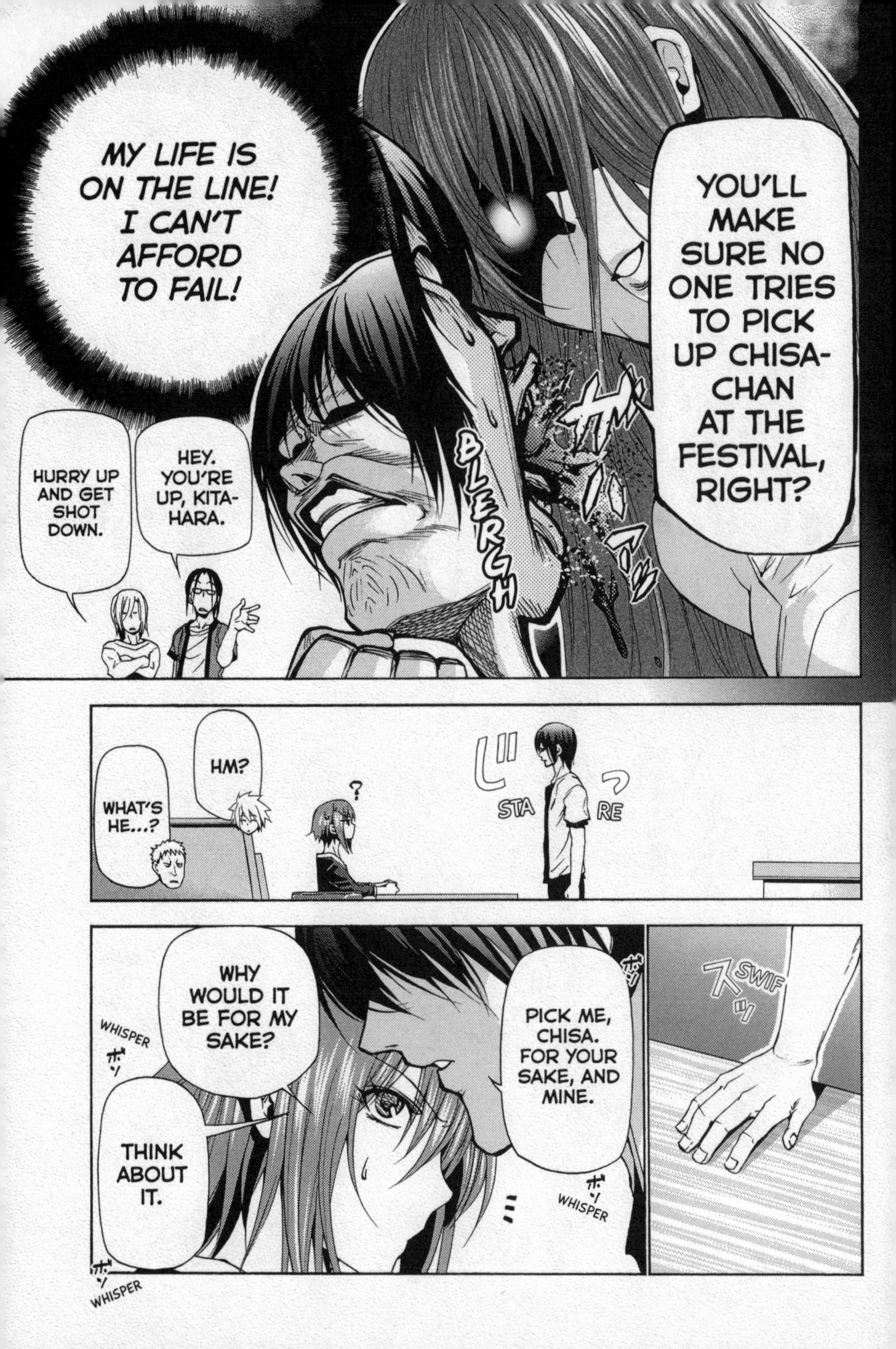
YOU'LL MAKE SURE NO ONE TRIES TO PICK UP CHISA-CHAN AT THE FESTIVAL, RIGHT?
BLERGH
MY LIFE IS ON THE LINE! I CAN'T AFFORD TO FAIL!
HEY. YOU'RE UP, KITA-HARA.
HURRY UP AND GET SHOT DOWN.
STA RE
?
HM?
WHAT'S HE...?
SWIF
PICK ME, CHISA. FOR YOUR SAKE, AND MINE.
WHISPER
WHY WOULD IT BE FOR MY SAKE?
WHISPER
THINK ABOUT IT.
WHISPER

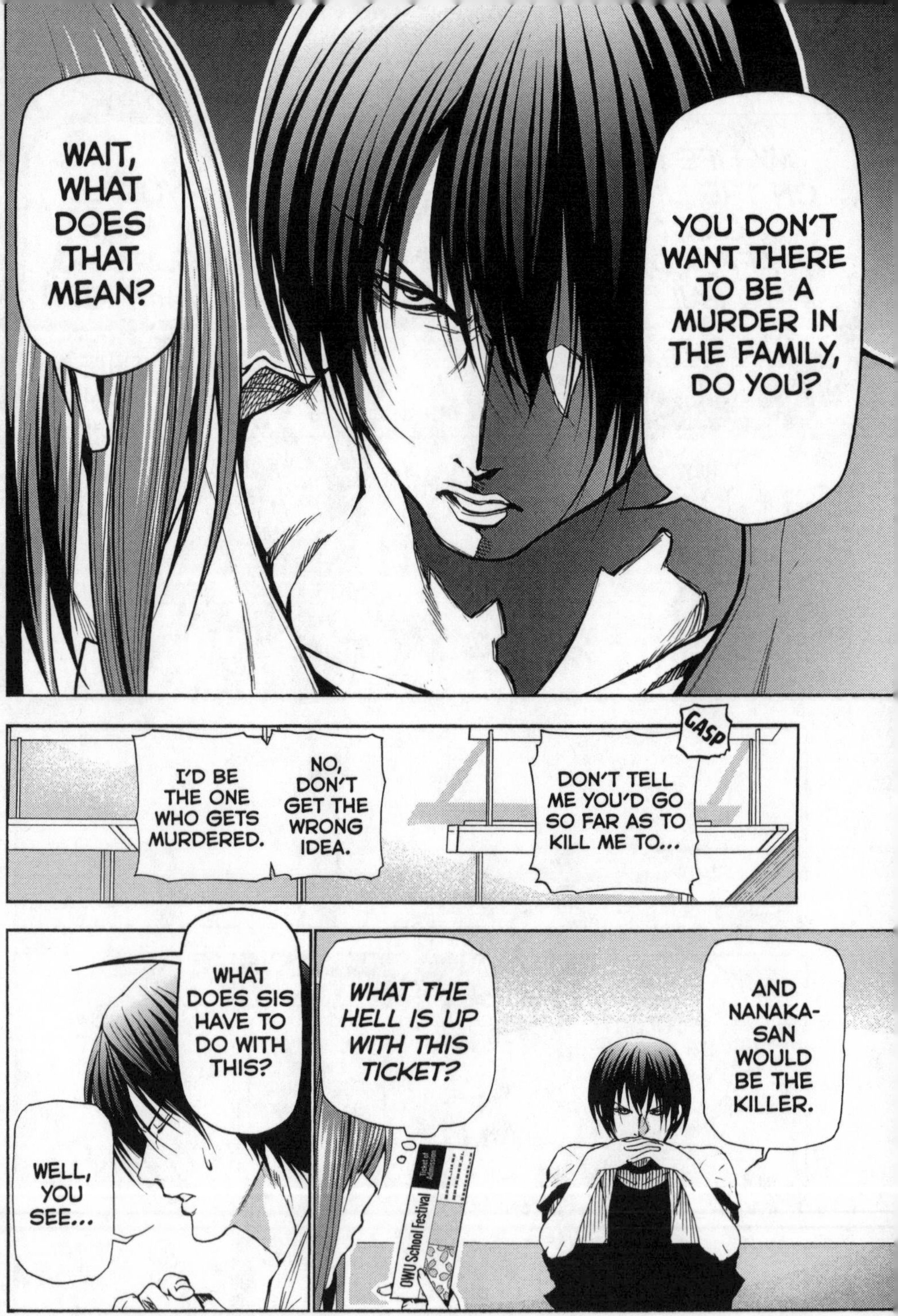
YOU DON'T WANT THERE TO BE A MURDER IN THE FAMILY, DO YOU?
WAIT, WHAT DOES THAT MEAN?
GASP
DON'T TELL ME YOU'D GO SO FAR AS TO KILL ME TO...
NO, DON'T GET THE WRONG IDEA.
I'D BE THE ONE WHO GETS MURDERED.
AND NANAKA-SAN WOULD BE THE KILLER.
WHAT THE HELL IS UP WITH THIS TICKET?
Ticket of Admission
OWU School Festival
WHAT DOES SIS HAVE TO DO WITH THIS?
WELL, YOU SEE...

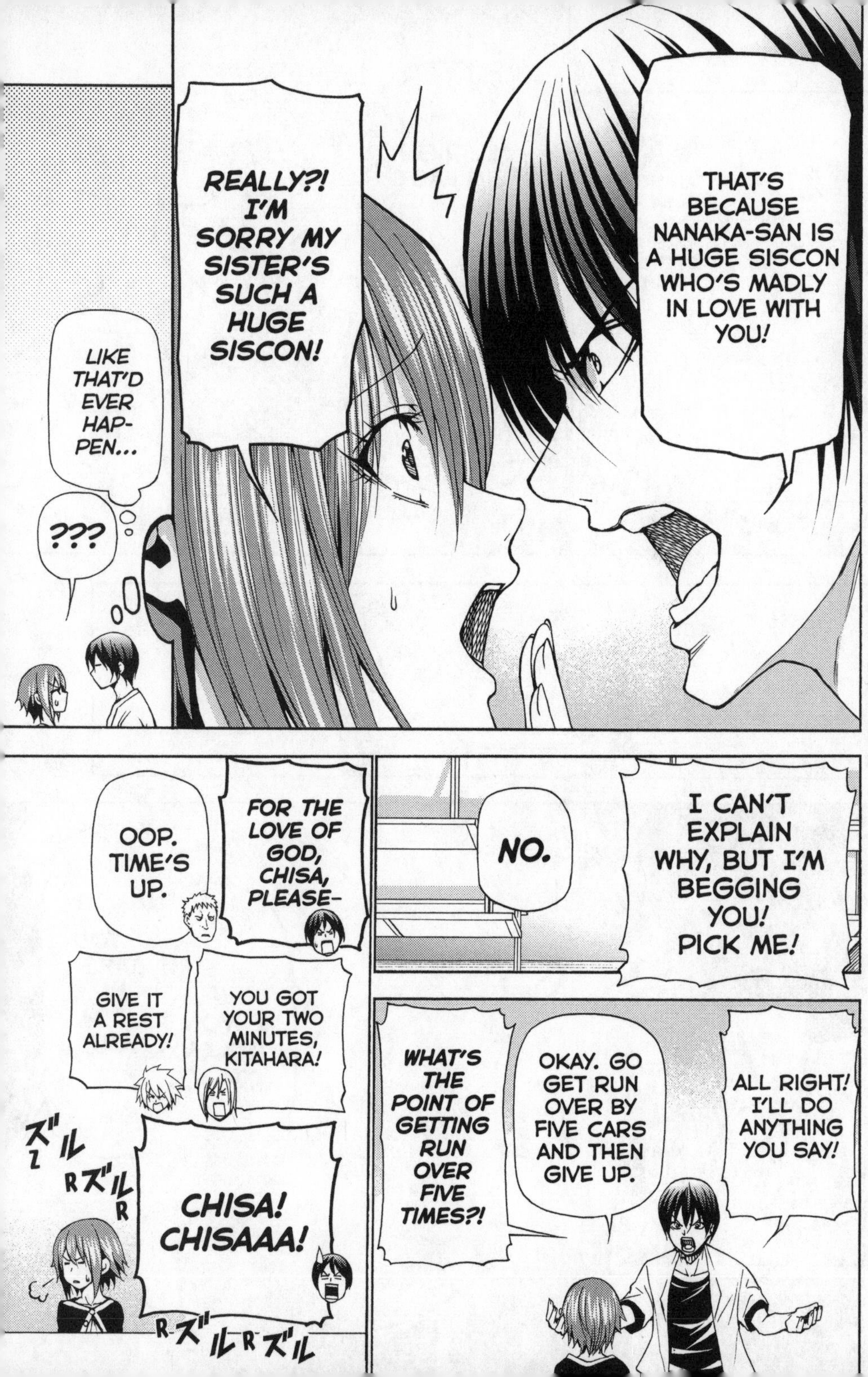
THAT'S BECAUSE NANAKA-SAN IS A HUGE SISCON WHO'S MADLY IN LOVE WITH YOU!
REALLY?! I'M SORRY MY SISTER'S SUCH A HUGE SISCON!
LIKE THAT'D EVER HAP-PEN...
???
I CAN'T EXPLAIN WHY, BUT I'M BEGGING YOU! PICK ME!
NO.
FOR THE LOVE OF GOD, CHISA, PLEASE-
OOP. TIME'S UP.
YOU GOT YOUR TWO MINUTES, KITAHARA!
GIVE IT A REST ALREADY!
ALL RIGHT! I'LL DO ANYTHING YOU SAY!
OKAY. GO GET RUN OVER BY FIVE CARS AND THEN GIVE UP.
WHAT'S THE POINT OF GETTING RUN OVER FIVE TIMES?!
CHISA! CHISAAA!
ズル Z
R ズル R
R ズル R ズル

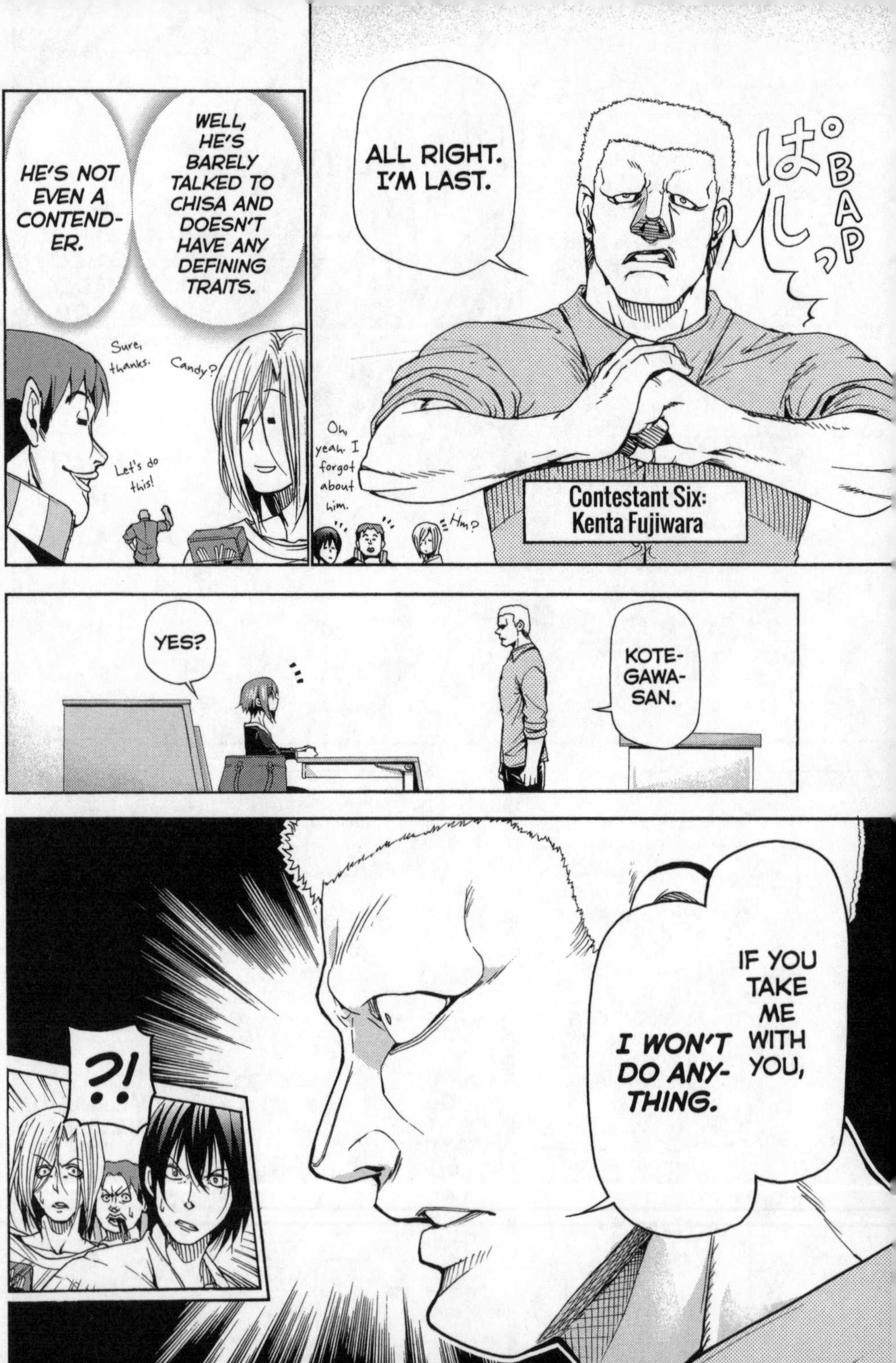
ぱしっ
BAP
ALL RIGHT. I'M LAST.
Contestant Six: Kenta Fujiwara
Oh yeah. I forgot about him.
Hm?
WELL, HE'S BARELY TALKED TO CHISA AND DOESN'T HAVE ANY DEFINING TRAITS.
HE'S NOT EVEN A CONTENDER.
Candy?
Sure, thanks.
Let's do this!
KOTE-GAWA-SAN.
YES?
IF YOU TAKE ME WITH YOU,
I WON'T DO ANYTHING.
?!

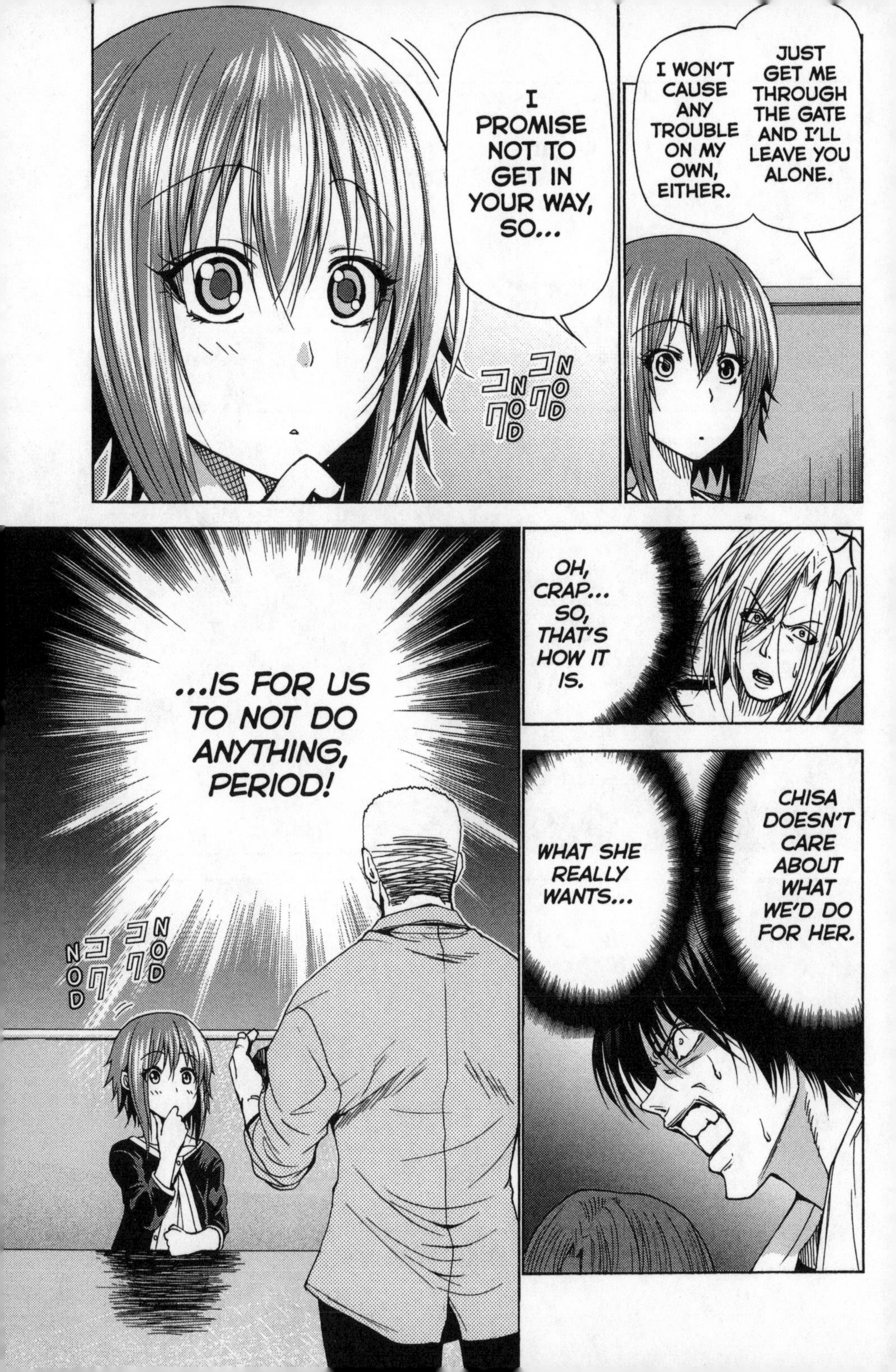
JUST GET ME THROUGH THE GATE AND I'LL LEAVE YOU ALONE.
I WON'T CAUSE ANY TROUBLE ON MY OWN, EITHER.
I PROMISE NOT TO GET IN YOUR WAY, SO...
NOD NOD
OH, CRAP... SO, THAT'S HOW IT IS.
CHISA DOESN'T CARE ABOUT WHAT WE'D DO FOR HER.
WHAT SHE REALLY WANTS...
...IS FOR US TO NOT DO ANYTHING, PERIOD!
NOD NOD

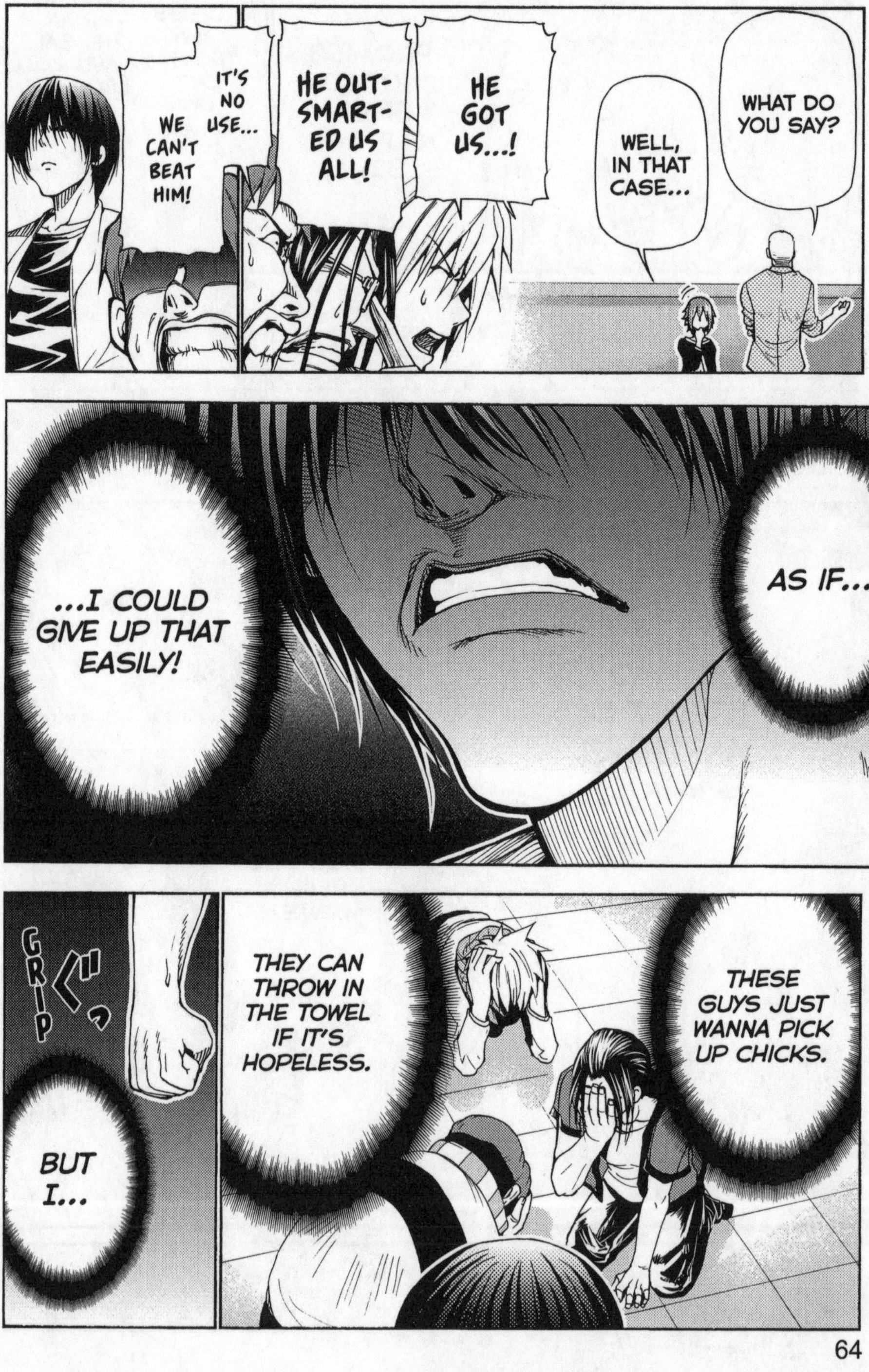
WHAT DO YOU SAY?
WELL, IN THAT CASE...
HE GOT US...!
HE OUT-SMART-ED US ALL!
IT'S NO USE...
WE CAN'T BEAT HIM!
AS IF...
...I COULD GIVE UP THAT EASILY!
THESE GUYS JUST WANNA PICK UP CHICKS.
THEY CAN THROW IN THE TOWEL IF IT'S HOPELESS.
ぐっ
GRIP
BUT I...

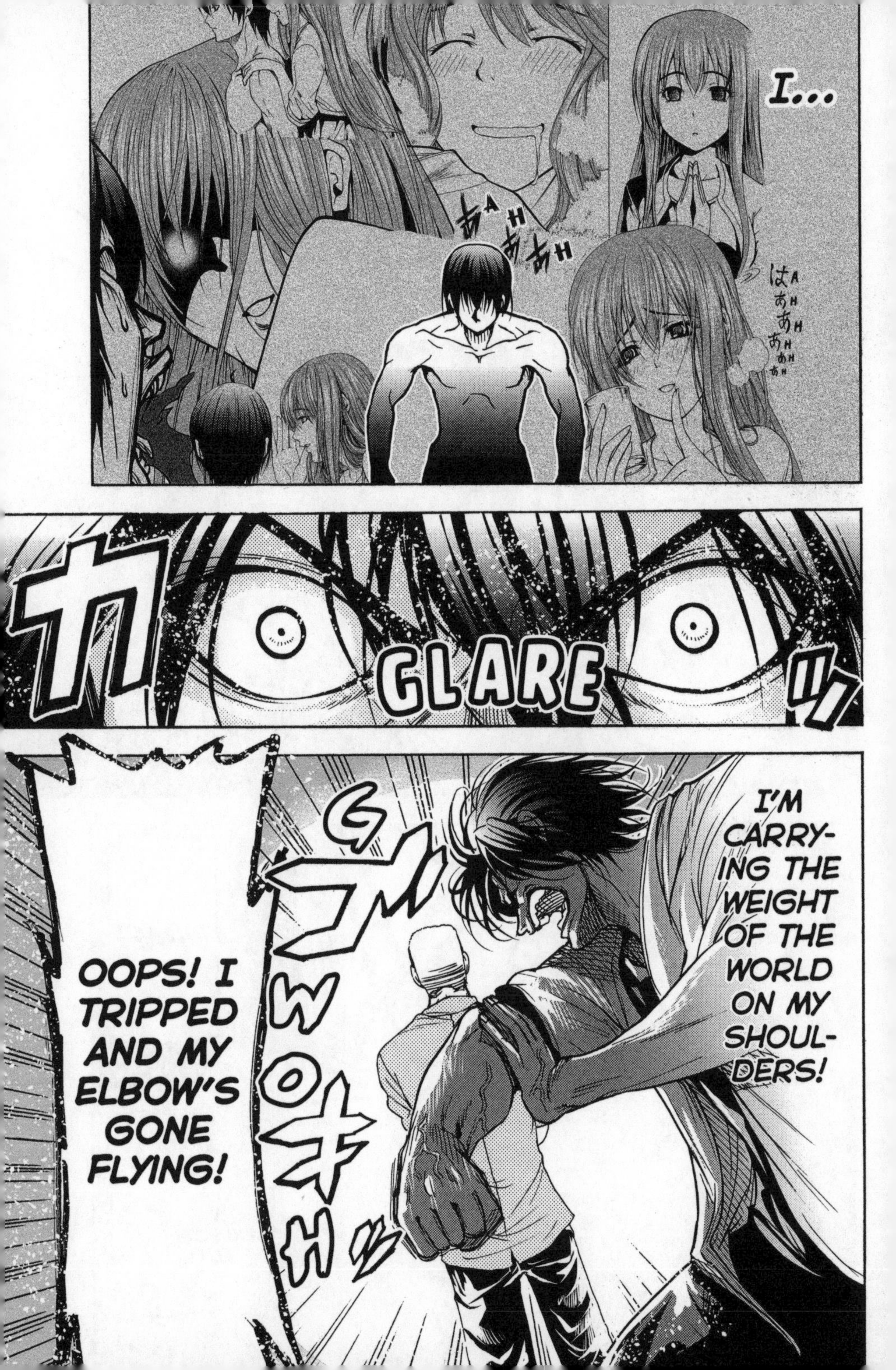
I...
CLARE
I'M CARRYING THE WEIGHT OF THE WORLD ON MY SHOULDERS!
GWOH
OOPS! I TRIPPED AND MY ELBOW'S GONE FLYING!

SON OF A...!

WHA?!

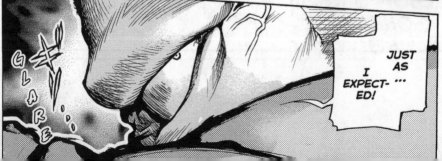

JUST AS I EXPECT-ED!

DON'T EVEN TRY.
I CAN READ YOU LIKE...
...A BOOK!
WHOOSH
BAP
...
YOU ...

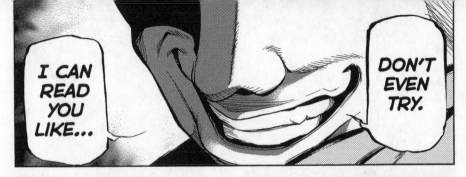

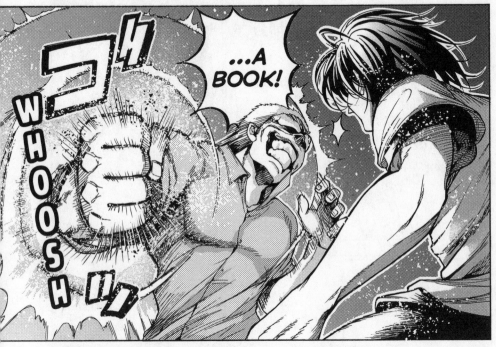

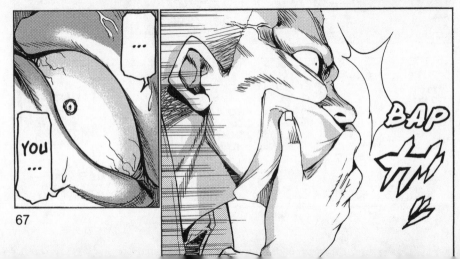

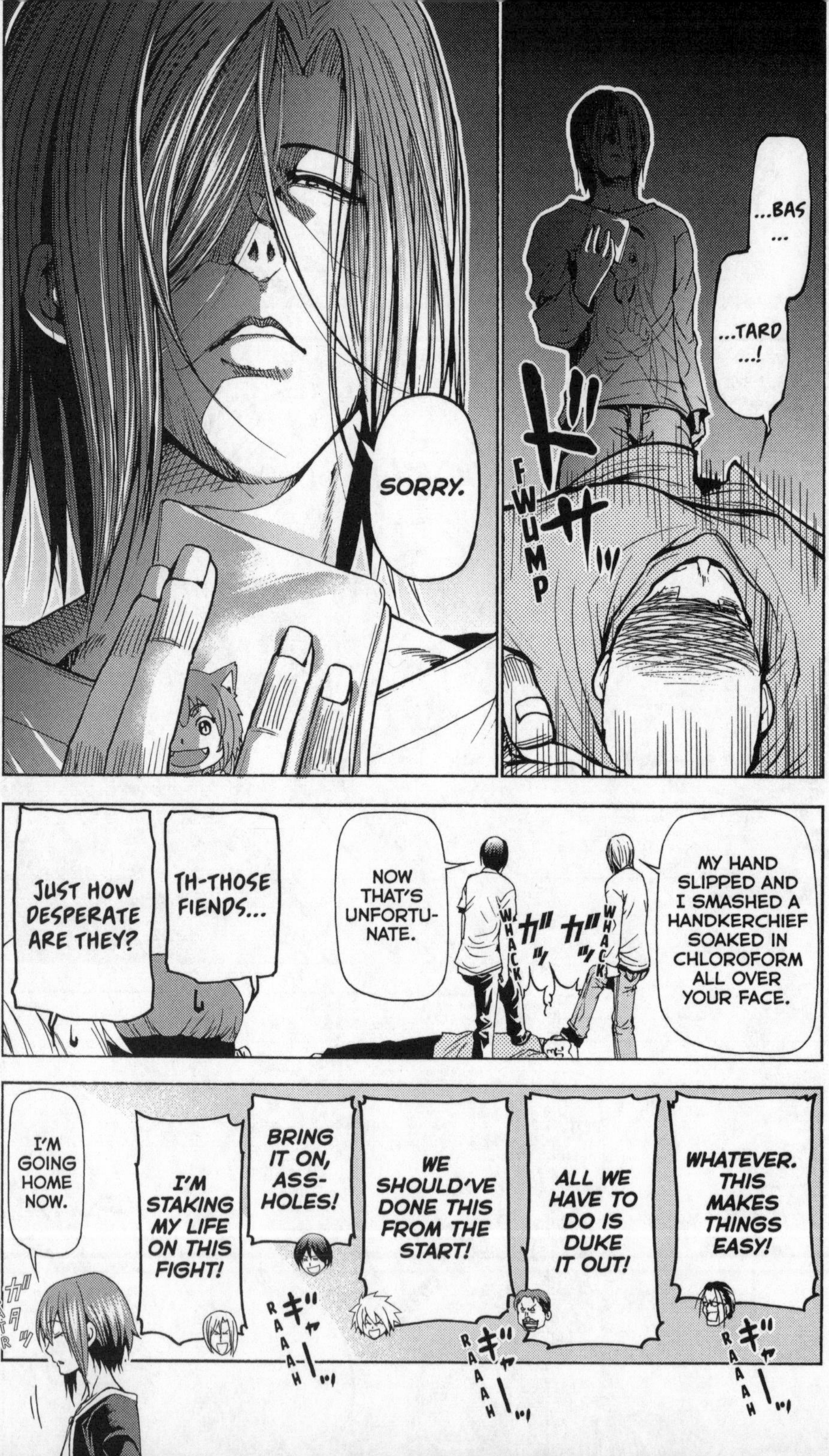
...BAS ...
...TARD ...!
FWUMP
SORRY.
MY HAND SLIPPED AND I SMASHED A HANDKERCHIEF SOAKED IN CHLOROFORM ALL OVER YOUR FACE.
WHACK
WHACK
NOW THAT'S UNFORTU-NATE.
TH-THOSE FIENDS...
JUST HOW DESPERATE ARE THEY?
WHATEVER. THIS MAKES THINGS EASY!
RAAAH
ALL WE HAVE TO DO IS DUKE IT OUT!
RAAAH
WE SHOULD'VE DONE THIS FROM THE START!
BRING IT ON, ASS-HOLES!
RAAAH
I'M STAKING MY LIFE ON THIS FIGHT!
I'M GOING HOME NOW.
CLATR

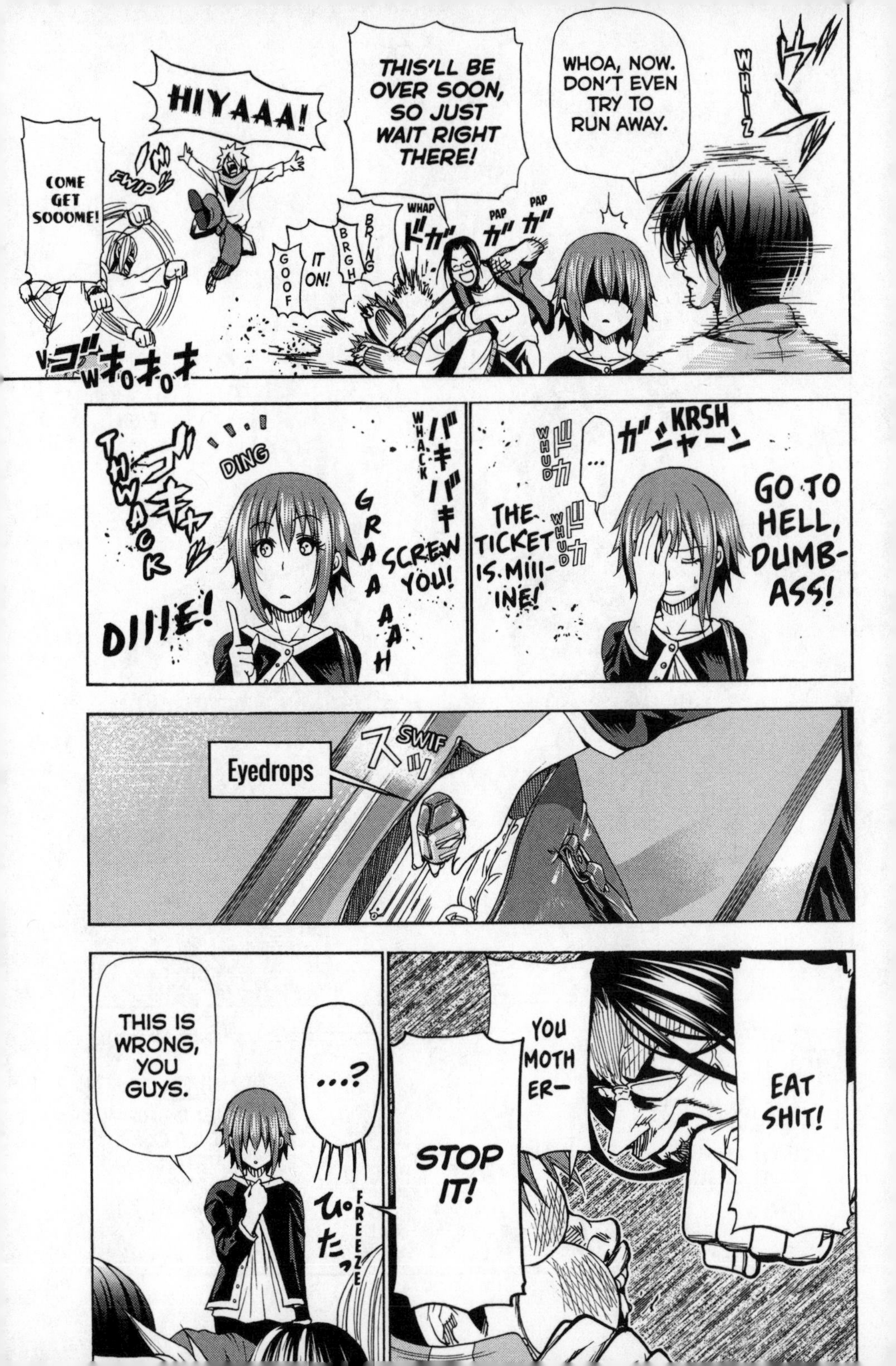
WHIZ
WHOA, NOW. DON'T EVEN TRY TO RUN AWAY.
PAP
PAP
WHAP
THIS'LL BE OVER SOON, SO JUST WAIT RIGHT THERE!
BRING
BRGH
IT ON!
GOOF
HIYAAA!
FWIP
COME GET SOOOME!
KRSH
...
WHUD
GO TO HELL, DUMB-ASS!
THE TICKET IS MIIII-INE!
WHUD
WHACK
SCREW YOU!
GRAAAAH
DING
THWACK
DIIIE!
SWIF
Eyedrops
EAT SHIT!
YOU MOTHER-
STOP IT!
FREEZE
...?
THIS IS WRONG, YOU GUYS.

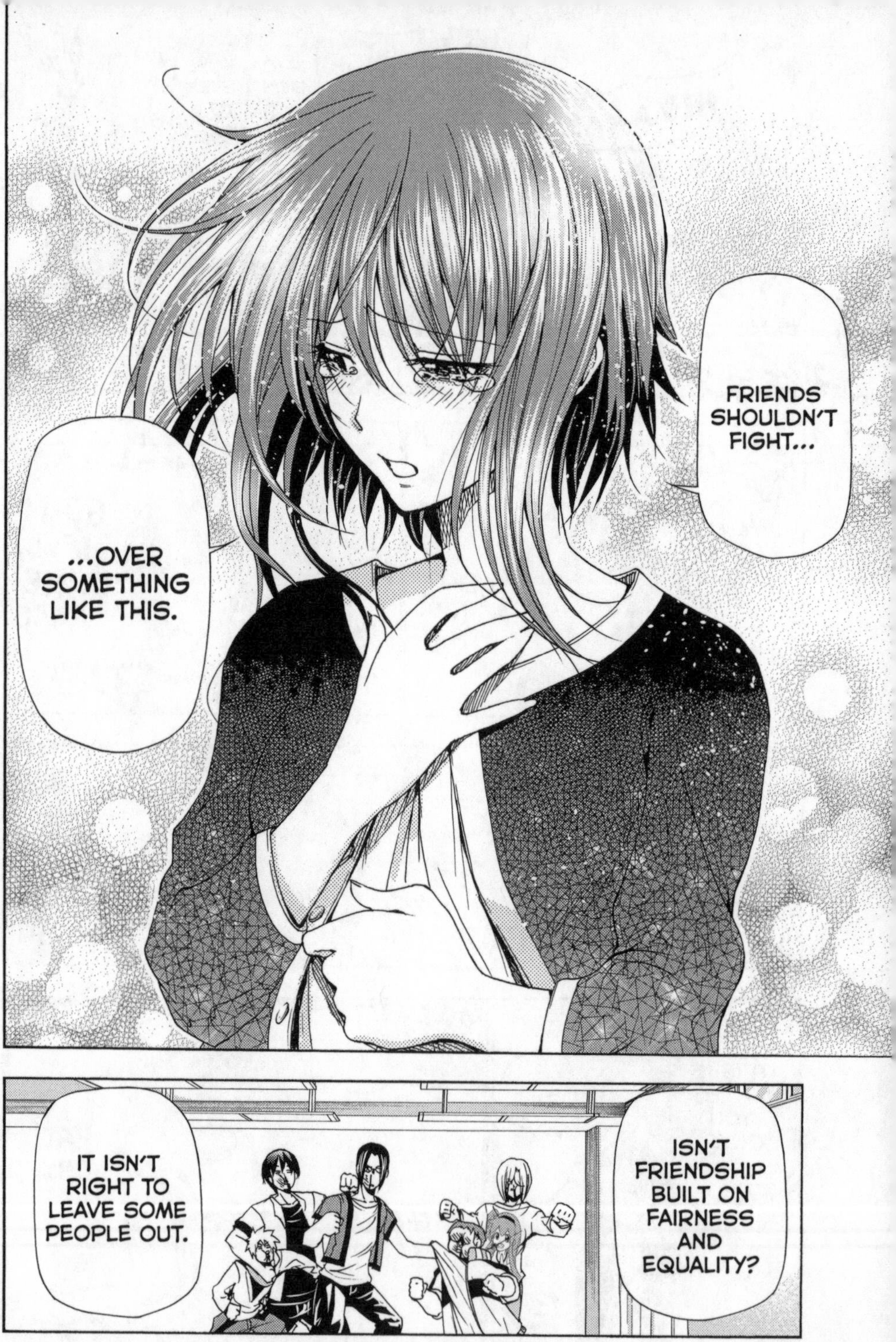
FRIENDS SHOULDN'T FIGHT...
...OVER SOMETHING LIKE THIS.
ISN'T FRIENDSHIP BUILT ON FAIRNESS AND EQUALITY?
IT ISN'T RIGHT TO LEAVE SOME PEOPLE OUT.

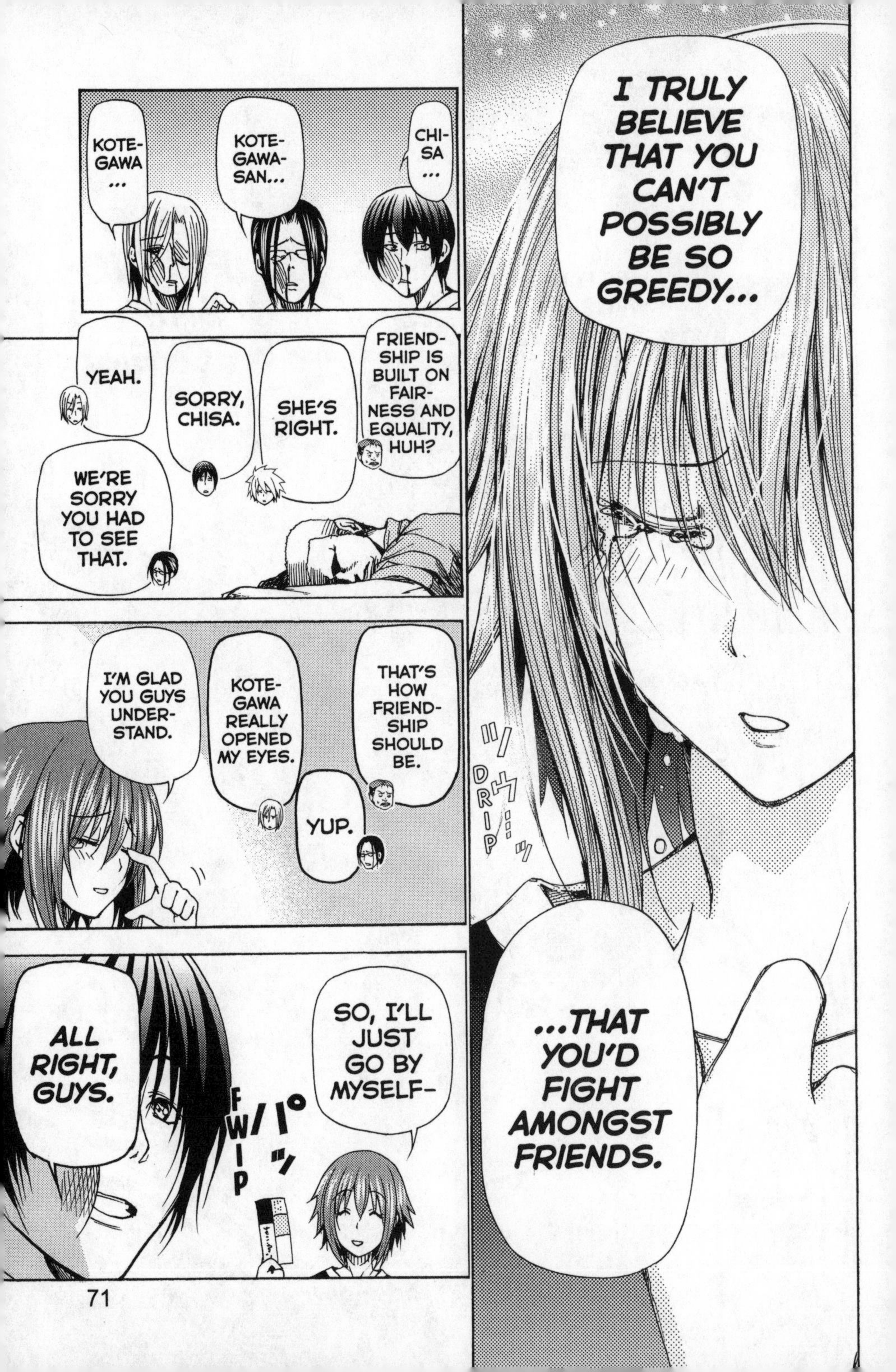

I TRULY BELIEVE THAT YOU CAN'T POSSIBLY BE SO GREEDY...
DRIP
...THAT YOU'D FIGHT AMONGST FRIENDS.
CHISA...
KOTEGAWA-SAN...
KOTEGAWA...
FRIENDSHIP IS BUILT ON FAIRNESS AND EQUALITY, HUH?
SHE'S RIGHT.
SORRY, CHISA.
YEAH.
WE'RE SORRY YOU HAD TO SEE THAT.
THAT'S HOW FRIENDSHIP SHOULD BE.
KOTEGAWA REALLY OPENED MY EYES.
YUP.
I'M GLAD YOU GUYS UNDERSTAND.
SO, I'LL JUST GO BY MYSELF-
FWIP
ALL RIGHT, GUYS.

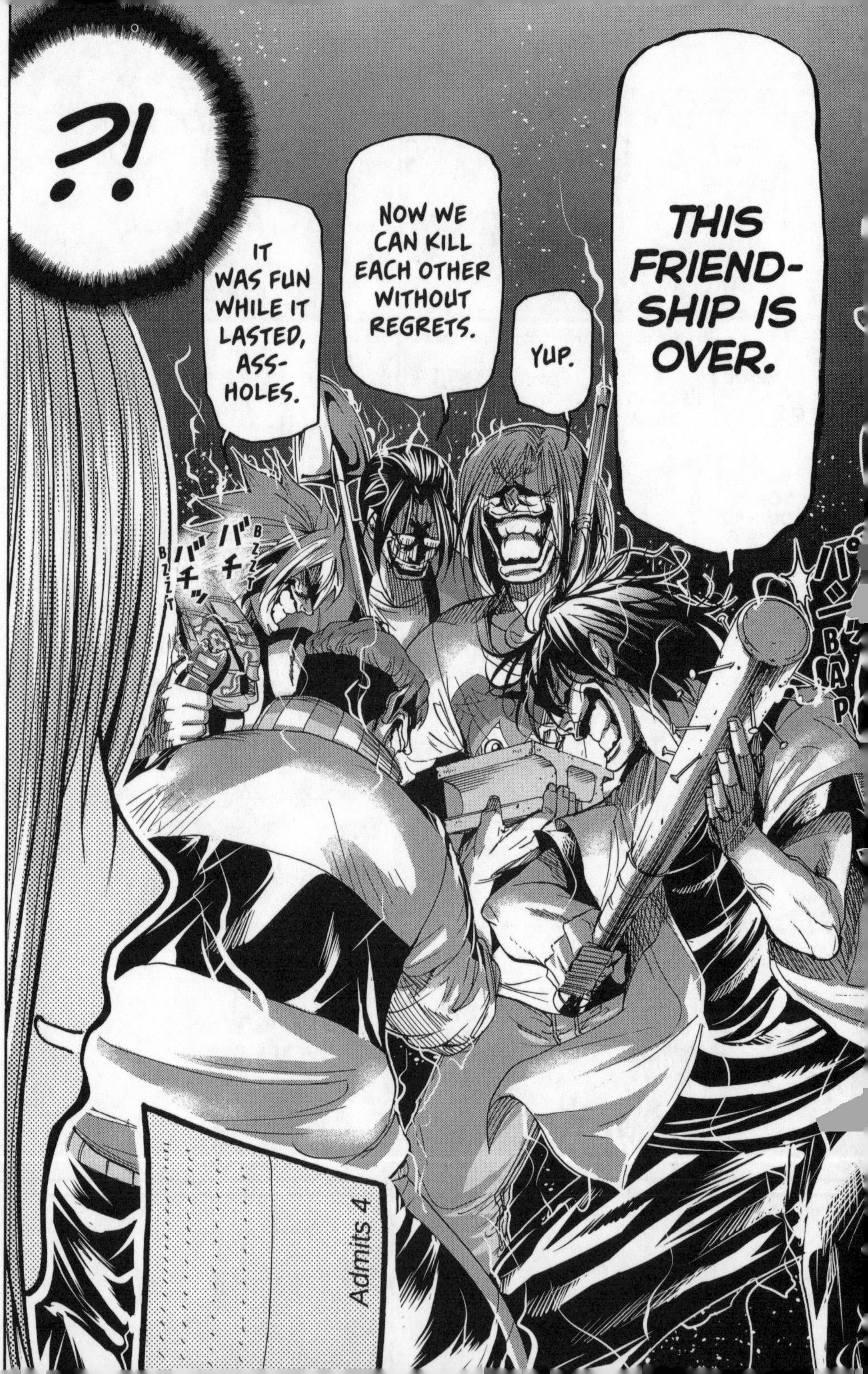
THIS FRIEND-SHIP IS OVER.
YUP.
NOW WE CAN KILL EACH OTHER WITHOUT REGRETS.
IT WAS FUN WHILE IT LASTED, ASS-HOLES.
?!
パンッ BAP
バチ BZZT
バチッ BZZT
Admits 4

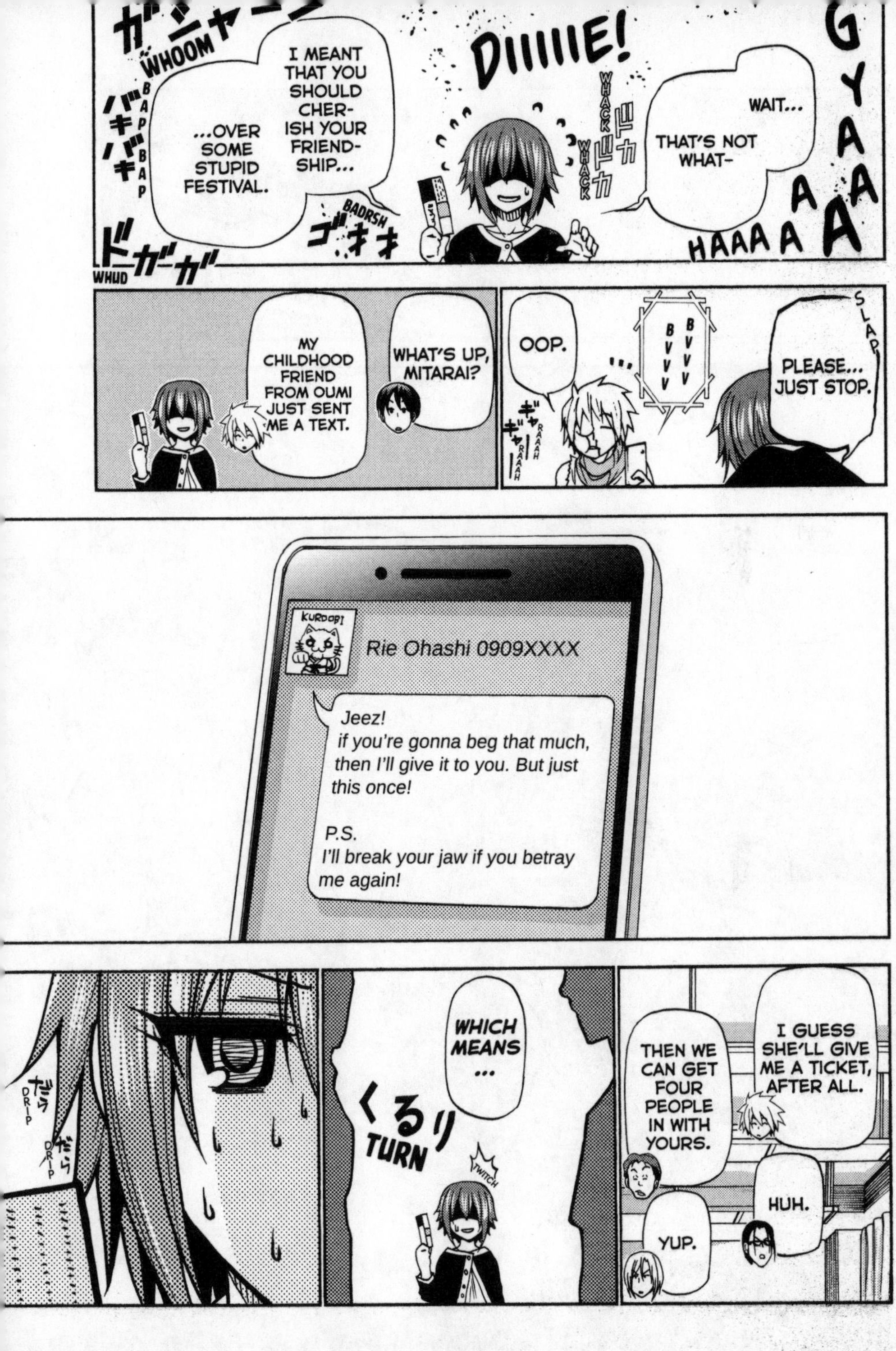
GYAAAAA
HAAAAA
WAIT... THAT'S NOT WHAT-
WHACK
WHACK
DIIIIIE!
I MEANT THAT YOU SHOULD CHERISH YOUR FRIENDSHIP...
...OVER SOME STUPID FESTIVAL.
BADRSH
BAP BAP
WHOOM
WHUD
SLAP
PLEASE... JUST STOP.
BVVV
BVVV
OOP.
RAAAH
RAAAH
WHAT'S UP, MITARAI?
MY CHILDHOOD FRIEND FROM OUMI JUST SENT ME A TEXT.
KURDOBI
Rie Ohashi 0909XXXX
Jeez!
if you're gonna beg that much, then I'll give it to you. But just this once!
P.S.
I'll break your jaw if you betray me again!
I GUESS SHE'LL GIVE ME A TICKET, AFTER ALL.
THEN WE CAN GET FOUR PEOPLE IN WITH YOURS.
HUH.
YUP.
WHICH MEANS...
TURN
TWITCH
DRIP
DRIP

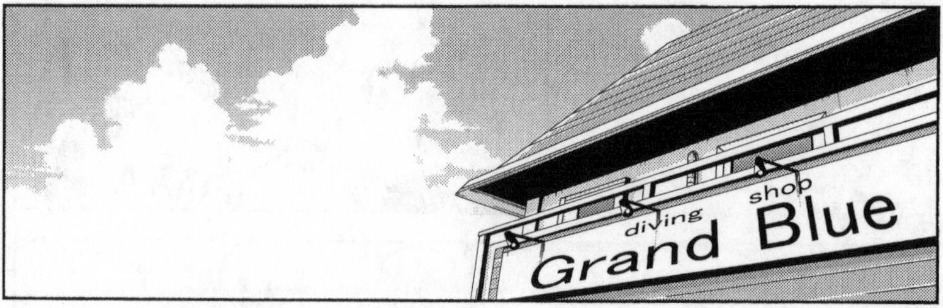
diving shop
Grand Blue

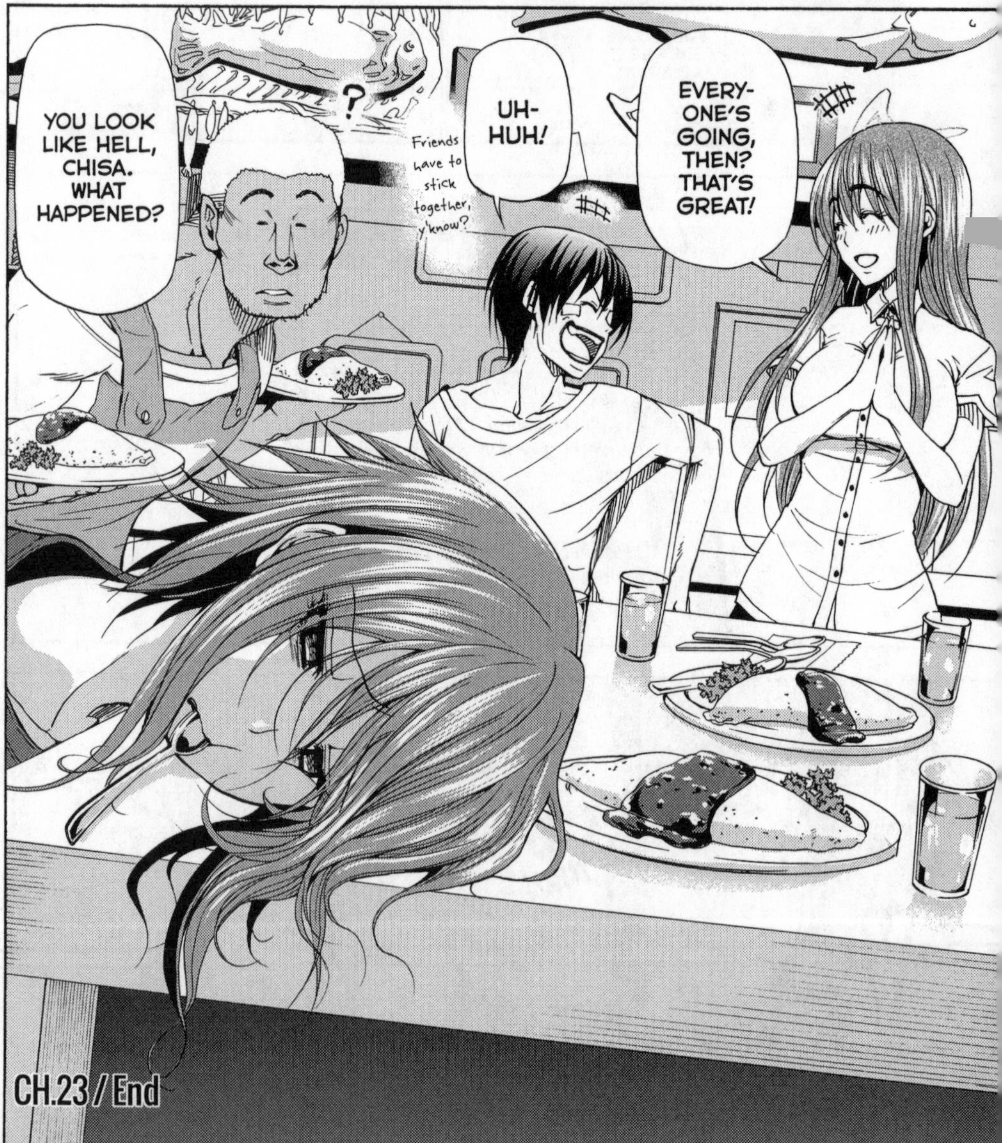
EVERY-ONE'S GOING, THEN? THAT'S GREAT!
UH-HUH!
Friends have to stick together, y'know?
YOU LOOK LIKE HELL, CHISA. WHAT HAPPENED?
CH.23 / End

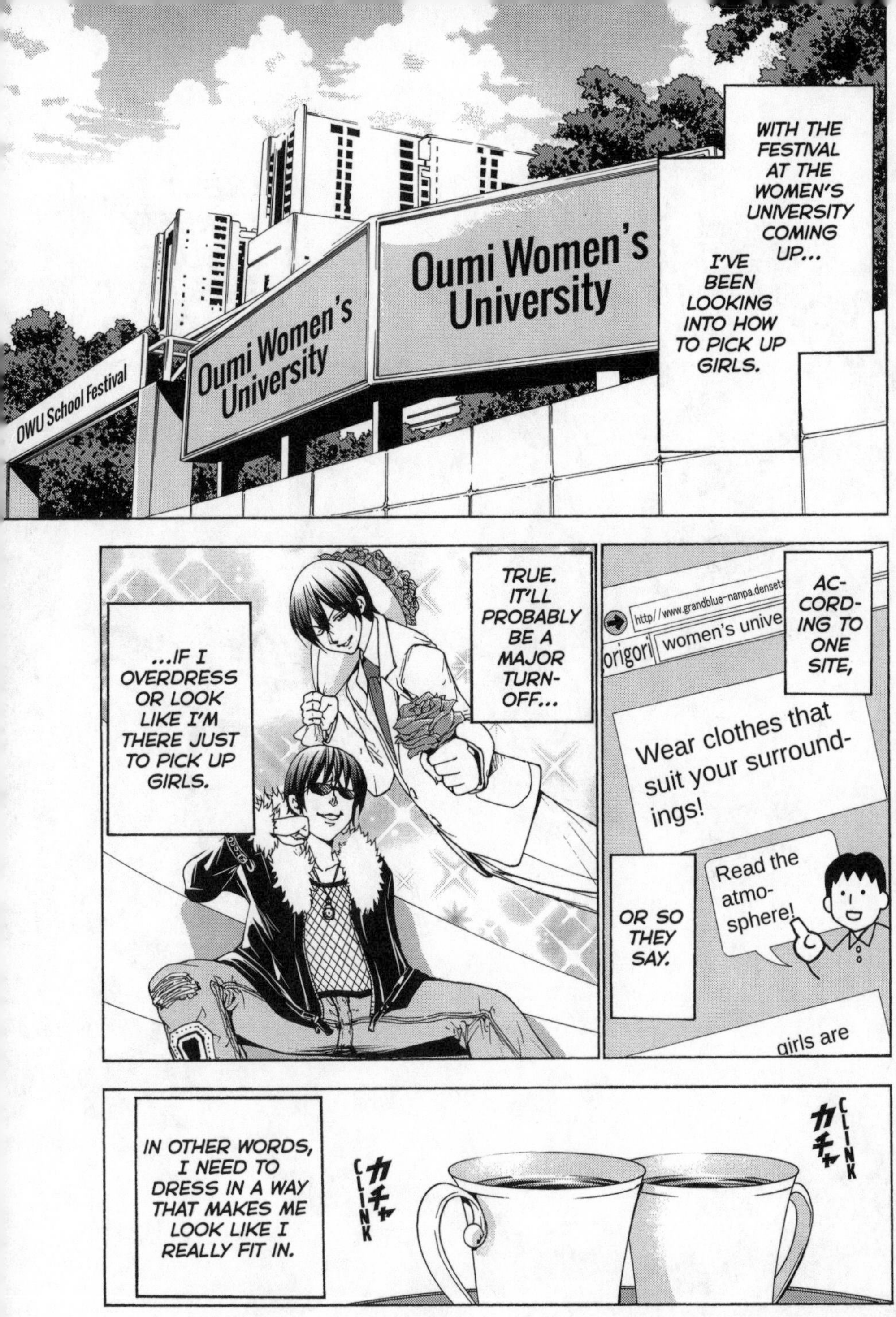
WITH THE FESTIVAL AT THE WOMEN'S UNIVERSITY COMING UP...
I'VE BEEN LOOKING INTO HOW TO PICK UP GIRLS.
Oumi Women's University
Oumi Women's University
OWU School Festival
ACCORDING TO ONE SITE,
http// www.grandblue-nanpa.densets
origori
women's unive
Wear clothes that suit your surroundings!
Read the atmosphere!
OR SO THEY SAY.
girls are
TRUE. IT'LL PROBABLY BE A MAJOR TURNOFF...
...IF I OVERDRESS OR LOOK LIKE I'M THERE JUST TO PICK UP GIRLS.
カチャ CLINK
カチャ CLINK
IN OTHER WORDS, I NEED TO DRESS IN A WAY THAT MAKES ME LOOK LIKE I REALLY FIT IN.

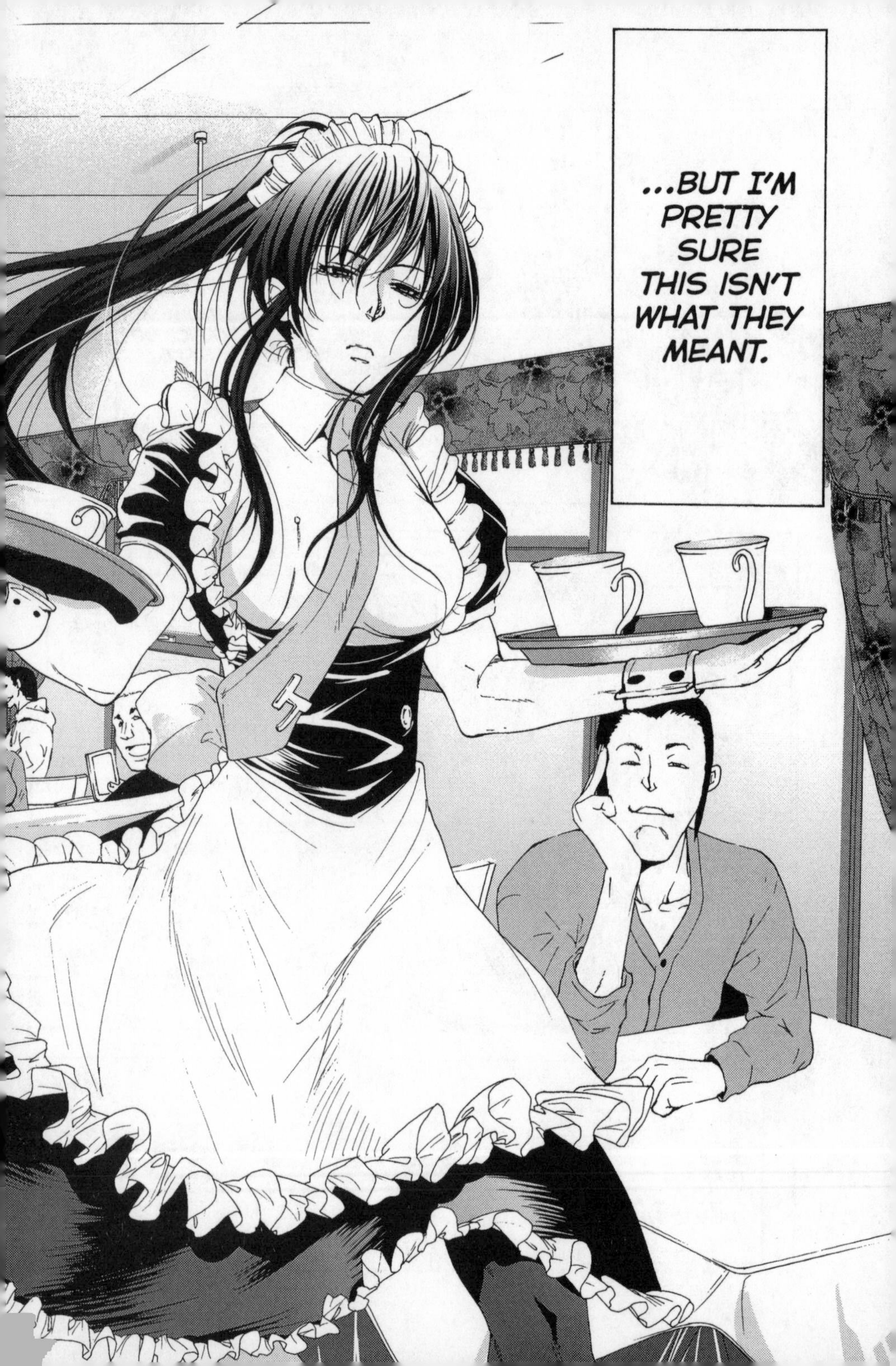
...BUT I'M PRETTY SURE THIS ISN'T WHAT THEY MEANT.

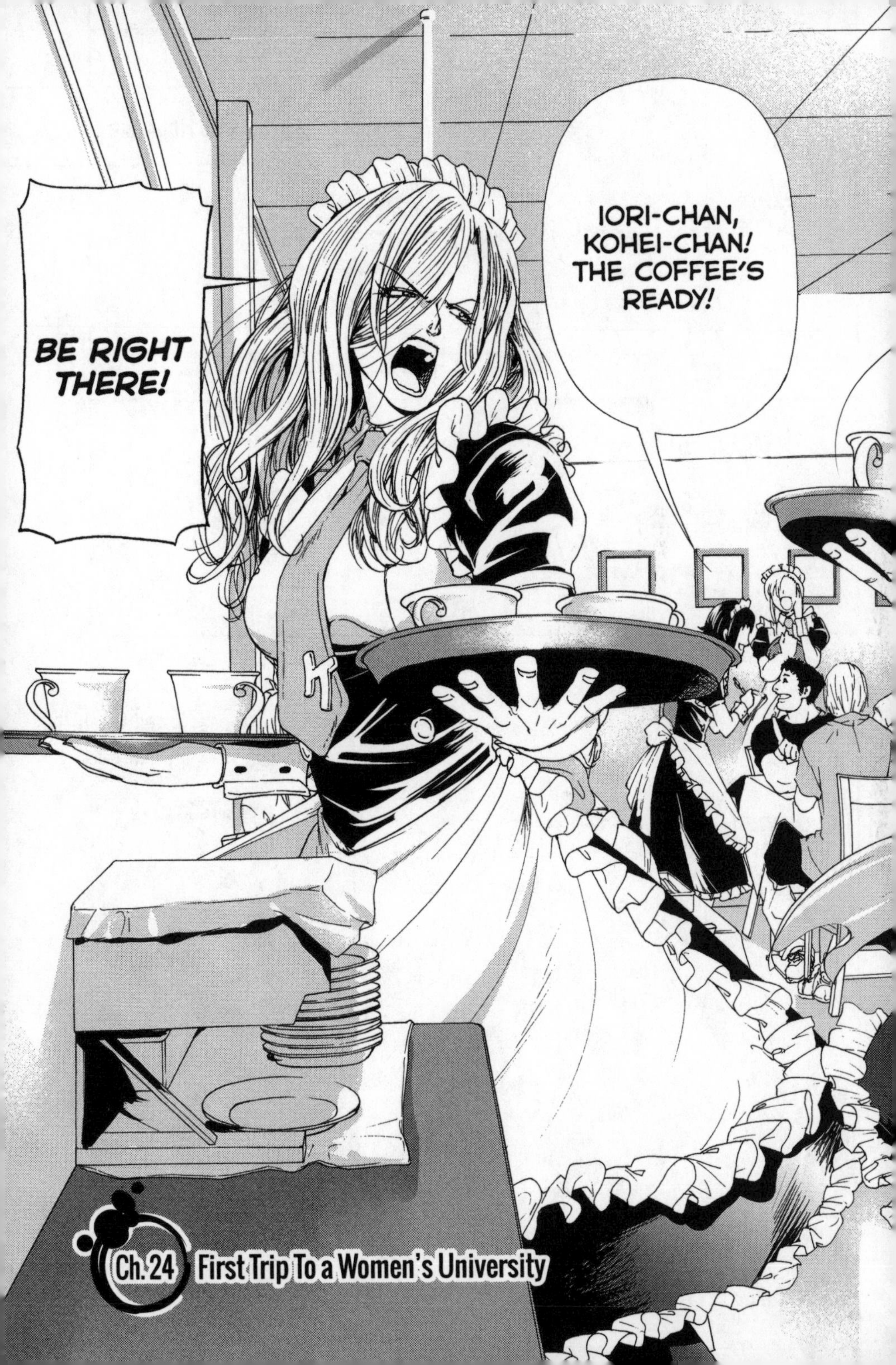
IORI-CHAN, KOHEI-CHAN! THE COFFEE'S READY!
BE RIGHT THERE!

Ch. 24 First Trip To a Women's University

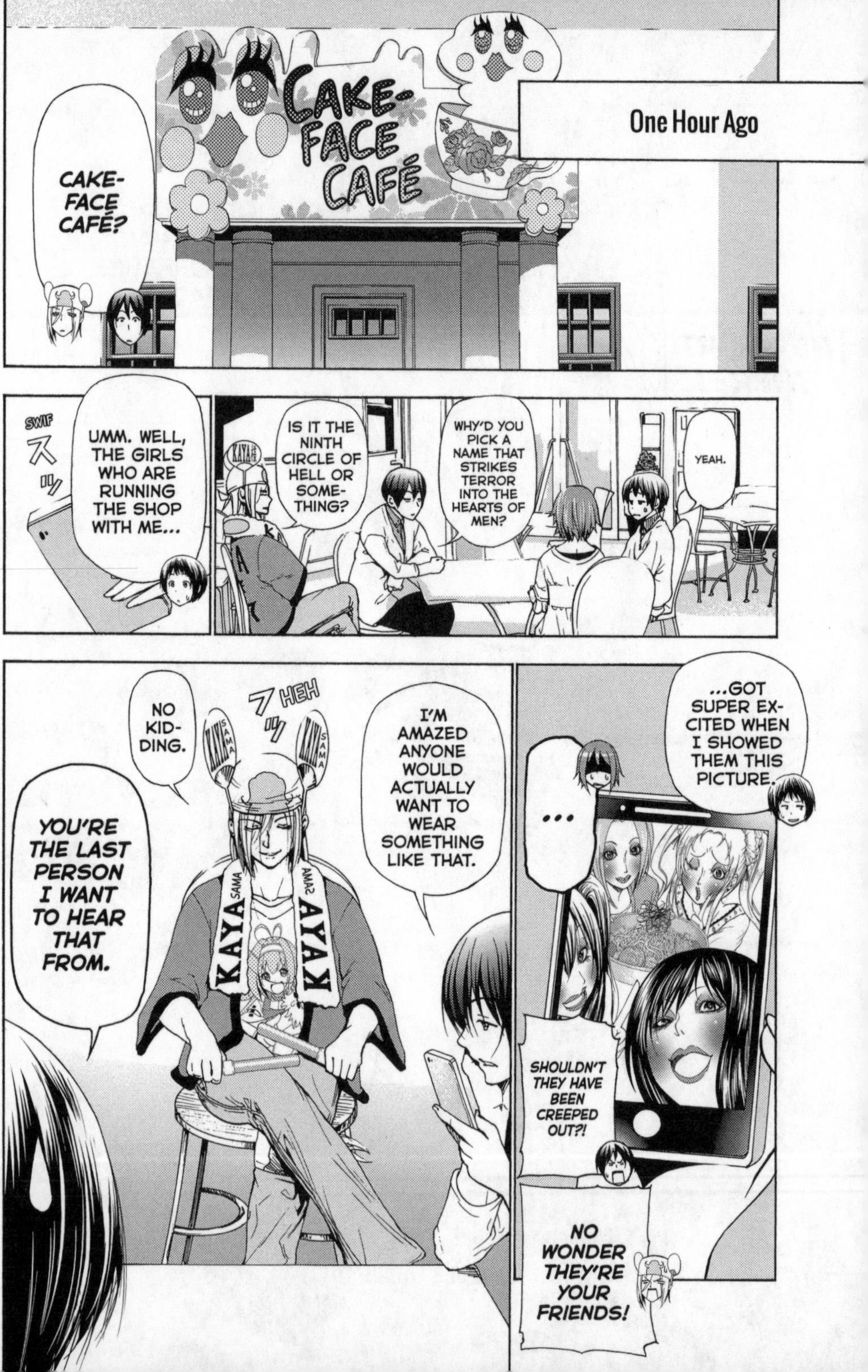

One Hour Ago
CAKE-FACE CAFÉ
CAKE-FACE CAFÉ?
YEAH.
WHY'D YOU PICK A NAME THAT STRIKES TERROR INTO THE HEARTS OF MEN?
IS IT THE NINTH CIRCLE OF HELL OR SOME-THING?
KAYA様
SWIF
UMM. WELL, THE GIRLS WHO ARE RUNNING THE SHOP WITH ME...
...GOT SUPER EX-CITED WHEN I SHOWED THEM THIS PICTURE.
...
SHOULDN'T THEY HAVE BEEN CREEPED OUT?!
NO WONDER THEY'RE YOUR FRIENDS!
I'M AMAZED ANYONE WOULD ACTUALLY WANT TO WEAR SOMETHING LIKE THAT.
HEH
NO KID-DING.
KAYA SAMA
YOU'RE THE LAST PERSON I WANT TO HEAR THAT FROM.

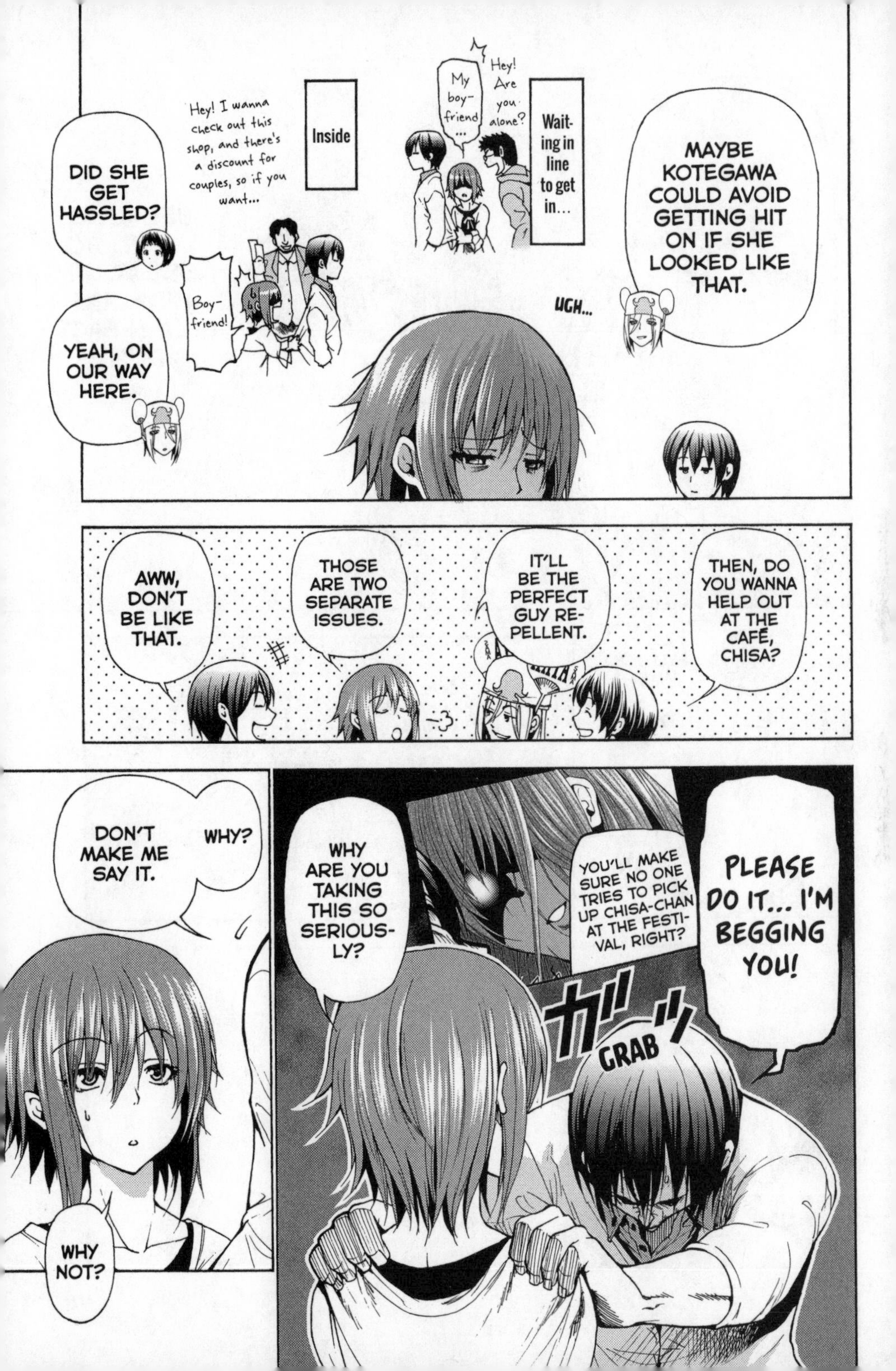
MAYBE KOTEGAWA COULD AVOID GETTING HIT ON IF SHE LOOKED LIKE THAT.
UGH...
Waiting in line to get in...
Hey! Are you alone?
My boyfriend...
Inside
Hey! I wanna check out this shop, and there's a discount for couples, so if you want...
Boyfriend!
DID SHE GET HASSLED?
YEAH, ON OUR WAY HERE.
THEN, DO YOU WANNA HELP OUT AT THE CAFÉ, CHISA?
IT'LL BE THE PERFECT GUY REPELLENT.
THOSE ARE TWO SEPARATE ISSUES.
AWW, DON'T BE LIKE THAT.
PLEASE DO IT... I'M BEGGING YOU!
ガッ
GRAB
YOU'LL MAKE SURE NO ONE TRIES TO PICK UP CHISA-CHAN AT THE FESTIVAL, RIGHT?
WHY ARE YOU TAKING THIS SO SERIOUSLY?
WHY?
DON'T MAKE ME SAY IT.
WHY NOT?

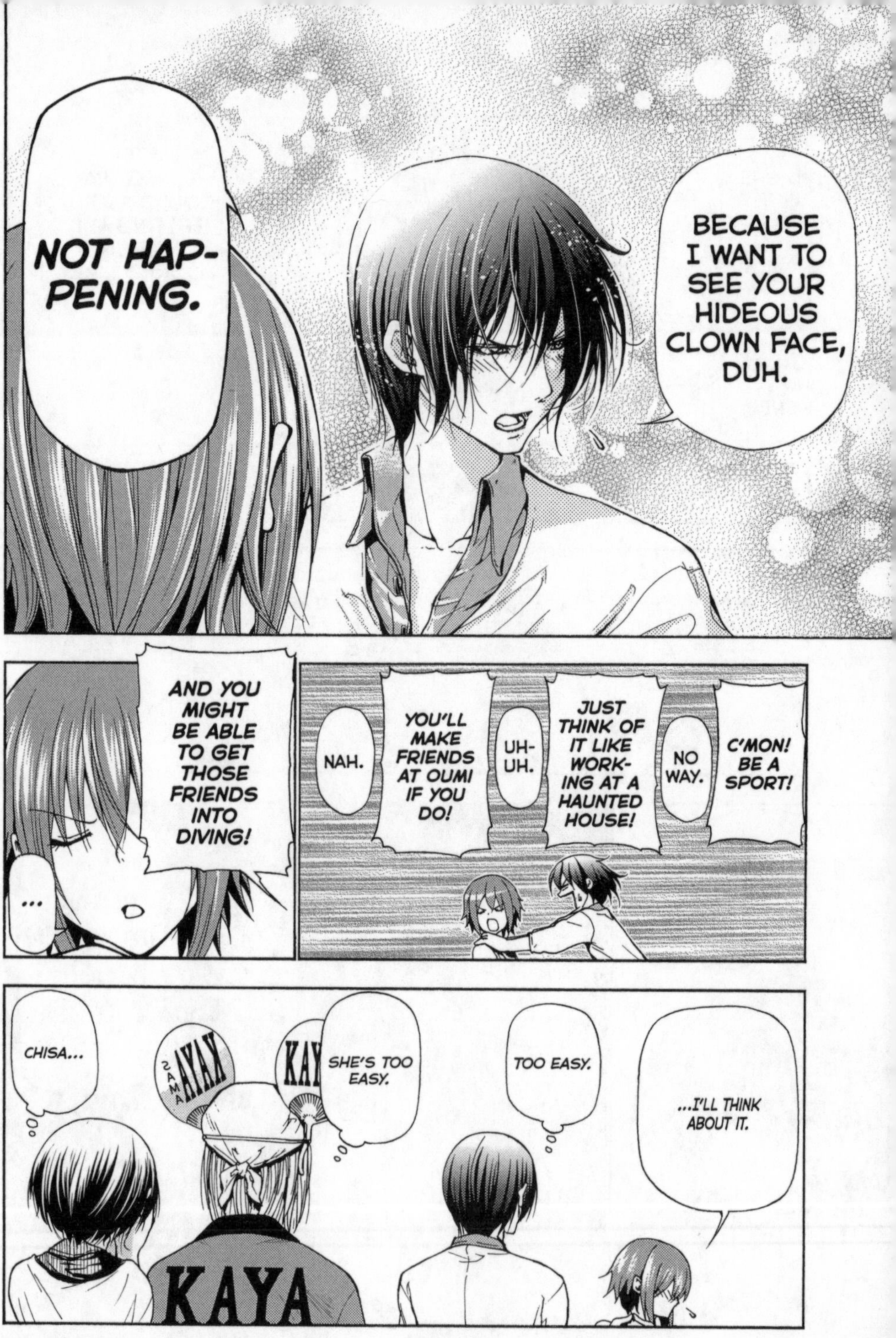
BECAUSE I WANT TO SEE YOUR HIDEOUS CLOWN FACE, DUH.
NOT HAP-PENING.
C'MON! BE A SPORT!
NO WAY.
JUST THINK OF IT LIKE WORK-ING AT A HAUNTED HOUSE!
UH-UH.
YOU'LL MAKE FRIENDS AT OUMI IF YOU DO!
NAH.
AND YOU MIGHT BE ABLE TO GET THOSE FRIENDS INTO DIVING!
...
...I'LL THINK ABOUT IT.
TOO EASY.
SHE'S TOO EASY.
CHISA...
KAYA

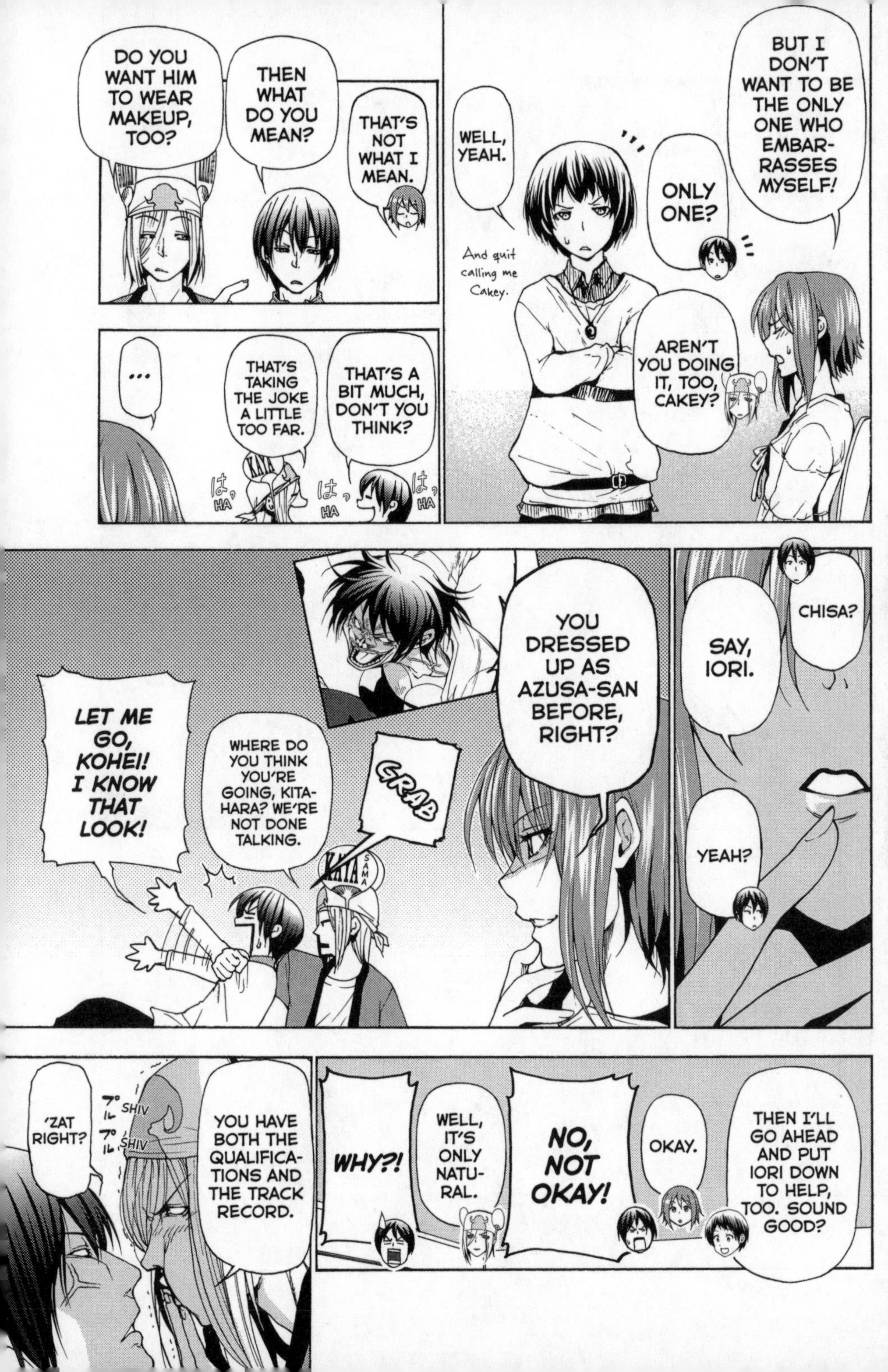
BUT I DON'T WANT TO BE THE ONLY ONE WHO EMBARRASSES MYSELF!
ONLY ONE?
AREN'T YOU DOING IT, TOO, CAKEY?
WELL, YEAH.
And quit calling me Cakey.
THAT'S NOT WHAT I MEAN.
THEN WHAT DO YOU MEAN?
DO YOU WANT HIM TO WEAR MAKEUP, TOO?
THAT'S A BIT MUCH, DON'T YOU THINK?
THAT'S TAKING THE JOKE A LITTLE TOO FAR.
は HA
は HA
は HA
KAYA
...
CHISA?
SAY, IORI.
YEAH?
YOU DRESSED UP AS AZUSA-SAN BEFORE, RIGHT?
GRAB
KAYA SAMA
WHERE DO YOU THINK YOU'RE GOING, KITAHARA? WE'RE NOT DONE TALKING.
LET ME GO, KOHEI! I KNOW THAT LOOK!
THEN I'LL GO AHEAD AND PUT IORI DOWN TO HELP, TOO. SOUND GOOD?
OKAY.
NO, NOT OKAY!
WELL, IT'S ONLY NATURAL.
WHY?!
YOU HAVE BOTH THE QUALIFICATIONS AND THE TRACK RECORD.
プル SHIV
プル SHIV
'ZAT RIGHT?

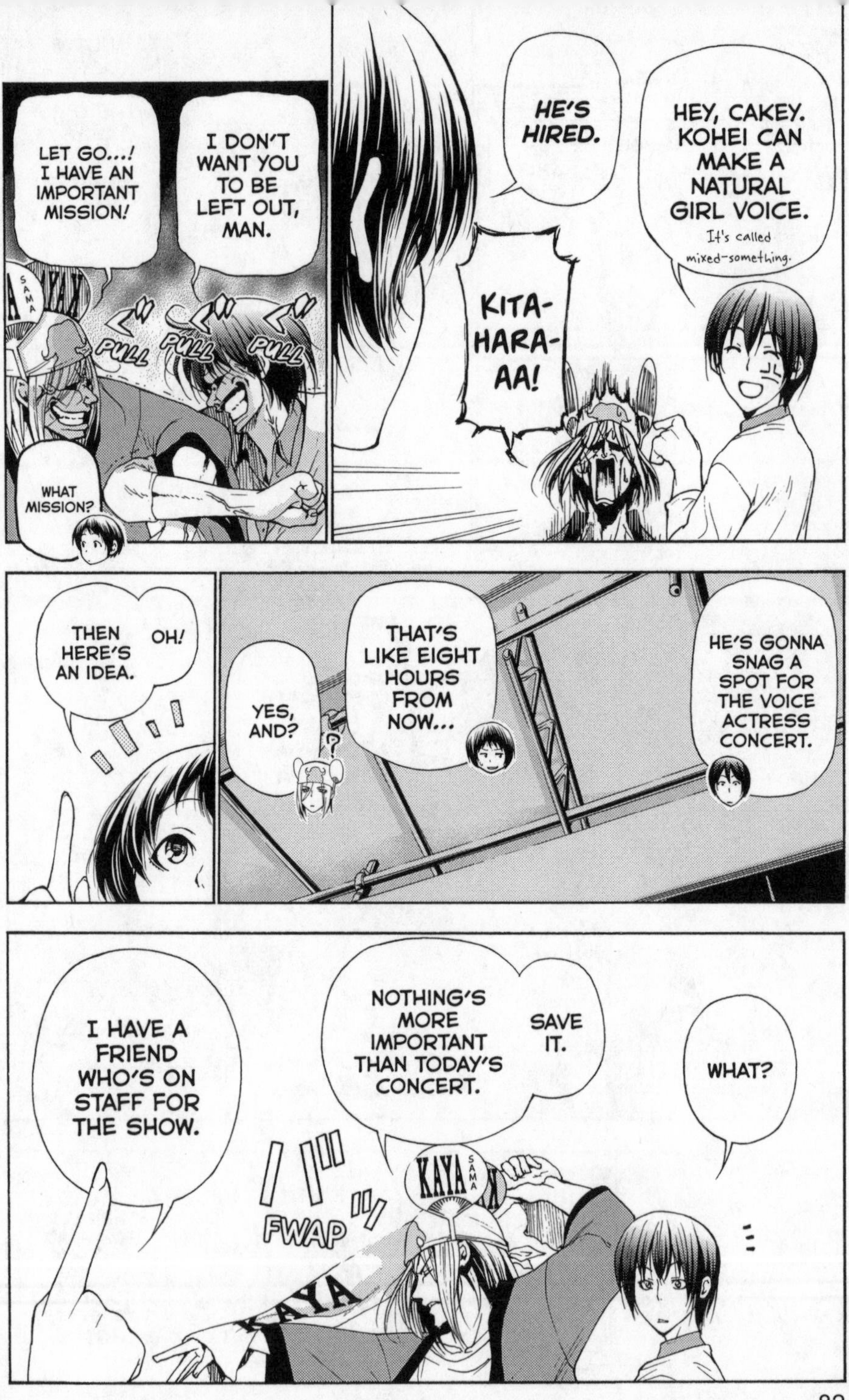
HEY, CAKEY. KOHEI CAN MAKE A NATURAL GIRL VOICE.
It's called mixed-something.
HE'S HIRED.
KITA-HARA-AA!
I DON'T WANT YOU TO BE LEFT OUT, MAN.
LET GO...! I HAVE AN IMPORTANT MISSION!
PULL
PULL
PULL
WHAT MISSION?
HE'S GONNA SNAG A SPOT FOR THE VOICE ACTRESS CONCERT.
THAT'S LIKE EIGHT HOURS FROM NOW...
YES, AND?
?
OH!
THEN HERE'S AN IDEA.
WHAT?
SAVE IT.
NOTHING'S MORE IMPORTANT THAN TODAY'S CONCERT.
KAYA SAMA
FWAP
I HAVE A FRIEND WHO'S ON STAFF FOR THE SHOW.

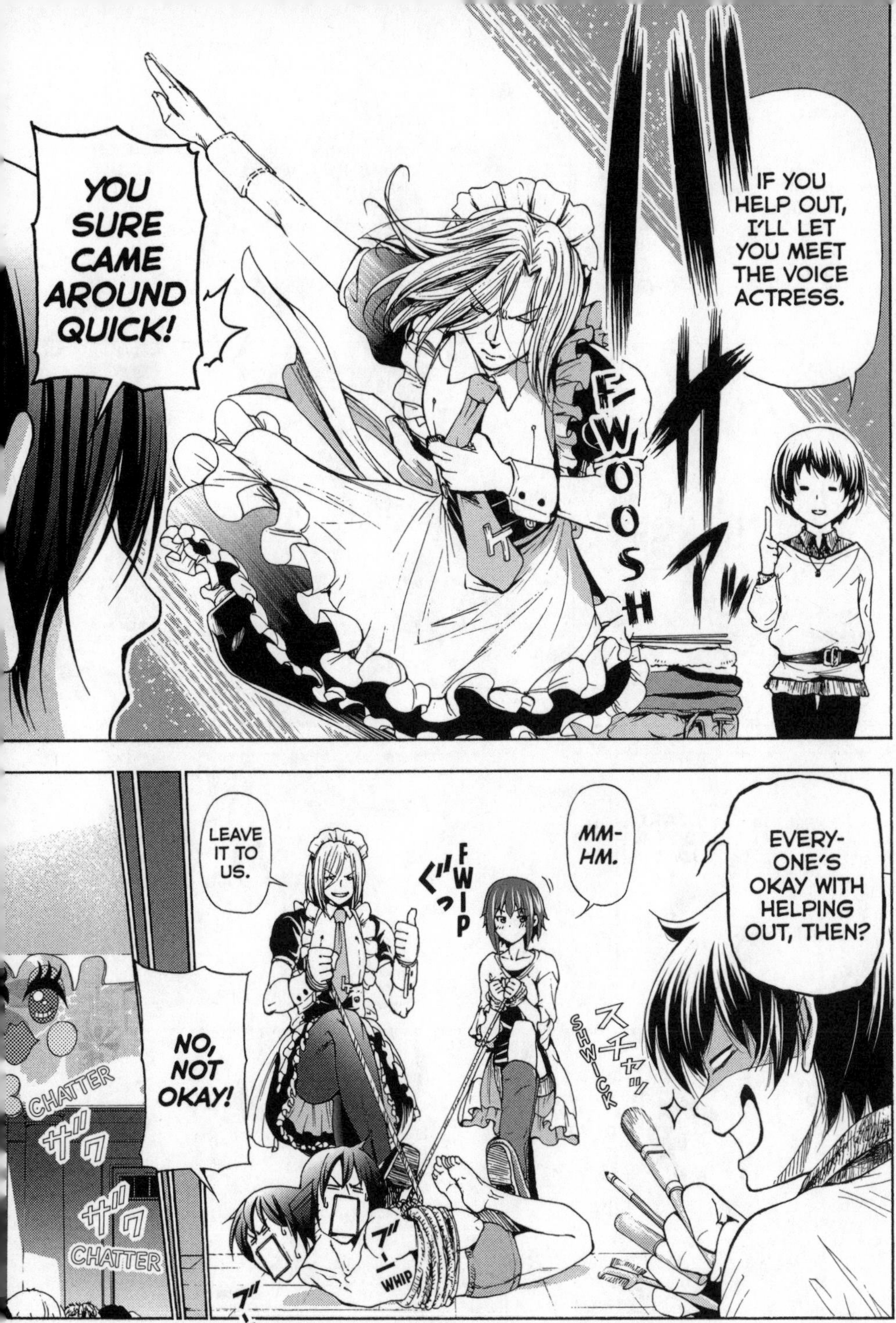
IF YOU HELP OUT, I'LL LET YOU MEET THE VOICE ACTRESS.
FWOOSH
YOU SURE CAME AROUND QUICK!
EVERY-ONE'S OKAY WITH HELPING OUT, THEN?
スチャッ
SHWICK
MM-HM.
ぐっ
FWIP
LEAVE IT TO US.
NO, NOT OKAY!
WHIP
WHIP
CHATTER
CHATTER

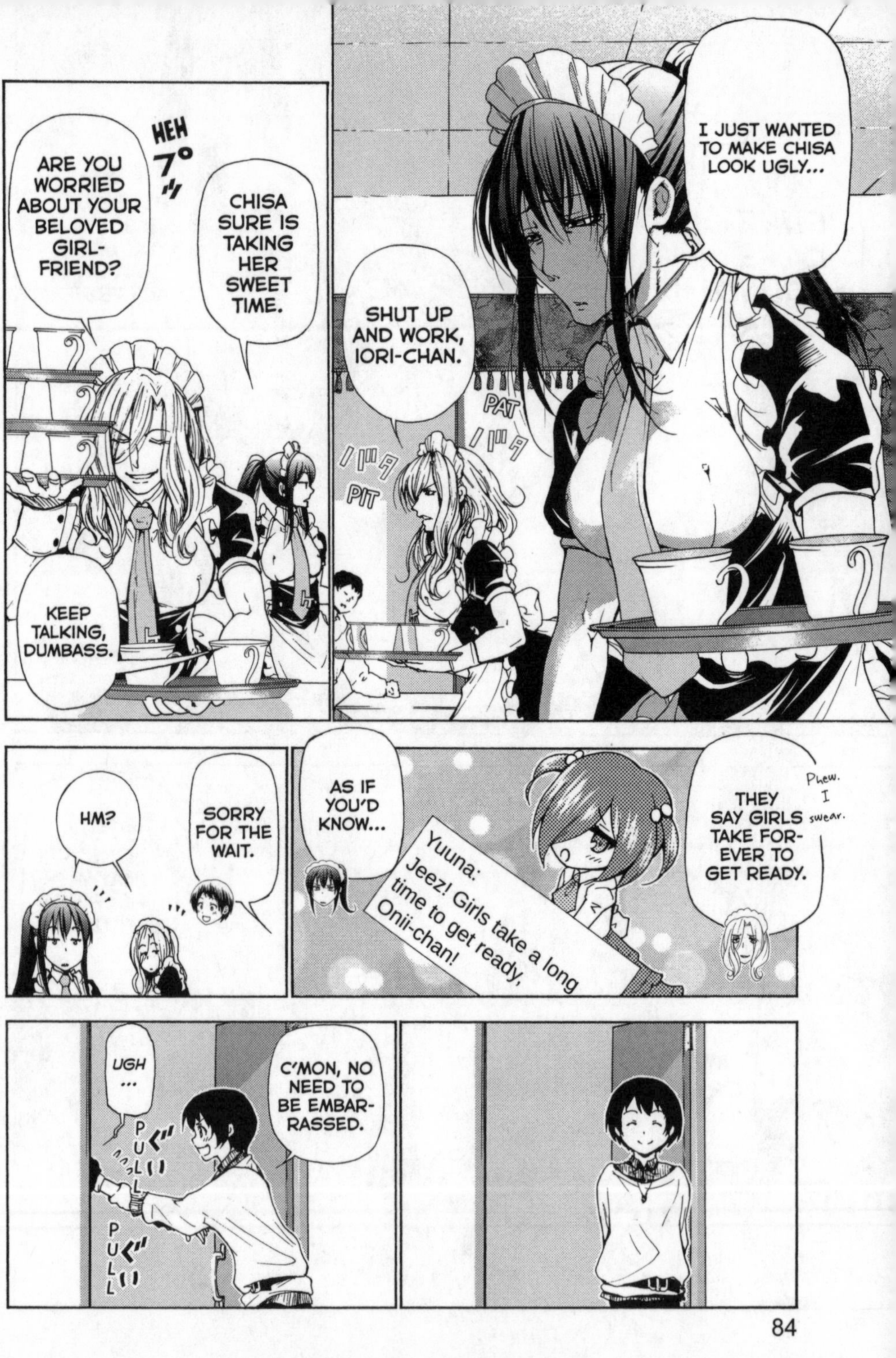

I JUST WANTED TO MAKE CHISA LOOK UGLY...
SHUT UP AND WORK, IORI-CHAN.
PAT
PIT
CHISA SURE IS TAKING HER SWEET TIME.
HEH
ARE YOU WORRIED ABOUT YOUR BELOVED GIRL-FRIEND?
KEEP TALKING, DUMBASS.
Phew. I swear.
THEY SAY GIRLS TAKE FOR-EVER TO GET READY.
Yuuna: Jeez! Girls take a long time to get ready, Onii-chan!
AS IF YOU'D KNOW...
SORRY FOR THE WAIT.
HM?
C'MON, NO NEED TO BE EMBAR-RASSED.
UGH ...
PULL
PULL

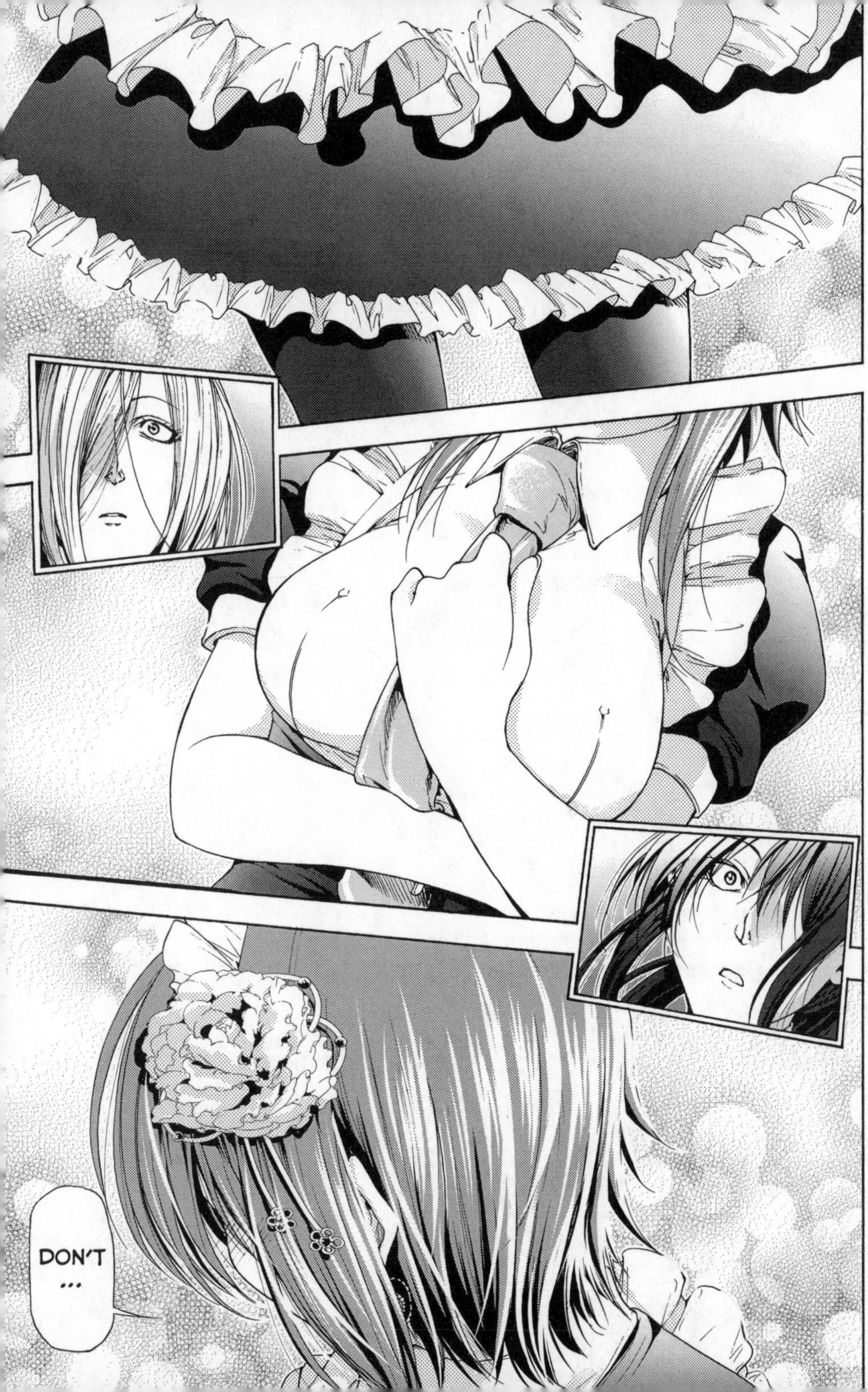
DON'T
...

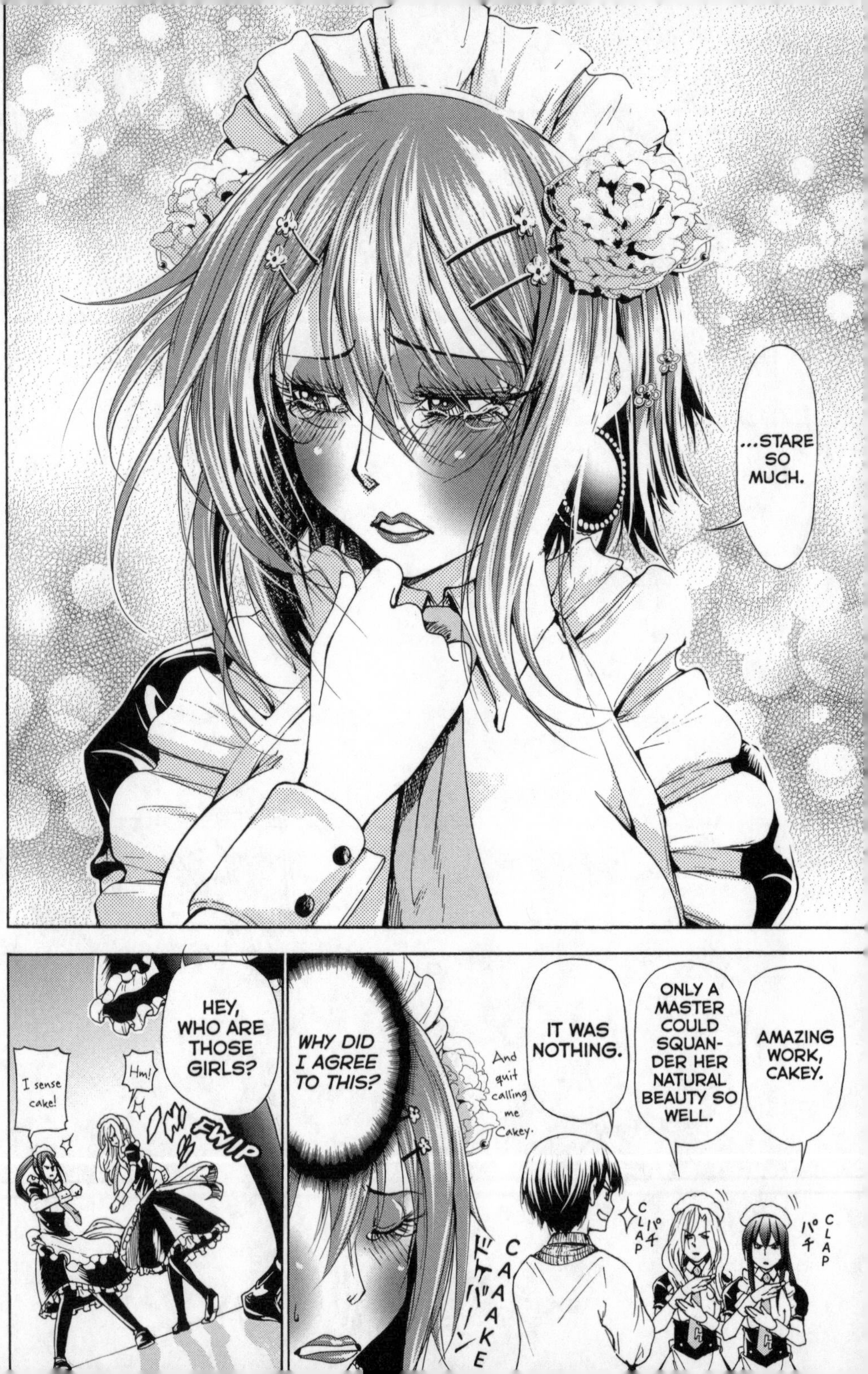
...STARE SO MUCH.
AMAZING WORK, CAKEY.
ONLY A MASTER COULD SQUANDER HER NATURAL BEAUTY SO WELL.
IT WAS NOTHING.
And quit calling me Cakey.
CLAP パチ
CLAP パチ
WHY DID I AGREE TO THIS?
CAAAAKE
HEY, WHO ARE THOSE GIRLS?
Hm!
I sense cake!
FWIP

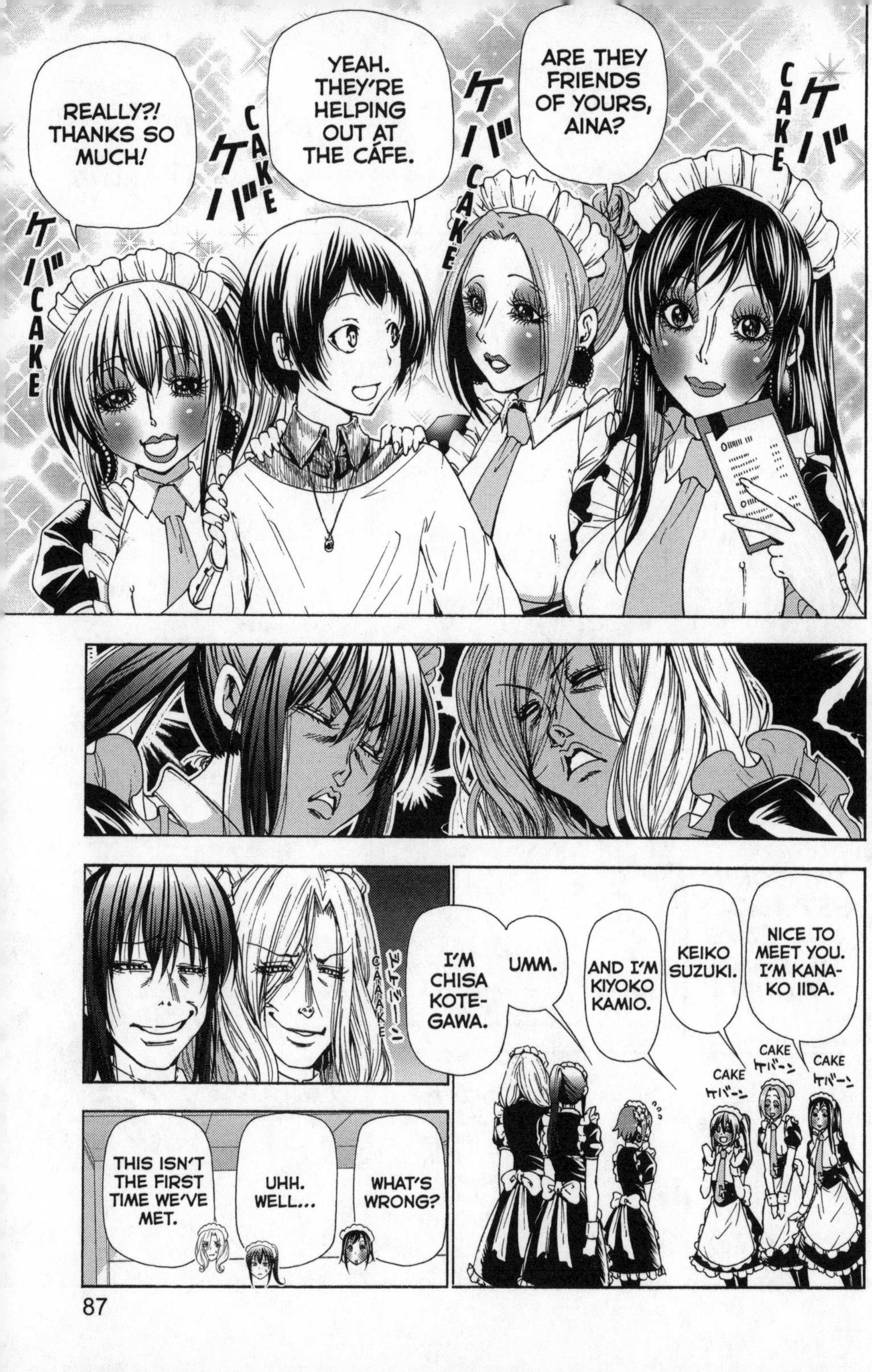
ケバ CAKE
ARE THEY FRIENDS OF YOURS, AINA?
ケバ CAKE
YEAH. THEY'RE HELPING OUT AT THE CÁFE.
ケバ CAKE
REALLY?! THANKS SO MUCH!
ケバ CAKE
NICE TO MEET YOU. I'M KANA-KO IIDA.
CAKE ケバーン
KEIKO SUZUKI.
CAKE ケバーン
AND I'M KIYOKO KAMIO.
UMM.
I'M CHISA KOTE-GAWA.
CAAAAKE
WHAT'S WRONG?
UHH. WELL...
THIS ISN'T THE FIRST TIME WE'VE MET.

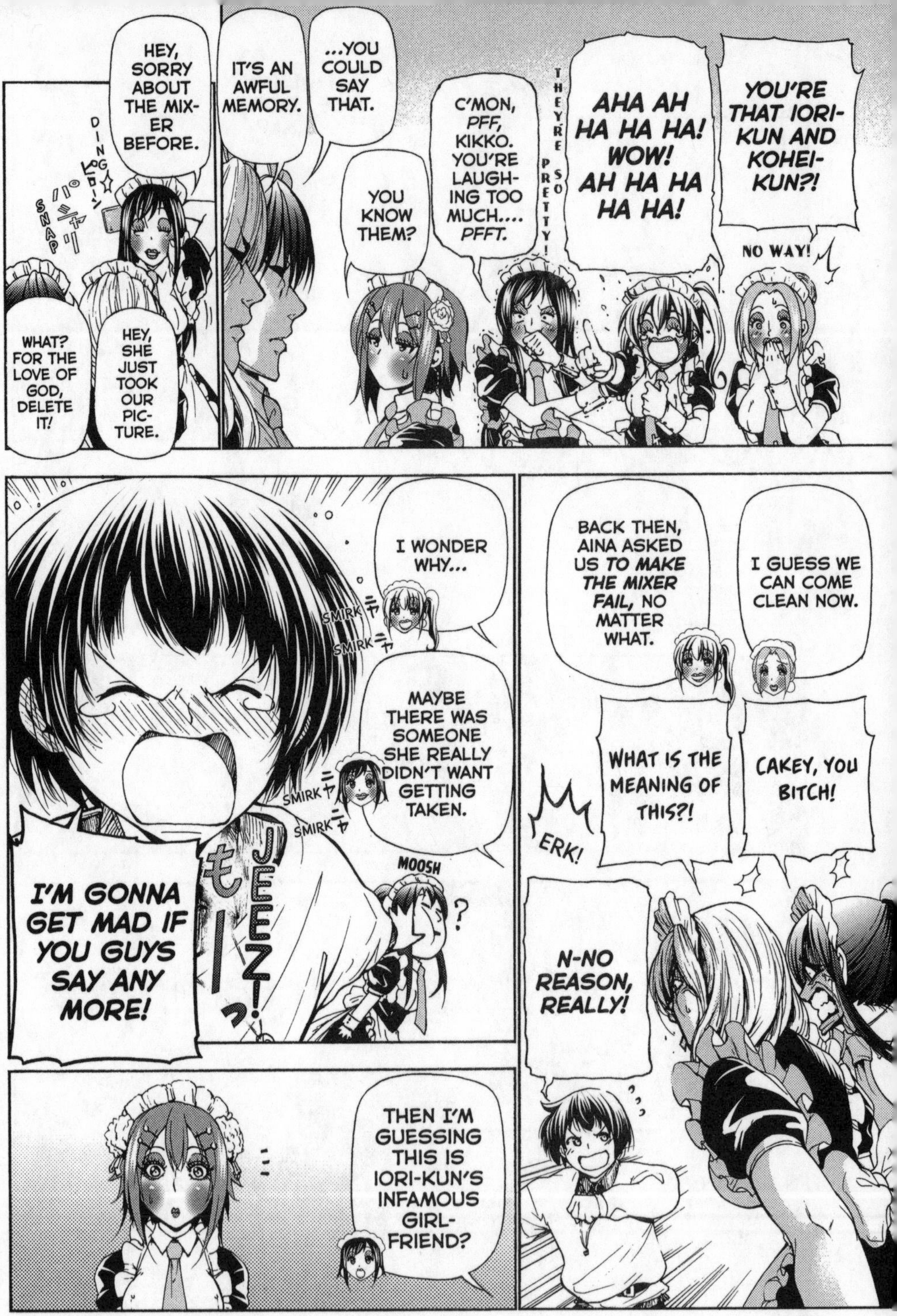
YOU'RE THAT IORI-KUN AND KOHEI-KUN?!
NO WAY!
AHA AH HA HA HA! WOW! AH HA HA HA HA!
THEY'RE SO PRETTY!
C'MON, PFF, KIKKO. YOU'RE LAUGHING TOO MUCH.... PFFT.
YOU KNOW THEM?
...YOU COULD SAY THAT.
IT'S AN AWFUL MEMORY.
HEY, SORRY ABOUT THE MIXER BEFORE.
DING
SNAP
HEY, SHE JUST TOOK OUR PICTURE.
WHAT? FOR THE LOVE OF GOD, DELETE IT!
I GUESS WE CAN COME CLEAN NOW.
BACK THEN, AINA ASKED US TO MAKE THE MIXER FAIL, NO MATTER WHAT.
CAKEY, YOU BITCH!
WHAT IS THE MEANING OF THIS?!
ERK!
N-NO REASON, REALLY!
I WONDER WHY...
SMIRK
SMIRK
MAYBE THERE WAS SOMEONE SHE REALLY DIDN'T WANT GETTING TAKEN.
SMIRK
SMIRK
JEEZ!
MOOSH
I'M GONNA GET MAD IF YOU GUYS SAY ANY MORE!
THEN I'M GUESSING THIS IS IORI-KUN'S INFAMOUS GIRLFRIEND?

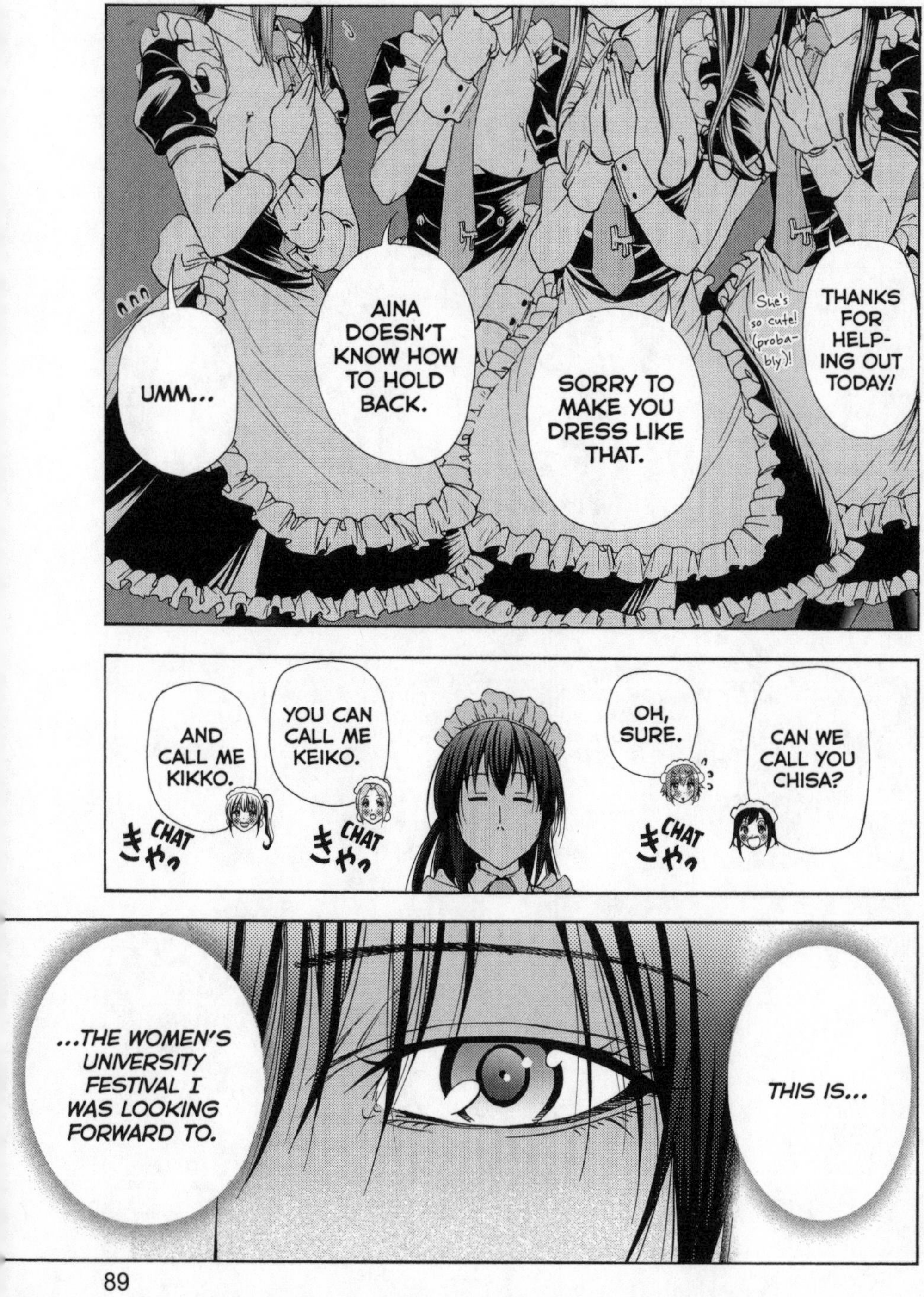
THANKS FOR HELPING OUT TODAY!
She's so cute! (probably)!
SORRY TO MAKE YOU DRESS LIKE THAT.
AINA DOESN'T KNOW HOW TO HOLD BACK.
UMM...
CAN WE CALL YOU CHISA?
OH, SURE.
CHAT きゃっ
YOU CAN CALL ME KEIKO.
CHAT きゃっ
AND CALL ME KIKKO.
CHAT きゃっ
THIS IS...
...THE WOMEN'S UNIVERSITY FESTIVAL I WAS LOOKING FORWARD TO.

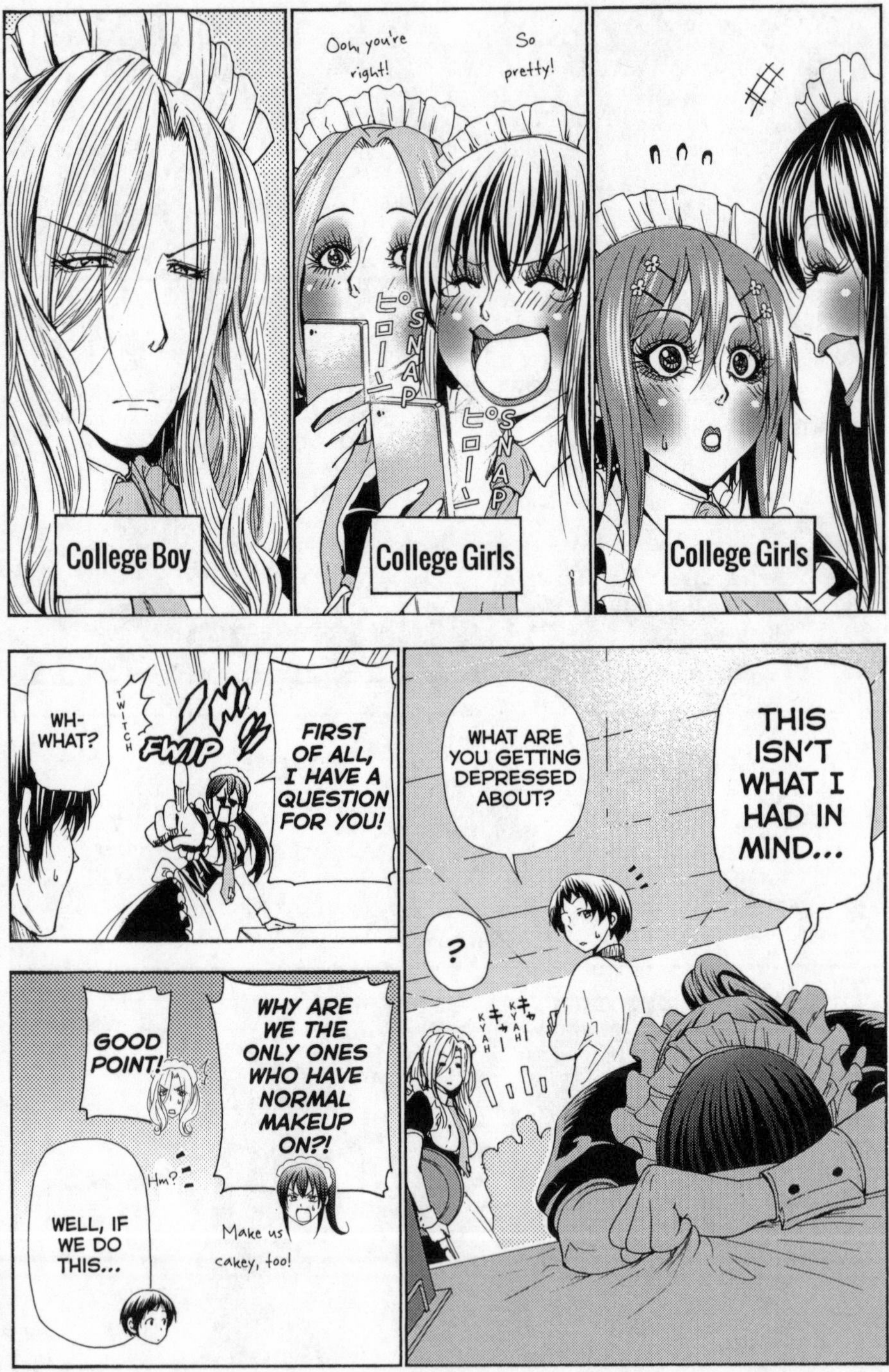
College Girls
So pretty!
Ooh, you're right!
SNAP
SNAP
College Girls
College Boy
THIS ISN'T WHAT I HAD IN MIND...
WHAT ARE YOU GETTING DEPRESSED ABOUT?
?
KYAH
KYAH
FIRST OF ALL, I HAVE A QUESTION FOR YOU!
FWIP
TWITCH
WH-WHAT?
WHY ARE WE THE ONLY ONES WHO HAVE NORMAL MAKEUP ON?!
GOOD POINT!
Hm?
Make us cakey, too!
WELL, IF WE DO THIS...

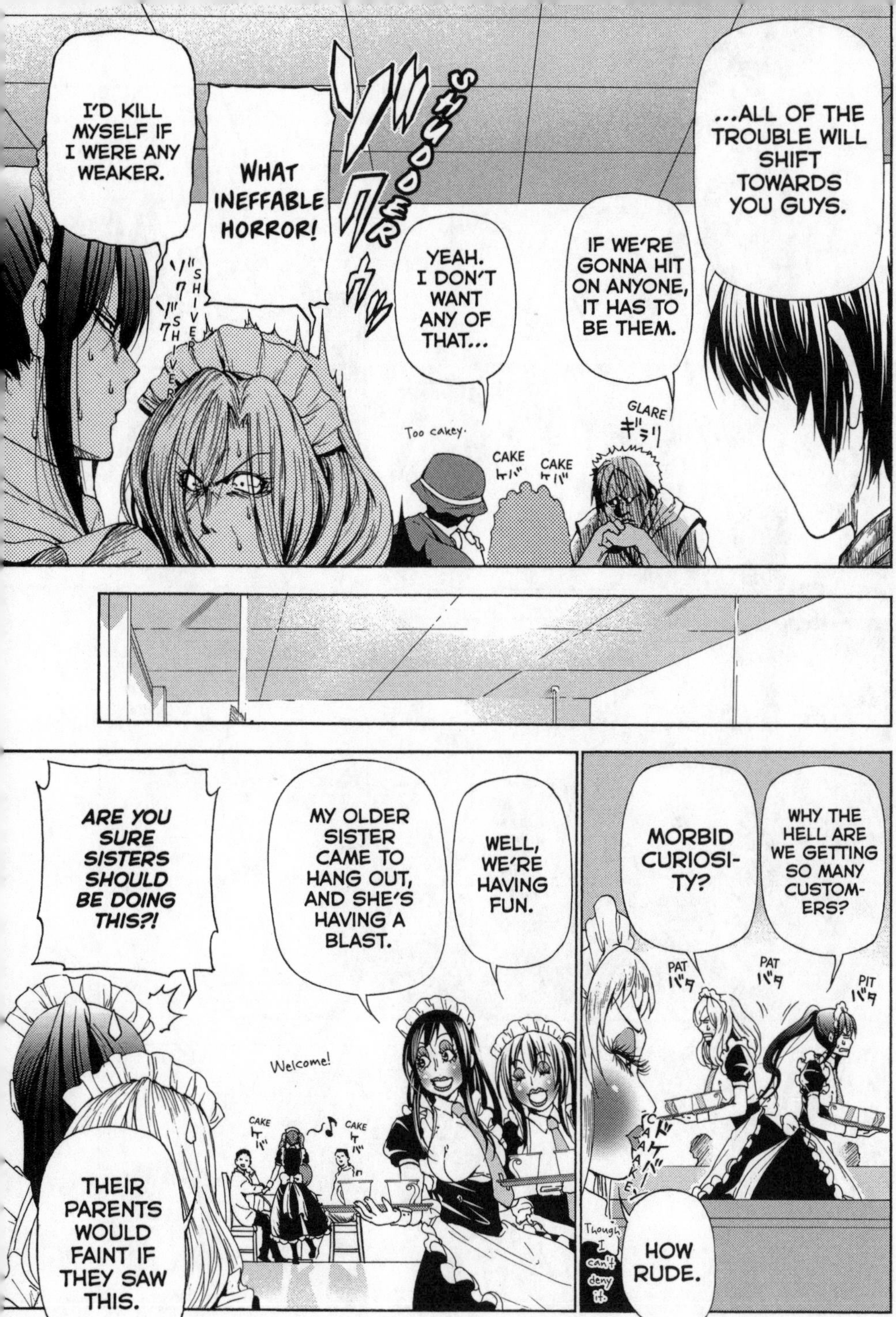
...ALL OF THE TROUBLE WILL SHIFT TOWARDS YOU GUYS.
IF WE'RE GONNA HIT ON ANYONE, IT HAS TO BE THEM.
GLARE
YEAH. I DON'T WANT ANY OF THAT...
SHUDDER
WHAT INEFFABLE HORROR!
I'D KILL MYSELF IF I WERE ANY WEAKER.
SHIVER SHIVER
CAKE
CAKE
Too cakey.
WHY THE HELL ARE WE GETTING SO MANY CUSTOMERS?
MORBID CURIOSI-TY?
PIT
PAT
PAT
CAKE CAKE
HOW RUDE.
Though I can't deny it.
WELL, WE'RE HAVING FUN.
MY OLDER SISTER CAME TO HANG OUT, AND SHE'S HAVING A BLAST.
ARE YOU SURE SISTERS SHOULD BE DOING THIS?!
Welcome!
CAKE
CAKE
THEIR PARENTS WOULD FAINT IF THEY SAW THIS.

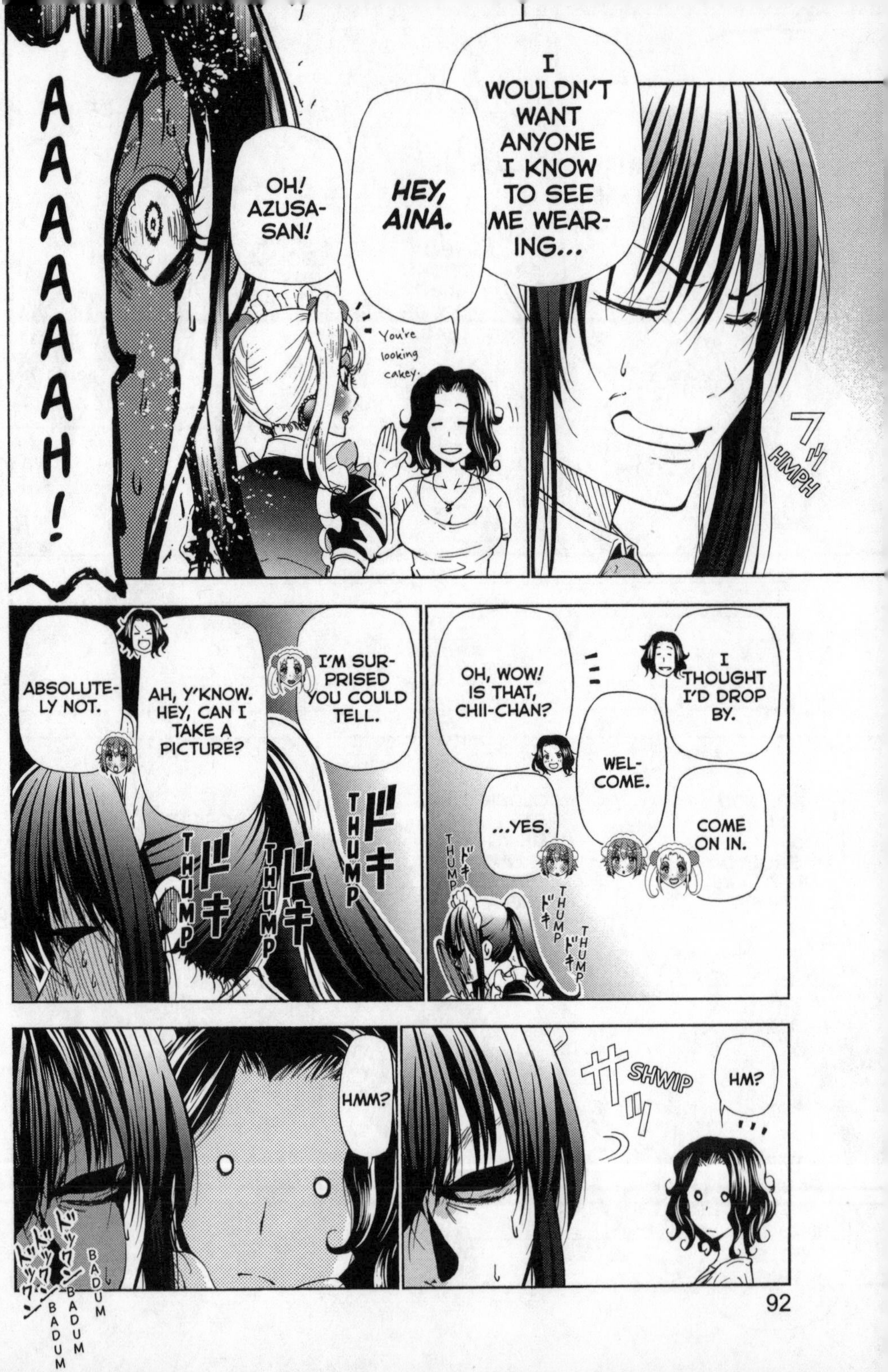
I WOULDN'T WANT ANYONE I KNOW TO SEE ME WEARING...
HMPH
HEY, AINA.
OH! AZUSA-SAN!
You're looking cakey.
AAAAAAAH!
I THOUGHT I'D DROP BY.
COME ON IN.
WELCOME.
OH, WOW! IS THAT, CHII-CHAN?
...YES.
THUMP THUMP THUMP
I'M SURPRISED YOU COULD TELL.
THUMP
AH, Y'KNOW. HEY, CAN I TAKE A PICTURE?
ABSOLUTELY NOT.
THUMP THUMP
HM?
SHWIP
HMM?
BADUM BADUM BADUM

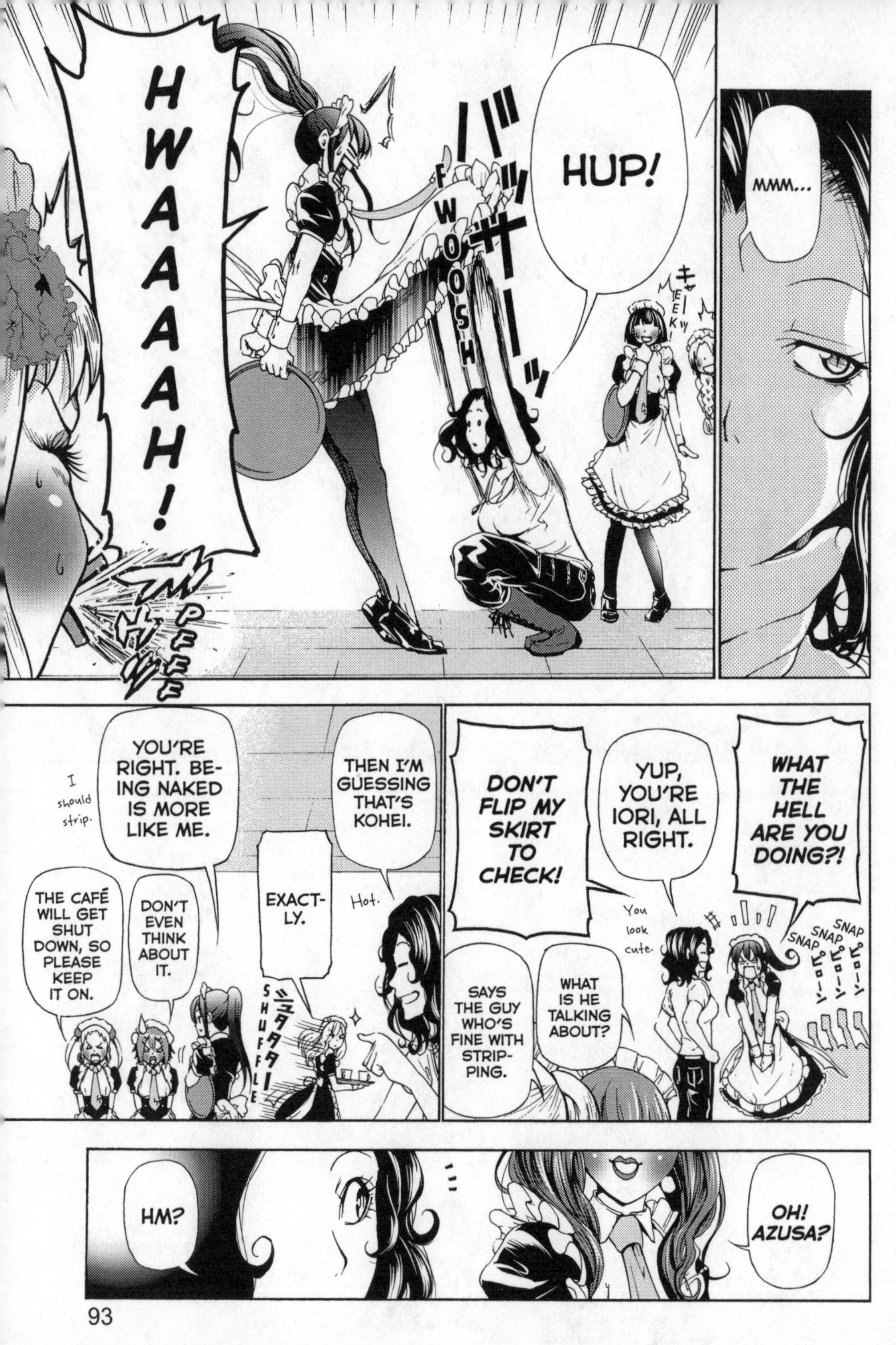
MMM...
HUP!
FWOOSH
EEK!
HWAAAAAH!
PFFFF
WHAT THE HELL ARE YOU DOING?!
SNAP SNAP SNAP
YUP, YOU'RE IORI, ALL RIGHT.
You look cute.
DON'T FLIP MY SKIRT TO CHECK!
WHAT IS HE TALKING ABOUT?
SAYS THE GUY WHO'S FINE WITH STRIP-PING.
THEN I'M GUESSING THAT'S KOHEI.
Hot.
EXACT-LY.
SHUFFLE
YOU'RE RIGHT. BE-ING NAKED IS MORE LIKE ME.
I should strip.
DON'T EVEN THINK ABOUT IT.
THE CAFÉ WILL GET SHUT DOWN, SO PLEASE KEEP IT ON.
OH! AZUSA?
HM?

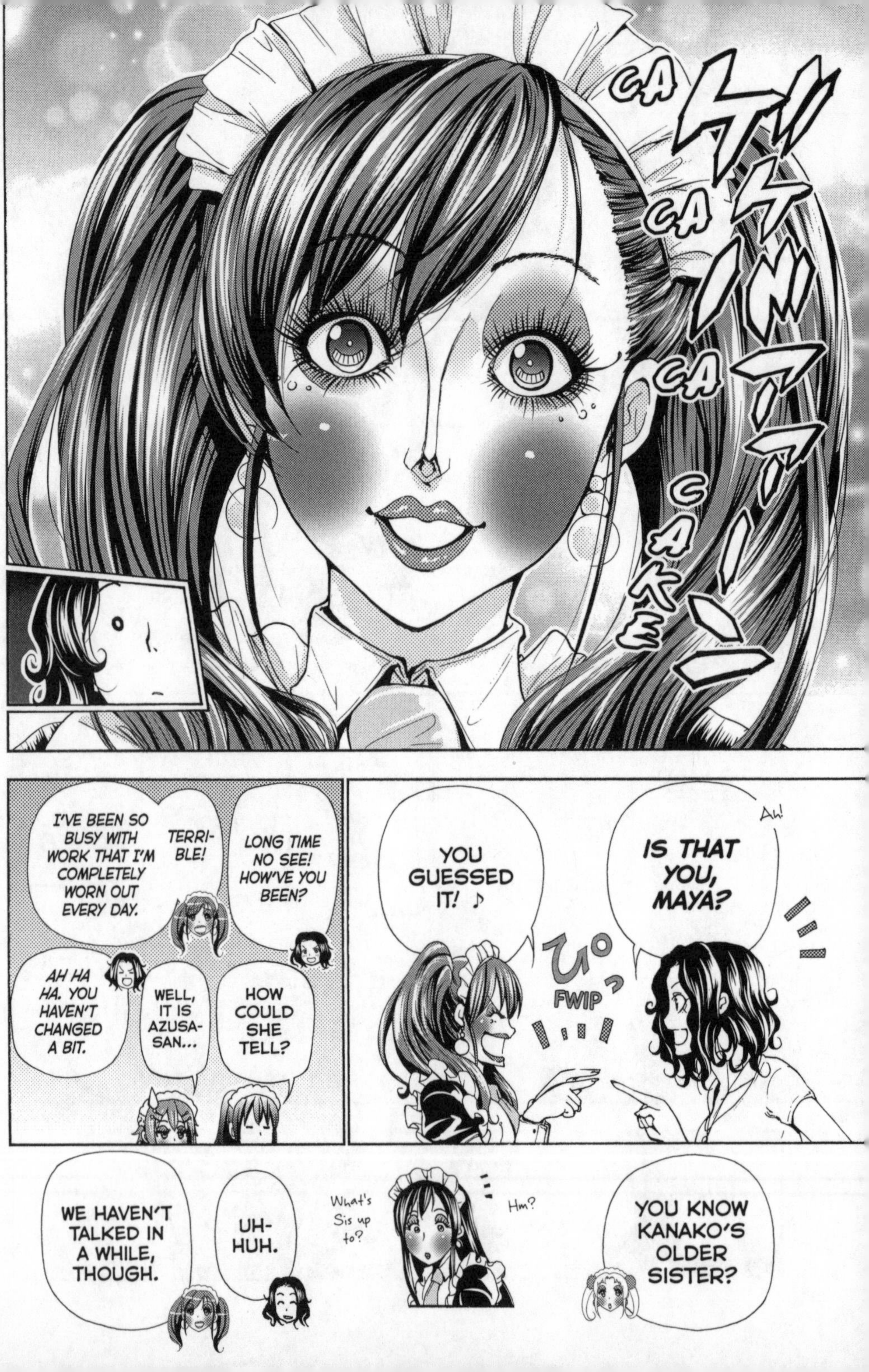
CA
CA
CA
CAKE
Ah!
IS THAT YOU, MAYA?
YOU GUESSED IT! ♪
FWIP
LONG TIME NO SEE! HOW'VE YOU BEEN?
TERRIBLE!
I'VE BEEN SO BUSY WITH WORK THAT I'M COMPLETELY WORN OUT EVERY DAY.
HOW COULD SHE TELL?
WELL, IT IS AZUSA-SAN...
AH HA HA. YOU HAVEN'T CHANGED A BIT.
YOU KNOW KANAKO'S OLDER SISTER?
Hm?
What's Sis up to?
UH-HUH.
WE HAVEN'T TALKED IN A WHILE, THOUGH.

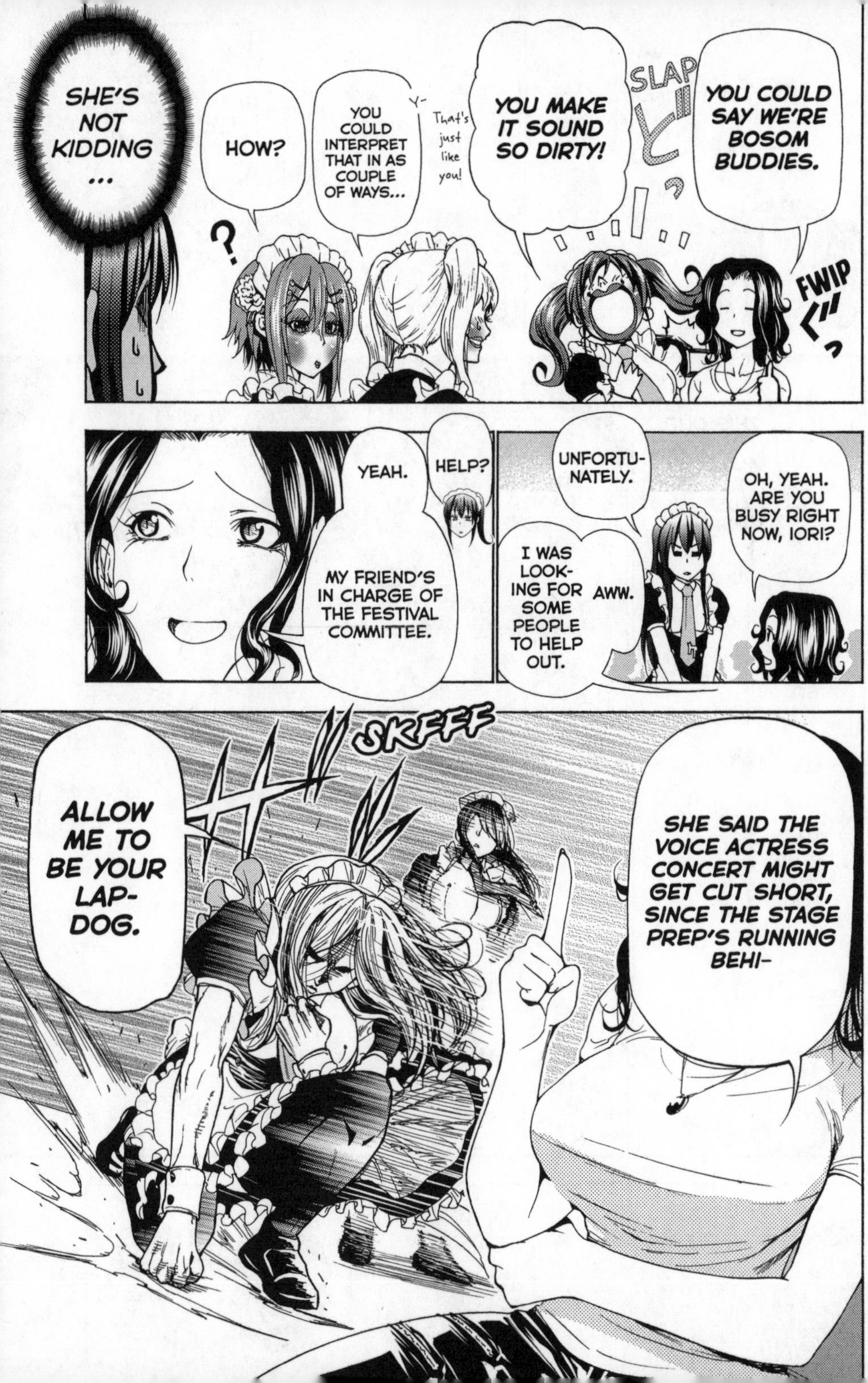
YOU COULD SAY WE'RE BOSOM BUDDIES.
FWIP
SLAP
YOU MAKE IT SOUND SO DIRTY!
That's just like you!
Y-
YOU COULD INTERPRET THAT IN AS COUPLE OF WAYS...
HOW?
SHE'S NOT KIDDING ...
OH, YEAH. ARE YOU BUSY RIGHT NOW, IORI?
UNFORTU-NATELY.
AWW.
I WAS LOOK-ING FOR SOME PEOPLE TO HELP OUT.
HELP?
YEAH.
MY FRIEND'S IN CHARGE OF THE FESTIVAL COMMITTEE.
SHE SAID THE VOICE ACTRESS CONCERT MIGHT GET CUT SHORT, SINCE THE STAGE PREP'S RUNNING BEHI-
SKFFF
ALLOW ME TO BE YOUR LAP-DOG.

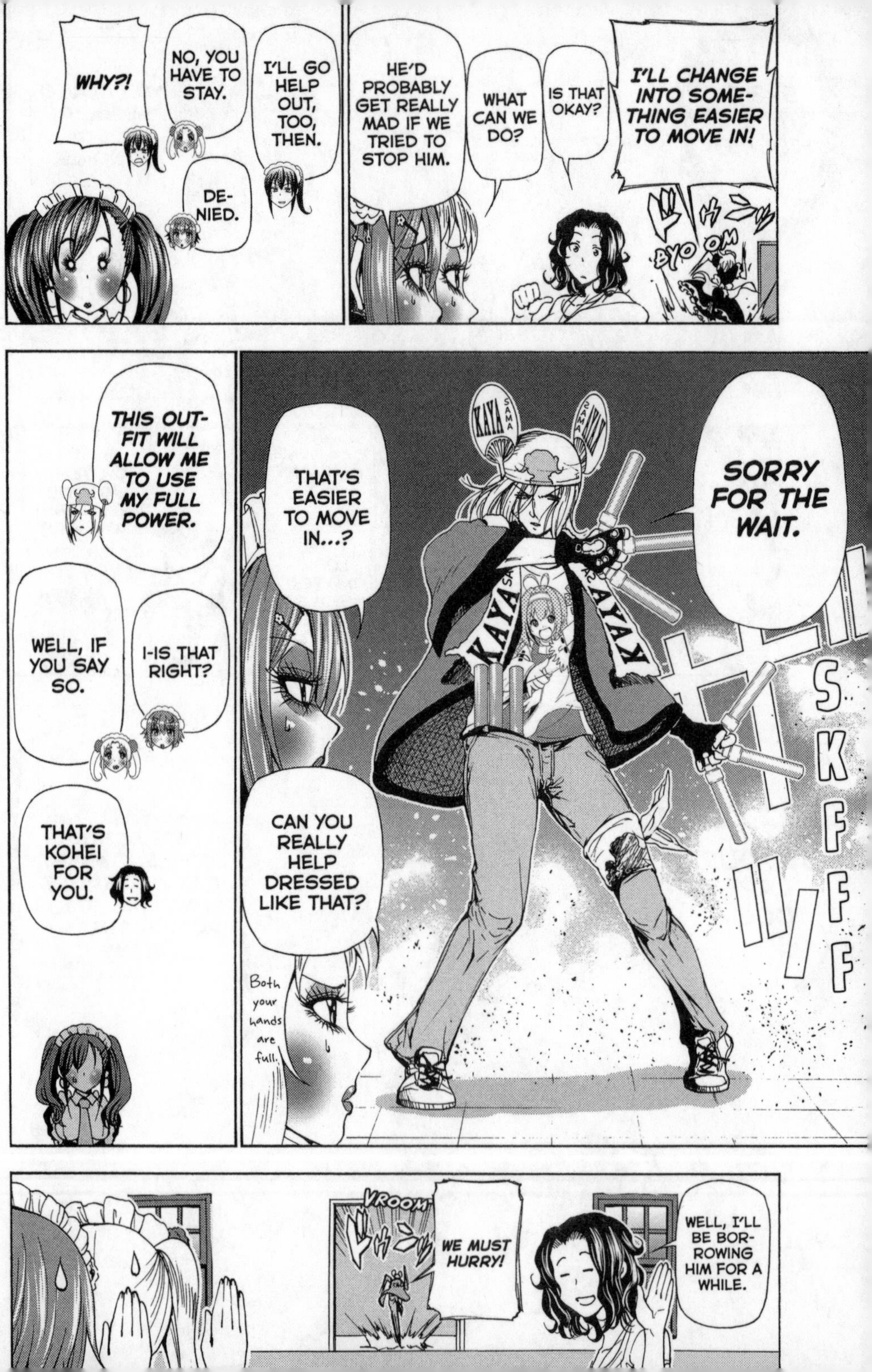
I'LL CHANGE INTO SOME-THING EASIER TO MOVE IN!
IS THAT OKAY?
WHAT CAN WE DO?
HE'D PROBABLY GET REALLY MAD IF WE TRIED TO STOP HIM.
BYO OM
I'LL GO HELP OUT, TOO, THEN.
NO, YOU HAVE TO STAY.
WHY?!
DE-NIED.
SORRY FOR THE WAIT.
SKFFF
THAT'S EASIER TO MOVE IN...?
CAN YOU REALLY HELP DRESSED LIKE THAT?
Both your hands are full.
THIS OUT-FIT WILL ALLOW ME TO USE MY FULL POWER.
I-IS THAT RIGHT?
WELL, IF YOU SAY SO.
THAT'S KOHEI FOR YOU.
WELL, I'LL BE BOR-ROWING HIM FOR A WHILE.
WE MUST HURRY!
VROOM

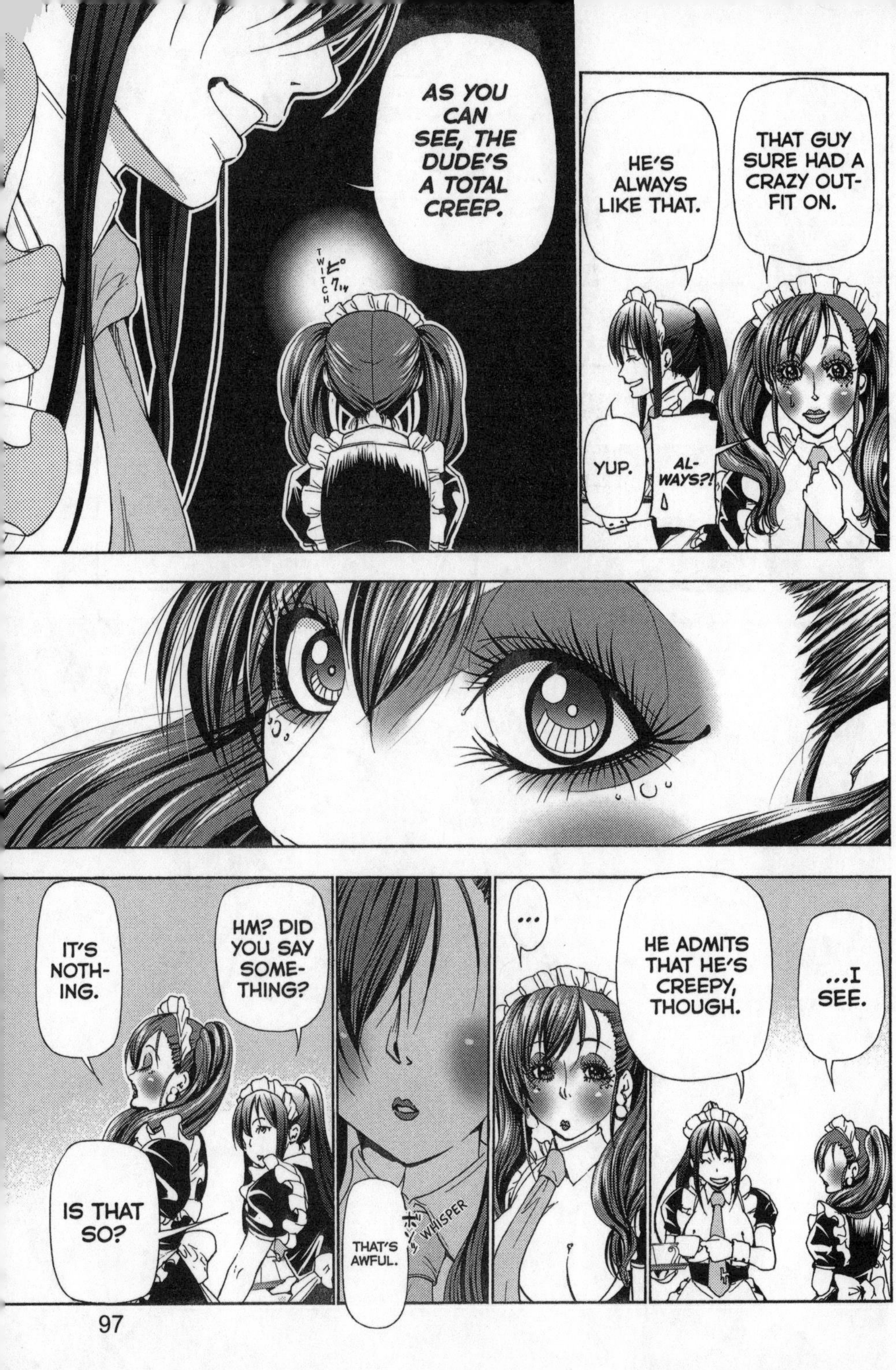
THAT GUY SURE HAD A CRAZY OUT-FIT ON.
HE'S ALWAYS LIKE THAT.
AL-WAYS?!
YUP.
AS YOU CAN SEE, THE DUDE'S A TOTAL CREEP.
TWITCH
...I SEE.
HE ADMITS THAT HE'S CREEPY, THOUGH.
...
WHISPER
THAT'S AWFUL.
HM? DID YOU SAY SOME-THING?
IT'S NOTH-ING.
IS THAT SO?

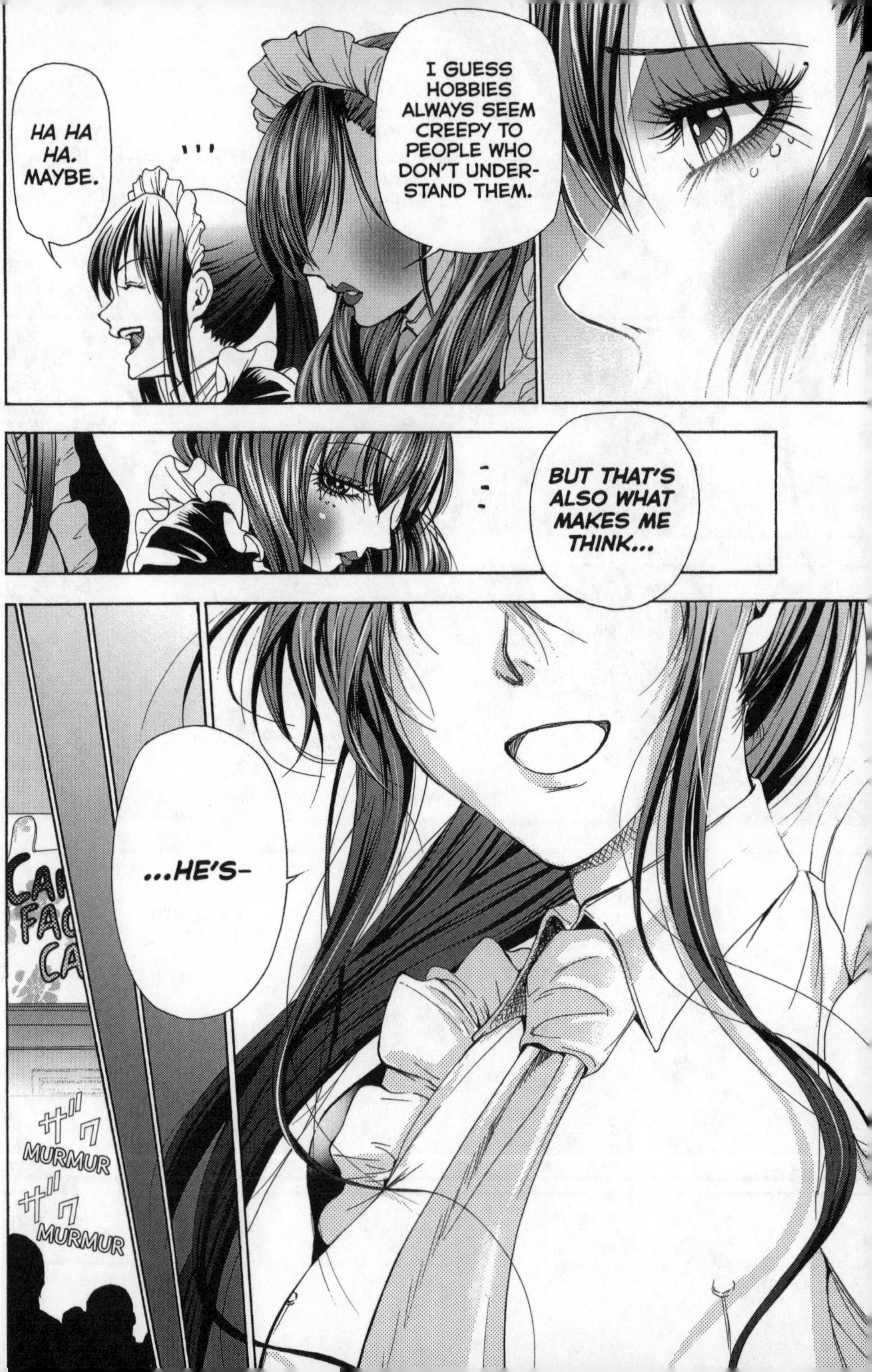
I GUESS HOBBIES ALWAYS SEEM CREEPY TO PEOPLE WHO DON'T UNDERSTAND THEM.
...
HA HA HA. MAYBE.
BUT THAT'S ALSO WHAT MAKES ME THINK...
...
...HE'S-
MURMUR
MURMUR

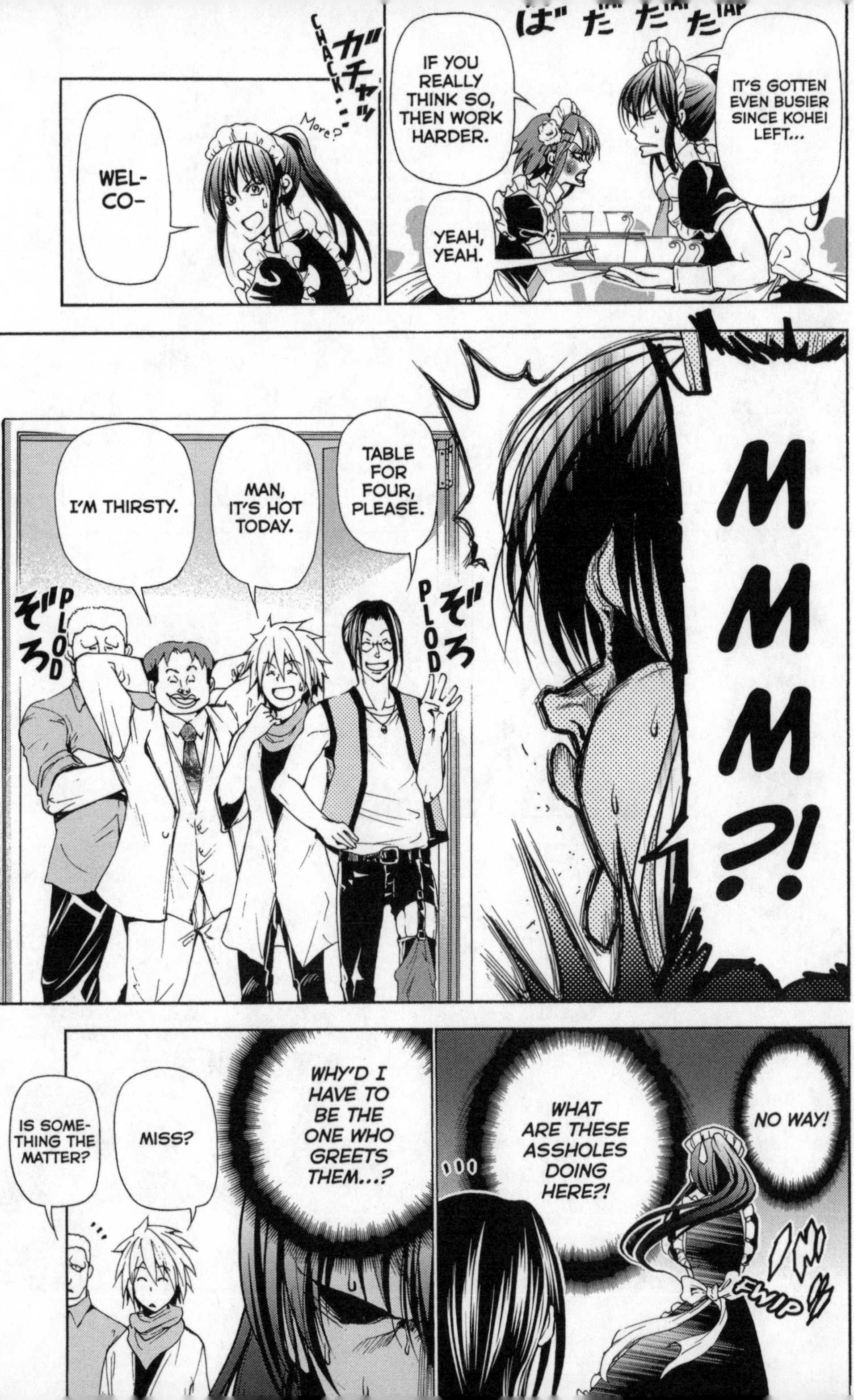

TAP
IT'S GOTTEN EVEN BUSIER SINCE KOHEI LEFT...
IF YOU REALLY THINK SO, THEN WORK HARDER.
YEAH, YEAH.
ガチャッ
CHACK
More?
WEL- CO-
MMM?!
TABLE FOR FOUR, PLEASE.
ぞろ
PLOD
MAN, IT'S HOT TODAY.
I'M THIRSTY.
ぞろ
PLOD
NO WAY!
WHAT ARE THESE ASSHOLES DOING HERE?!
FWIP
WHY'D I HAVE TO BE THE ONE WHO GREETS THEM...?
MISS?
IS SOME- THING THE MATTER?

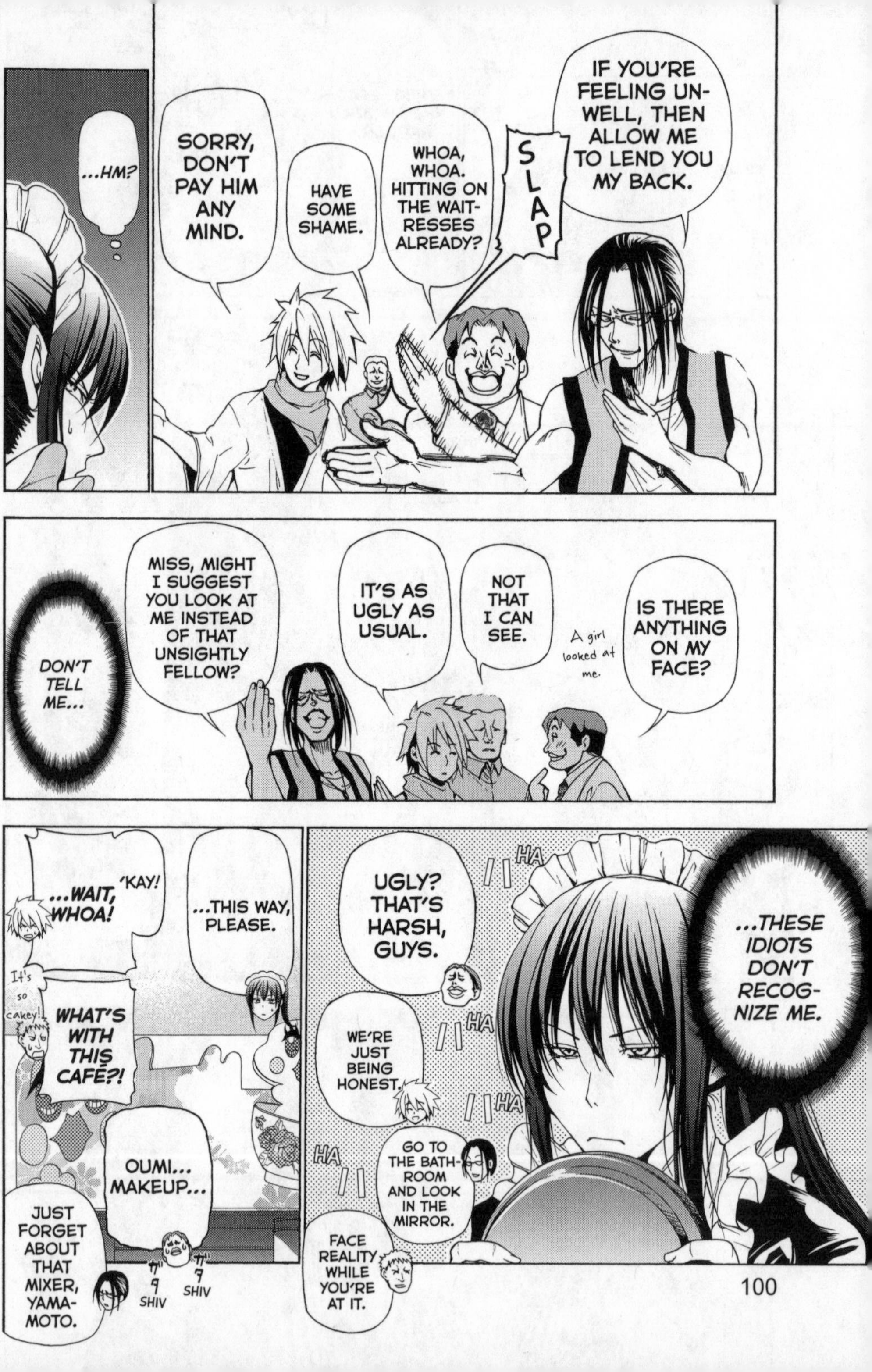
IF YOU'RE FEELING UN-WELL, THEN ALLOW ME TO LEND YOU MY BACK.
SLAP
WHOA, WHOA. HITTING ON THE WAIT-RESSES ALREADY?
HAVE SOME SHAME.
SORRY, DON'T PAY HIM ANY MIND.
...HM?
IS THERE ANYTHING ON MY FACE?
A girl looked at me.
NOT THAT I CAN SEE.
IT'S AS UGLY AS USUAL.
MISS, MIGHT I SUGGEST YOU LOOK AT ME INSTEAD OF THAT UNSIGHTLY FELLOW?
DON'T TELL ME...
...THESE IDIOTS DON'T RECOG-NIZE ME.
HA
UGLY? THAT'S HARSH, GUYS.
HA
WE'RE JUST BEING HONEST.
HA
HA
GO TO THE BATH-ROOM AND LOOK IN THE MIRROR.
FACE REALITY WHILE YOU'RE AT IT.
...THIS WAY, PLEASE.
'KAY!
...WAIT, WHOA!
It's so cakey!
WHAT'S WITH THIS CAFÉ?!
OUMI... MAKEUP...
SHIV
SHIV
JUST FORGET ABOUT THAT MIXER, YAMA-MOTO.

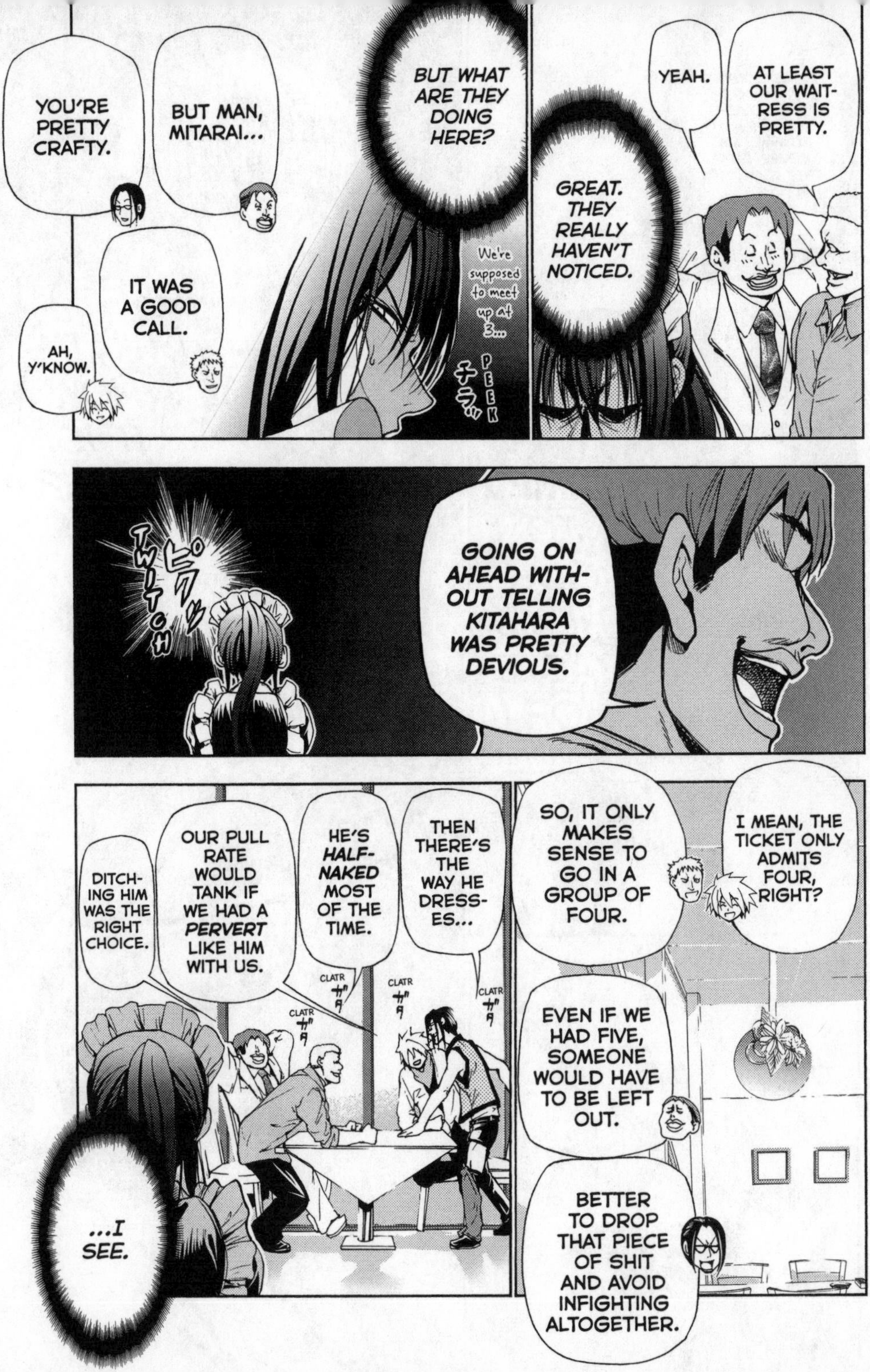
AT LEAST OUR WAITRESS IS PRETTY.
YEAH.
GREAT. THEY REALLY HAVEN'T NOTICED.
BUT WHAT ARE THEY DOING HERE?
We're supposed to meet up at 3...
PEEK
BUT MAN, MITARAI...
YOU'RE PRETTY CRAFTY.
IT WAS A GOOD CALL.
AH, Y'KNOW.
GOING ON AHEAD WITHOUT TELLING KITAHARA WAS PRETTY DEVIOUS.
TWITCH
I MEAN, THE TICKET ONLY ADMITS FOUR, RIGHT?
SO, IT ONLY MAKES SENSE TO GO IN A GROUP OF FOUR.
EVEN IF WE HAD FIVE, SOMEONE WOULD HAVE TO BE LEFT OUT.
BETTER TO DROP THAT PIECE OF SHIT AND AVOID INFIGHTING ALTOGETHER.
THEN THERE'S THE WAY HE DRESSES...
CLATR
HE'S HALF-NAKED MOST OF THE TIME.
CLATR
OUR PULL RATE WOULD TANK IF WE HAD A PERVERT LIKE HIM WITH US.
CLATR
DITCHING HIM WAS THE RIGHT CHOICE.
...I SEE.

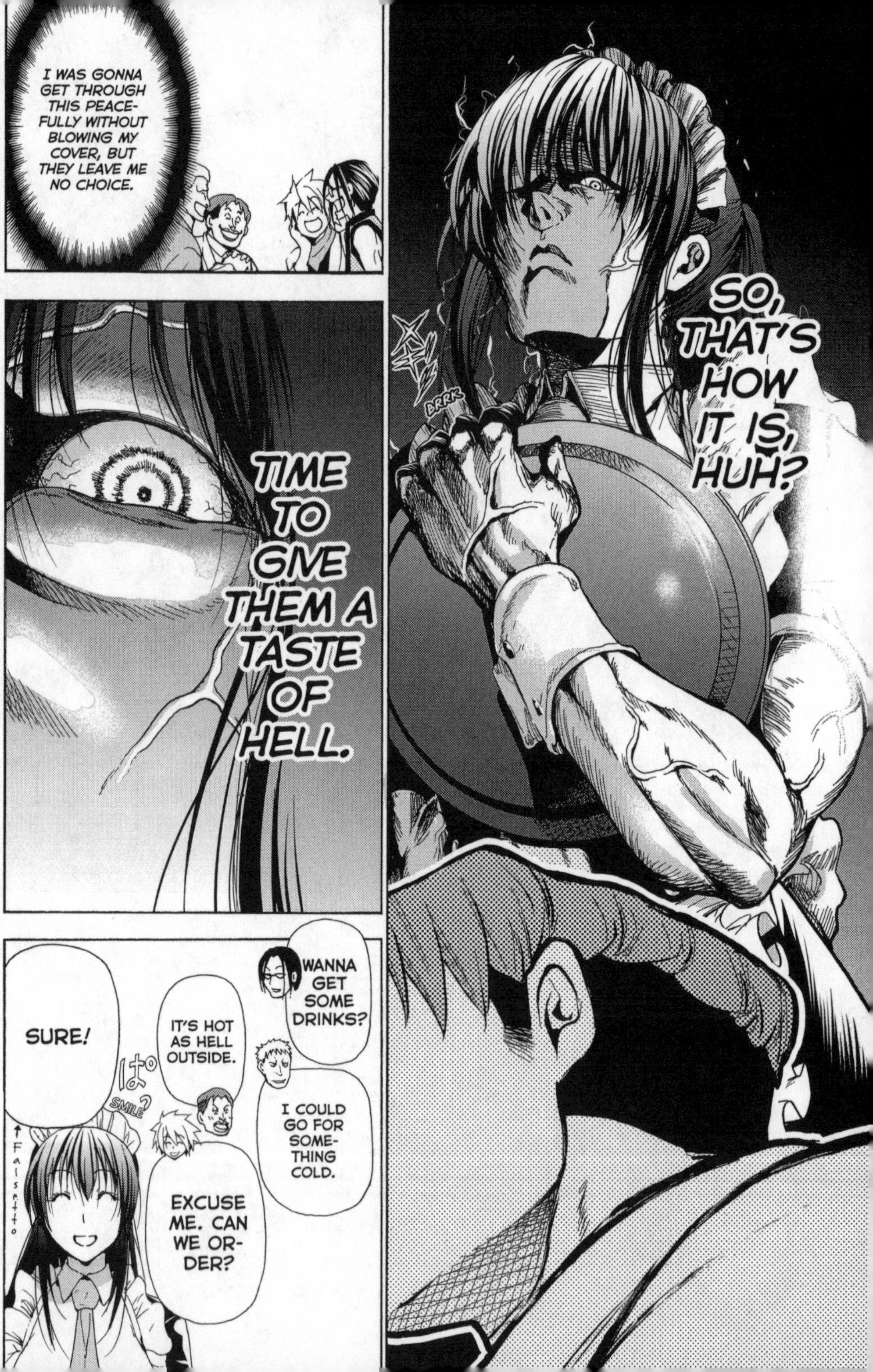

SO, THAT'S HOW IT IS, HUH?
BRRK
I WAS GONNA GET THROUGH THIS PEACE-FULLY WITHOUT BLOWING MY COVER, BUT THEY LEAVE ME NO CHOICE.
TIME TO GIVE THEM A TASTE OF HELL.
WANNA GET SOME DRINKS?
I COULD GO FOR SOME-THING COLD.
IT'S HOT AS HELL OUTSIDE.
EXCUSE ME. CAN WE OR-DER?
SURE!
SMILE
↑Falsetto

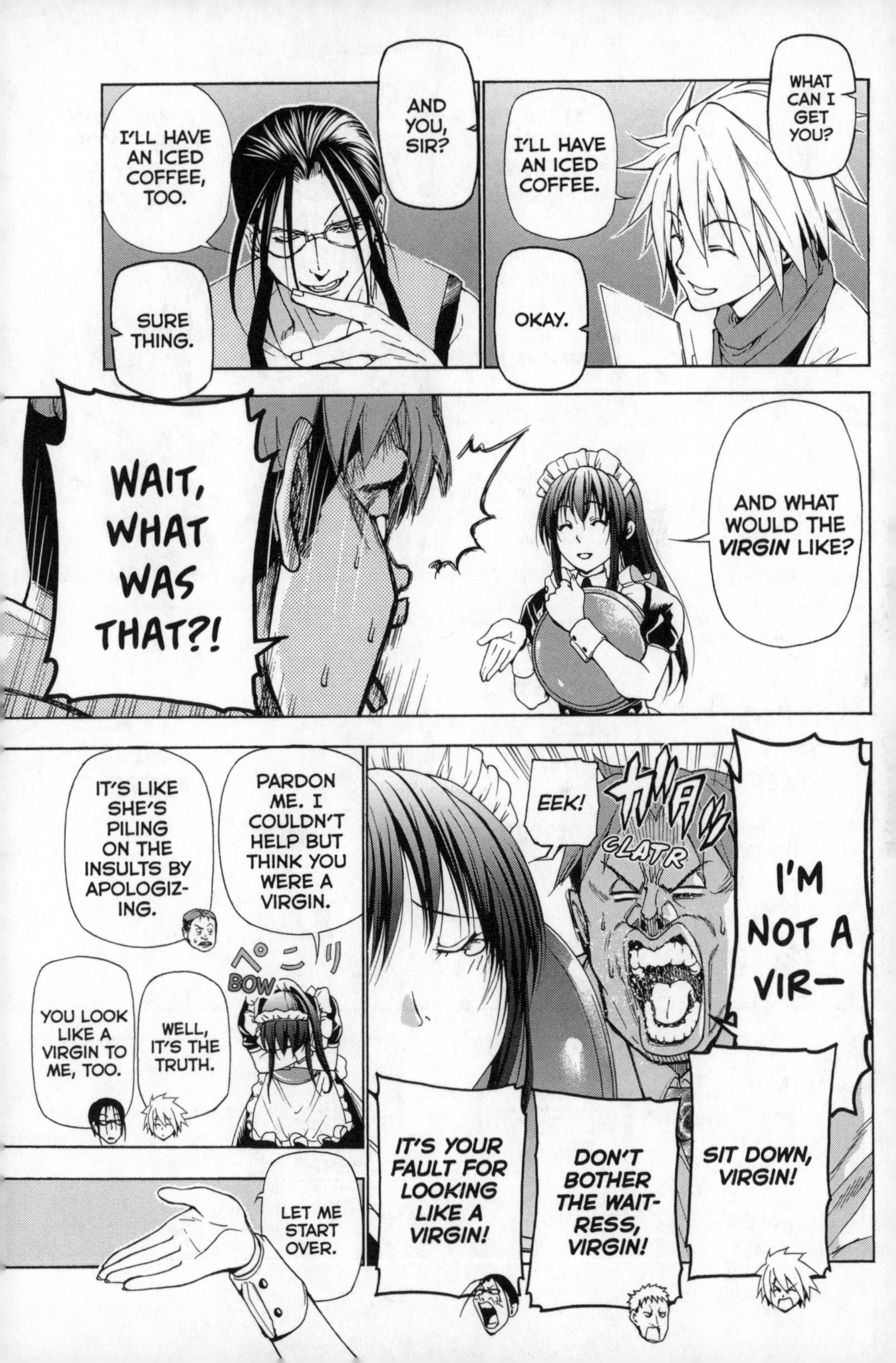
WHAT CAN I GET YOU?
I'LL HAVE AN ICED COFFEE.
OKAY.
AND YOU, SIR?
I'LL HAVE AN ICED COFFEE, TOO.
SURE THING.
AND WHAT WOULD THE VIRGIN LIKE?
WAIT, WHAT WAS THAT?!
I'M NOT A VIR—
EEK!
GLATR
SIT DOWN, VIRGIN!
DON'T BOTHER THE WAITRESS, VIRGIN!
IT'S YOUR FAULT FOR LOOKING LIKE A VIRGIN!
PARDON ME. I COULDN'T HELP BUT THINK YOU WERE A VIRGIN.
IT'S LIKE SHE'S PILING ON THE INSULTS BY APOLOGIZING.
BOW
WELL, IT'S THE TRUTH.
YOU LOOK LIKE A VIRGIN TO ME, TOO.
LET ME START OVER.

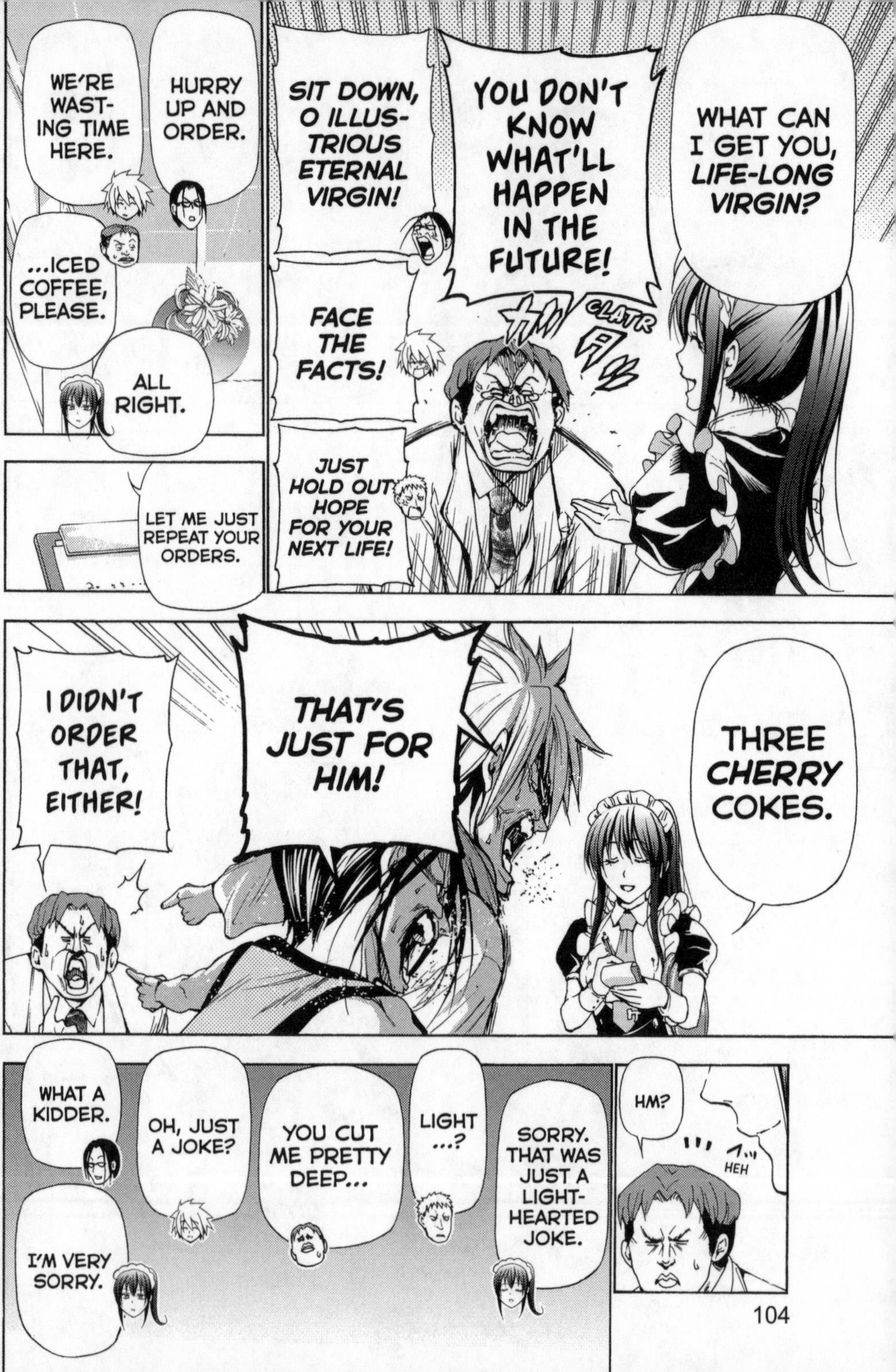
WHAT CAN I GET YOU, LIFE-LONG VIRGIN?
YOU DON'T KNOW WHAT'LL HAPPEN IN THE FUTURE!
CLATR
SIT DOWN, O ILLUS-TRIOUS ETERNAL VIRGIN!
FACE THE FACTS!
JUST HOLD OUT HOPE FOR YOUR NEXT LIFE!
HURRY UP AND ORDER.
WE'RE WAST-ING TIME HERE.
...ICED COFFEE, PLEASE.
ALL RIGHT.
LET ME JUST REPEAT YOUR ORDERS.
THREE CHERRY COKES.
THAT'S JUST FOR HIM!
I DIDN'T ORDER THAT, EITHER!
HM?
HEH
SORRY. THAT WAS JUST A LIGHT-HEARTED JOKE.
LIGHT ...?
YOU CUT ME PRETTY DEEP...
OH, JUST A JOKE?
WHAT A KIDDER.
I'M VERY SORRY.

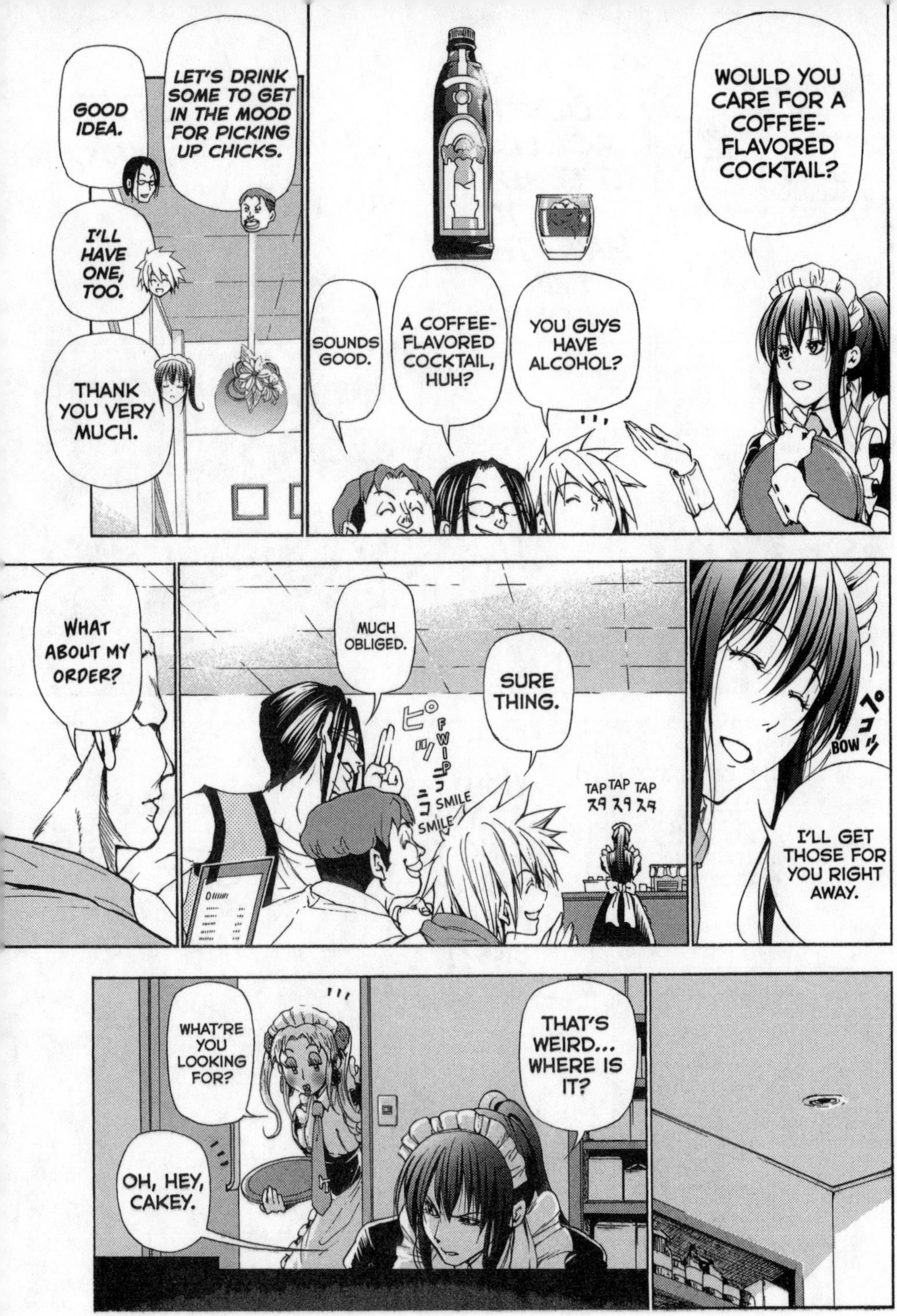
WOULD YOU CARE FOR A COFFEE-FLAVORED COCKTAIL?
YOU GUYS HAVE ALCOHOL?
A COFFEE-FLAVORED COCKTAIL, HUH?
SOUNDS GOOD.
LET'S DRINK SOME TO GET IN THE MOOD FOR PICKING UP CHICKS.
GOOD IDEA.
I'LL HAVE ONE, TOO.
THANK YOU VERY MUCH.
BOW
I'LL GET THOSE FOR YOU RIGHT AWAY.
TAP TAP TAP
SURE THING.
SMILE SMILE
FWIP
MUCH OBLIGED.
WHAT ABOUT MY ORDER?
THAT'S WEIRD... WHERE IS IT?
WHAT'RE YOU LOOKING FOR?
OH, HEY, CAKEY.

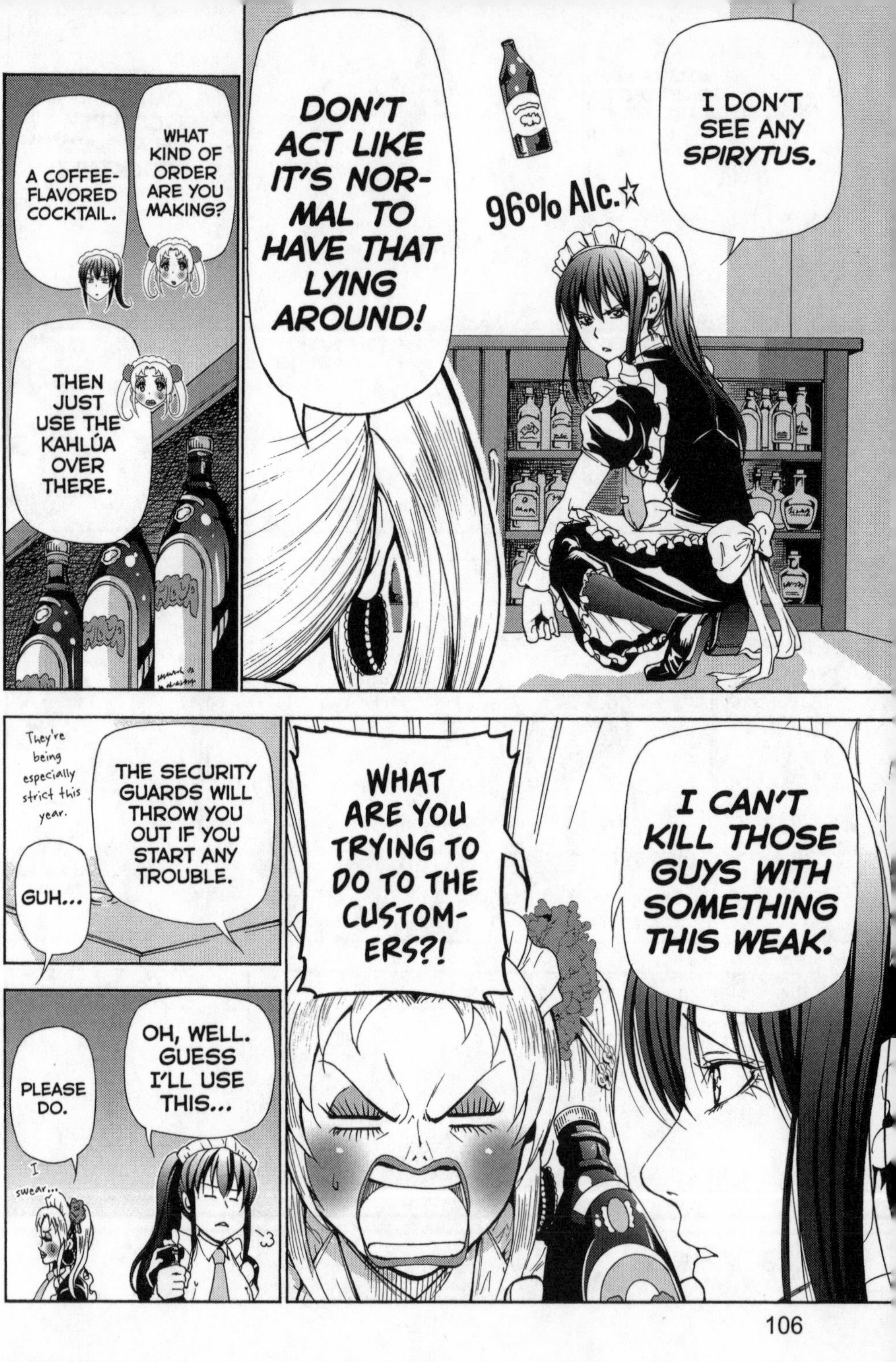
I DON'T SEE ANY SPIRYTUS.
96% Alc.☆
DON'T ACT LIKE IT'S NOR-MAL TO HAVE THAT LYING AROUND!
WHAT KIND OF ORDER ARE YOU MAKING?
A COFFEE-FLAVORED COCKTAIL.
THEN JUST USE THE KAHLÚA OVER THERE.
I CAN'T KILL THOSE GUYS WITH SOMETHING THIS WEAK.
WHAT ARE YOU TRYING TO DO TO THE CUSTOM-ERS?!
THE SECURITY GUARDS WILL THROW YOU OUT IF YOU START ANY TROUBLE.
They're being especially strict this year.
GUH...
OH, WELL. GUESS I'LL USE THIS...
PLEASE DO.
I swear...

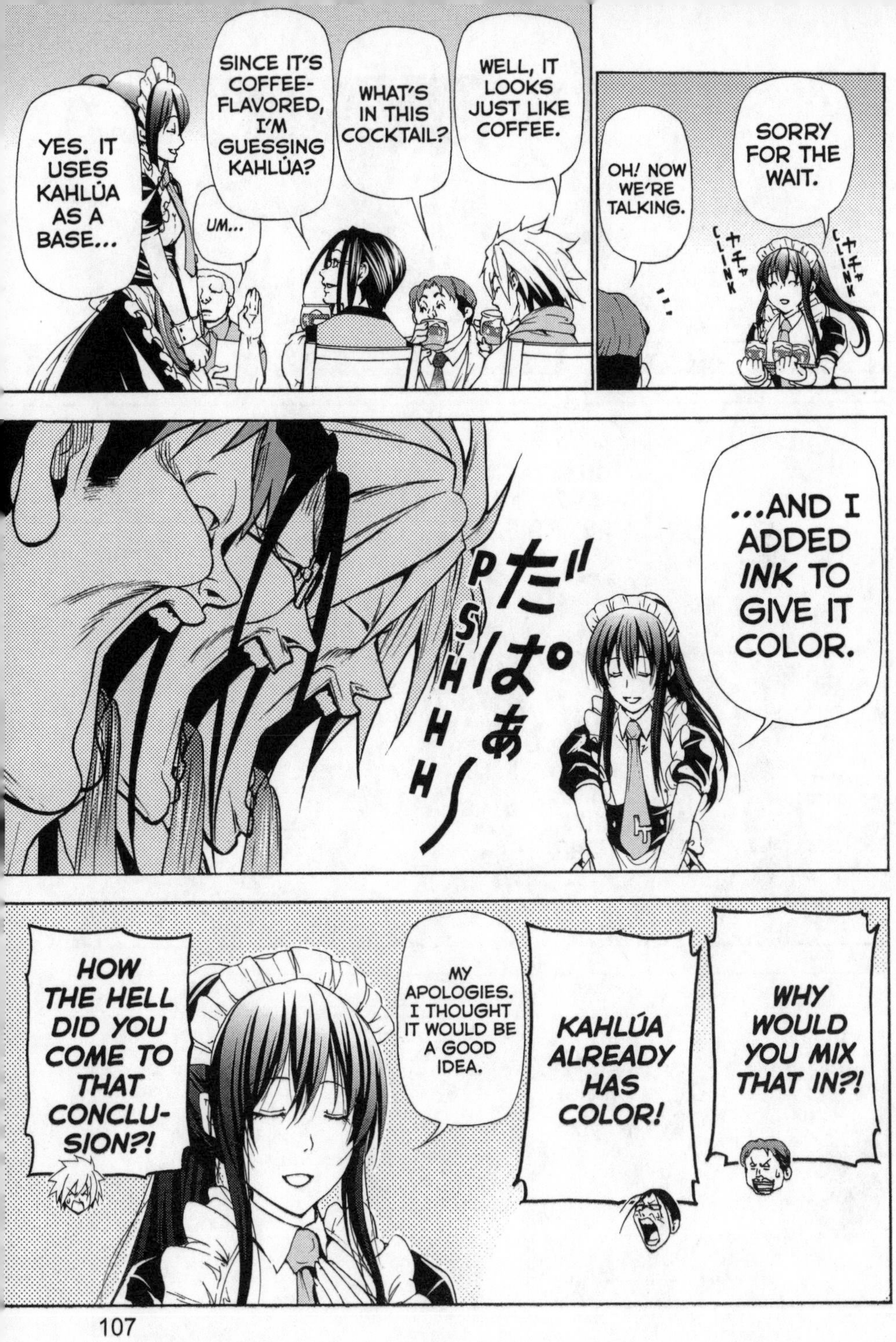
SORRY FOR THE WAIT.
カチャ CLINK
カチャ CLINK
OH! NOW WE'RE TALKING.
...
WELL, IT LOOKS JUST LIKE COFFEE.
WHAT'S IN THIS COCKTAIL?
SINCE IT'S COFFEE-FLAVORED, I'M GUESSING KAHLÚA?
UM...
YES. IT USES KAHLÚA AS A BASE...
...AND I ADDED INK TO GIVE IT COLOR.
だばぁ～
PSHHHH
WHY WOULD YOU MIX THAT IN?!
KAHLÚA ALREADY HAS COLOR!
MY APOLOGIES. I THOUGHT IT WOULD BE A GOOD IDEA.
HOW THE HELL DID YOU COME TO THAT CONCLUSION?!

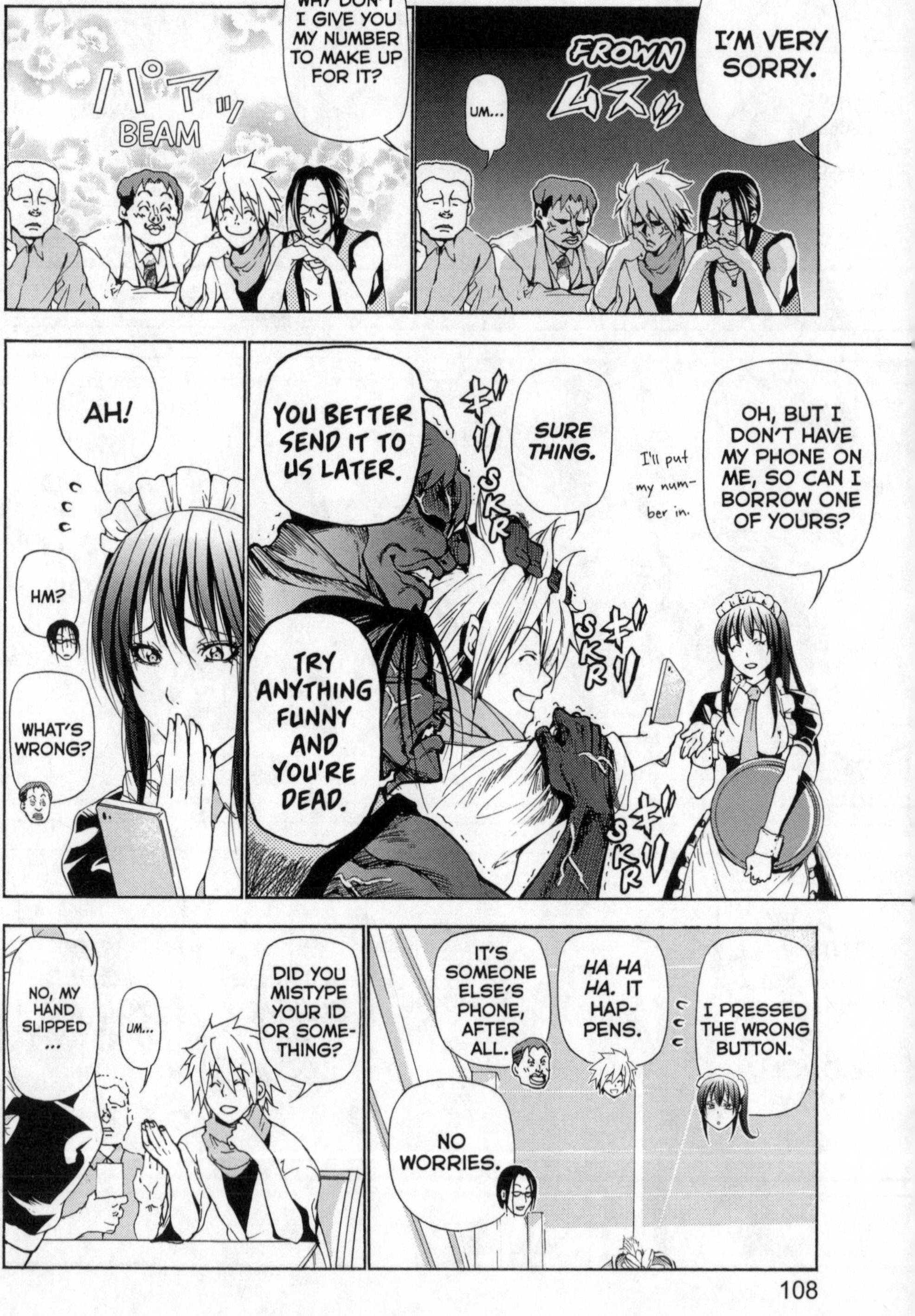
I'M VERY SORRY.
FROWN
ムスッ
UM...
WHY DON'T I GIVE YOU MY NUMBER TO MAKE UP FOR IT?
パアッ
BEAM
OH, BUT I DON'T HAVE MY PHONE ON ME, SO CAN I BORROW ONE OF YOURS?
I'll put my num-ber in.
SURE THING.
ギリ
SKR
YOU BETTER SEND IT TO US LATER.
TRY ANYTHING FUNNY AND YOU'RE DEAD.
AH!
HM?
WHAT'S WRONG?
I PRESSED THE WRONG BUTTON.
HA HA HA. IT HAP-PENS.
IT'S SOMEONE ELSE'S PHONE, AFTER ALL.
NO WORRIES.
DID YOU MISTYPE YOUR ID OR SOME-THING?
UM...
NO, MY HAND SLIPPED ...

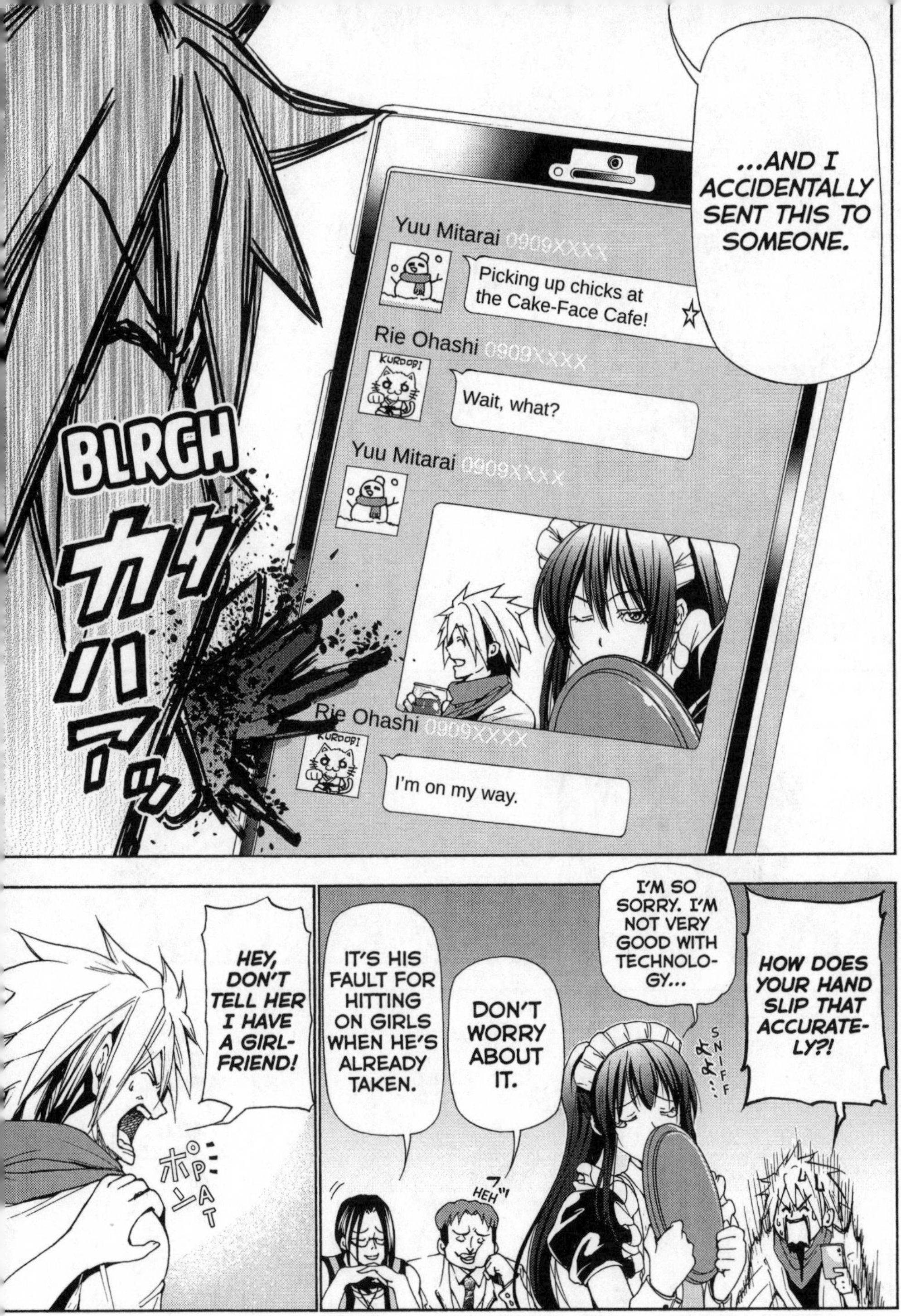

...AND I ACCIDENTALLY SENT THIS TO SOMEONE.
Yuu Mitarai 0909XXXX
Picking up chicks at the Cake-Face Cafe! ☆
Rie Ohashi 0909XXXX
KURODDPI
Wait, what?
Yuu Mitarai 0909XXXX
Rie Ohashi 0909XXXX
I'm on my way.
BLRGH
HOW DOES YOUR HAND SLIP THAT ACCURATE-LY?!
I'M SO SORRY. I'M NOT VERY GOOD WITH TECHNOLO-GY...
SNIFF
DON'T WORRY ABOUT IT.
HEH
IT'S HIS FAULT FOR HITTING ON GIRLS WHEN HE'S ALREADY TAKEN.
HEY, DON'T TELL HER I HAVE A GIRL-FRIEND!
PAT

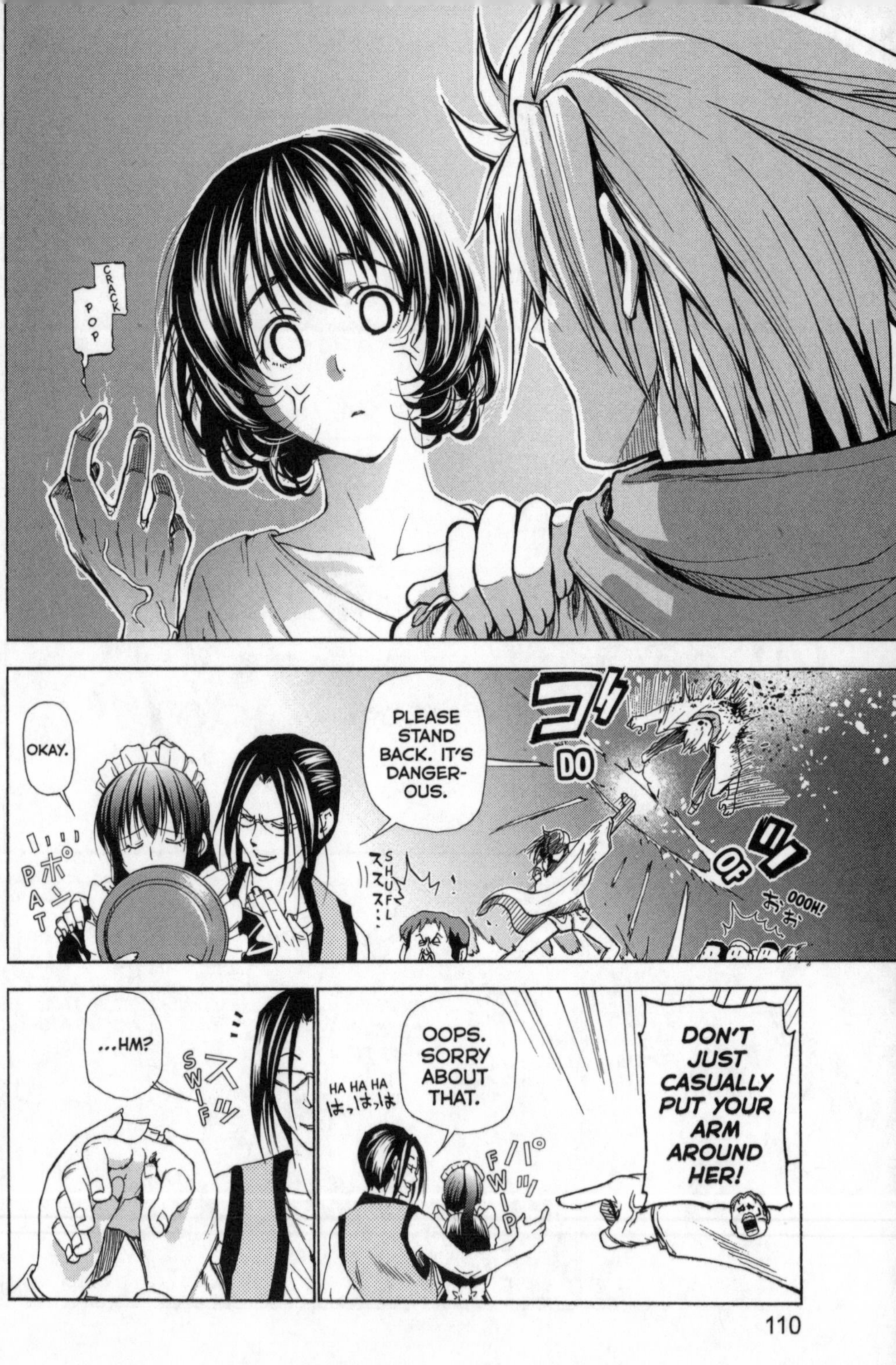
CRACK
POP
DO
OF
OOOH!
PLEASE STAND BACK. IT'S DANGER- OUS.
SHUFFL
OKAY.
PAT
DON'T JUST CASUALLY PUT YOUR ARM AROUND HER!
FWIP
OOPS. SORRY ABOUT THAT.
HA HA HA
はっはっは
SWIF
...HM?

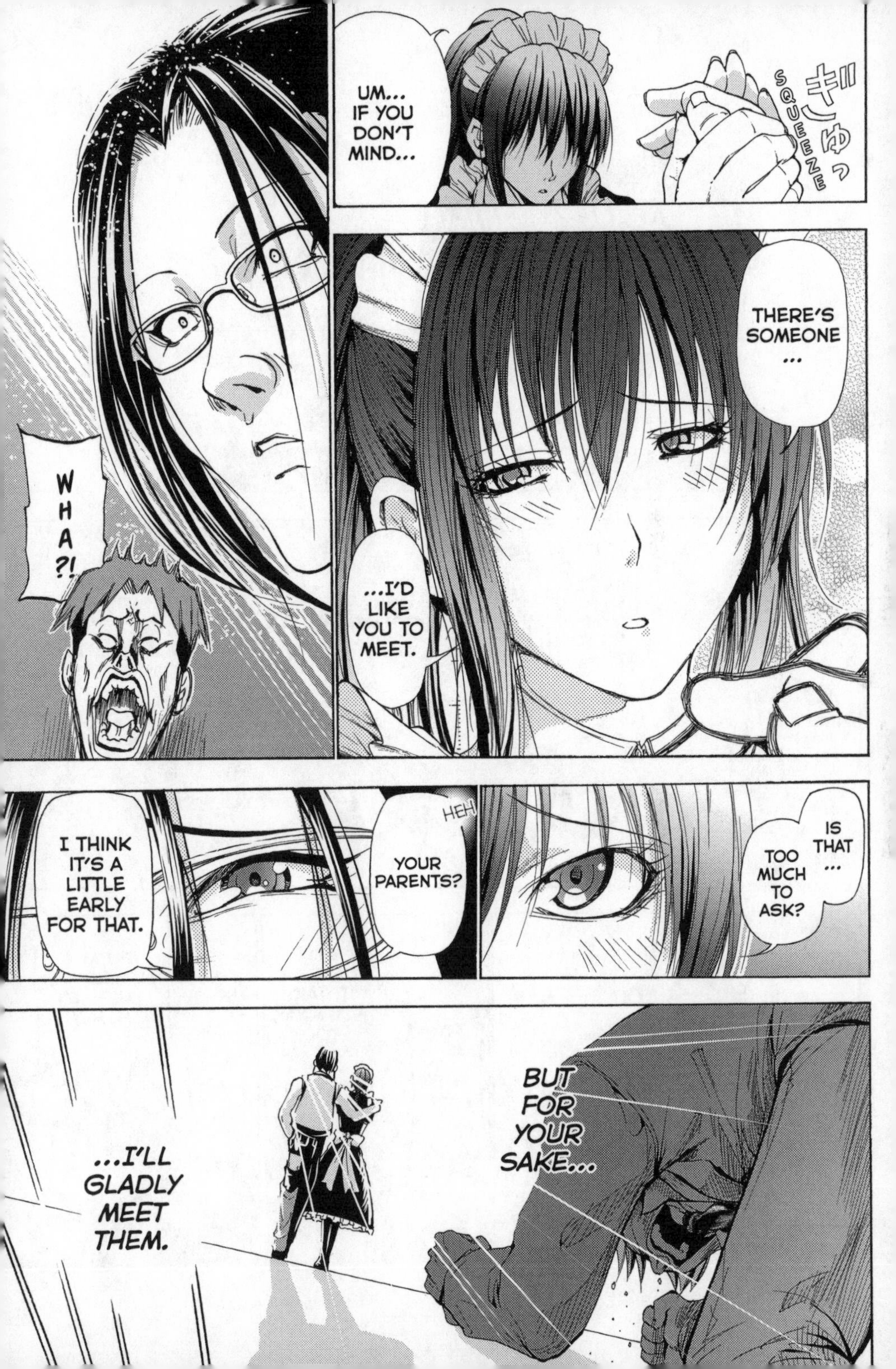
ぎゅっ
SQUEEZE
UM... IF YOU DON'T MIND...
THERE'S SOMEONE ...
...I'D LIKE YOU TO MEET.
WHA?!
IS THAT ... TOO MUCH TO ASK?
HEH
YOUR PARENTS?
I THINK IT'S A LITTLE EARLY FOR THAT.
BUT FOR YOUR SAKE...
...I'LL GLADLY MEET THEM.

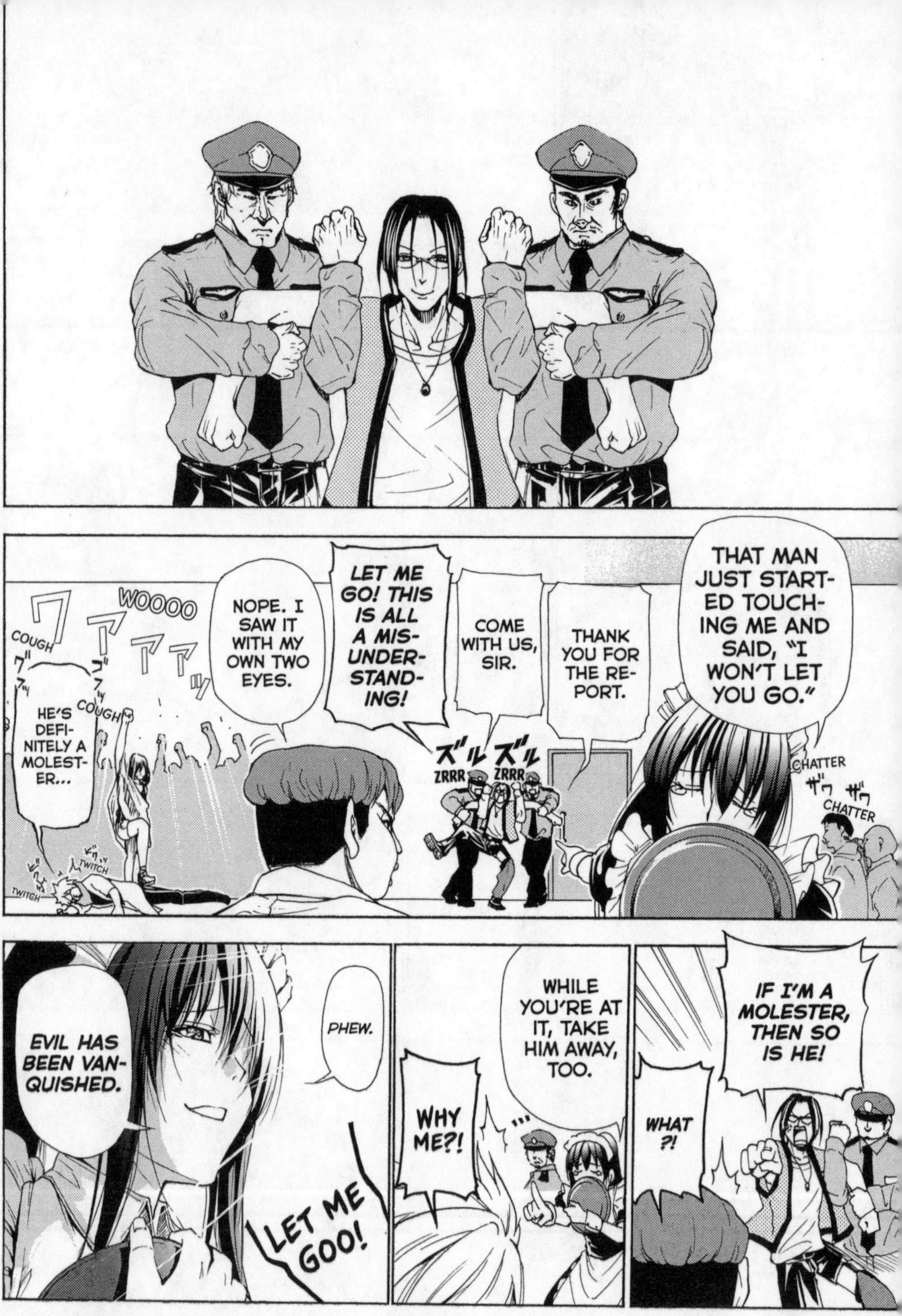
THAT MAN JUST STARTED TOUCHING ME AND SAID, "I WON'T LET YOU GO."
CHATTER
CHATTER
THANK YOU FOR THE REPORT.
COME WITH US, SIR.
ZRRR
ZRRR
LET ME GO! THIS IS ALL A MISUNDERSTANDING!
NOPE. I SAW IT WITH MY OWN TWO EYES.
WOOOO
COUGH
COUGH
HE'S DEFINITELY A MOLESTER...
TWITCH
TWITCH
IF I'M A MOLESTER, THEN SO IS HE!
WHAT?!
WHILE YOU'RE AT IT, TAKE HIM AWAY, TOO.
...
WHY ME?!
PHEW.
EVIL HAS BEEN VANQUISHED.
LET ME GOO!

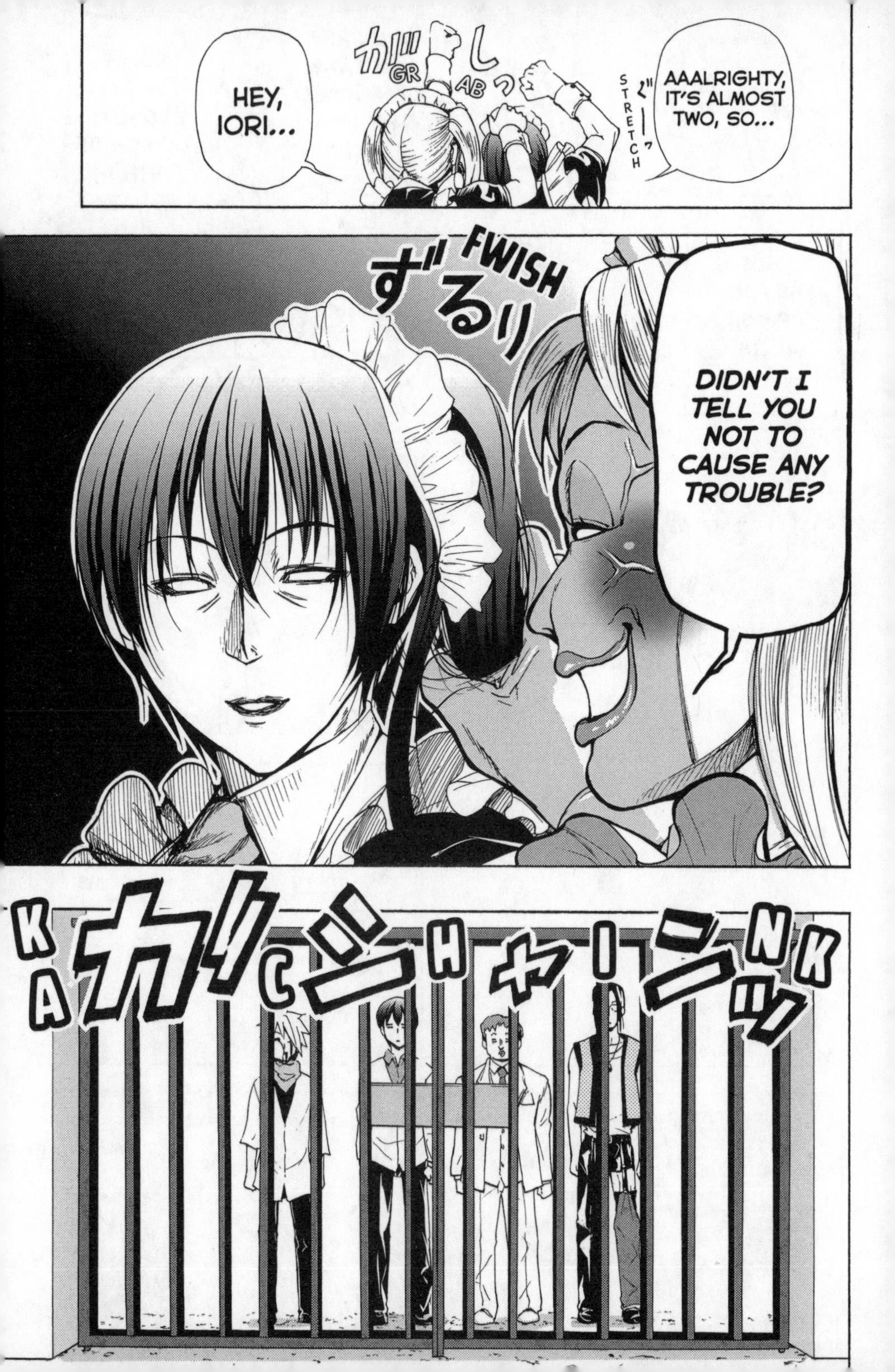
AAALRIGHTY, IT'S ALMOST TWO, SO...
STRETCH
GRAB
HEY, IORI...
FWISH
DIDN'T I TELL YOU NOT TO CAUSE ANY TROUBLE?
KACHINK

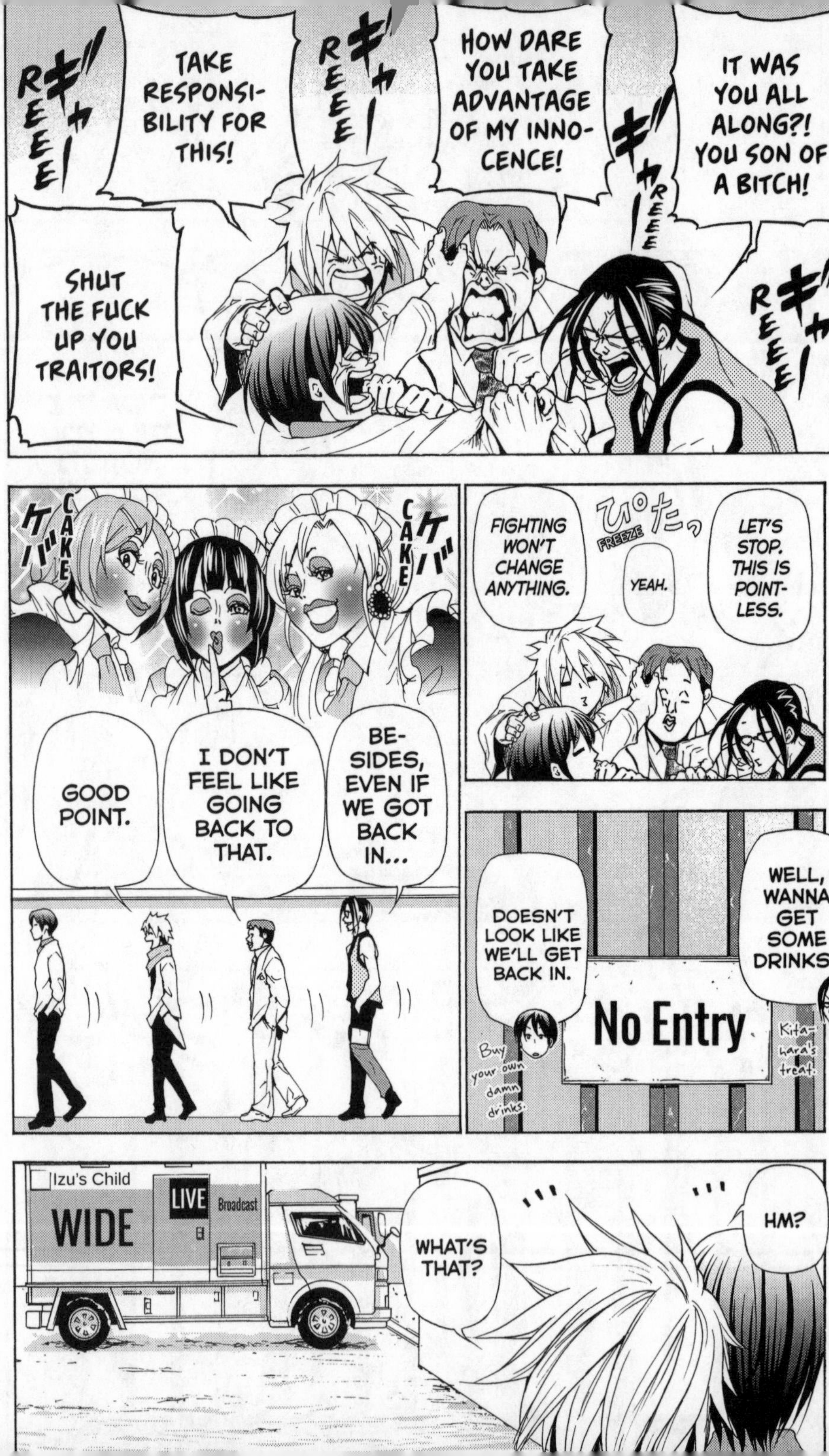
IT WAS YOU ALL ALONG?! YOU SON OF A BITCH!
ギャーREEEE
ギャーREEEE
HOW DARE YOU TAKE ADVANTAGE OF MY INNO-CENCE!
ギャーREEEE
TAKE RESPONSI-BILITY FOR THIS!
ギャーREEEE
SHUT THE FUCK UP YOU TRAITORS!
LET'S STOP. THIS IS POINT-LESS.
ぴたっ FREEZE
YEAH.
FIGHTING WON'T CHANGE ANYTHING.
ケバ CAKE
ケバ CAKE
BE-SIDES, EVEN IF WE GOT BACK IN...
I DON'T FEEL LIKE GOING BACK TO THAT.
GOOD POINT.
WELL, WANNA GET SOME DRINKS?
Kita-hara's treat.
DOESN'T LOOK LIKE WE'LL GET BACK IN.
No Entry
Buy your own damn drinks.
HM?
...
...
WHAT'S THAT?
Izu's Child
LIVE Broadcast
WIDE

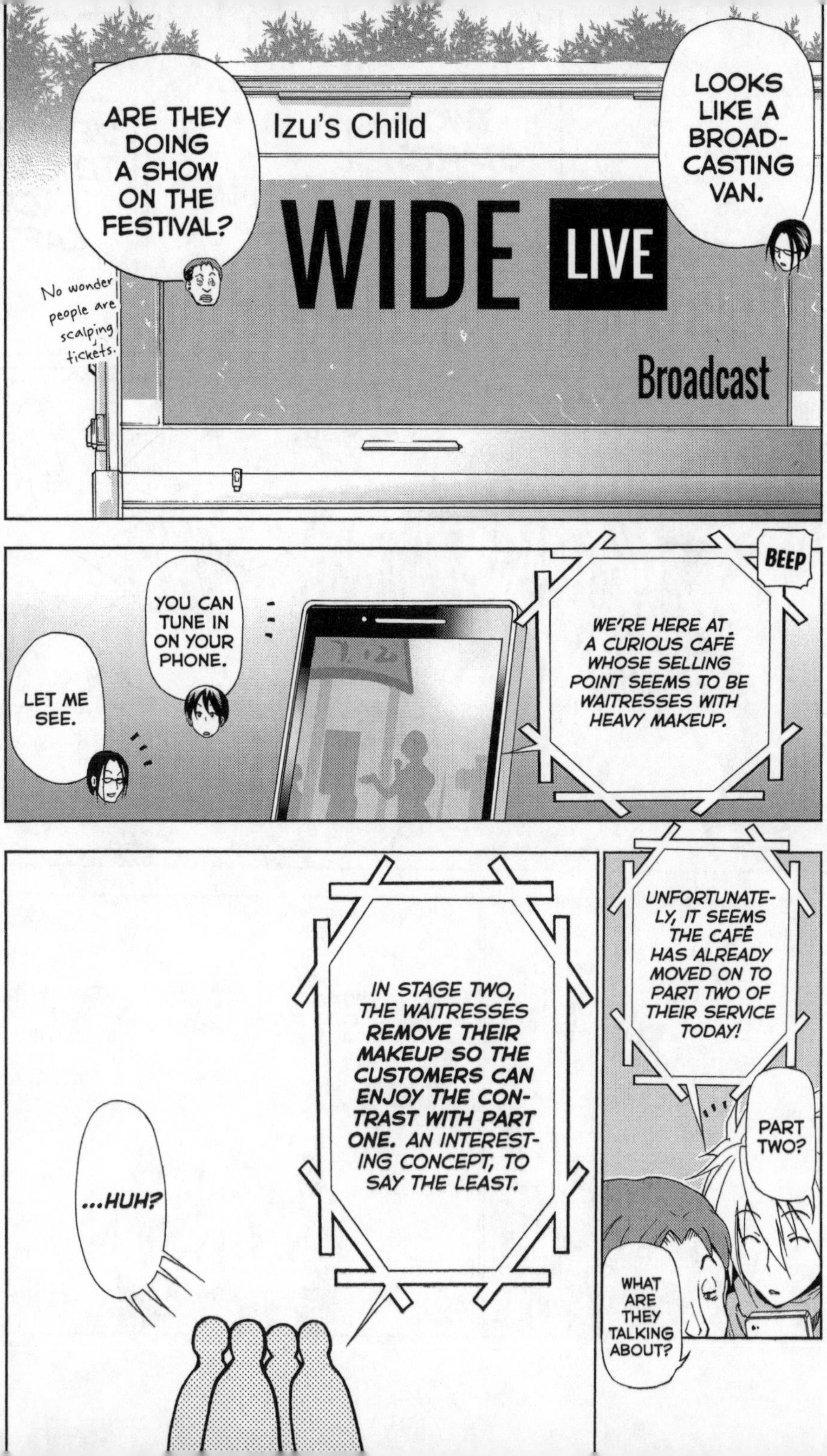
LOOKS LIKE A BROAD-CASTING VAN.
Izu's Child
WIDE LIVE
Broadcast
ARE THEY DOING A SHOW ON THE FESTIVAL?
No wonder people are scalping tickets.
BEEP
WE'RE HERE AT A CURIOUS CAFÉ WHOSE SELLING POINT SEEMS TO BE WAITRESSES WITH HEAVY MAKEUP.
YOU CAN TUNE IN ON YOUR PHONE.
LET ME SEE.
UNFORTUNATE-LY, IT SEEMS THE CAFÉ HAS ALREADY MOVED ON TO PART TWO OF THEIR SERVICE TODAY!
PART TWO?
WHAT ARE THEY TALKING ABOUT?
IN STAGE TWO, THE WAITRESSES REMOVE THEIR MAKEUP SO THE CUSTOMERS CAN ENJOY THE CON-TRAST WITH PART ONE. AN INTEREST-ING CONCEPT, TO SAY THE LEAST.
...HUH?

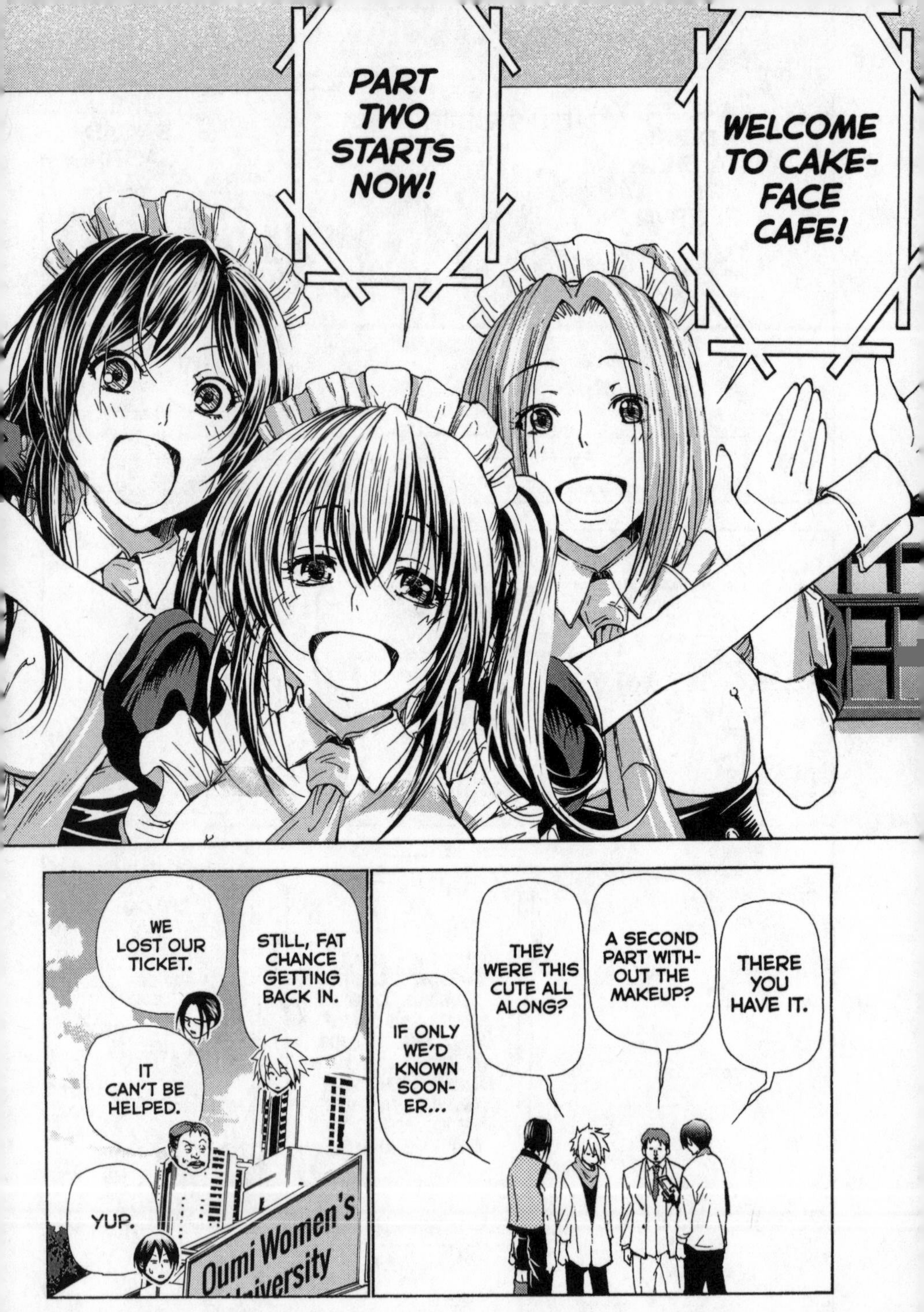
WELCOME TO CAKE-FACE CAFE!
PART TWO STARTS NOW!
THERE YOU HAVE IT.
A SECOND PART WITH-OUT THE MAKEUP?
THEY WERE THIS CUTE ALL ALONG?
IF ONLY WE'D KNOWN SOON-ER...
STILL, FAT CHANCE GETTING BACK IN.
WE LOST OUR TICKET.
IT CAN'T BE HELPED.
YUP.
Oumi Women's University

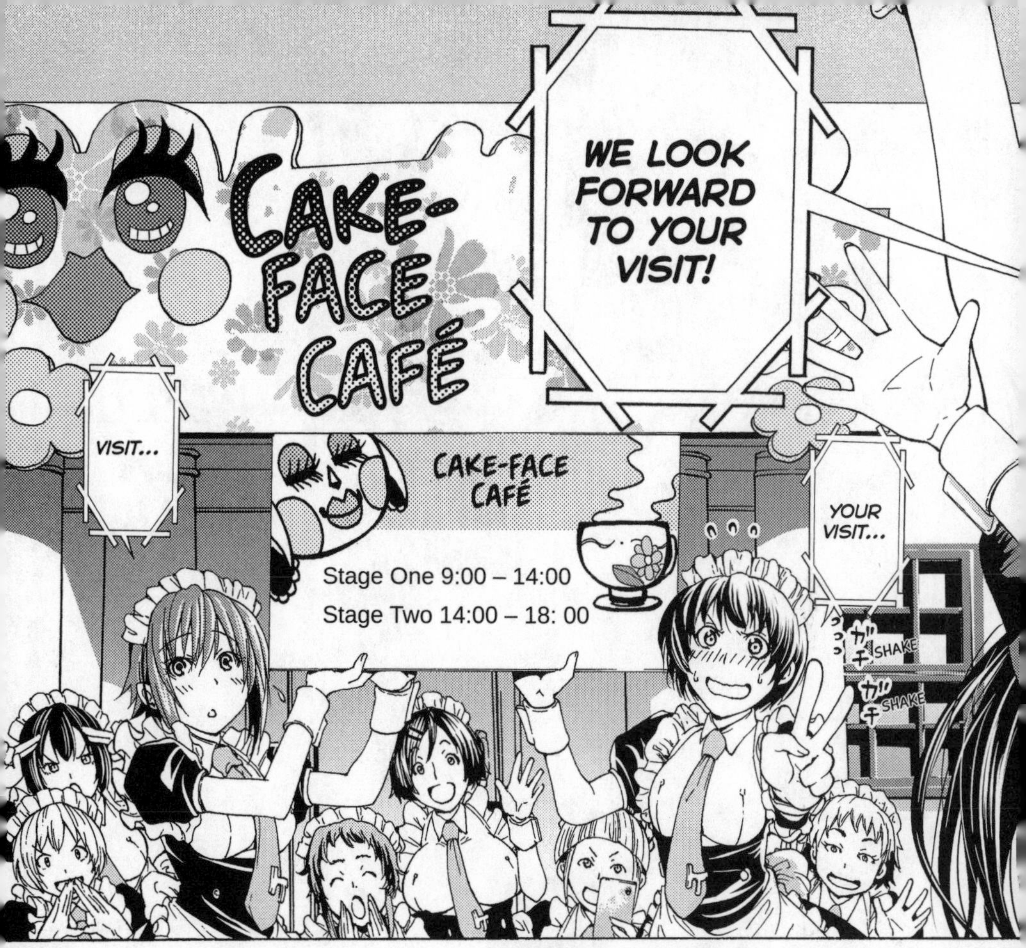
WE LOOK FORWARD TO YOUR VISIT!
YOUR VISIT...
CAKE-FACE CAFÉ
VISIT...
CAKE-FACE CAFÉ
Stage One 9:00 – 14:00
Stage Two 14:00 – 18: 00
SHAKE
SHAKE
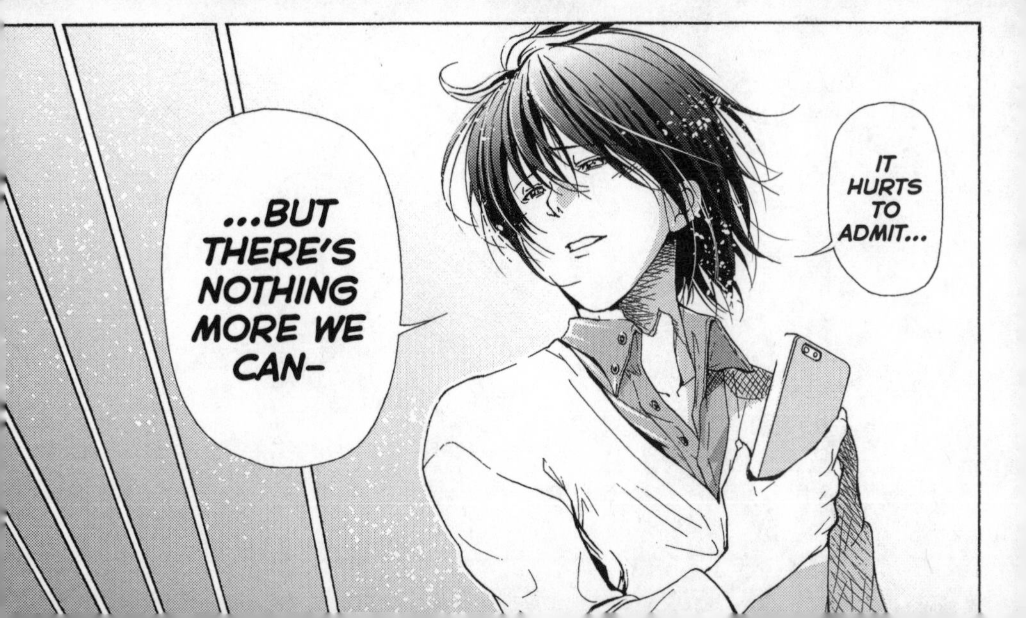
IT HURTS TO ADMIT...
...BUT THERE'S NOTHING MORE WE CAN-

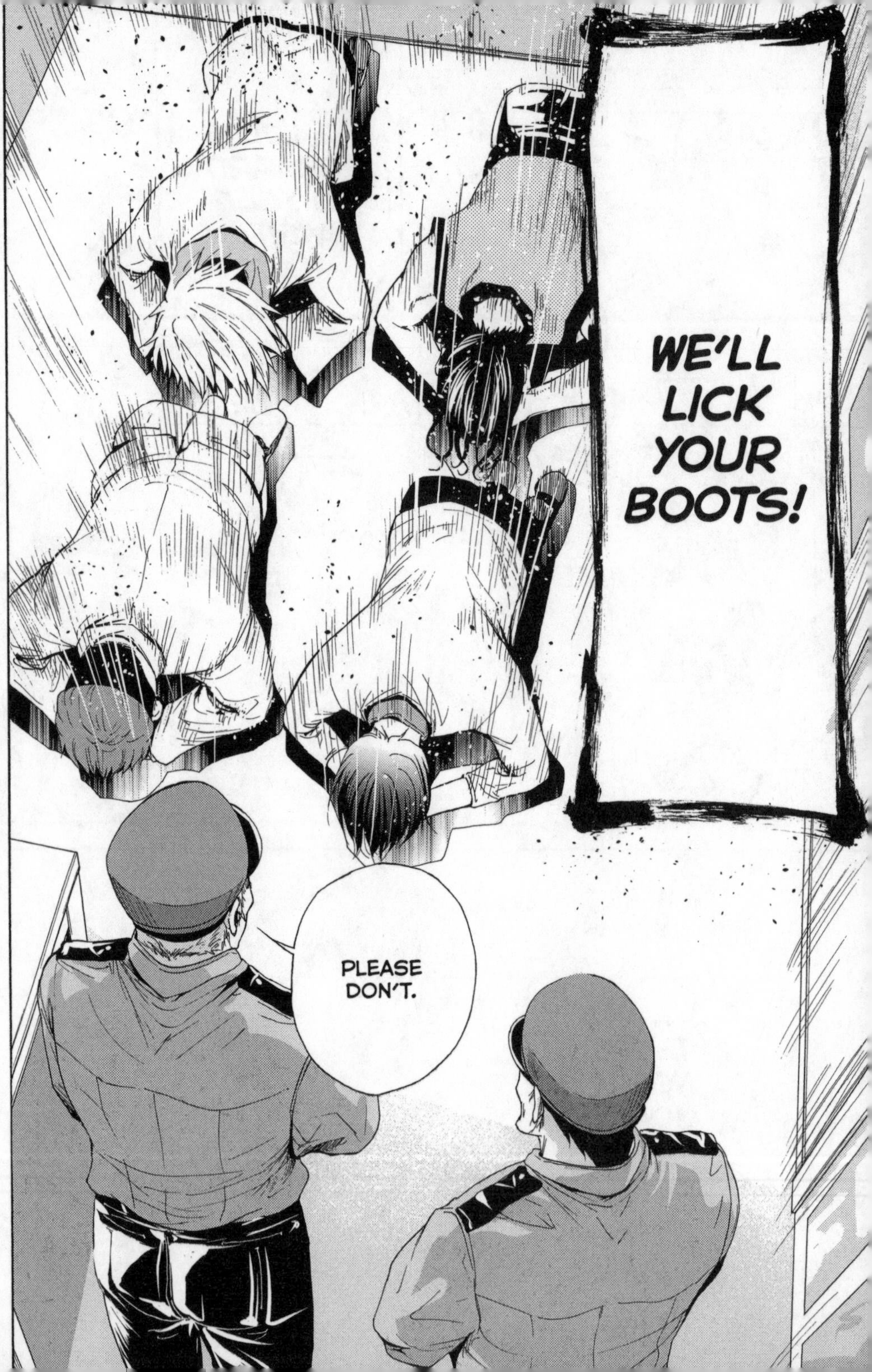
WE'LL LICK YOUR BOOTS!
PLEASE DON'T.

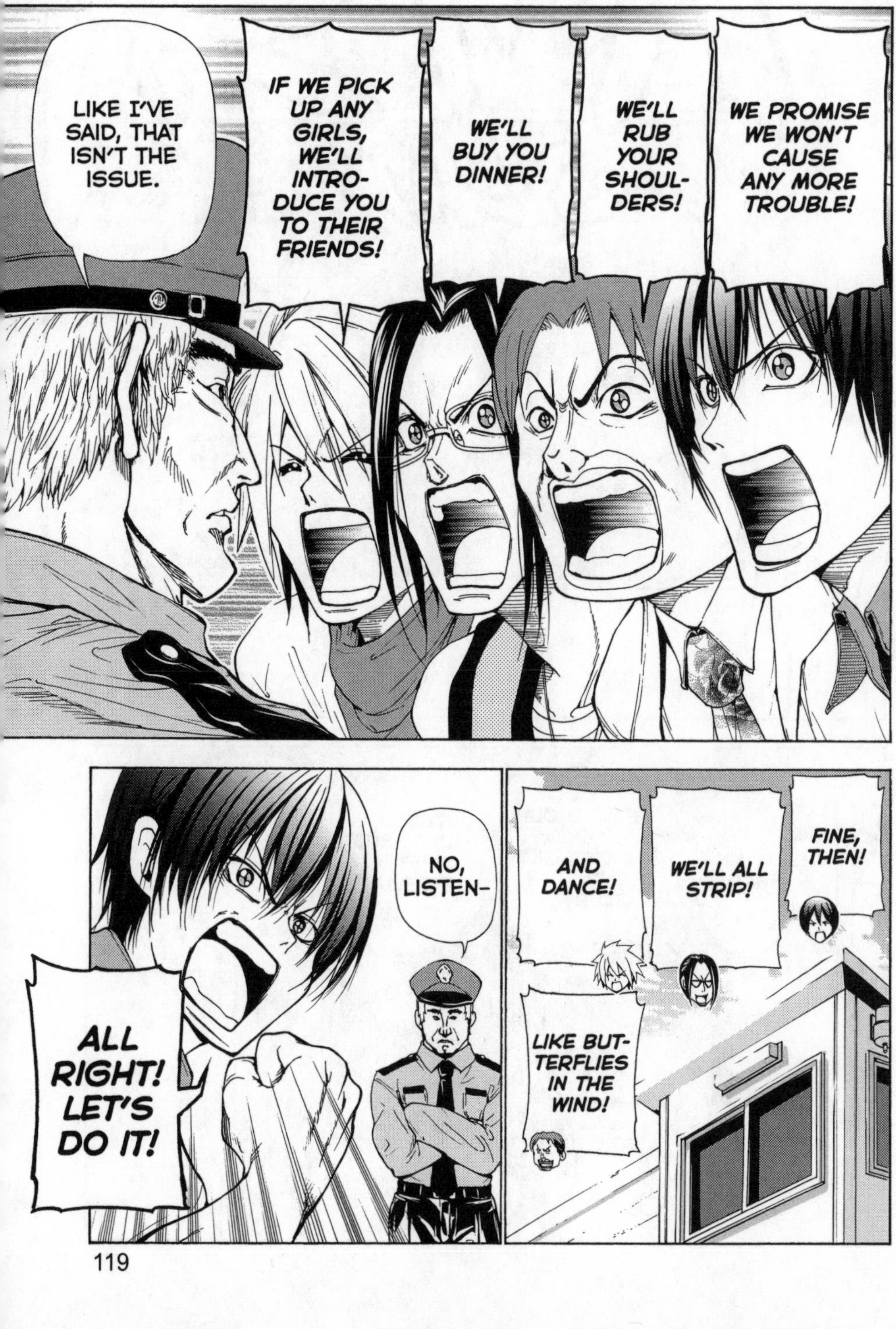
WE PROMISE WE WON'T CAUSE ANY MORE TROUBLE!
WE'LL RUB YOUR SHOUL-DERS!
WE'LL BUY YOU DINNER!
IF WE PICK UP ANY GIRLS, WE'LL INTRO-DUCE YOU TO THEIR FRIENDS!
LIKE I'VE SAID, THAT ISN'T THE ISSUE.
FINE, THEN!
WE'LL ALL STRIP!
AND DANCE!
LIKE BUT-TERFLIES IN THE WIND!
NO, LISTEN-
ALL RIGHT! LET'S DO IT!

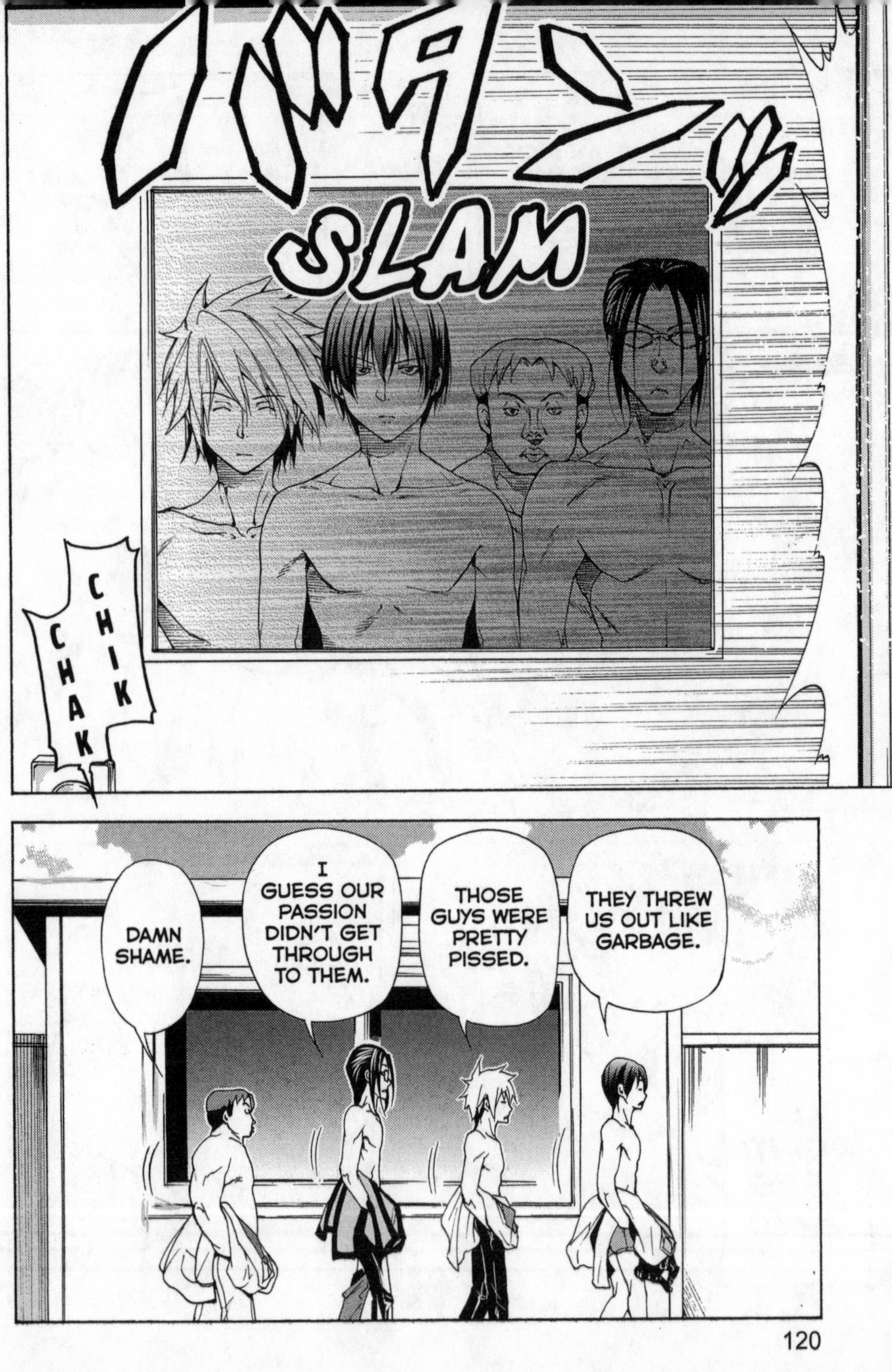
SLAM
CHIK CHAK
THEY THREW US OUT LIKE GARBAGE.
THOSE GUYS WERE PRETTY PISSED.
I GUESS OUR PASSION DIDN'T GET THROUGH TO THEM.
DAMN SHAME.

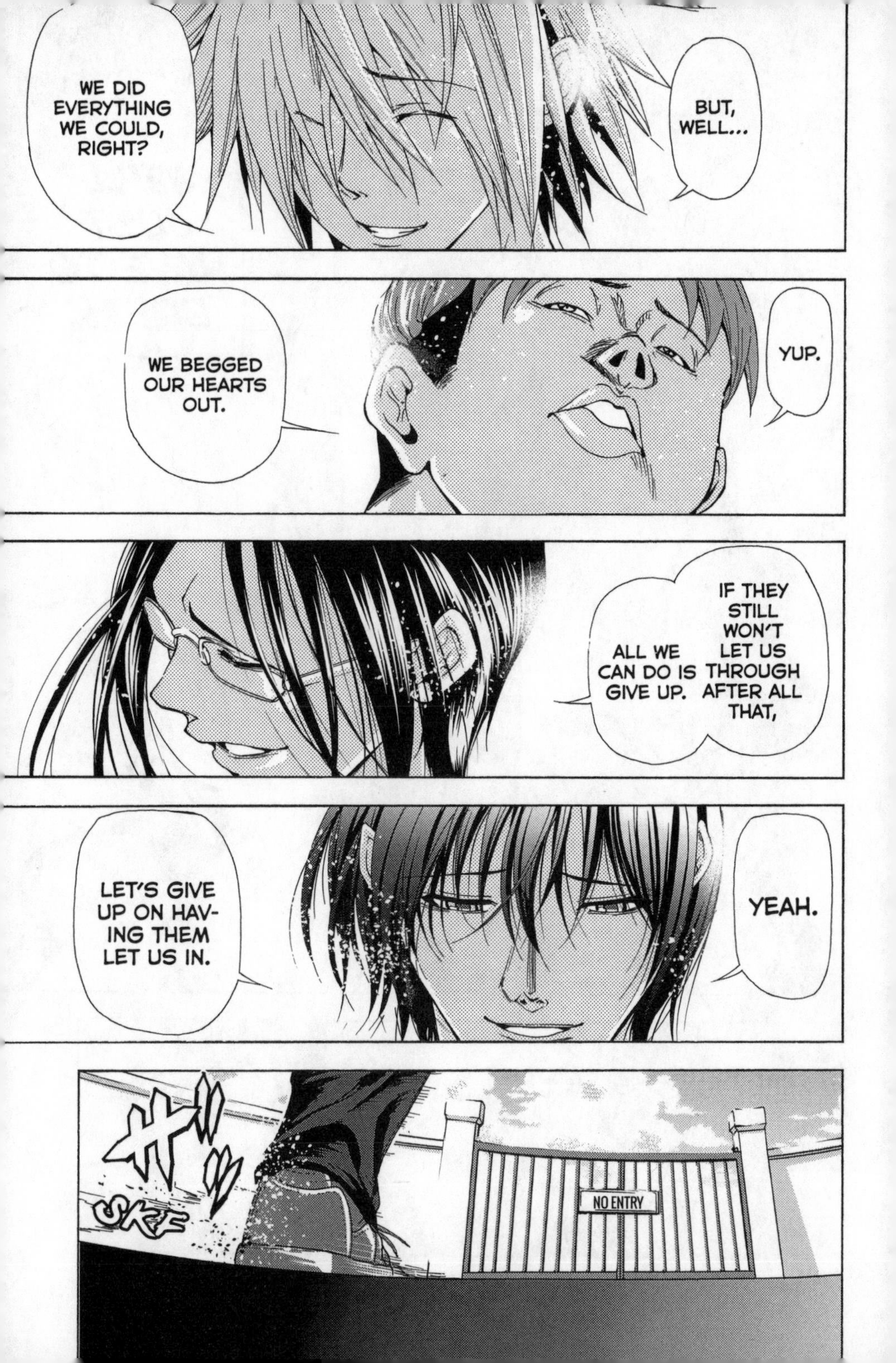
BUT, WELL...
WE DID EVERYTHING WE COULD, RIGHT?
YUP.
WE BEGGED OUR HEARTS OUT.
IF THEY STILL WON'T LET US THROUGH AFTER ALL THAT,
ALL WE CAN DO IS GIVE UP.
YEAH.
LET'S GIVE UP ON HAV-ING THEM LET US IN.
NO ENTRY
SKF

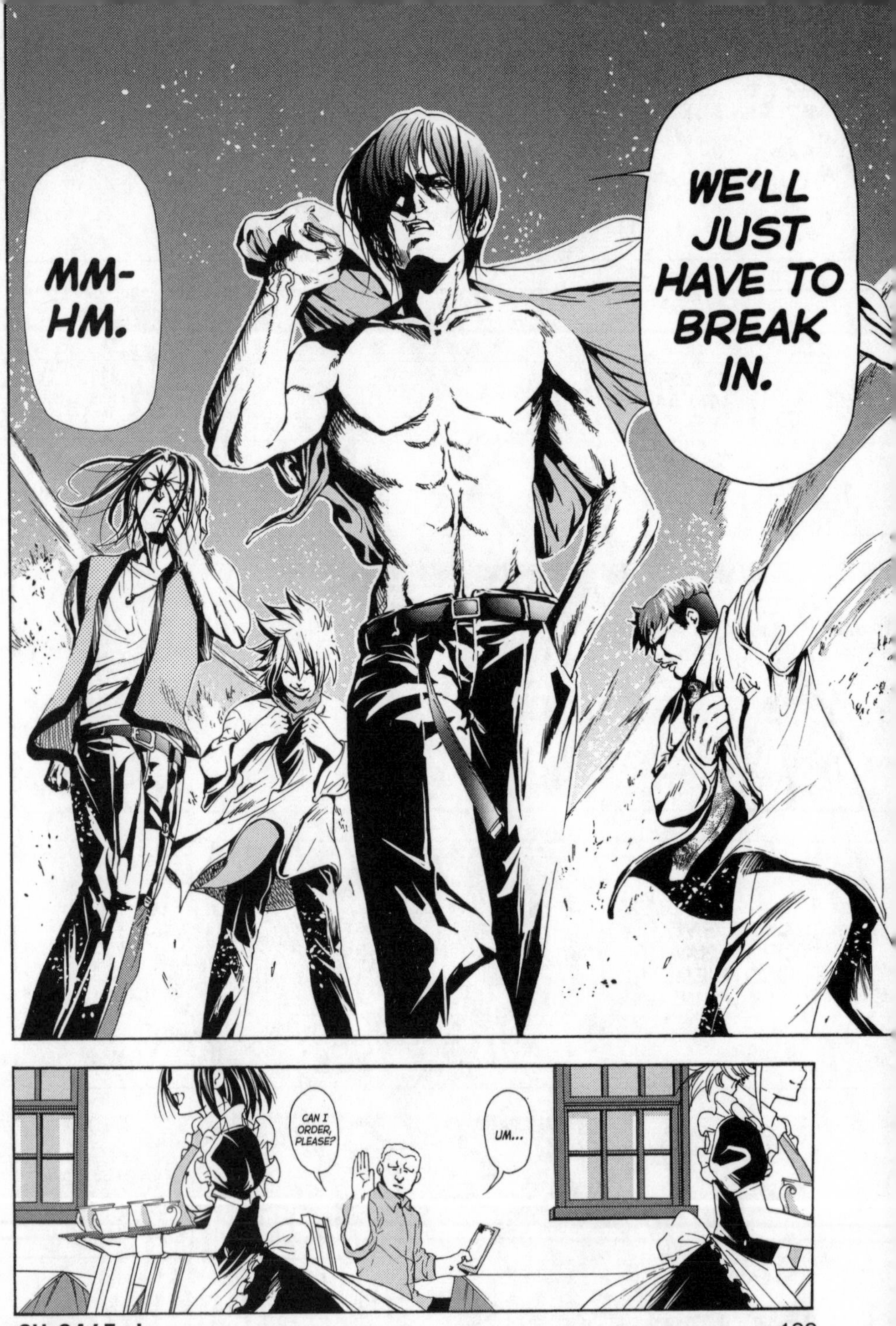
WE'LL JUST HAVE TO BREAK IN.
MM-HM.
UM...
CAN I ORDER, PLEASE?

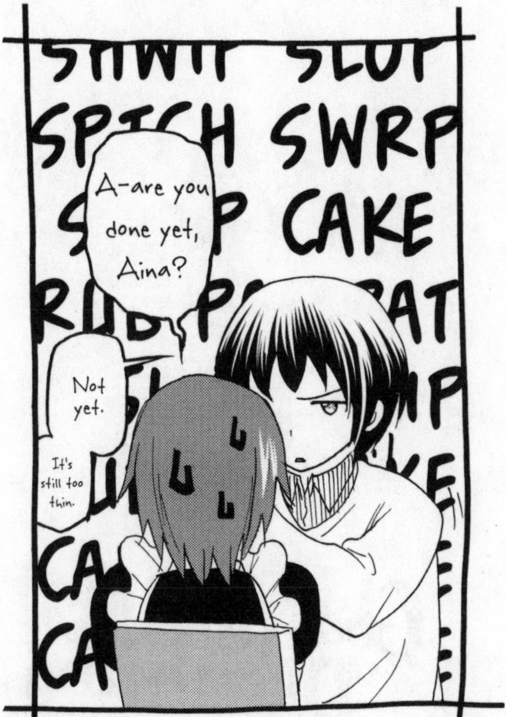
SPTCH
SWRP
CAKE
A-are you done yet, Aina?
Not yet.
It's still too thin.

Grand Blue
Dreaming

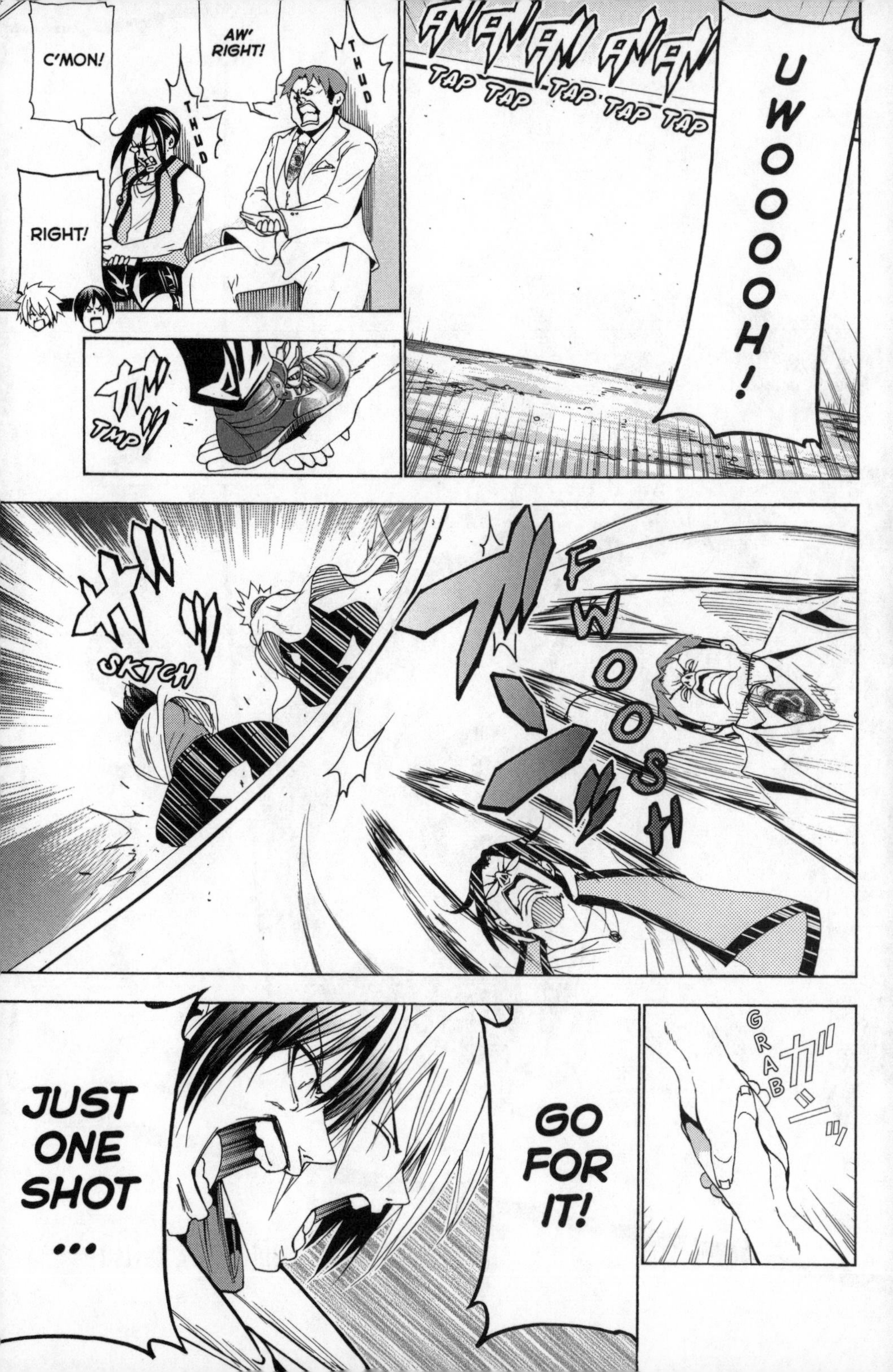

TAP TAP TAP TAP TAP
UWOOOOOH!
THUD
AW' RIGHT!
C'MON!
THUD
RIGHT!
TMP
FWOOSH
SKTCH
GRAB
GO FOR IT!
JUST ONE SHOT ...

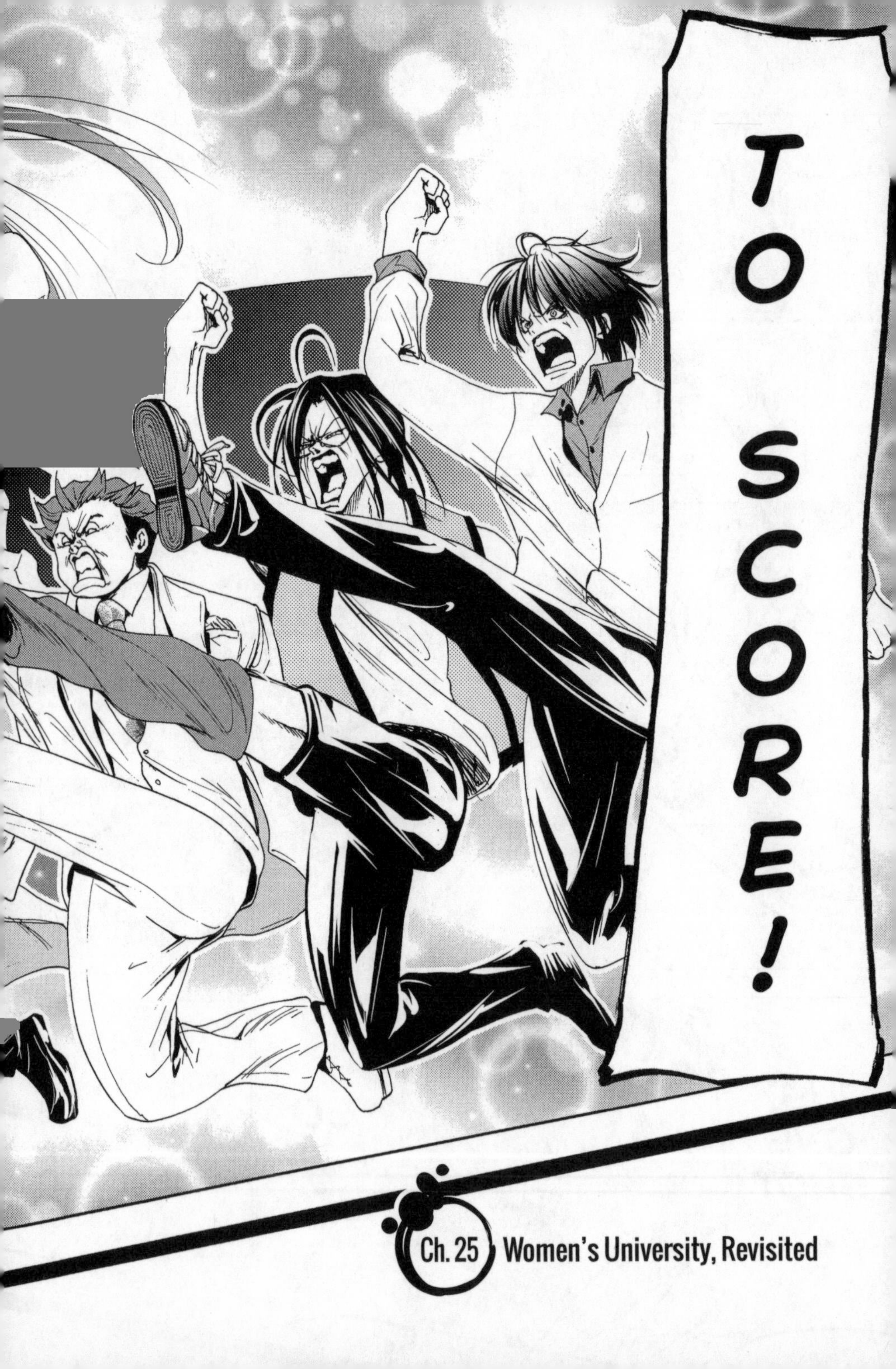
TO SCORE!

Ch. 25 Women's University, Revisited

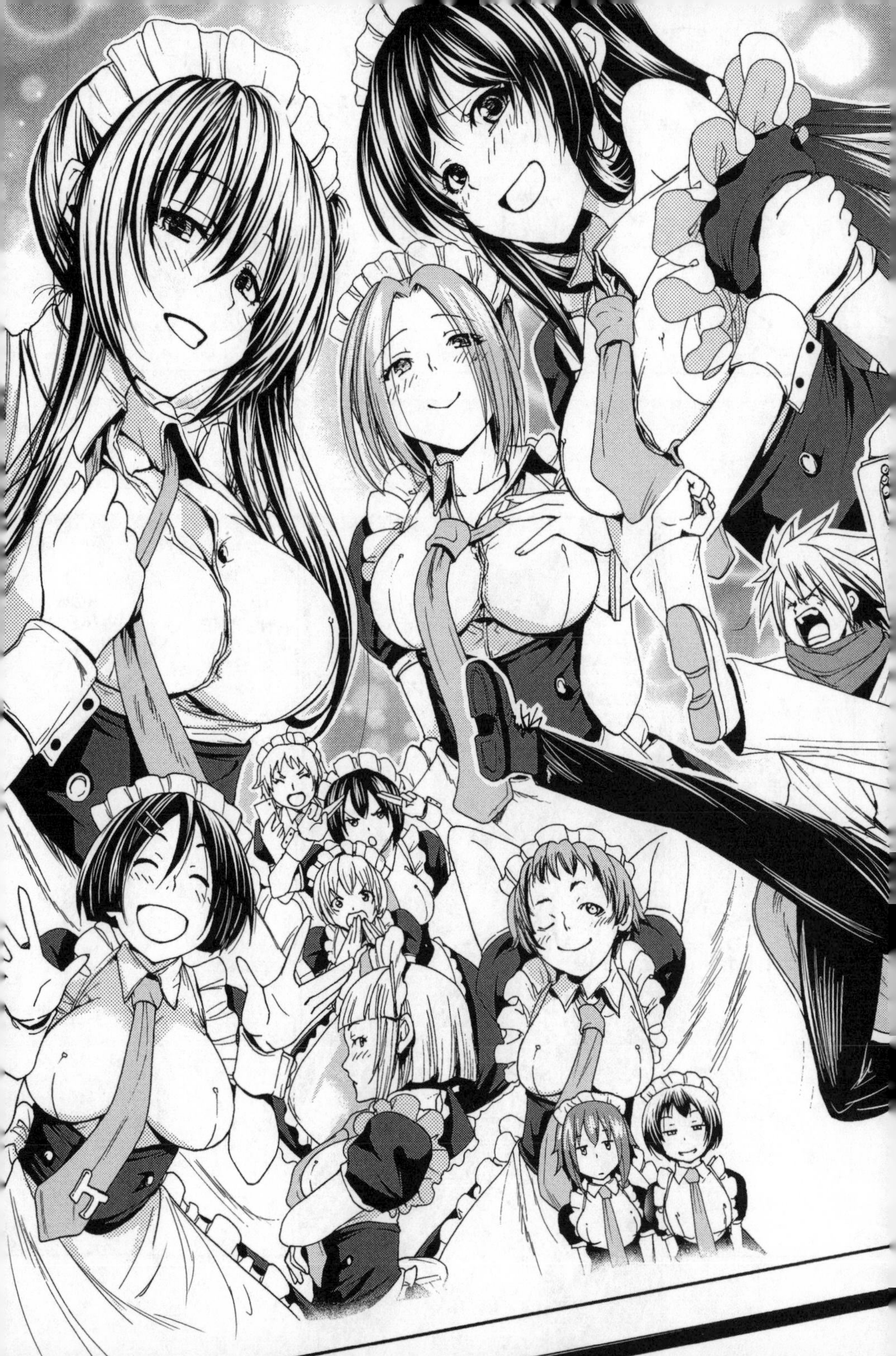

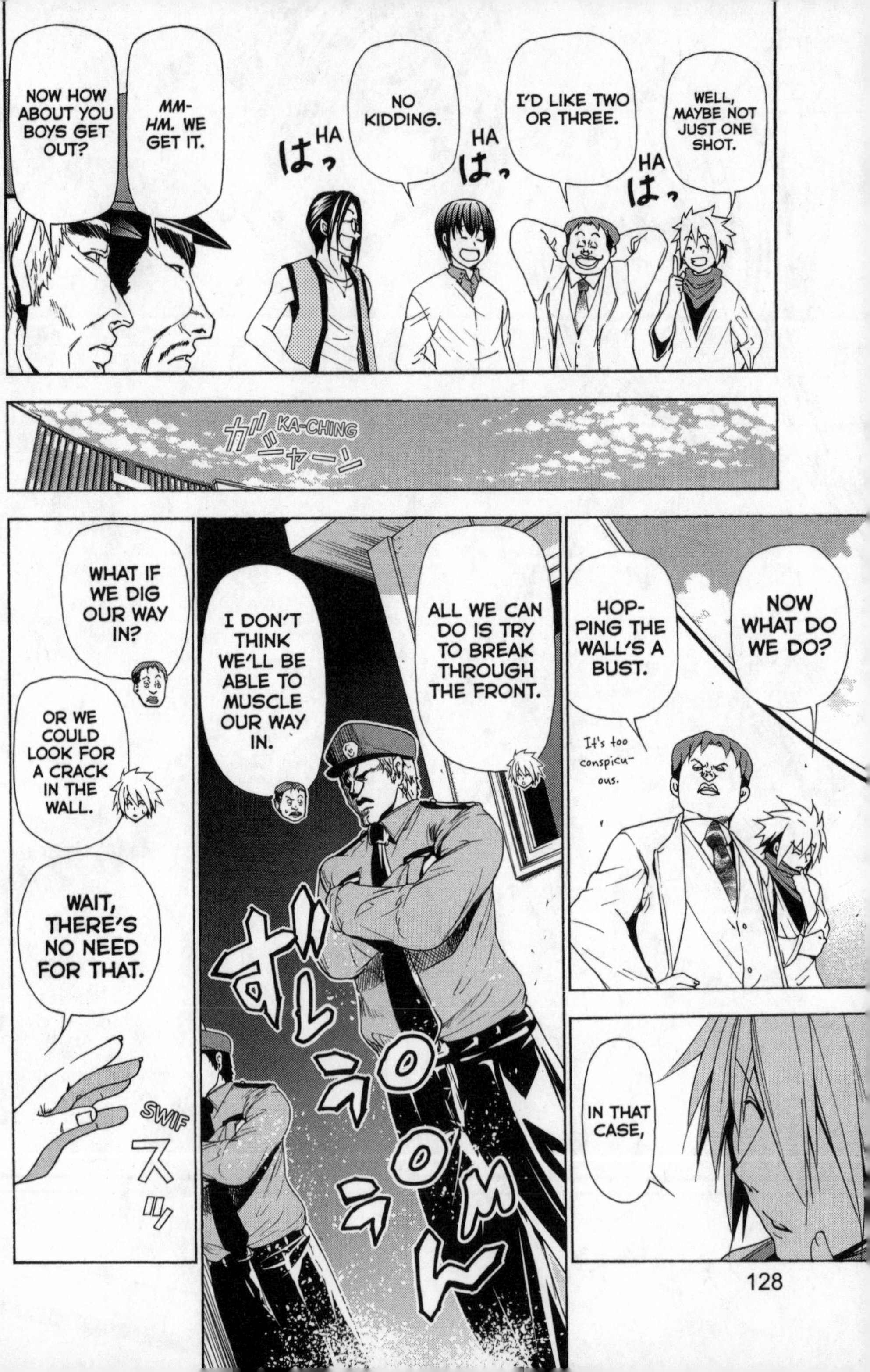

WELL, MAYBE NOT JUST ONE SHOT.
HA
I'D LIKE TWO OR THREE.
HA
NO KIDDING.
HA
MM-HM. WE GET IT.
NOW HOW ABOUT YOU BOYS GET OUT?
KA-CHING
NOW WHAT DO WE DO?
HOP-PING THE WALL'S A BUST.
It's too conspicu-ous.
IN THAT CASE,
ALL WE CAN DO IS TRY TO BREAK THROUGH THE FRONT.
I DON'T THINK WE'LL BE ABLE TO MUSCLE OUR WAY IN.
WHAT IF WE DIG OUR WAY IN?
OR WE COULD LOOK FOR A CRACK IN THE WALL.
WAIT, THERE'S NO NEED FOR THAT.
SWIF

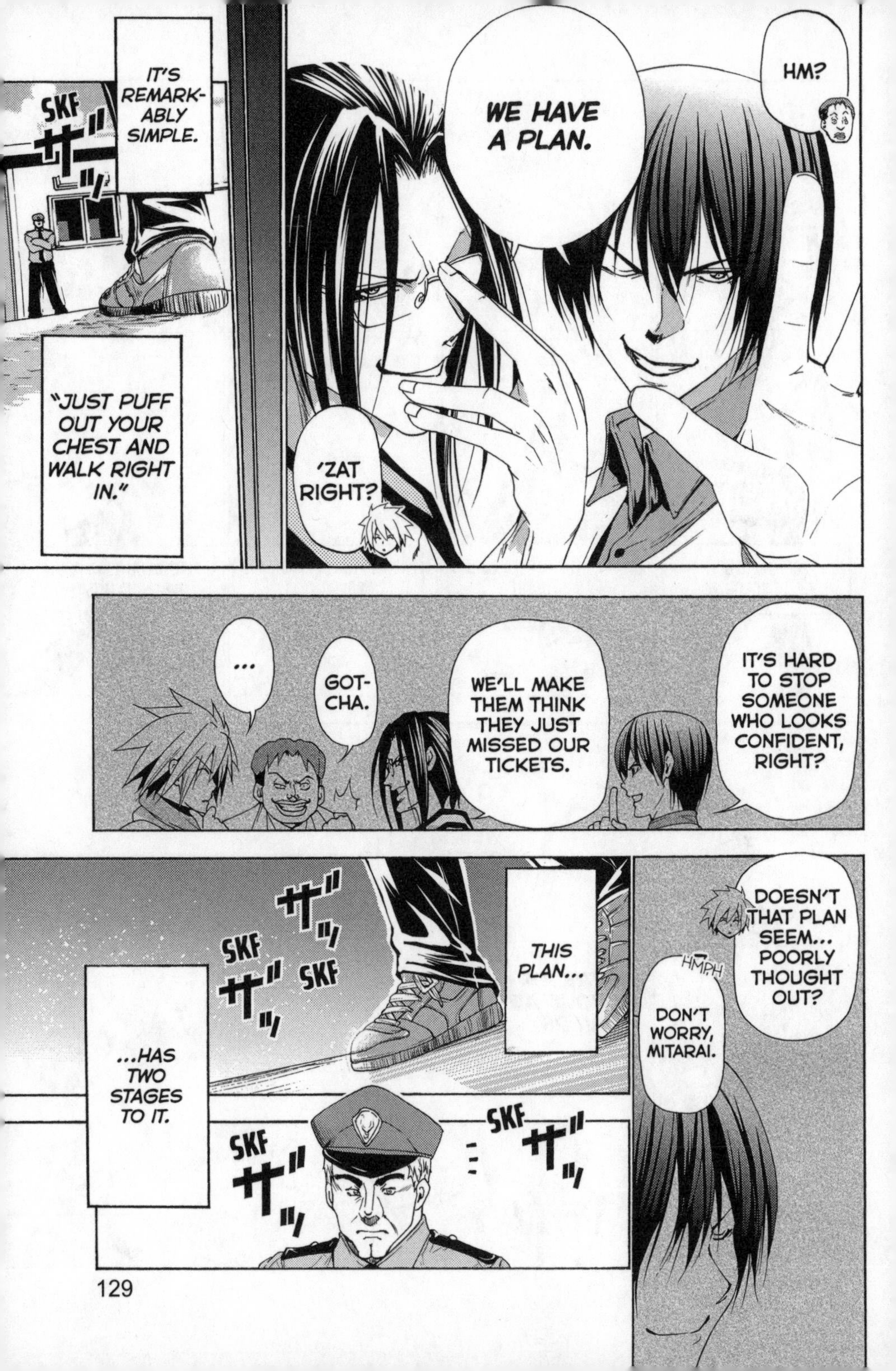
HM?
WE HAVE A PLAN.
'ZAT RIGHT?
IT'S REMARKABLY SIMPLE.
SKF
"JUST PUFF OUT YOUR CHEST AND WALK RIGHT IN."
IT'S HARD TO STOP SOMEONE WHO LOOKS CONFIDENT, RIGHT?
WE'LL MAKE THEM THINK THEY JUST MISSED OUR TICKETS.
GOT-CHA.
...
DOESN'T THAT PLAN SEEM... POORLY THOUGHT OUT?
HMPH
DON'T WORRY, MITARAI.
THIS PLAN...
SKF
SKF
...HAS TWO STAGES TO IT.
SKF
SKF

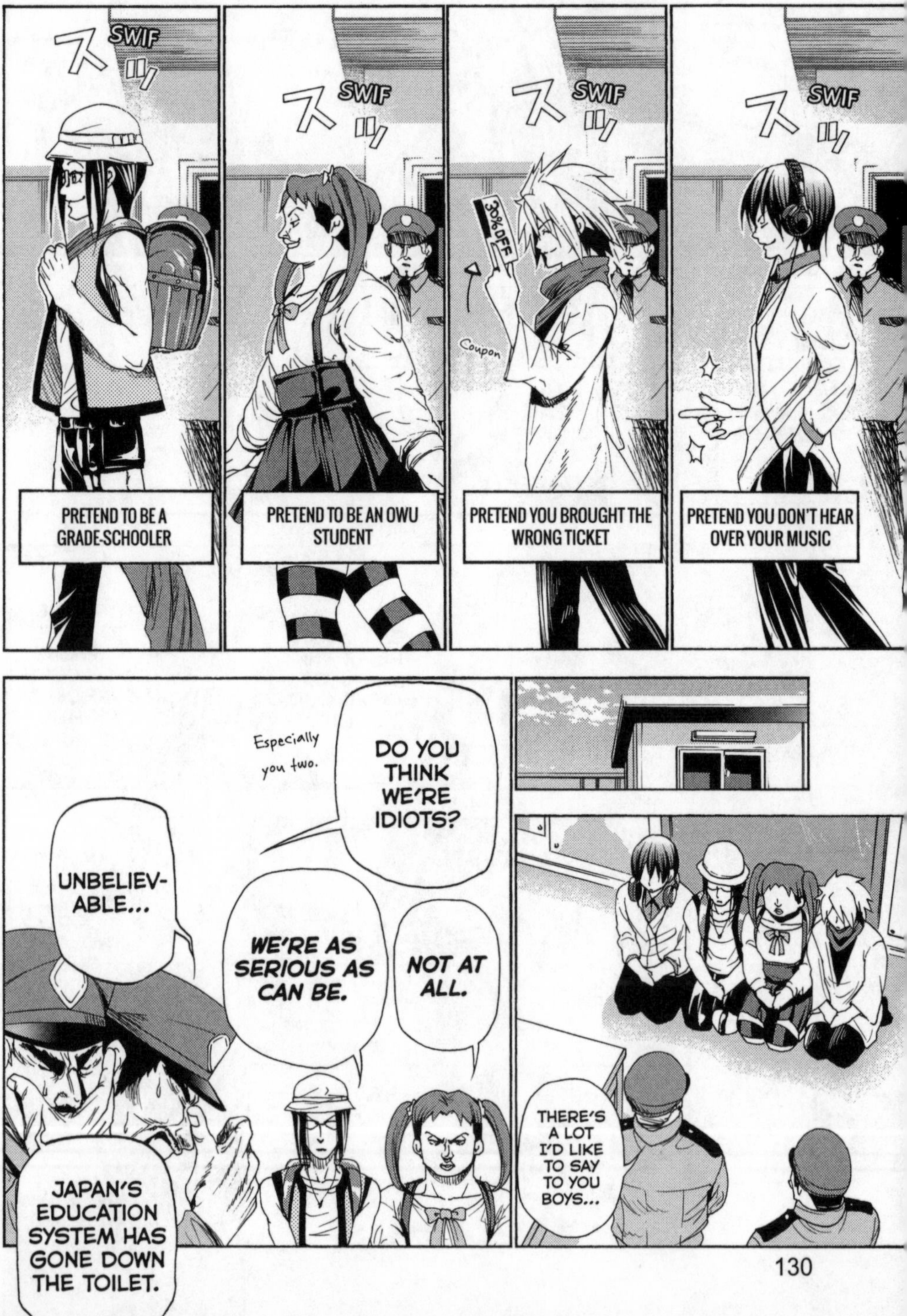
スッ
SWIF
PRETEND YOU DON'T HEAR OVER YOUR MUSIC
スッ
SWIF
30% OFF
Coupon
PRETEND YOU BROUGHT THE WRONG TICKET
スッ
SWIF
PRETEND TO BE AN OWU STUDENT
スッ
SWIF
PRETEND TO BE A GRADE-SCHOOLER
THERE'S A LOT I'D LIKE TO SAY TO YOU BOYS...
DO YOU THINK WE'RE IDIOTS?
Especially you two.
NOT AT ALL.
WE'RE AS SERIOUS AS CAN BE.
UNBELIEVABLE...
JAPAN'S EDUCATION SYSTEM HAS GONE DOWN THE TOILET.

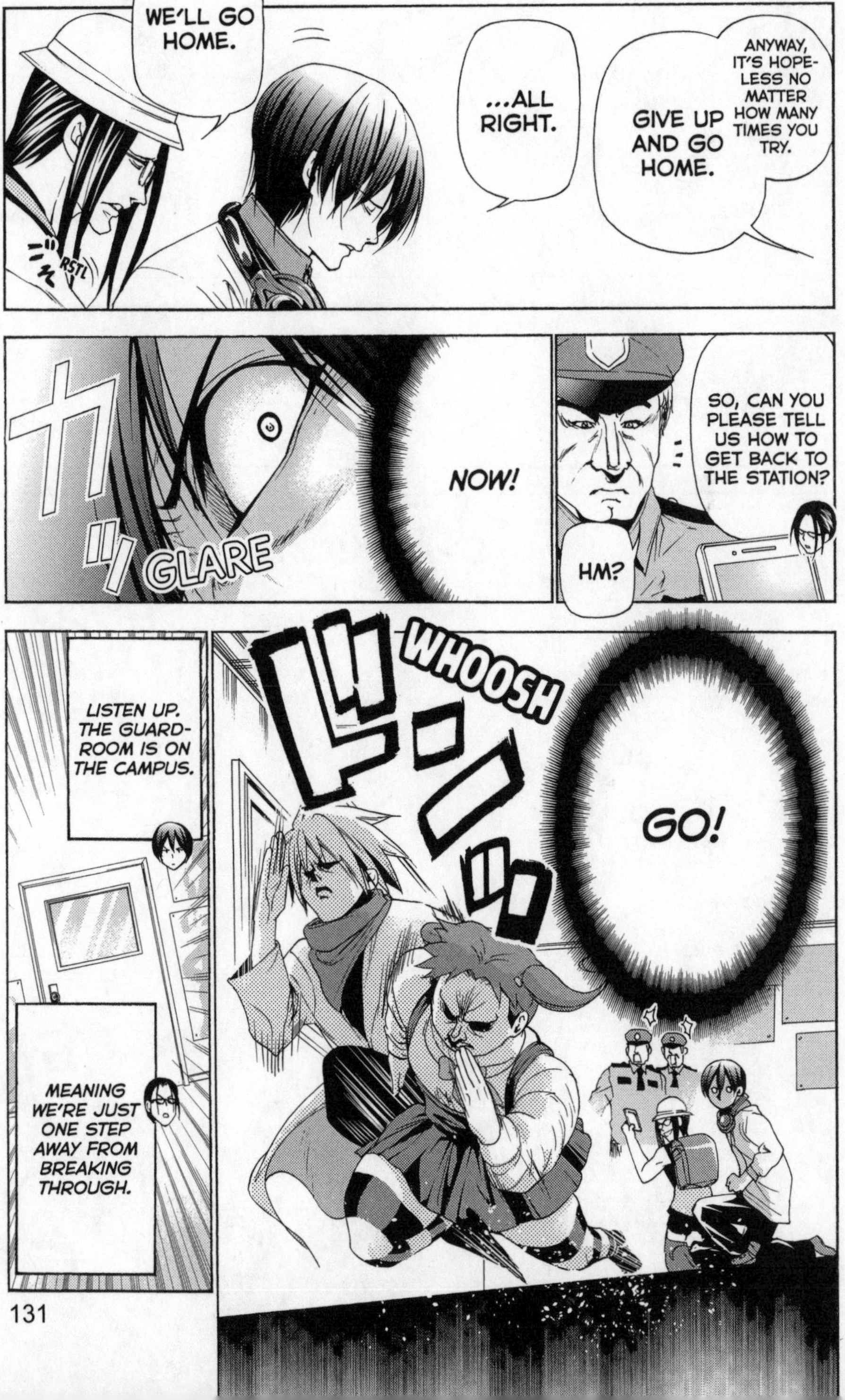
ANYWAY, IT'S HOPE-LESS NO MATTER HOW MANY TIMES YOU TRY.
GIVE UP AND GO HOME.
...ALL RIGHT.
WE'LL GO HOME.
RSTL
SO, CAN YOU PLEASE TELL US HOW TO GET BACK TO THE STATION?
HM?
NOW!
GLARE
WHOOSH
GO!
LISTEN UP. THE GUARD-ROOM IS ON THE CAMPUS.
MEANING WE'RE JUST ONE STEP AWAY FROM BREAKING THROUGH.

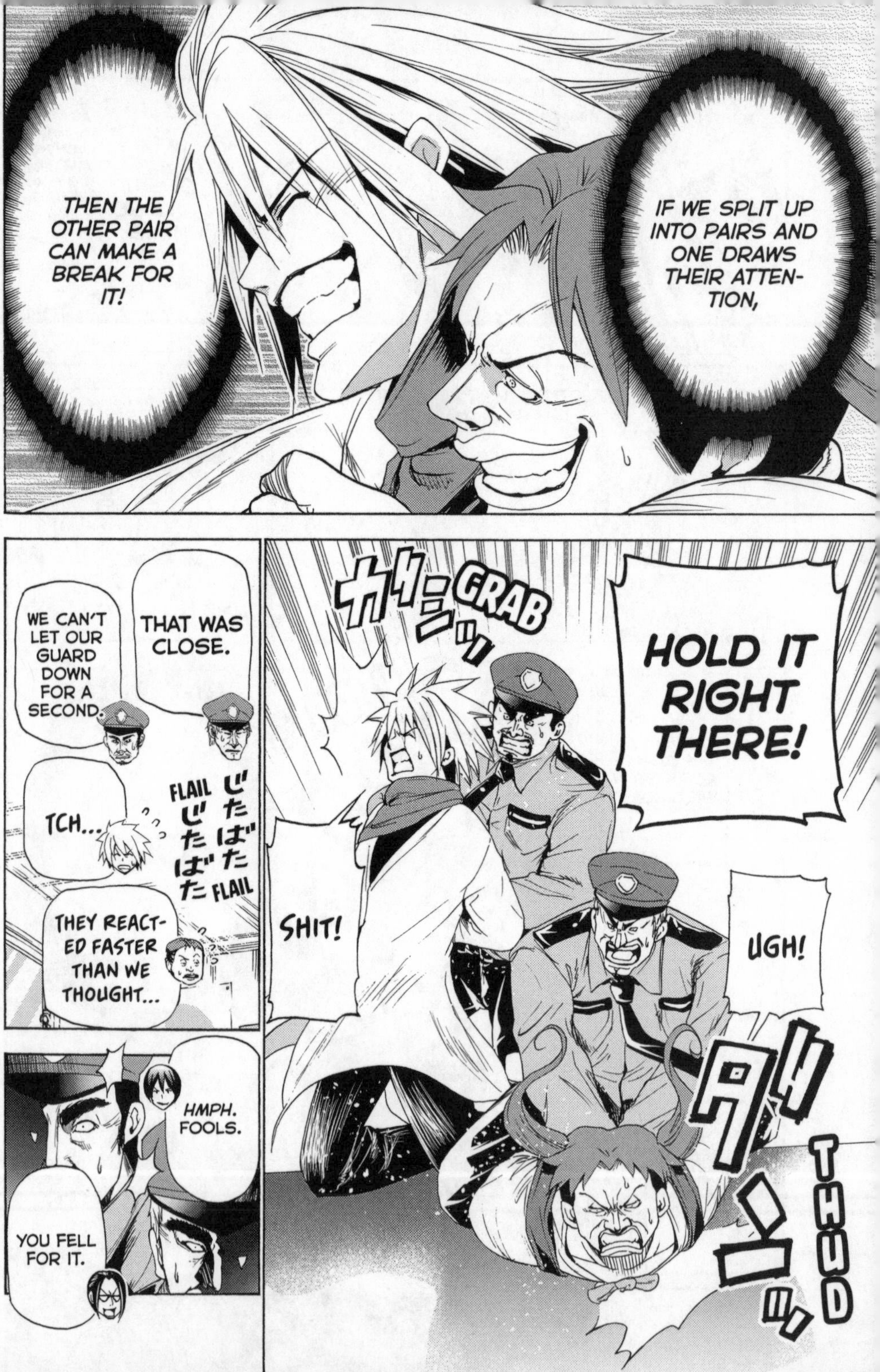
IF WE SPLIT UP INTO PAIRS AND ONE DRAWS THEIR ATTEN-TION,
THEN THE OTHER PAIR CAN MAKE A BREAK FOR IT!
GRAB
HOLD IT RIGHT THERE!
SHIT!
UGH!
THUD
THAT WAS CLOSE.
WE CAN'T LET OUR GUARD DOWN FOR A SECOND.
じたばた じたばた
FLAIL FLAIL
TCH...
THEY REACT-ED FASTER THAN WE THOUGHT...
HMPH. FOOLS.
YOU FELL FOR IT.

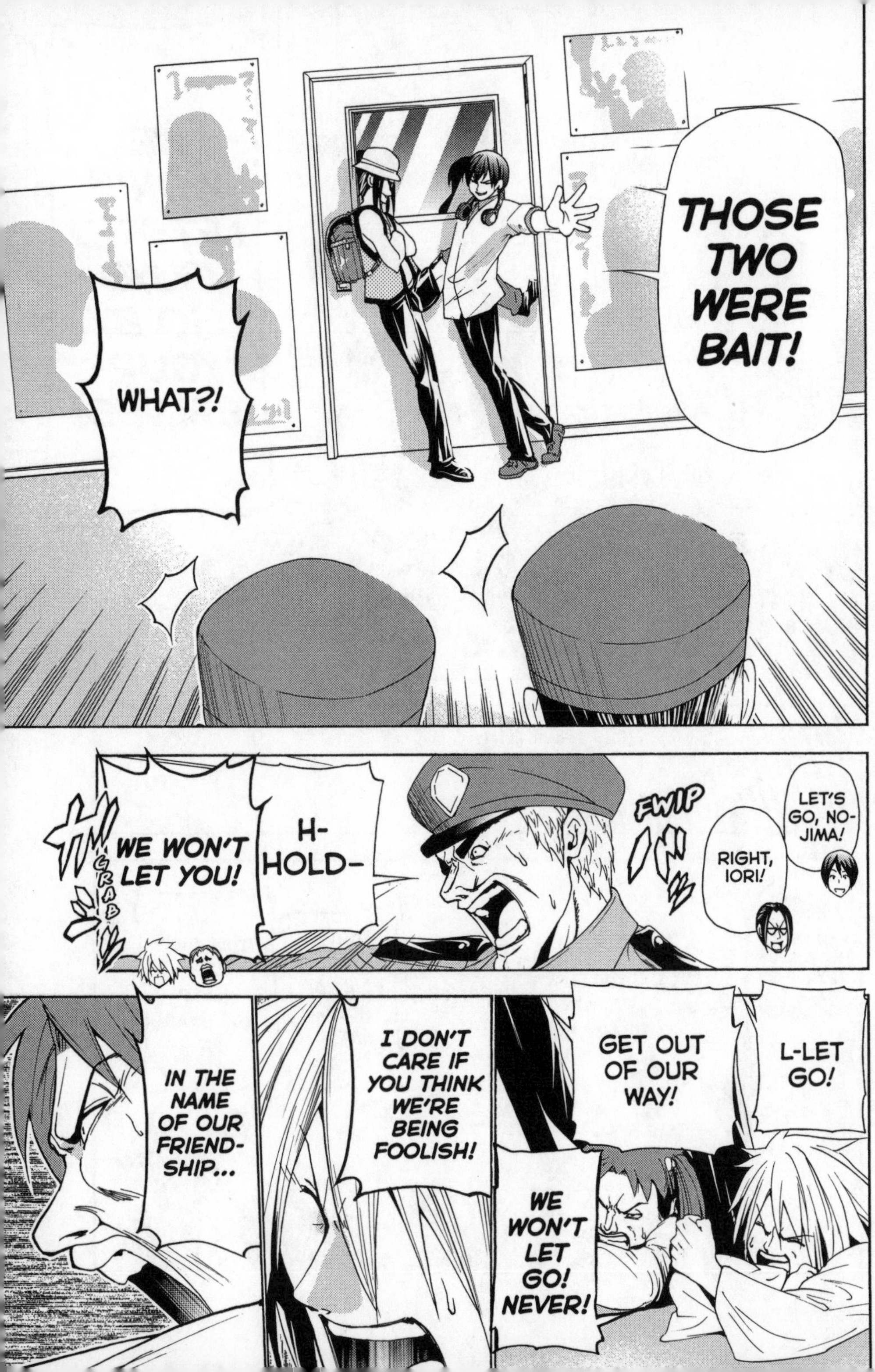
THOSE TWO WERE BAIT!
WHAT?!
LET'S GO, NO-JIMA!
RIGHT, IORI!
FWIP
H-HOLD-
WE WON'T LET YOU!
GRAB
L-LET GO!
GET OUT OF OUR WAY!
WE WON'T LET GO! NEVER!
I DON'T CARE IF YOU THINK WE'RE BEING FOOLISH!
IN THE NAME OF OUR FRIEND-SHIP...

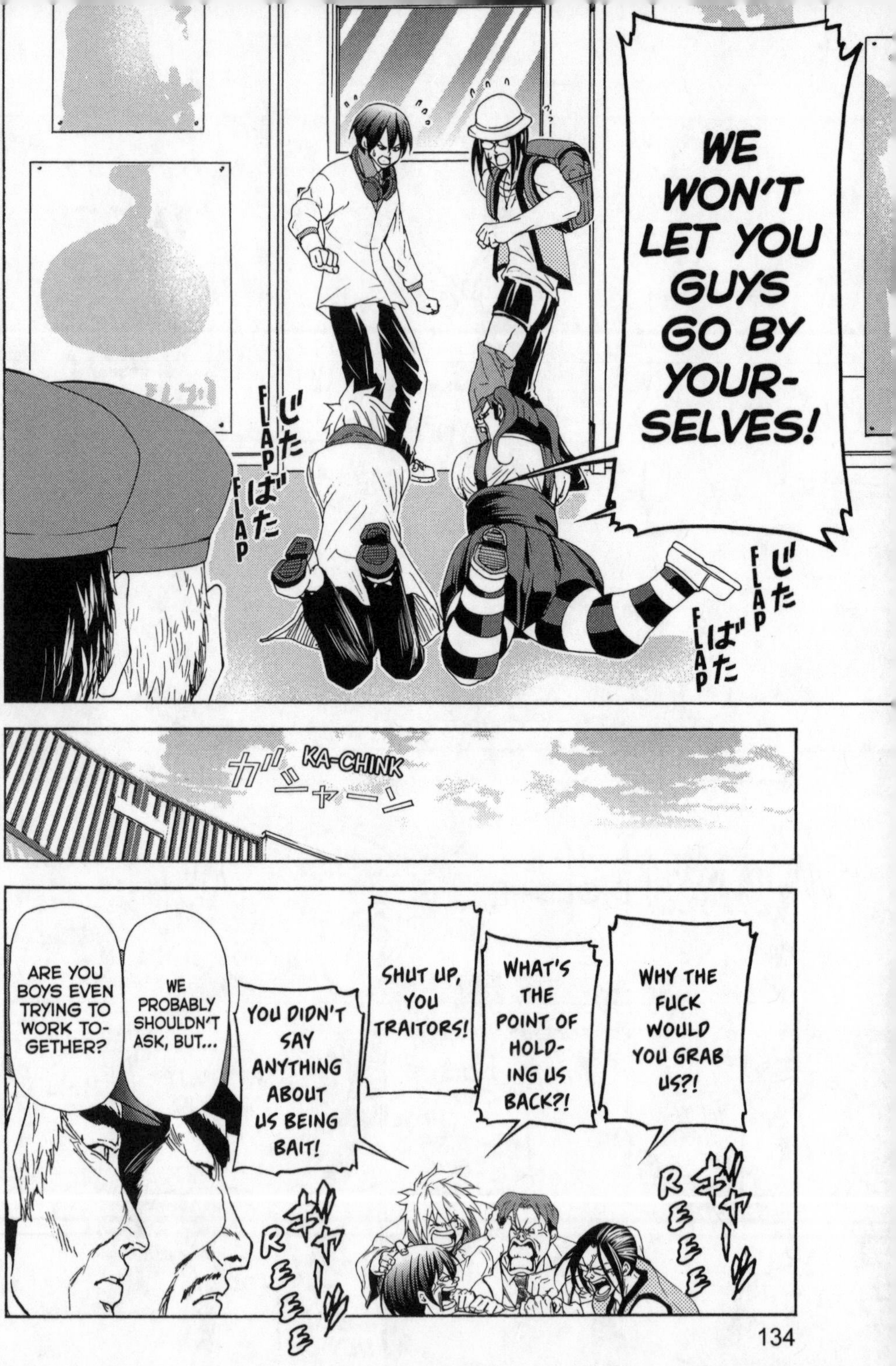
WE WON'T LET YOU GUYS GO BY YOUR-SELVES!
じた ばた
FLAP FLAP
じた ばた
FLAP FLAP
ガシャーン
KA-CHINK
WHY THE FUCK WOULD YOU GRAB US?!
WHAT'S THE POINT OF HOLD-ING US BACK?!
SHUT UP, YOU TRAITORS!
YOU DIDN'T SAY ANYTHING ABOUT US BEING BAIT!
WE PROBABLY SHOULDN'T ASK, BUT...
ARE YOU BOYS EVEN TRYING TO WORK TO-GETHER?
ギャー
REEE
ギャー
REEE

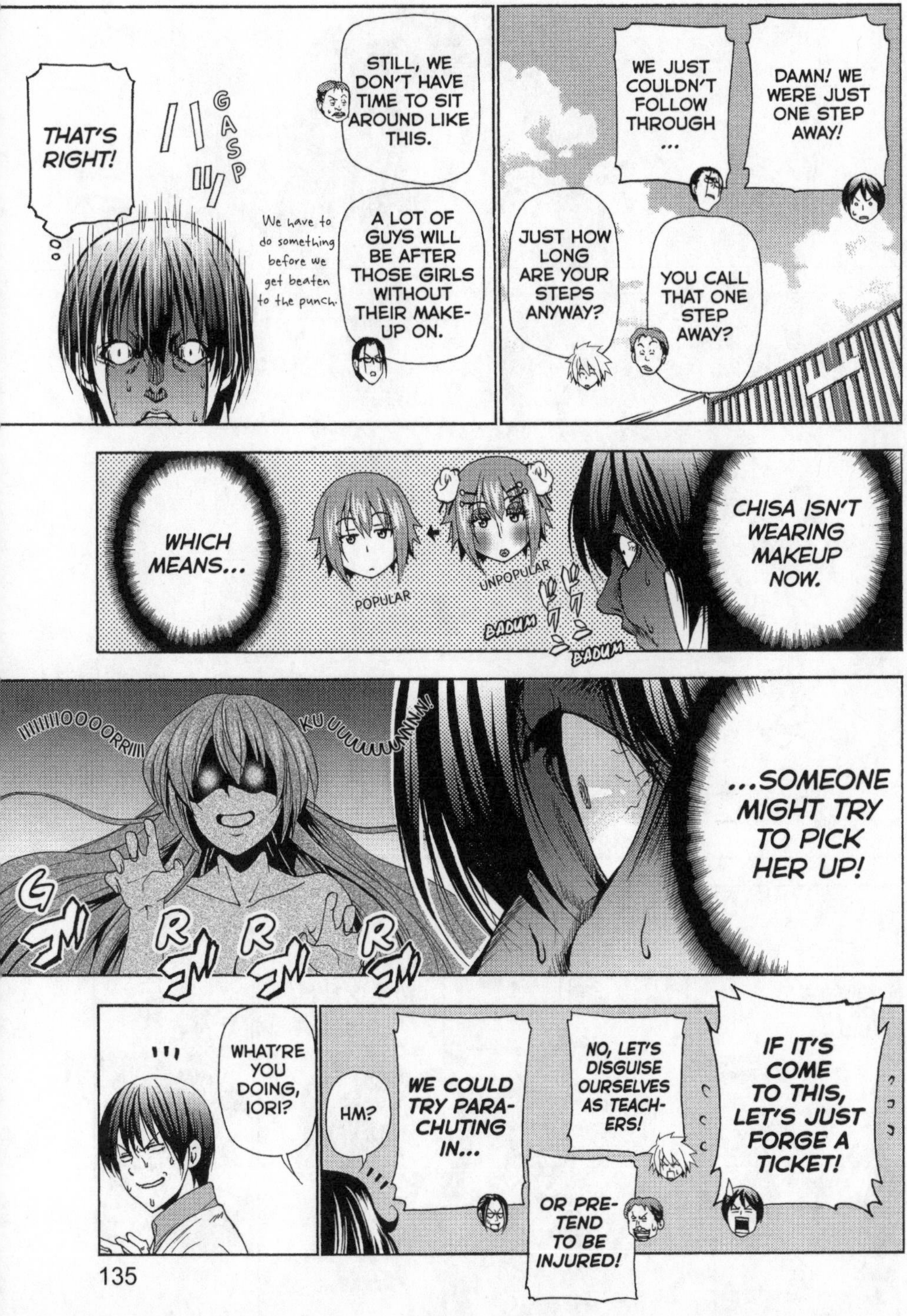
DAMN! WE WERE JUST ONE STEP AWAY!
WE JUST COULDN'T FOLLOW THROUGH...
YOU CALL THAT ONE STEP AWAY?
JUST HOW LONG ARE YOUR STEPS ANYWAY?
STILL, WE DON'T HAVE TIME TO SIT AROUND LIKE THIS.
A LOT OF GUYS WILL BE AFTER THOSE GIRLS WITHOUT THEIR MAKE-UP ON.
We have to do something before we get beaten to the punch.
GASP
THAT'S RIGHT!
CHISA ISN'T WEARING MAKEUP NOW.
BADUM
BADUM
UNPOPULAR
POPULAR
WHICH MEANS...
...SOMEONE MIGHT TRY TO PICK HER UP!
KU UUUUUUNNN!
IIIIIIIOOOOORRIII
G R R R
IF IT'S COME TO THIS, LET'S JUST FORGE A TICKET!
NO, LET'S DISGUISE OURSELVES AS TEACH-ERS!
OR PRE-TEND TO BE INJURED!
WE COULD TRY PARA-CHUTING IN...
HM?
WHAT'RE YOU DOING, IORI?

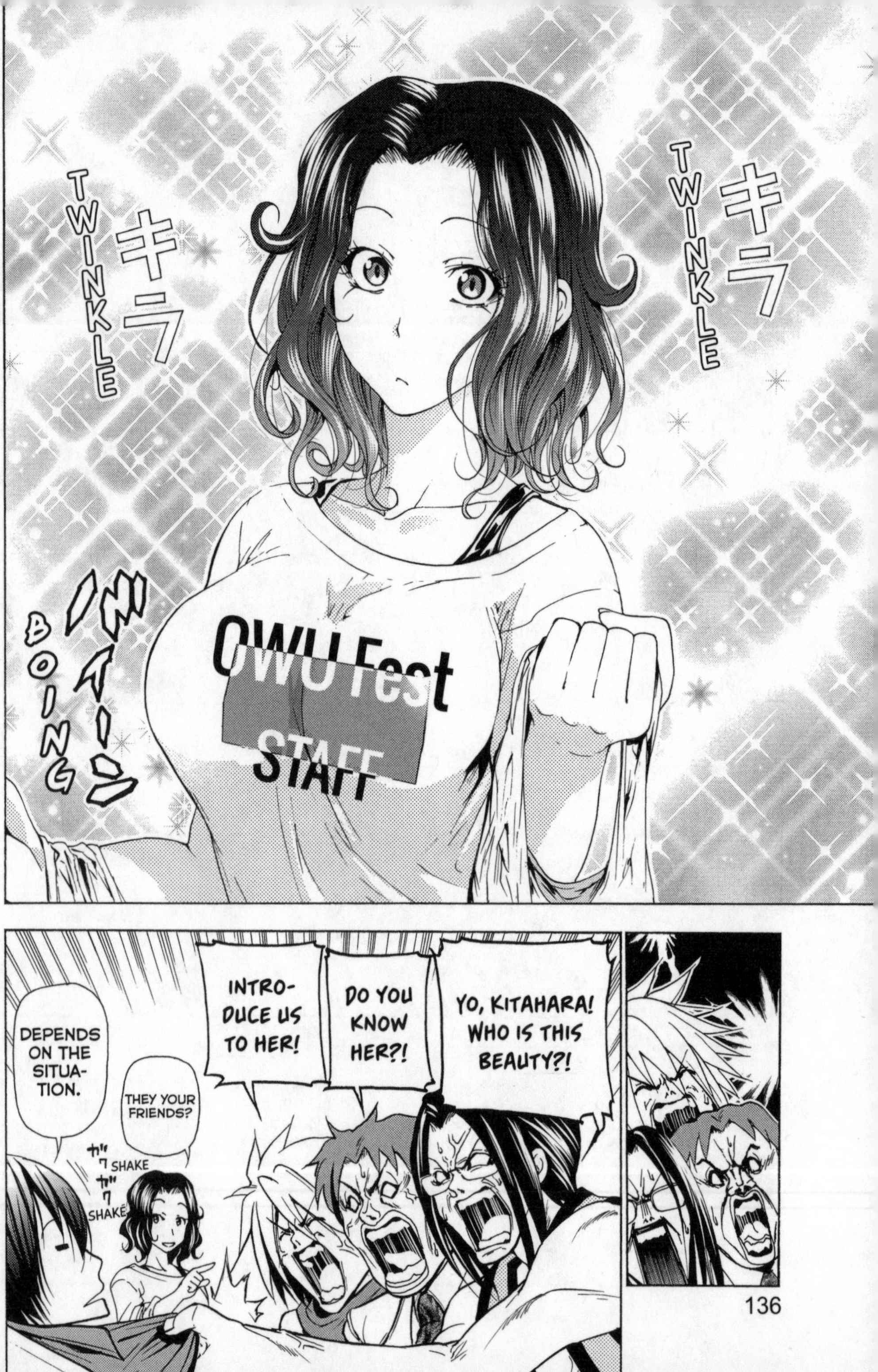
キラ
TWINKLE
キラ
TWINKLE
BOING
OWU Fest
STAFF
YO, KITAHARA! WHO IS THIS BEAUTY?!
DO YOU KNOW HER?!
INTRO-DUCE US TO HER!
THEY YOUR FRIENDS?
SHAKE
SHAKE
DEPENDS ON THE SITUA-TION.

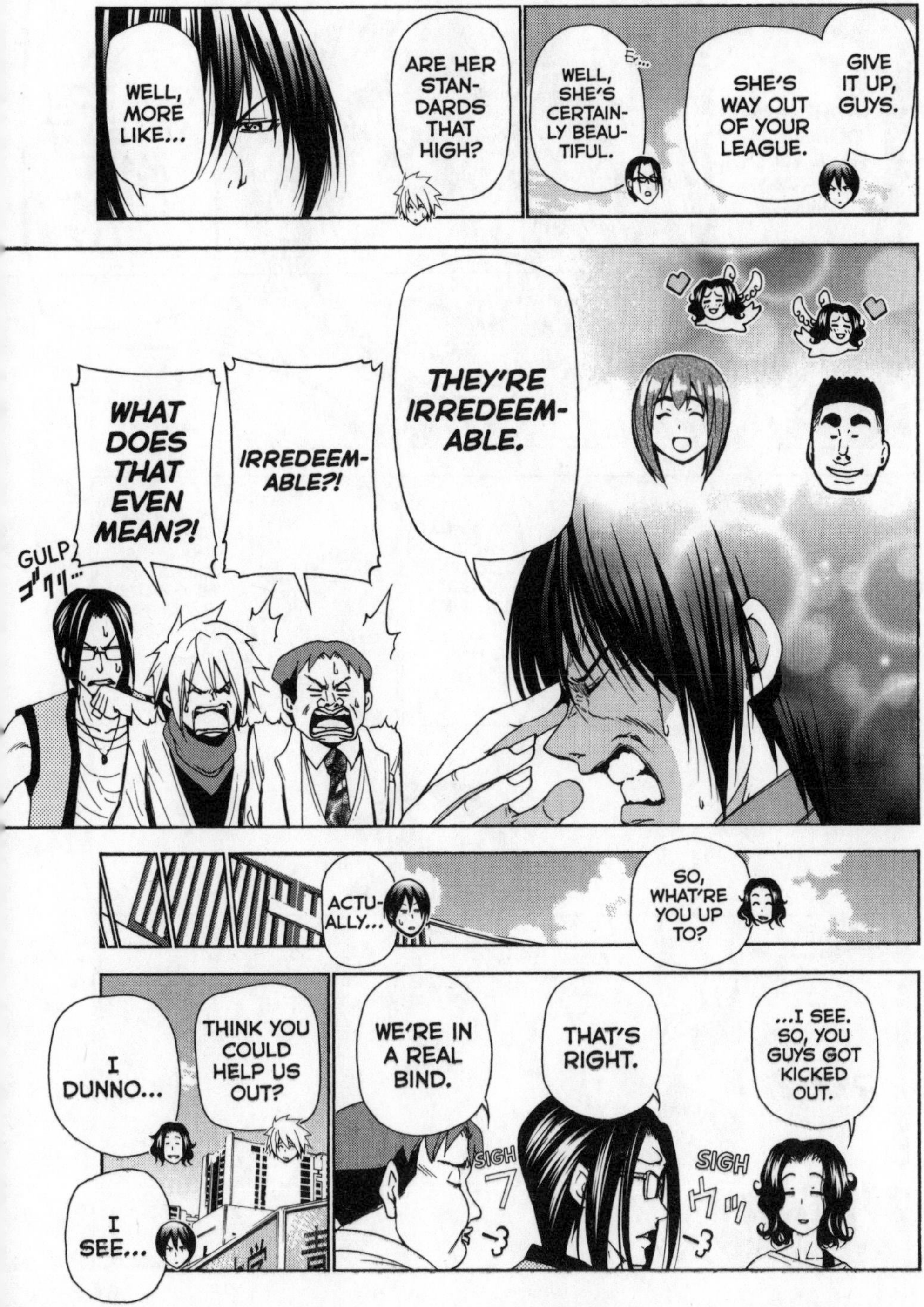
GIVE IT UP, GUYS.
SHE'S WAY OUT OF YOUR LEAGUE.
Er...
WELL, SHE'S CERTAIN-LY BEAU-TIFUL.
ARE HER STAN-DARDS THAT HIGH?
WELL, MORE LIKE...
THEY'RE IRREDEEM-ABLE.
IRREDEEM-ABLE?!
WHAT DOES THAT EVEN MEAN?!
GULP
SO, WHAT'RE YOU UP TO?
ACTU-ALLY...
...I SEE. SO, YOU GUYS GOT KICKED OUT.
SIGH
THAT'S RIGHT.
SIGH
WE'RE IN A REAL BIND.
THINK YOU COULD HELP US OUT?
I DUNNO...
I SEE...

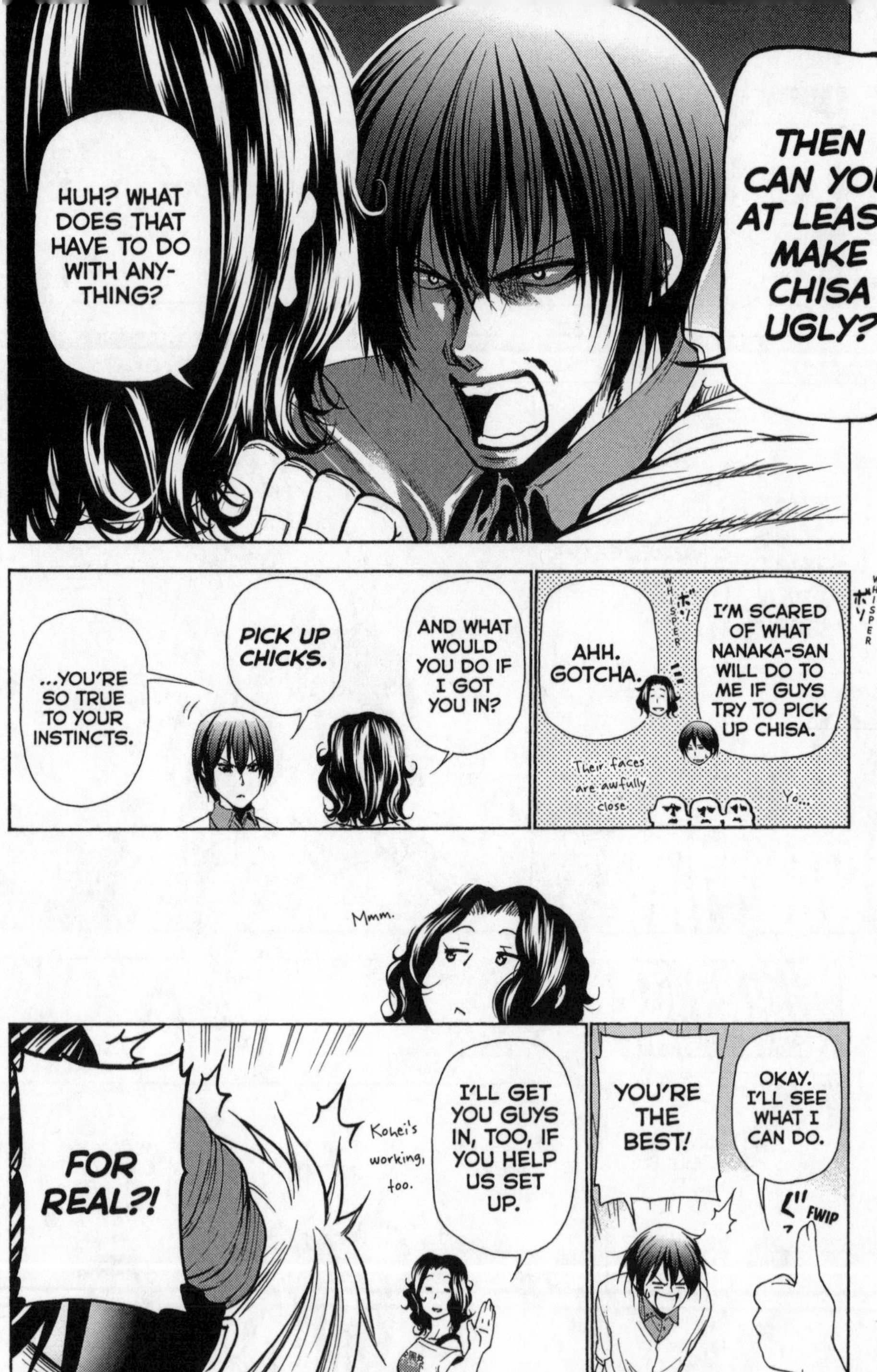
THEN CAN YOU AT LEAST MAKE CHISA UGLY?
HUH? WHAT DOES THAT HAVE TO DO WITH ANY-THING?
WHISPER
I'M SCARED OF WHAT NANAKA-SAN WILL DO TO ME IF GUYS TRY TO PICK UP CHISA.
WHISPER
AHH. GOTCHA.
Yo...
Their faces are awfully close.
AND WHAT WOULD YOU DO IF I GOT YOU IN?
PICK UP CHICKS.
...YOU'RE SO TRUE TO YOUR INSTINCTS.
Mmm.
OKAY. I'LL SEE WHAT I CAN DO.
FWIP
YOU'RE THE BEST!
I'LL GET YOU GUYS IN, TOO, IF YOU HELP US SET UP.
Kohei's working, too.
FOR REAL?!

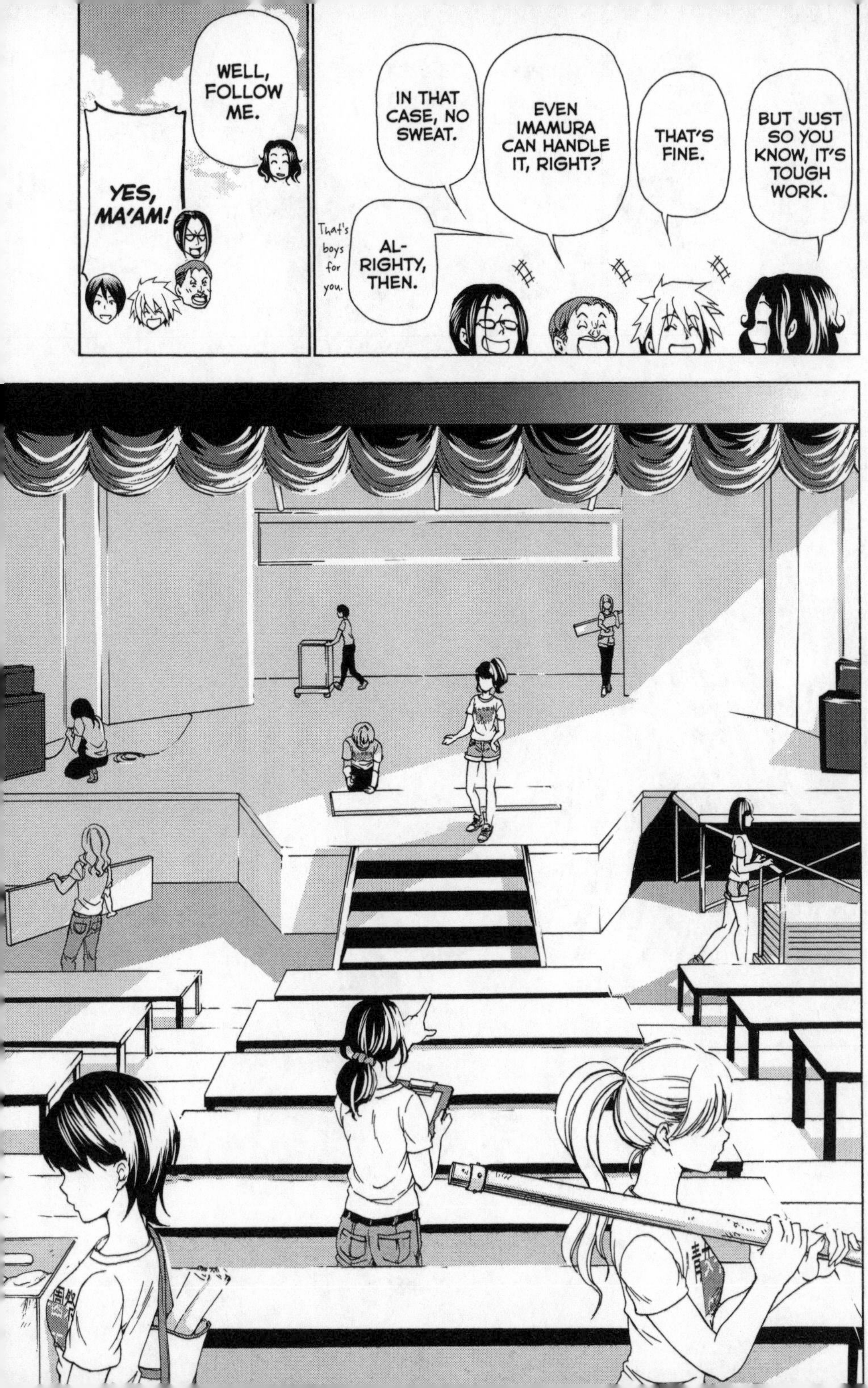
BUT JUST SO YOU KNOW, IT'S TOUGH WORK.
THAT'S FINE.
EVEN IMAMURA CAN HANDLE IT, RIGHT?
IN THAT CASE, NO SWEAT.
AL-RIGHTY, THEN.
That's boys for you.
WELL, FOLLOW ME.
YES, MA'AM!

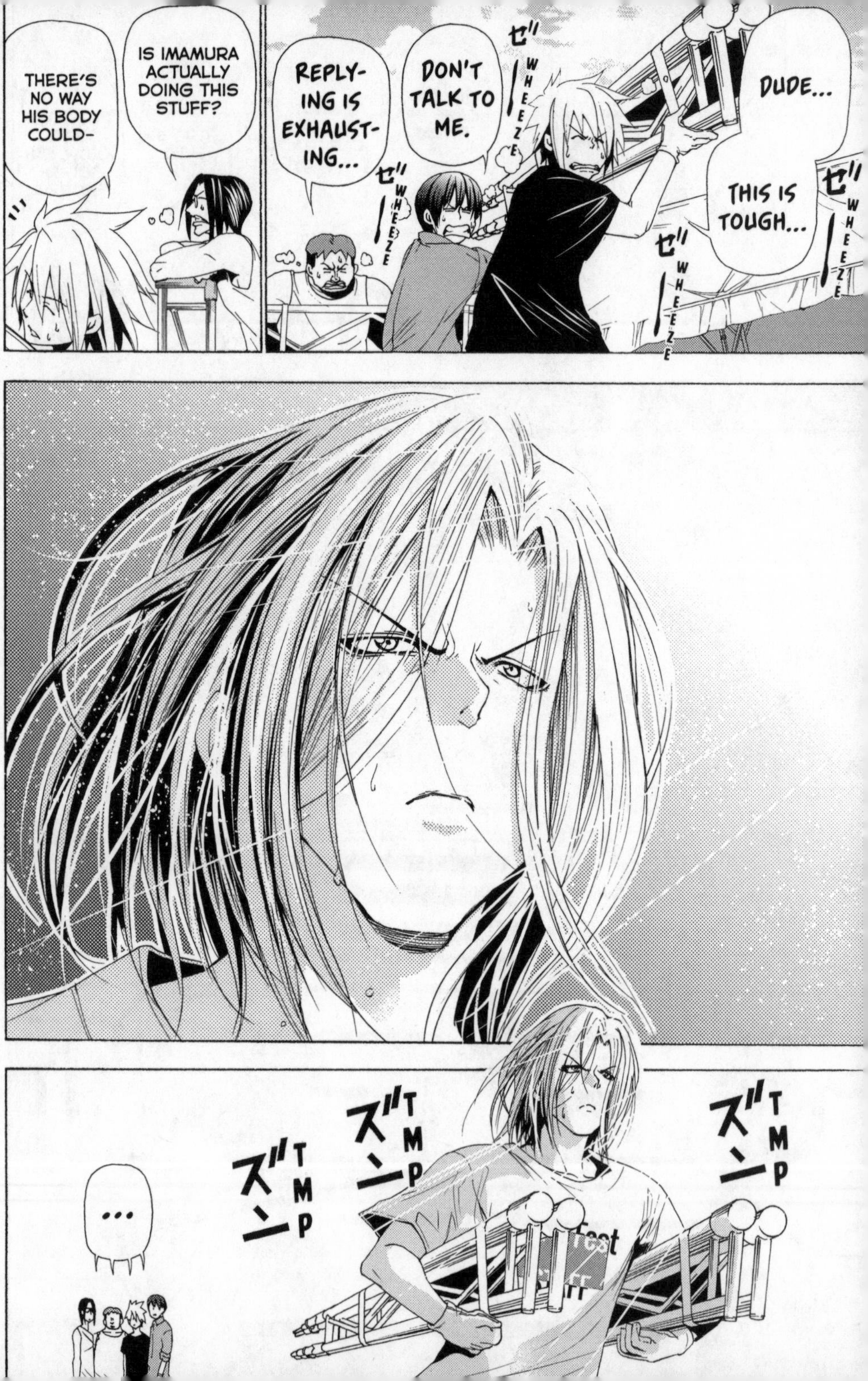
DUDE...
THIS IS TOUGH...
ゼー WHEEZE
ゼー WHEEZE
ゼー WHEEZE
DON'T TALK TO ME.
REPLY-ING IS EXHAUST-ING...
ゼー WHEEZE
IS IMAMURA ACTUALLY DOING THIS STUFF?
THERE'S NO WAY HIS BODY COULD-
ズン TMP
ズン TMP
ズン TMP
...

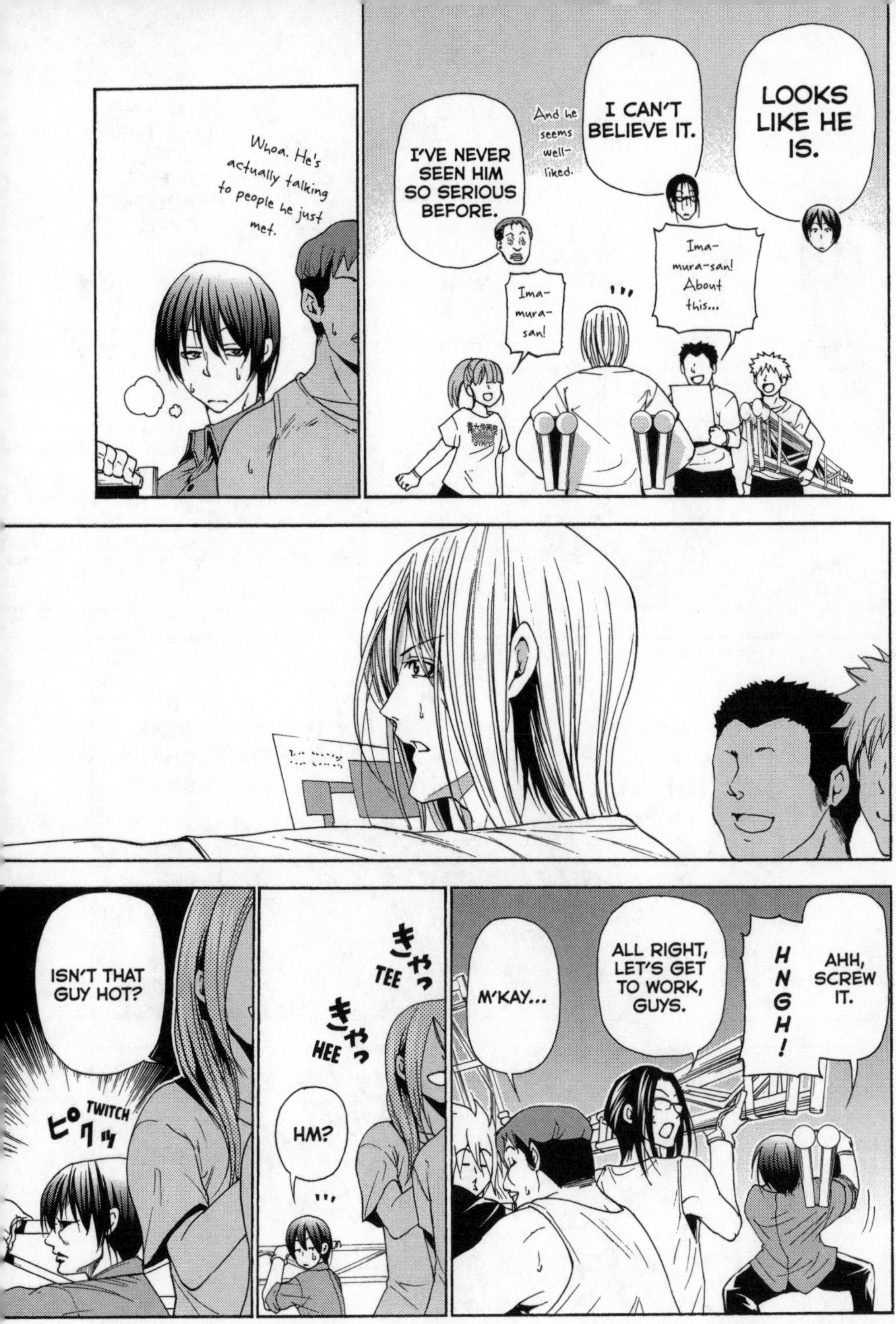

LOOKS LIKE HE IS.
I CAN'T BELIEVE IT.
And he seems well-liked.
I'VE NEVER SEEN HIM SO SERIOUS BEFORE.
Ima-mura-san! About this...
...
Ima-mura-san!
Whoa. He's actually talking to people he just met.
AHH, SCREW IT.
HNGH!
ALL RIGHT, LET'S GET TO WORK, GUYS.
M'KAY...
きゃっ TEE
きゃっ HEE
HM?
...
ISN'T THAT GUY HOT?
ピクッ TWITCH

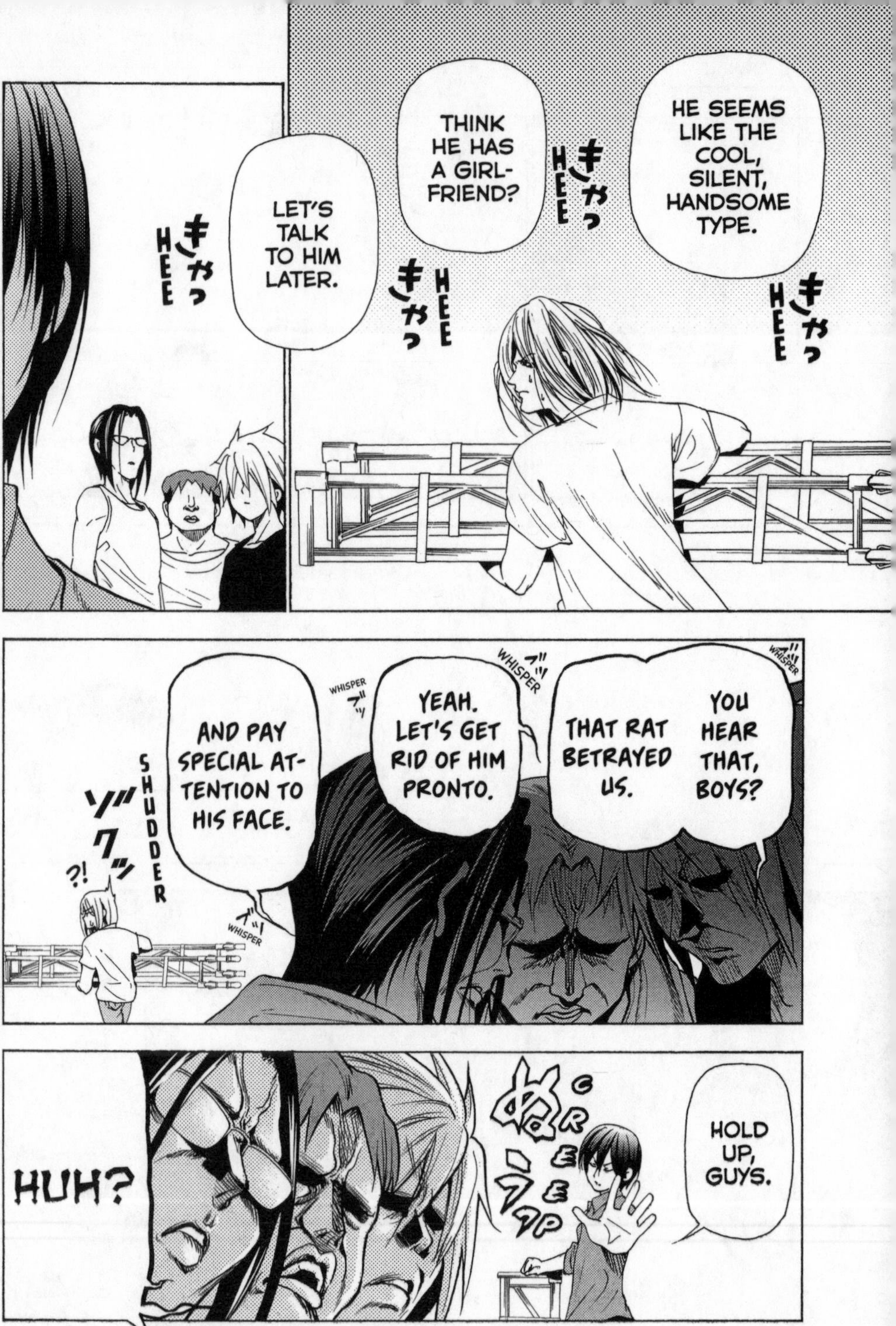
HE SEEMS LIKE THE COOL, SILENT, HANDSOME TYPE.
キャっ HEE
THINK HE HAS A GIRL-FRIEND?
キャっ HEE
キャっ HEE
LET'S TALK TO HIM LATER.
キャっ HEE
WHISPER ブツ
YOU HEAR THAT, BOYS?
THAT RAT BETRAYED US.
WHISPER ブツ
YEAH. LET'S GET RID OF HIM PRONTO.
WHISPER ブツ
AND PAY SPECIAL AT-TENTION TO HIS FACE.
WHISPER ズッ
ゾクッ SHUDDER
?!
HOLD UP, GUYS.
ぬぅっ CREEP
HUH?

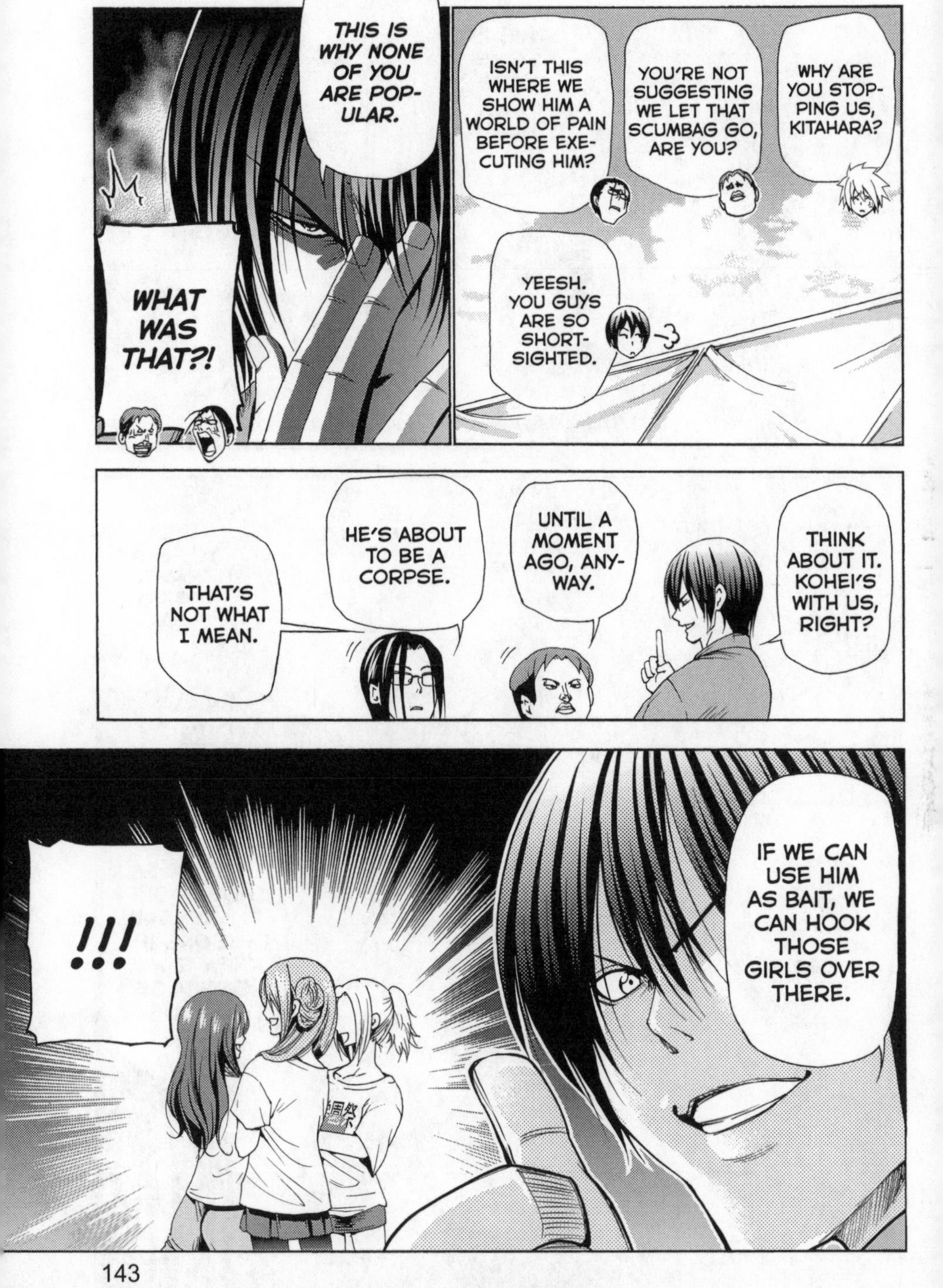
WHY ARE YOU STOP-PING US, KITAHARA?
YOU'RE NOT SUGGESTING WE LET THAT SCUMBAG GO, ARE YOU?
ISN'T THIS WHERE WE SHOW HIM A WORLD OF PAIN BEFORE EXE-CUTING HIM?
YEESH. YOU GUYS ARE SO SHORT-SIGHTED.
THIS IS WHY NONE OF YOU ARE POP-ULAR.
WHAT WAS THAT?!
THINK ABOUT IT. KOHEI'S WITH US, RIGHT?
UNTIL A MOMENT AGO, ANY-WAY.
HE'S ABOUT TO BE A CORPSE.
THAT'S NOT WHAT I MEAN.
IF WE CAN USE HIM AS BAIT, WE CAN HOOK THOSE GIRLS OVER THERE.
!!!

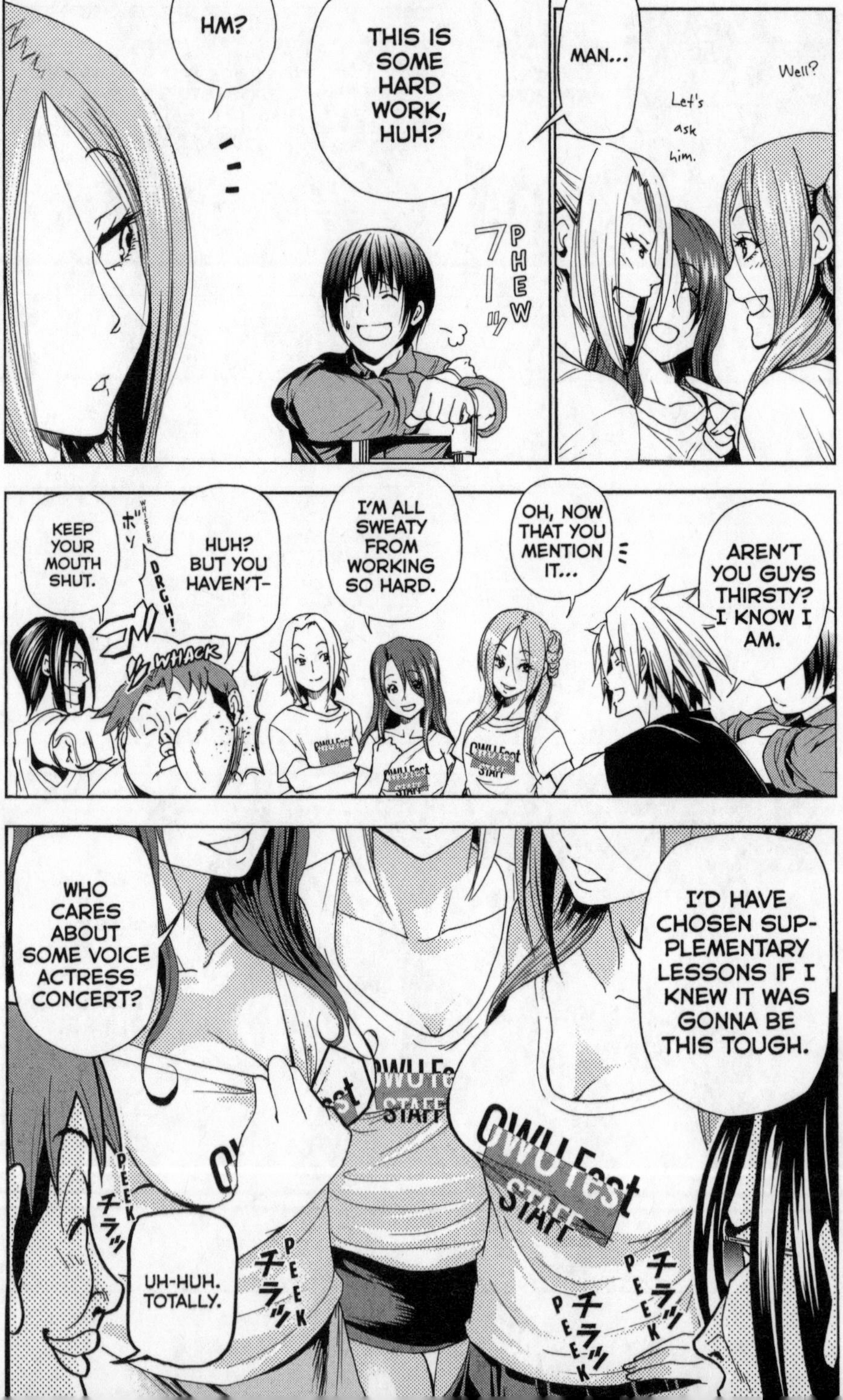
MAN...
Well?
Let's ask him.
THIS IS SOME HARD WORK, HUH?
PHEW
HM?
AREN'T YOU GUYS THIRSTY? I KNOW I AM.
OH, NOW THAT YOU MENTION IT...
I'M ALL SWEATY FROM WORKING SO HARD.
HUH? BUT YOU HAVEN'T-
WHISPER
DRGH!
WHACK
KEEP YOUR MOUTH SHUT.
I'D HAVE CHOSEN SUP-PLEMENTARY LESSONS IF I KNEW IT WAS GONNA BE THIS TOUGH.
PEEK
PEEK
WHO CARES ABOUT SOME VOICE ACTRESS CONCERT?
PEEK
UH-HUH. TOTALLY.
PEEK

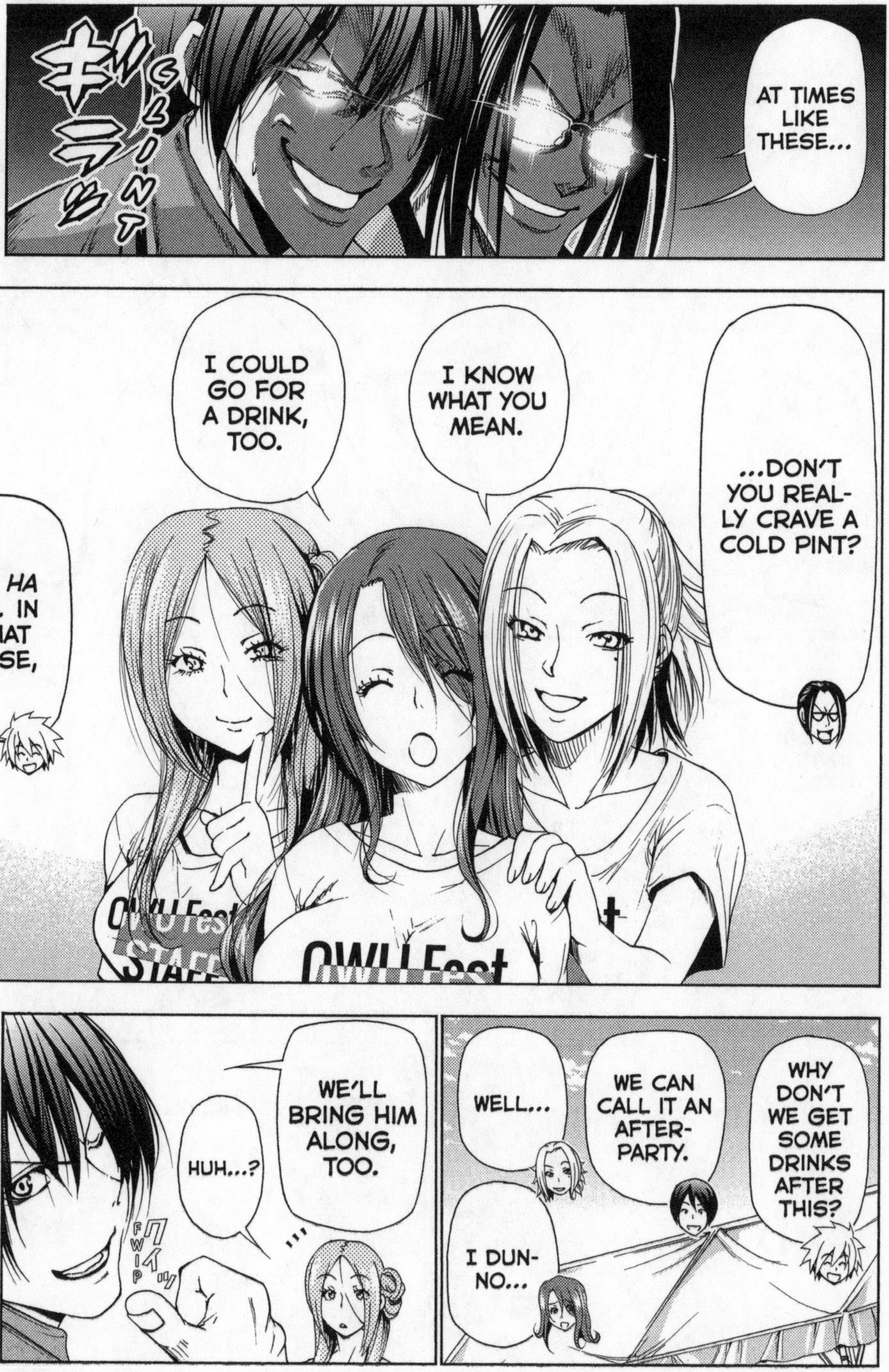
AT TIMES LIKE THESE...
キラッ
GLINT
...DON'T YOU REAL-LY CRAVE A COLD PINT?
I KNOW WHAT YOU MEAN.
I COULD GO FOR A DRINK, TOO.
AH HA HA. IN THAT CASE,
OWU Fest STAFF
OWU Fest
WHY DON'T WE GET SOME DRINKS AFTER THIS?
WE CAN CALL IT AN AFTER-PARTY.
WELL...
I DUN-NO...
WE'LL BRING HIM ALONG, TOO.
HUH...?
クイッ
FWIP

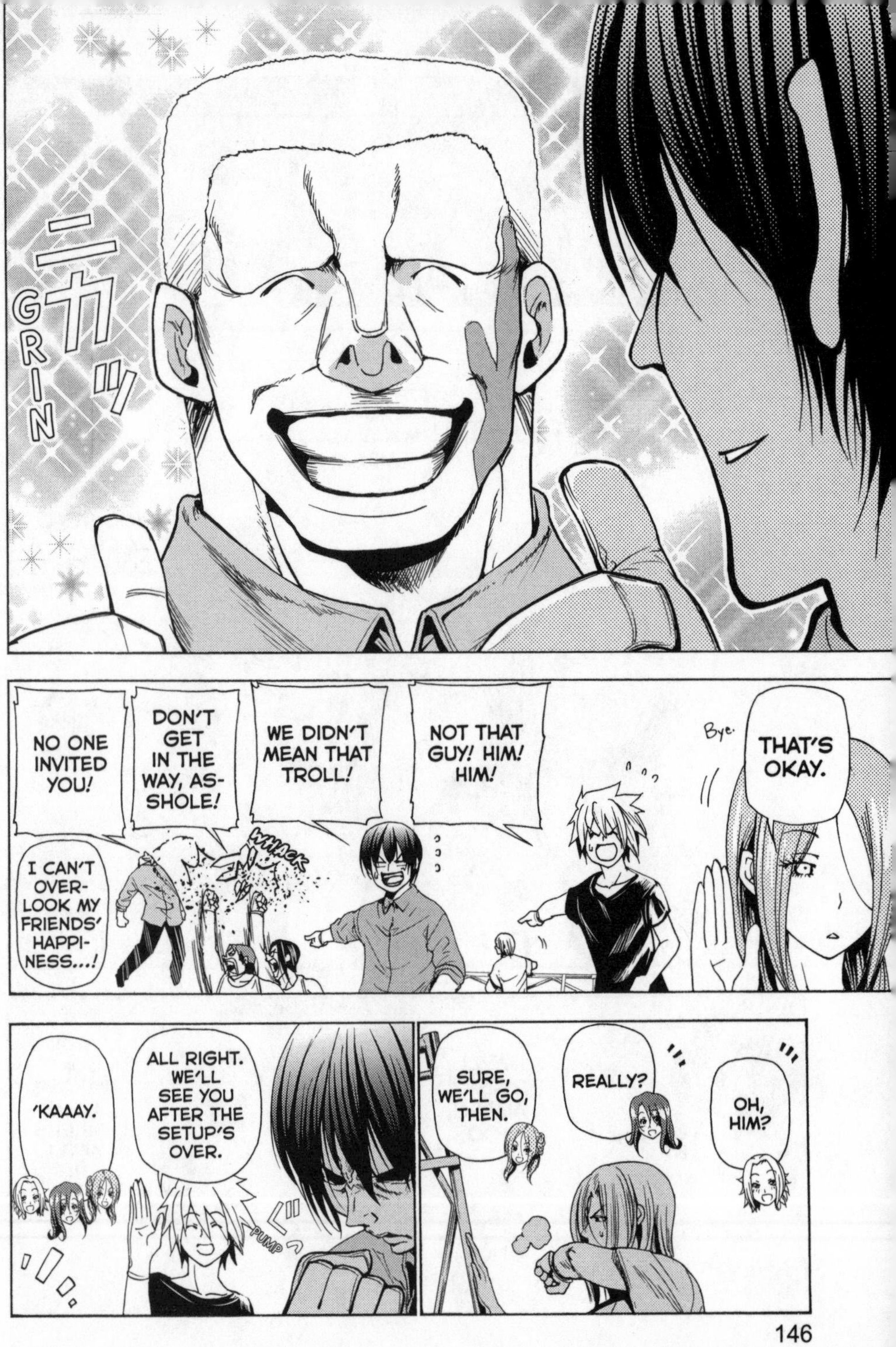
ニカッ
GRIN
Bye.
THAT'S OKAY.
NOT THAT GUY! HIM! HIM!
WE DIDN'T MEAN THAT TROLL!
WHACK
DON'T GET IN THE WAY, AS-SHOLE!
NO ONE INVITED YOU!
I CAN'T OVER-LOOK MY FRIENDS' HAPPI-NESS...!
OH, HIM?
REALLY?
SURE, WE'LL GO, THEN.
ALL RIGHT. WE'LL SEE YOU AFTER THE SETUP'S OVER.
PUMP
'KAAAY.

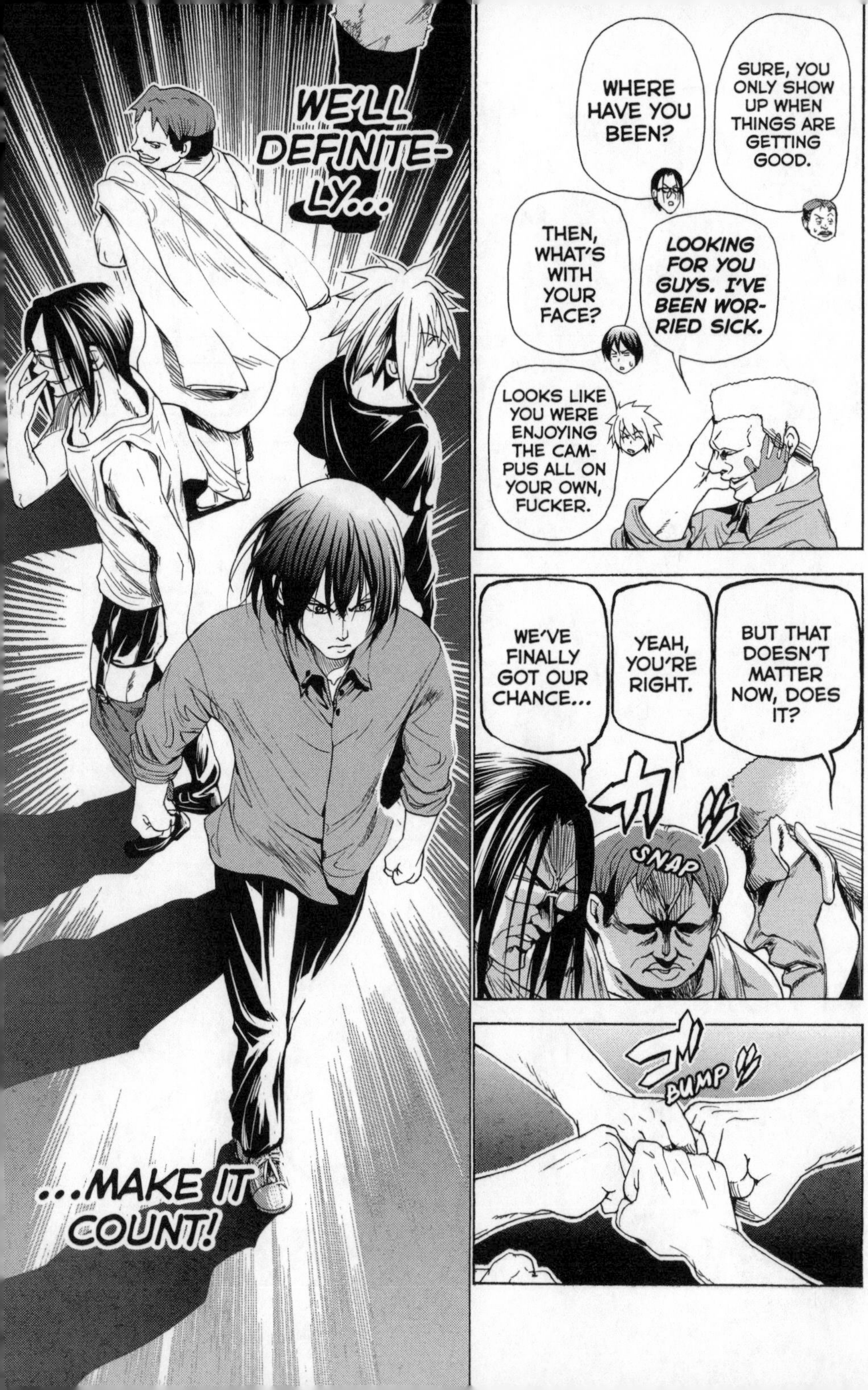
SURE, YOU ONLY SHOW UP WHEN THINGS ARE GETTING GOOD.
WHERE HAVE YOU BEEN?
LOOKING FOR YOU GUYS. I'VE BEEN WOR-RIED SICK.
THEN, WHAT'S WITH YOUR FACE?
LOOKS LIKE YOU WERE ENJOYING THE CAM-PUS ALL ON YOUR OWN, FUCKER.
BUT THAT DOESN'T MATTER NOW, DOES IT?
YEAH, YOU'RE RIGHT.
WE'VE FINALLY GOT OUR CHANCE...
SNAP
BUMP
WE'LL DEFINITE-LY...
...MAKE IT COUNT!

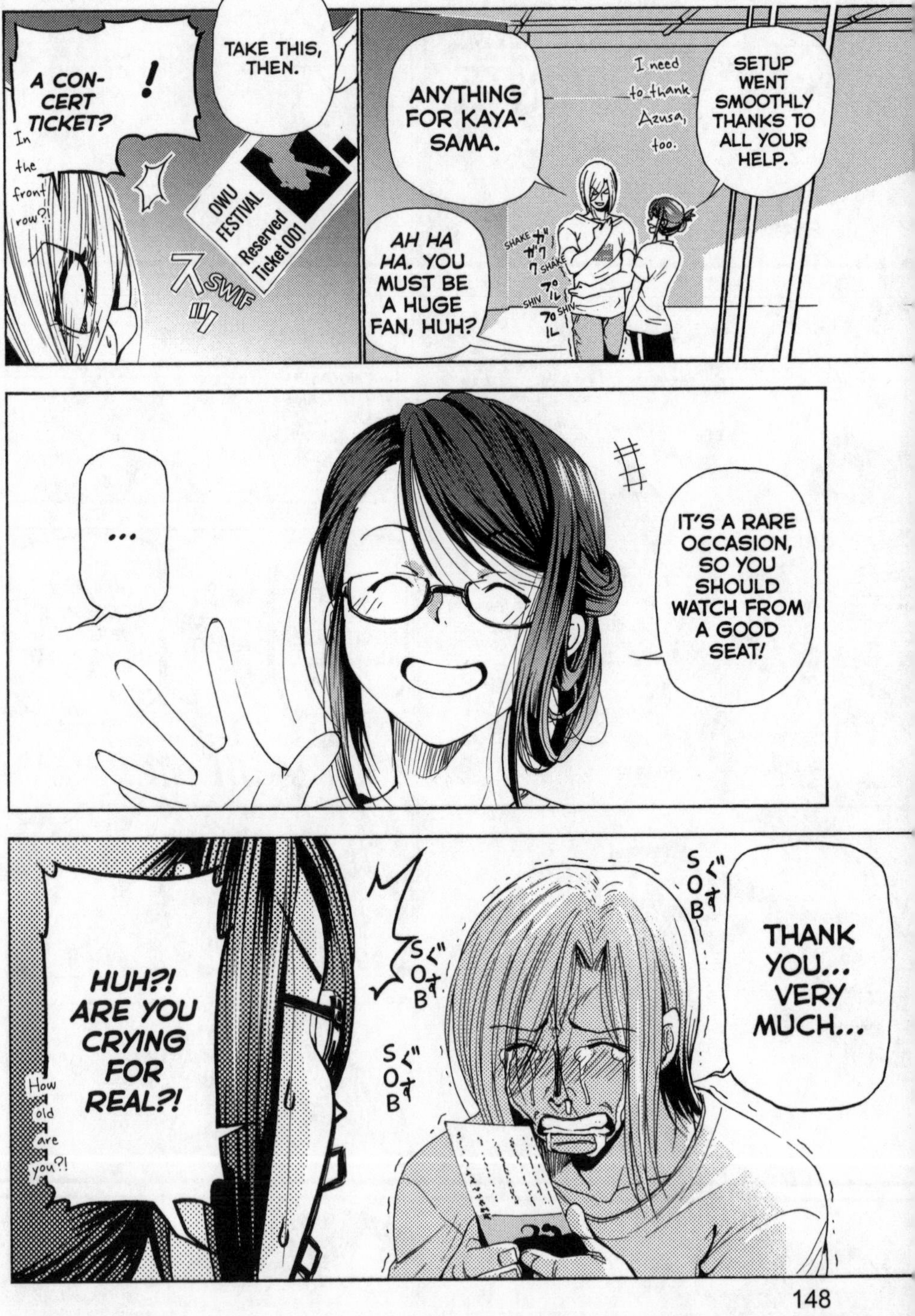
SETUP WENT SMOOTHLY THANKS TO ALL YOUR HELP.
I need to thank Azusa, too.
ANYTHING FOR KAYA-SAMA.
SHAKE SHAKE
SHIV SHIV
AH HA HA. YOU MUST BE A HUGE FAN, HUH?
TAKE THIS, THEN.
!
A CON-CERT TICKET?
In the front row?!
OWU FESTIVAL Reserved Ticket 001
SWIF
IT'S A RARE OCCASION, SO YOU SHOULD WATCH FROM A GOOD SEAT!
...
THANK YOU... VERY MUCH...
SOB
SOB
SOB
HUH?! ARE YOU CRYING FOR REAL?!
How old are you?!

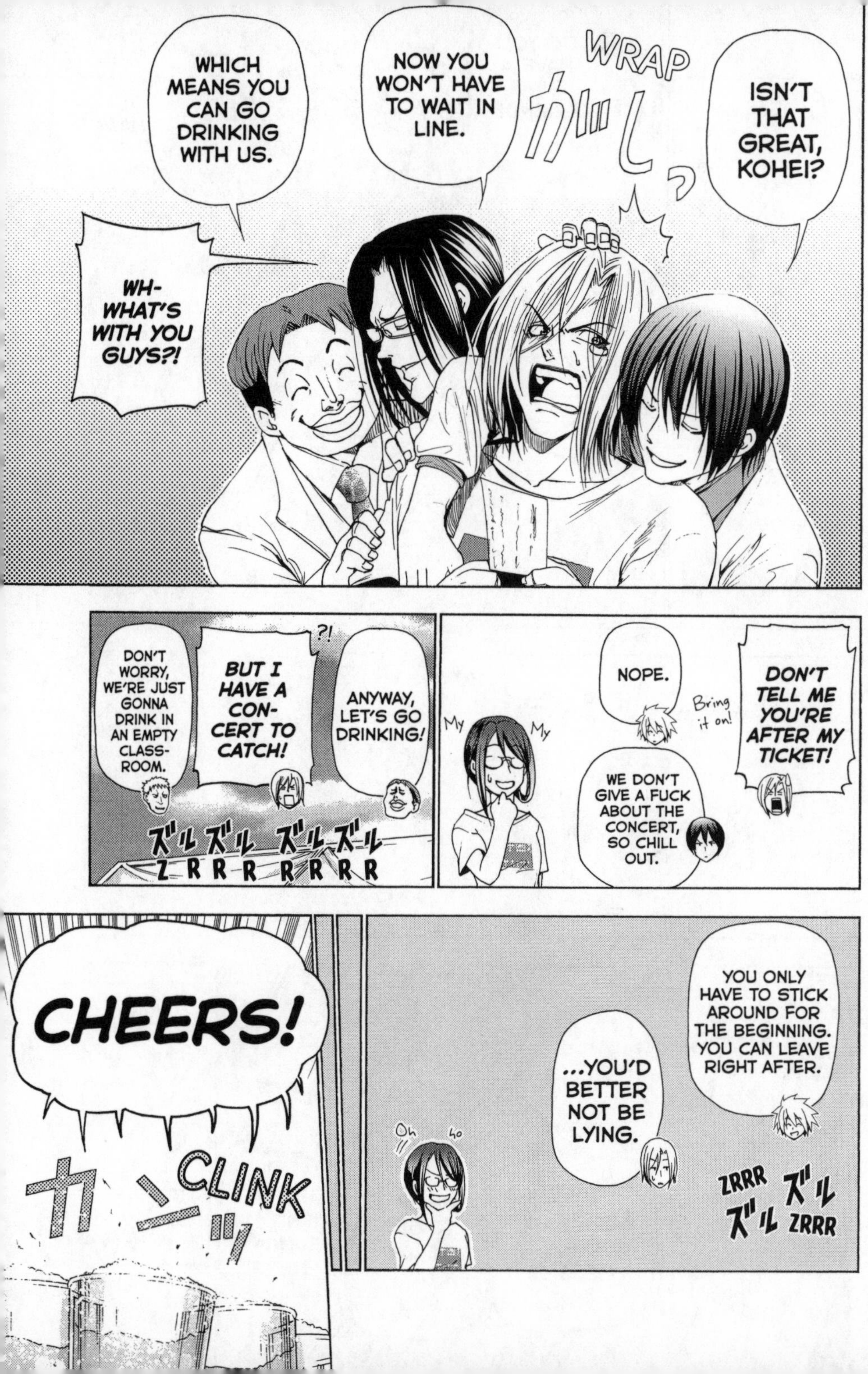

ISN'T THAT GREAT, KOHEI?
WRAP
NOW YOU WON'T HAVE TO WAIT IN LINE.
WHICH MEANS YOU CAN GO DRINKING WITH US.
WH-WHAT'S WITH YOU GUYS?!
DON'T TELL ME YOU'RE AFTER MY TICKET!
Bring it on!
NOPE.
My My
WE DON'T GIVE A FUCK ABOUT THE CONCERT, SO CHILL OUT.
?!
ANYWAY, LET'S GO DRINKING!
BUT I HAVE A CONCERT TO CATCH!
DON'T WORRY, WE'RE JUST GONNA DRINK IN AN EMPTY CLASSROOM.
ZRRR RRRR
YOU ONLY HAVE TO STICK AROUND FOR THE BEGINNING. YOU CAN LEAVE RIGHT AFTER.
...YOU'D BETTER NOT BE LYING.
Oh ho
ZRRR ZRRR
CHEERS!
CLINK

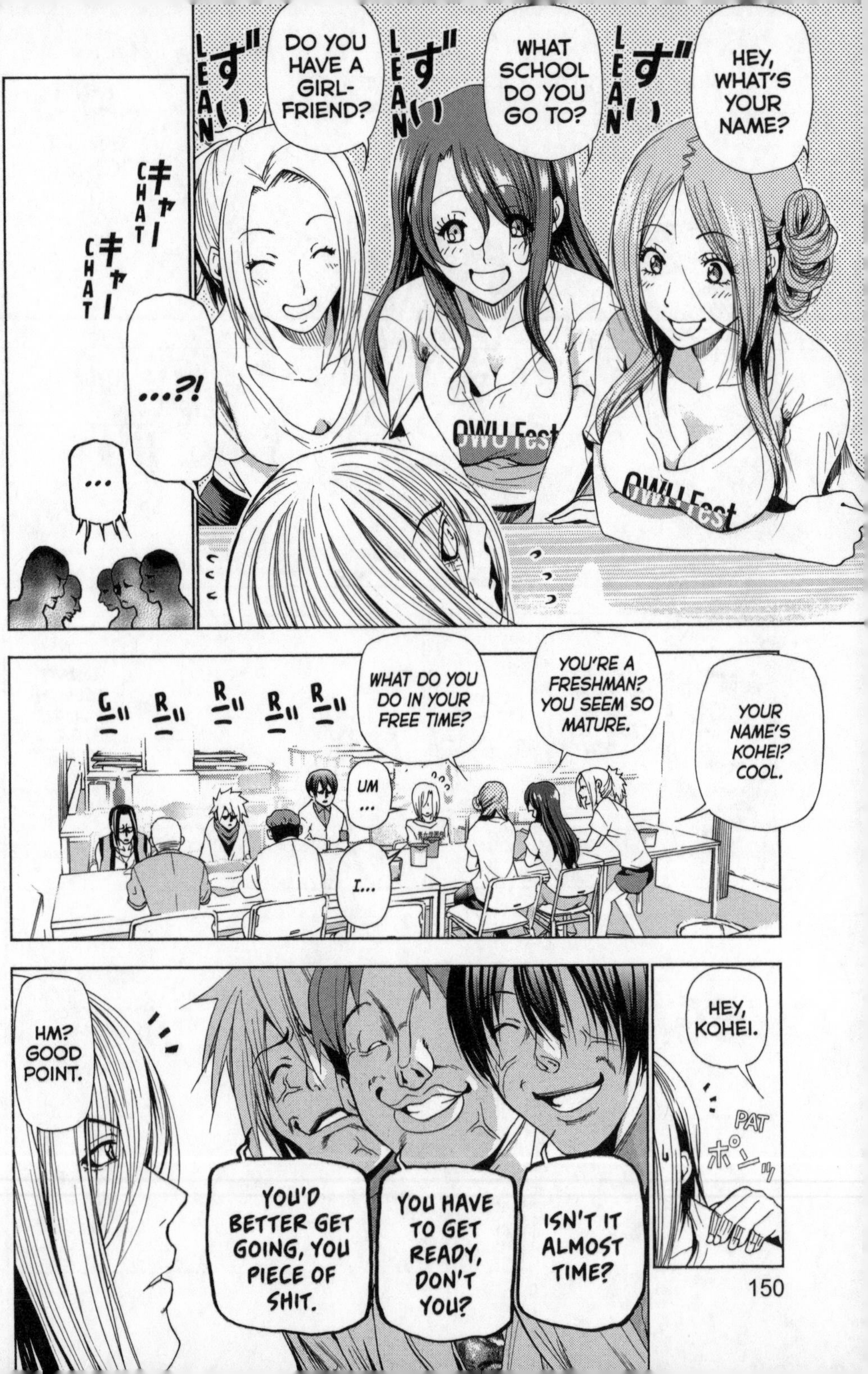
HEY, WHAT'S YOUR NAME?
LEAN
ず"
WHAT SCHOOL DO YOU GO TO?
LEAN
ず"
DO YOU HAVE A GIRL-FRIEND?
LEAN
ず"
CHAT
キャー
CHAT
キャー
...?!
...
YOUR NAME'S KOHEI? COOL.
YOU'RE A FRESHMAN? YOU SEEM SO MATURE.
WHAT DO YOU DO IN YOUR FREE TIME?
UM ...
I...
G" R" R" R" R"
HEY, KOHEI.
PAT
ポンッ
ISN'T IT ALMOST TIME?
YOU HAVE TO GET READY, DON'T YOU?
YOU'D BETTER GET GOING, YOU PIECE OF SHIT.
HM? GOOD POINT.

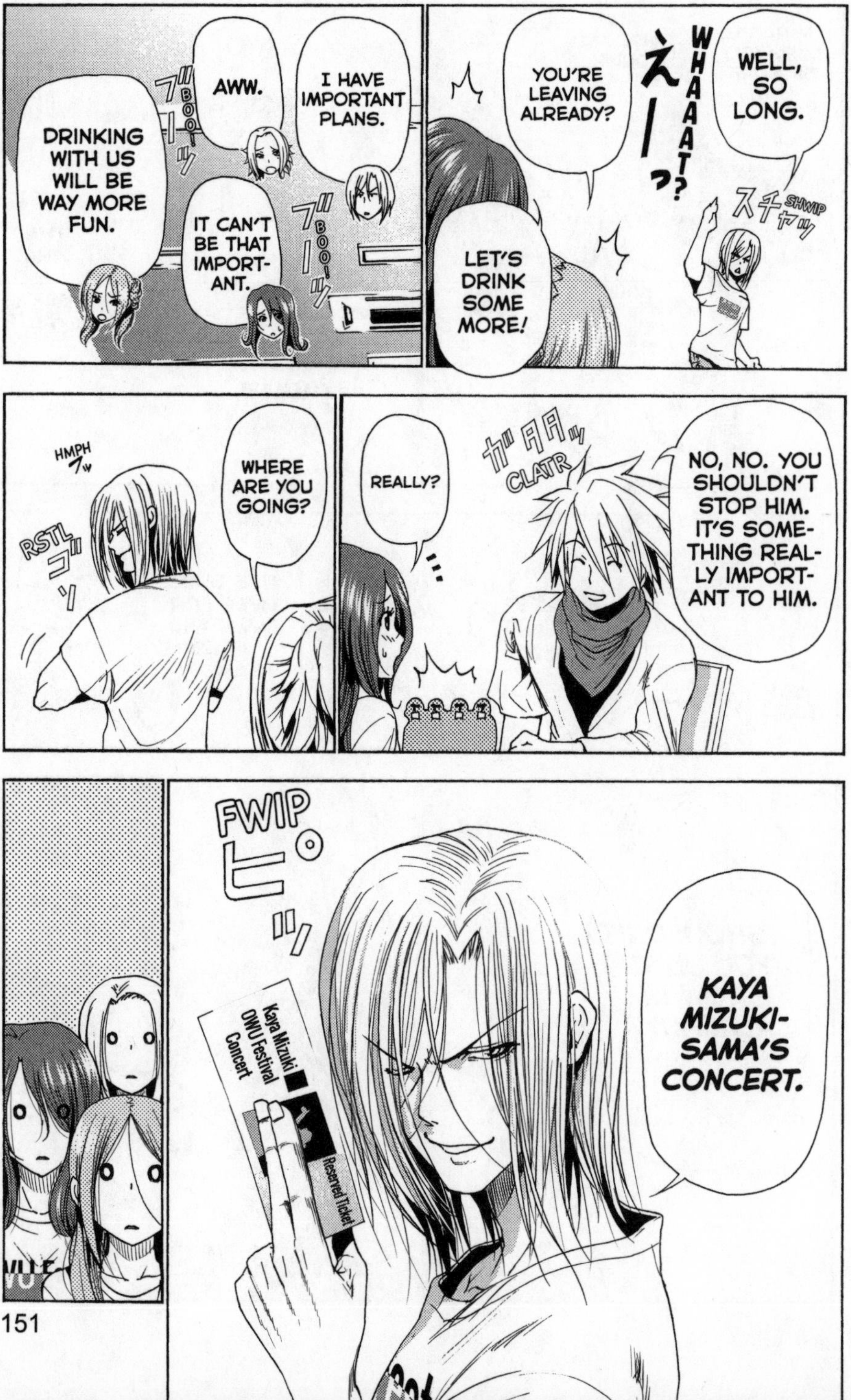
WELL, SO LONG.
SHWIP スチャッ
WHAAAT? えーっ
YOU'RE LEAVING ALREADY?
LET'S DRINK SOME MORE!
I HAVE IMPORTANT PLANS.
AWW.
BOO! ブーッ
IT CAN'T BE THAT IMPORT-ANT.
BOO! ブーッ
DRINKING WITH US WILL BE WAY MORE FUN.
NO, NO. YOU SHOULDN'T STOP HIM. IT'S SOME-THING REAL-LY IMPORT-ANT TO HIM.
CLATR ガタタッ
REALLY?
WHERE ARE YOU GOING?
HMPH フッ
RSTL ゴソ
FWIP ピッ
Kaya Mizuki OWU Festival Concert
Reserved Ticket
KAYA MIZUKI-SAMA'S CONCERT.

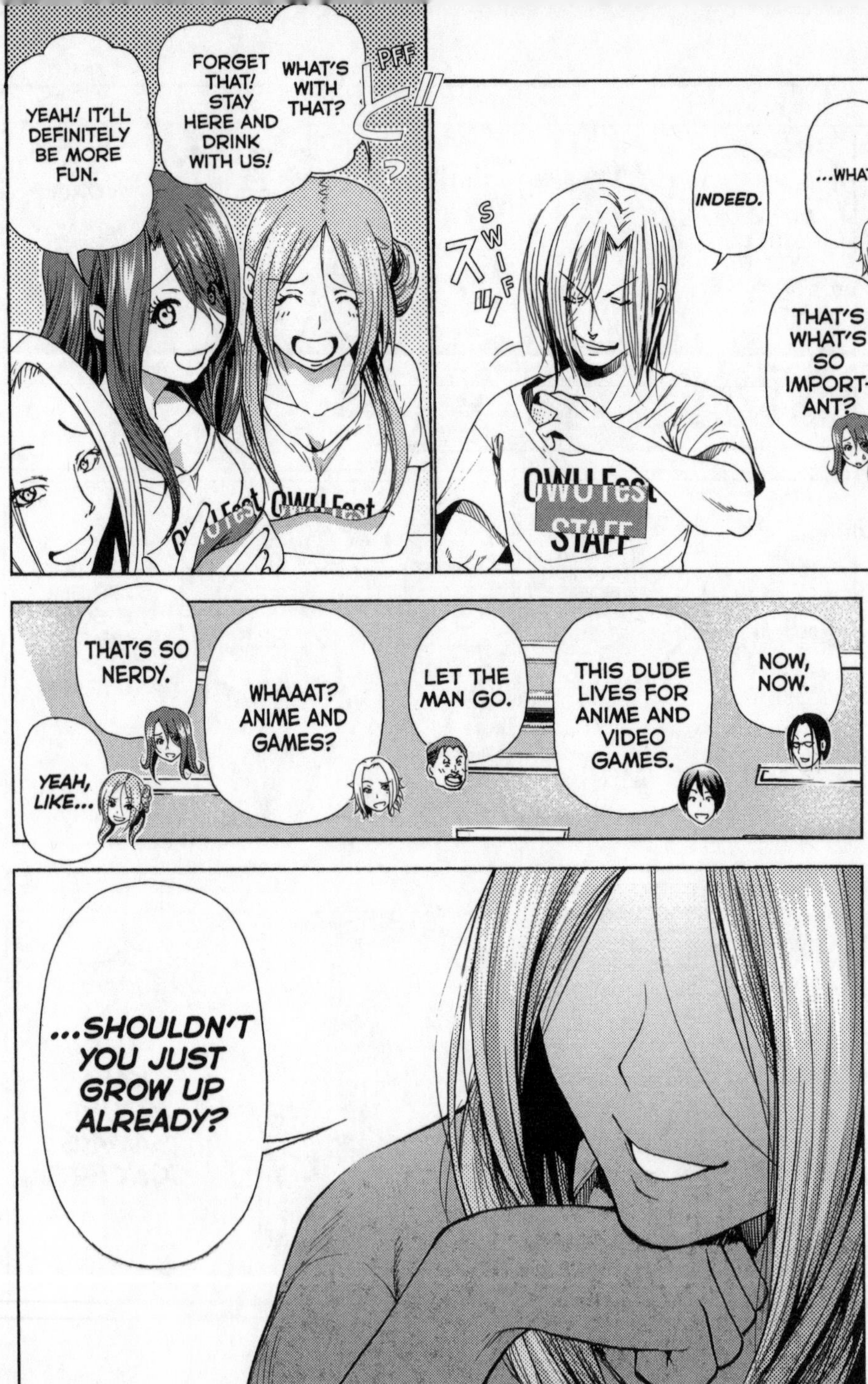
...WHAT?
INDEED.
THAT'S WHAT'S SO IMPORT-ANT?
SWIF
PFF
WHAT'S WITH THAT?
FORGET THAT! STAY HERE AND DRINK WITH US!
YEAH! IT'LL DEFINITELY BE MORE FUN.
OWU Fest
STAFF
NOW, NOW.
THIS DUDE LIVES FOR ANIME AND VIDEO GAMES.
LET THE MAN GO.
WHAAAT? ANIME AND GAMES?
THAT'S SO NERDY.
YEAH, LIKE...
...SHOULDN'T YOU JUST GROW UP ALREADY?

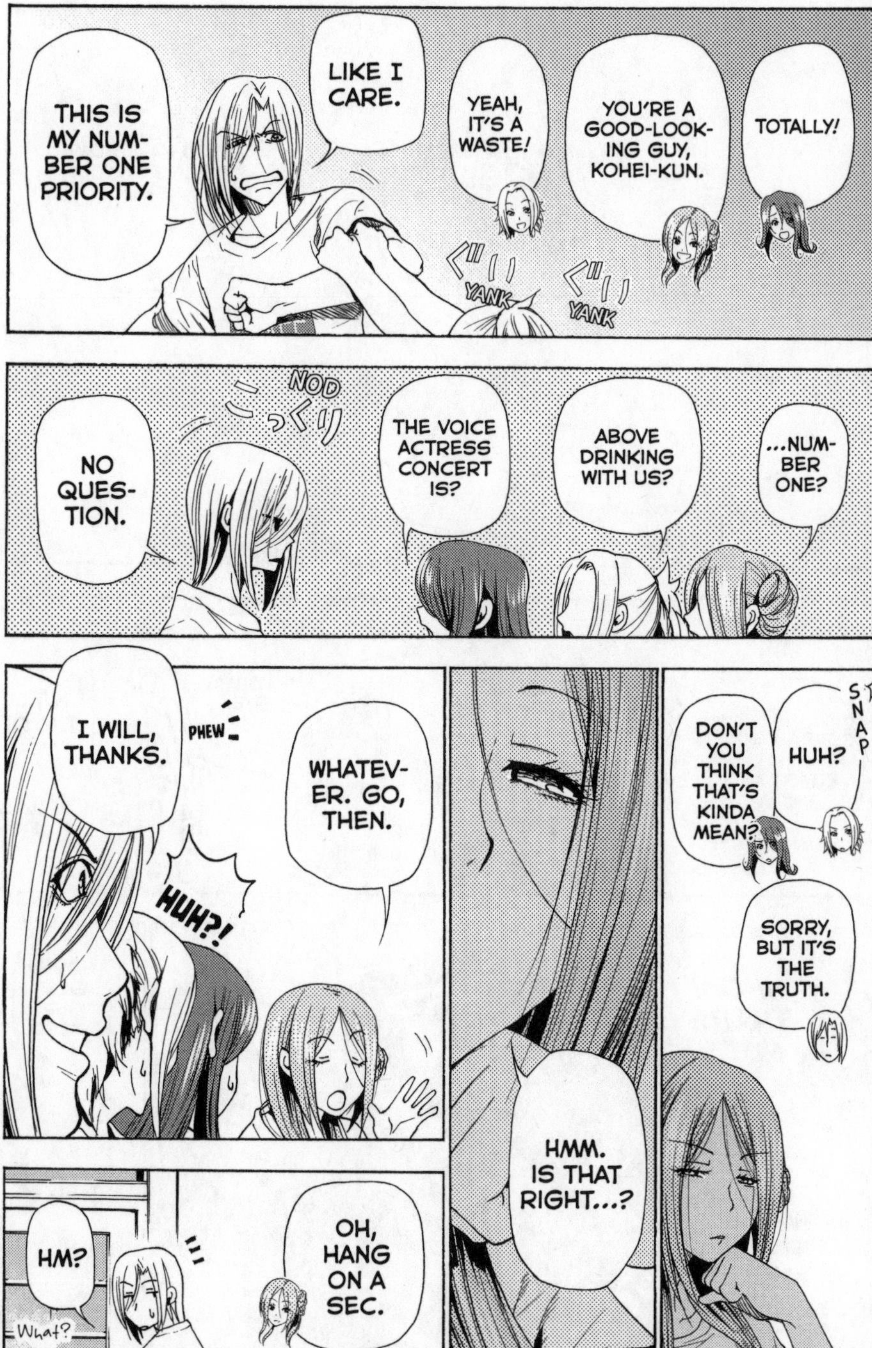
TOTALLY!
YOU'RE A GOOD-LOOKING GUY, KOHEI-KUN.
YEAH, IT'S A WASTE!
YANK
YANK
LIKE I CARE.
THIS IS MY NUMBER ONE PRIORITY.
...NUMBER ONE?
ABOVE DRINKING WITH US?
THE VOICE ACTRESS CONCERT IS?
NOD
NO QUESTION.
SNAP
HUH?
DON'T YOU THINK THAT'S KINDA MEAN?
SORRY, BUT IT'S THE TRUTH.
HMM. IS THAT RIGHT...?
WHATEVER. GO, THEN.
PHEW
I WILL, THANKS.
HUH?!
OH, HANG ON A SEC.
HM?
What?

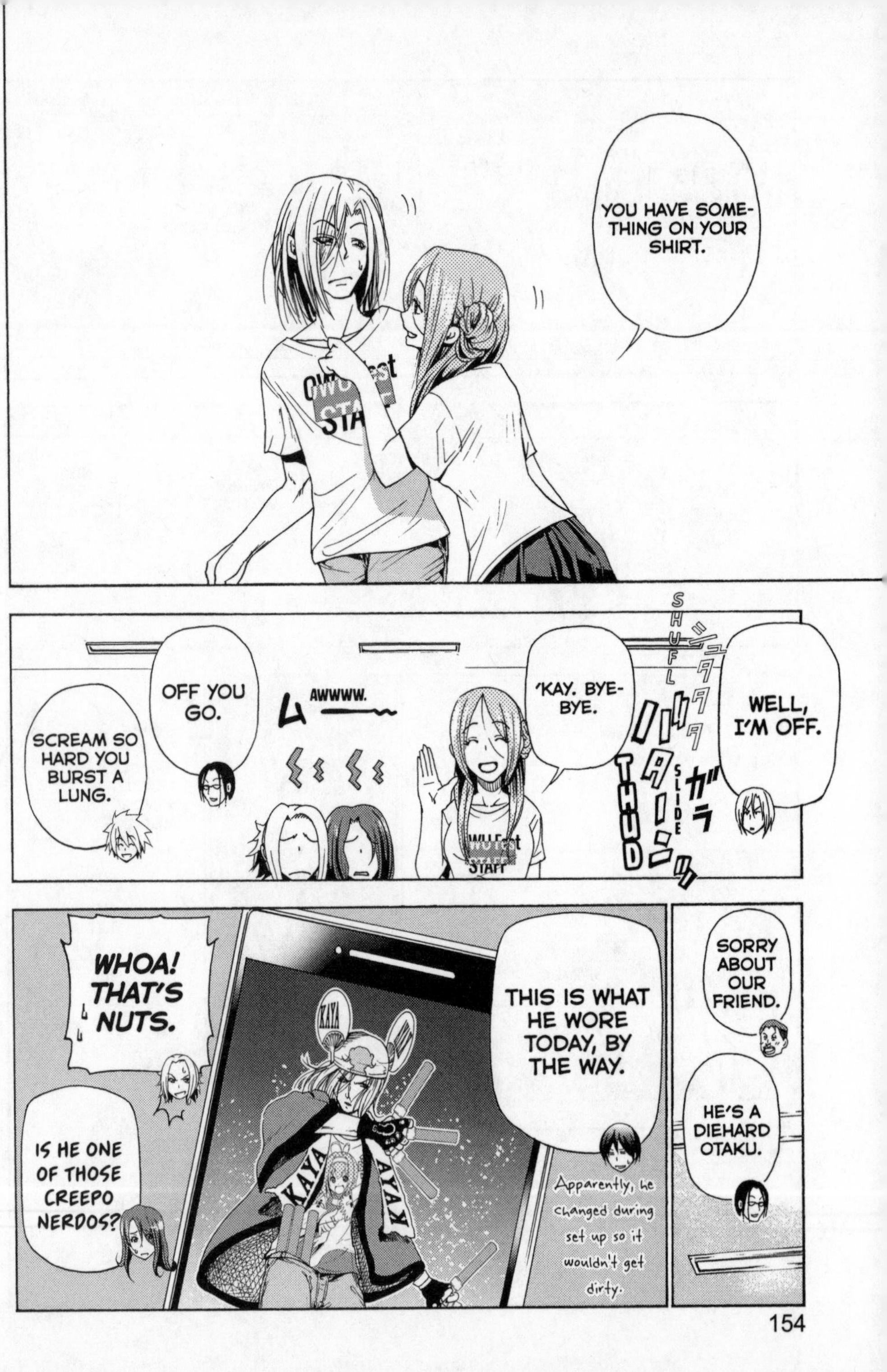
YOU HAVE SOMETHING ON YOUR SHIRT.
WELL, I'M OFF.
SHUFL
SLIDE
THUD
'KAY. BYE-BYE.
AWWWW.
OFF YOU GO.
SCREAM SO HARD YOU BURST A LUNG.
SORRY ABOUT OUR FRIEND.
HE'S A DIEHARD OTAKU.
THIS IS WHAT HE WORE TODAY, BY THE WAY.
Apparently, he changed during set up so it wouldn't get dirty.
WHOA! THAT'S NUTS.
IS HE ONE OF THOSE CREEPO NERDOS?

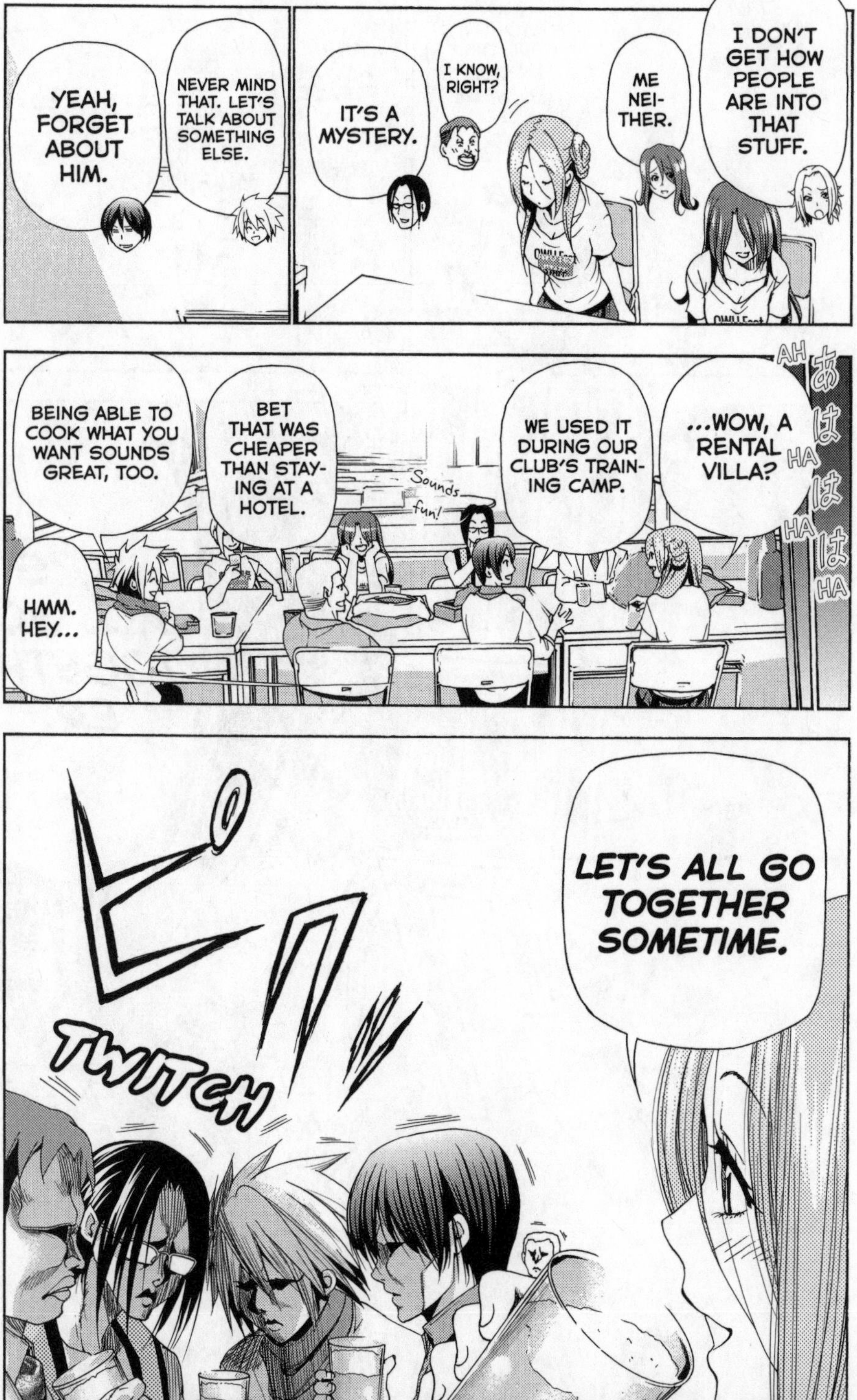
I DON'T GET HOW PEOPLE ARE INTO THAT STUFF.
ME NEI-THER.
I KNOW, RIGHT?
IT'S A MYSTERY.
NEVER MIND THAT. LET'S TALK ABOUT SOMETHING ELSE.
YEAH, FORGET ABOUT HIM.
AH HA HA HA
あははは
...WOW, A RENTAL VILLA?
WE USED IT DURING OUR CLUB'S TRAIN-ING CAMP.
Sounds fun!
BET THAT WAS CHEAPER THAN STAY-ING AT A HOTEL.
BEING ABLE TO COOK WHAT YOU WANT SOUNDS GREAT, TOO.
HMM. HEY...
LET'S ALL GO TOGETHER SOMETIME.
TWITCH

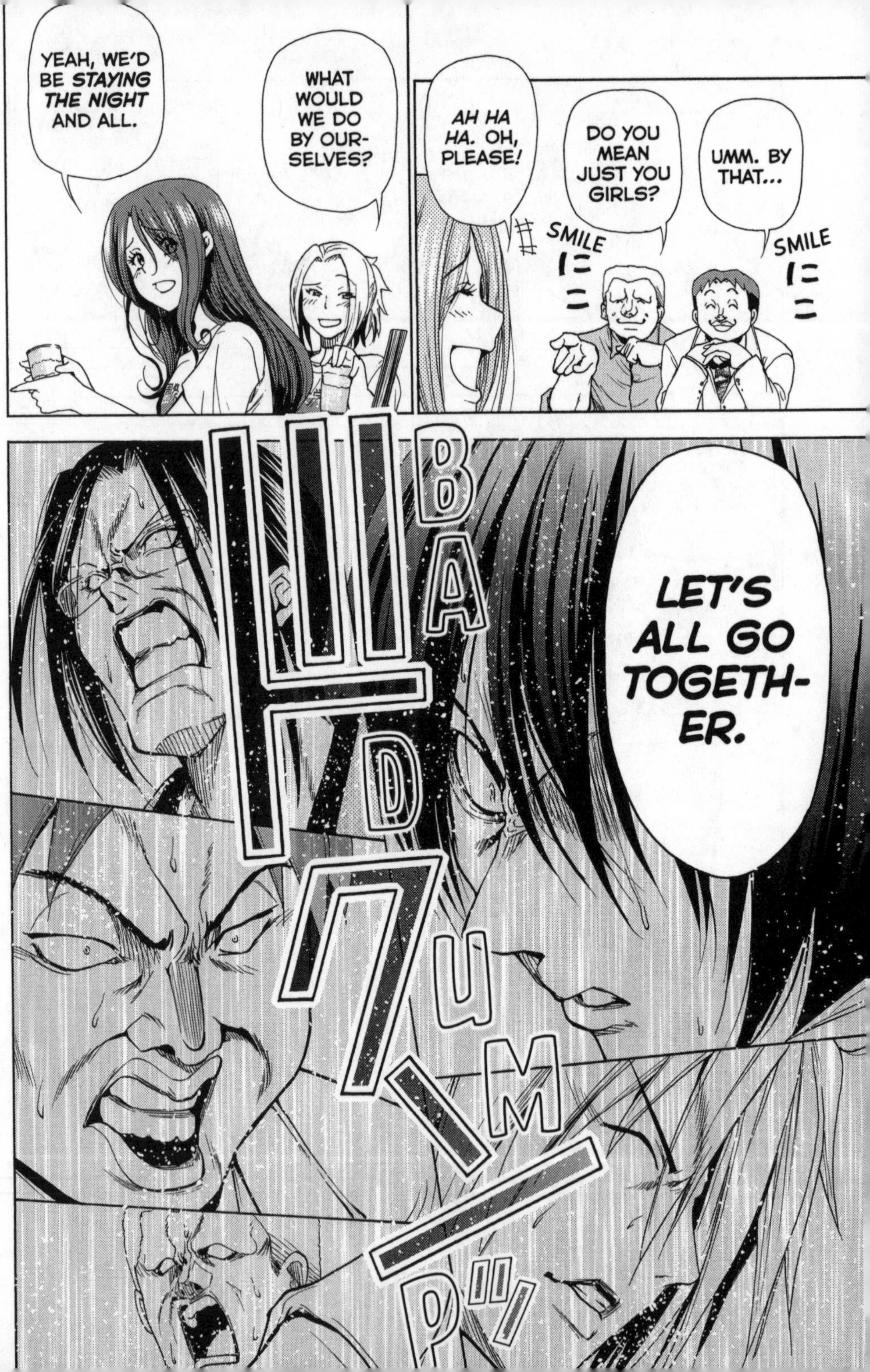
UMM. BY THAT...
SMILE
DO YOU MEAN JUST YOU GIRLS?
SMILE
AH HA HA. OH, PLEASE!
WHAT WOULD WE DO BY OURSELVES?
YEAH, WE'D BE *STAYING THE NIGHT* AND ALL.
LET'S ALL GO TOGETHER.
BA-DUMP

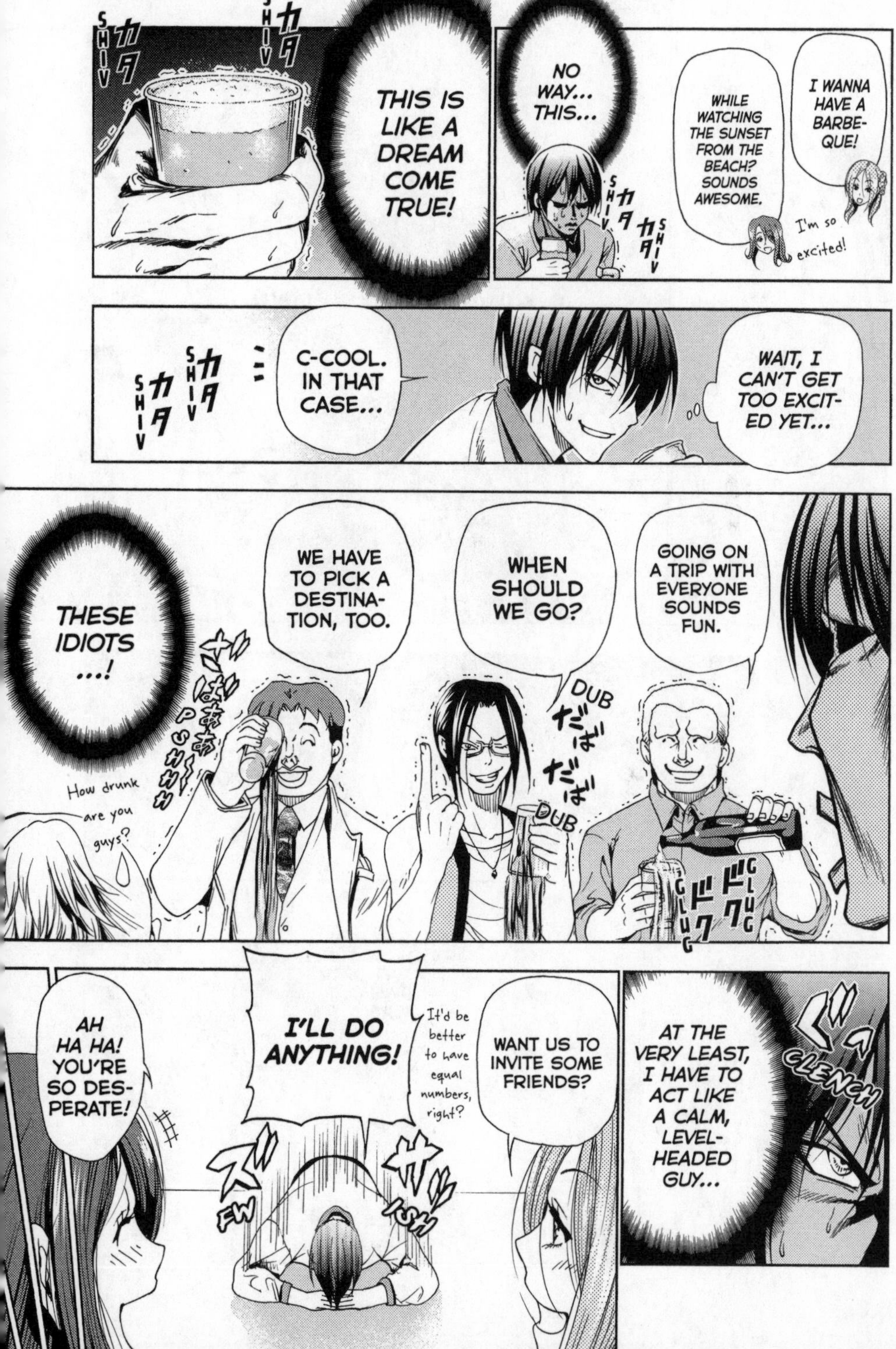
I WANNA HAVE A BARBE-QUE!
WHILE WATCHING THE SUNSET FROM THE BEACH? SOUNDS AWESOME.
I'm so excited!
NO WAY... THIS...
SHIV SHIV
THIS IS LIKE A DREAM COME TRUE!
SHIV
WAIT, I CAN'T GET TOO EXCITED YET...
C-COOL. IN THAT CASE...
SHIV SHIV
GOING ON A TRIP WITH EVERYONE SOUNDS FUN.
WHEN SHOULD WE GO?
WE HAVE TO PICK A DESTINATION, TOO.
GLUG GLUG
DUB DUB
PSHHH
THESE IDIOTS...!
How drunk are you guys?
AT THE VERY LEAST, I HAVE TO ACT LIKE A CALM, LEVEL-HEADED GUY...
CLENCH
WANT US TO INVITE SOME FRIENDS?
It'd be better to have equal numbers, right?
I'LL DO ANYTHING!
FWISH
AH HA HA! YOU'RE SO DESPERATE!

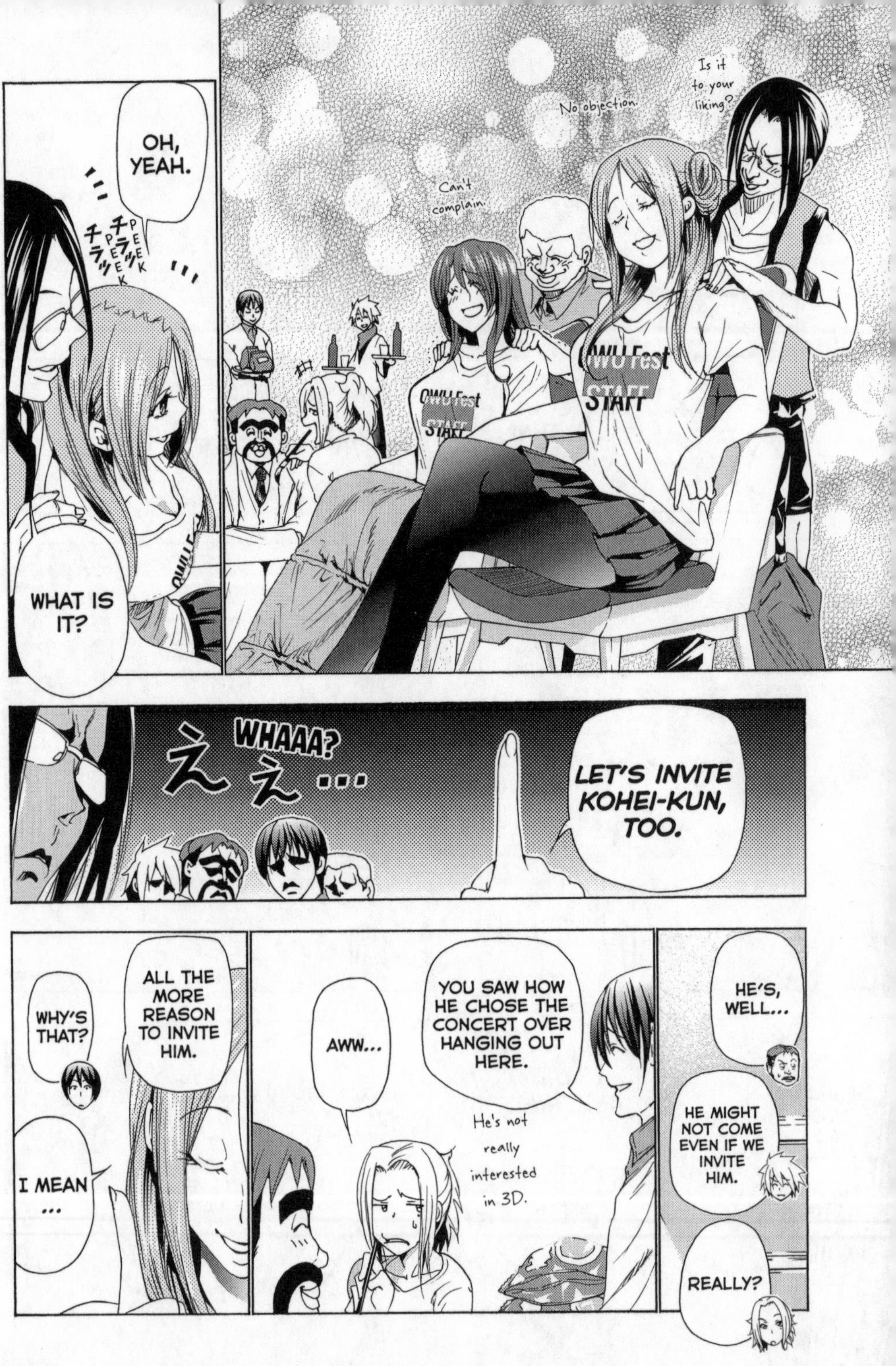
Is it to your liking?
No objection.
Can't complain.
OH, YEAH.
チラッチラッ
PEEK PEEK
WHAT IS IT?
LET'S INVITE KOHEI-KUN, TOO.
WHAAA?
えぇ...
HE'S, WELL...
HE MIGHT NOT COME EVEN IF WE INVITE HIM.
REALLY?
YOU SAW HOW HE CHOSE THE CONCERT OVER HANGING OUT HERE.
AWW...
He's not really interested in 3D.
ALL THE MORE REASON TO INVITE HIM.
WHY'S THAT?
I MEAN...

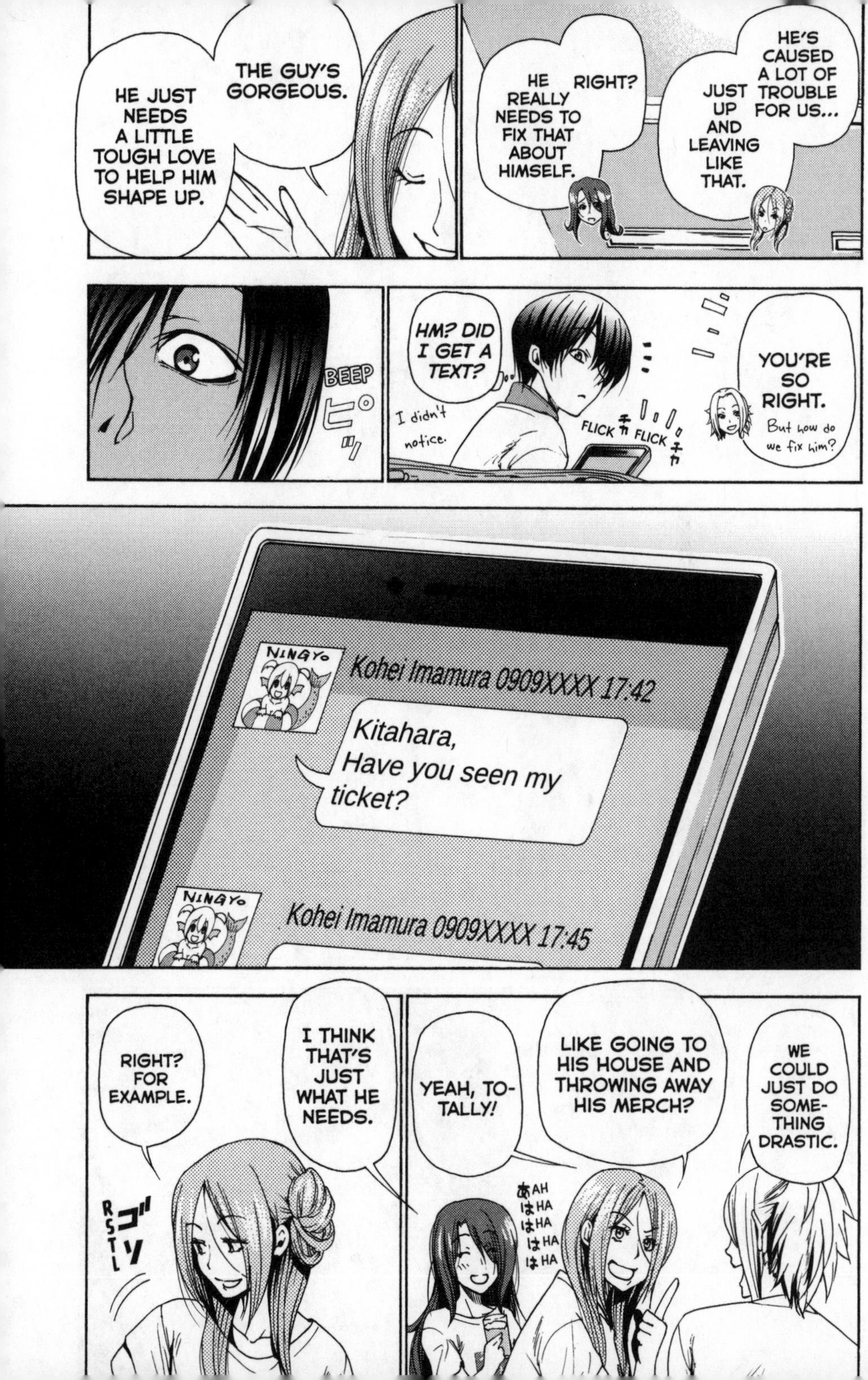
HE'S CAUSED A LOT OF TROUBLE FOR US...
JUST UP AND LEAVING LIKE THAT.
RIGHT?
HE REALLY NEEDS TO FIX THAT ABOUT HIMSELF.
THE GUY'S GORGEOUS.
HE JUST NEEDS A LITTLE TOUGH LOVE TO HELP HIM SHAPE UP.
YOU'RE SO RIGHT.
But how do we fix him?
FLICK FLICK
HM? DID I GET A TEXT?
I didn't notice.
BEEP
NINGYO
Kohei Imamura 0909XXXX 17:42
Kitahara,
Have you seen my ticket?
NINGYO
Kohei Imamura 0909XXXX 17:45
WE COULD JUST DO SOMETHING DRASTIC.
LIKE GOING TO HIS HOUSE AND THROWING AWAY HIS MERCH?
YEAH, TOTALLY!
AH HA HA HA HA
I THINK THAT'S JUST WHAT HE NEEDS.
RIGHT? FOR EXAMPLE.
RSTL

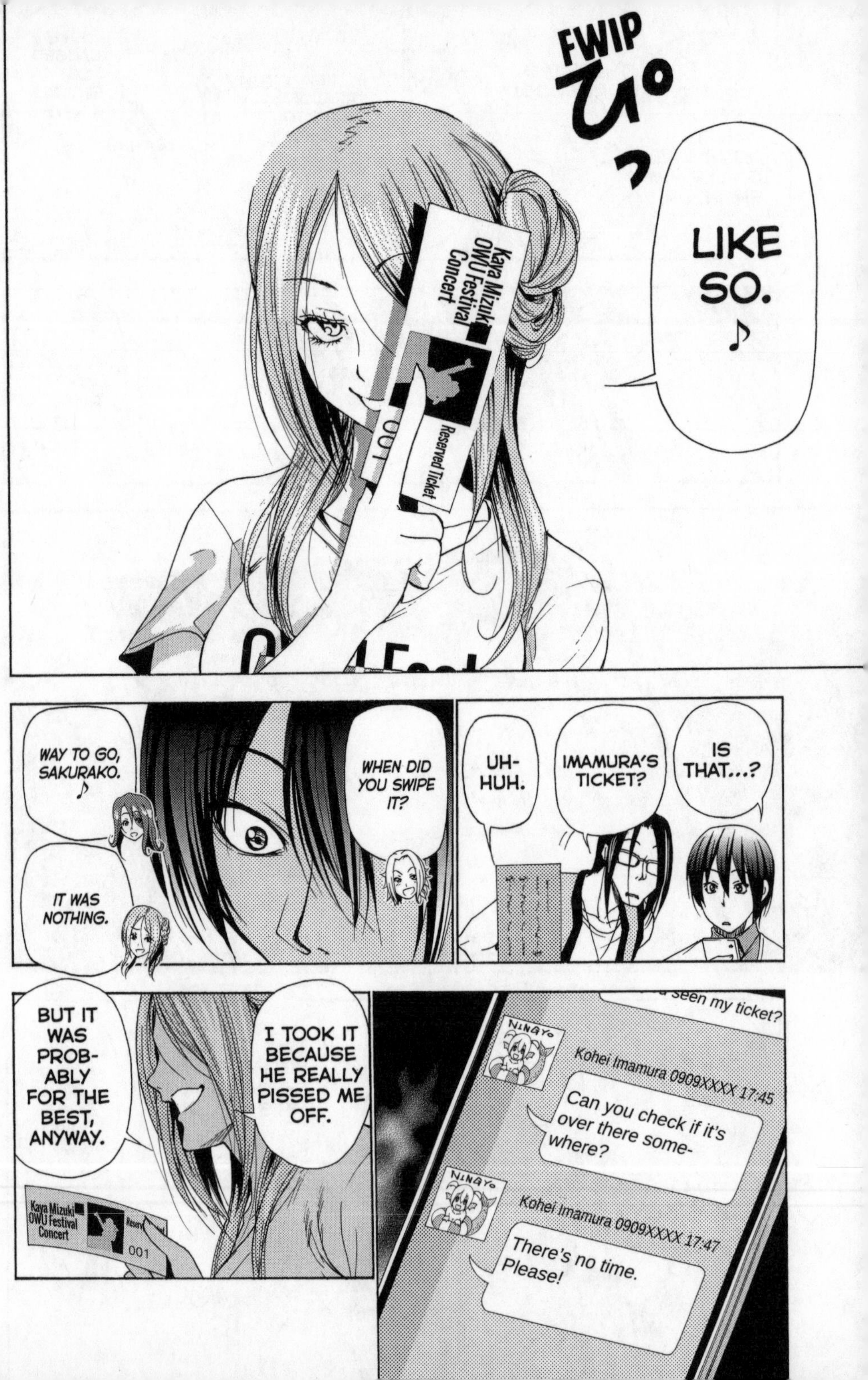
FWIP
ぴっ
LIKE SO. ♪
Kaya Mizuki OWU Festival Concert
Reserved Ticket
001
IS THAT...?
IMAMURA'S TICKET?
UH-HUH.
WHEN DID YOU SWIPE IT?
WAY TO GO, SAKURAKO. ♪
IT WAS NOTHING.
seen my ticket?
Kohei Imamura 0909XXXX 17:45
Can you check if it's over there some-where?
Kohei Imamura 0909XXXX 17:47
There's no time. Please!
I TOOK IT BECAUSE HE REALLY PISSED ME OFF.
BUT IT WAS PROB-ABLY FOR THE BEST, ANYWAY.
Kaya Mizuki OWU Festival Concert
001

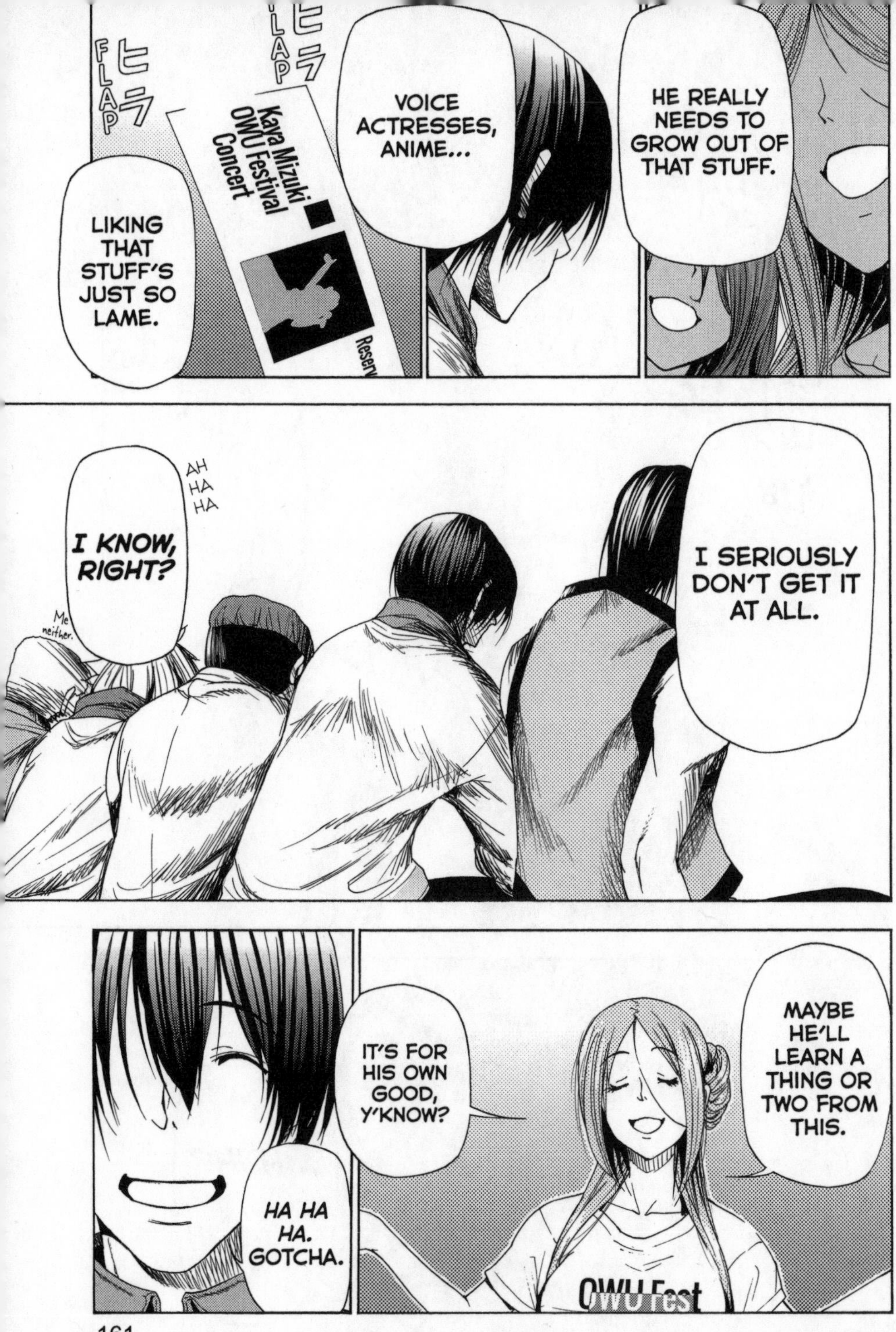
HE REALLY NEEDS TO GROW OUT OF THAT STUFF.
VOICE ACTRESSES, ANIME...
ヒラ FLAP
ヒラ FLAP
Kaya Mizuki OWU Festival Concert
Reserv
LIKING THAT STUFF'S JUST SO LAME.
I SERIOUSLY DON'T GET IT AT ALL.
AH HA HA
I KNOW, RIGHT?
Me neither.
MAYBE HE'LL LEARN A THING OR TWO FROM THIS.
IT'S FOR HIS OWN GOOD, Y'KNOW?
OWU Fest
HA HA HA. GOTCHA.

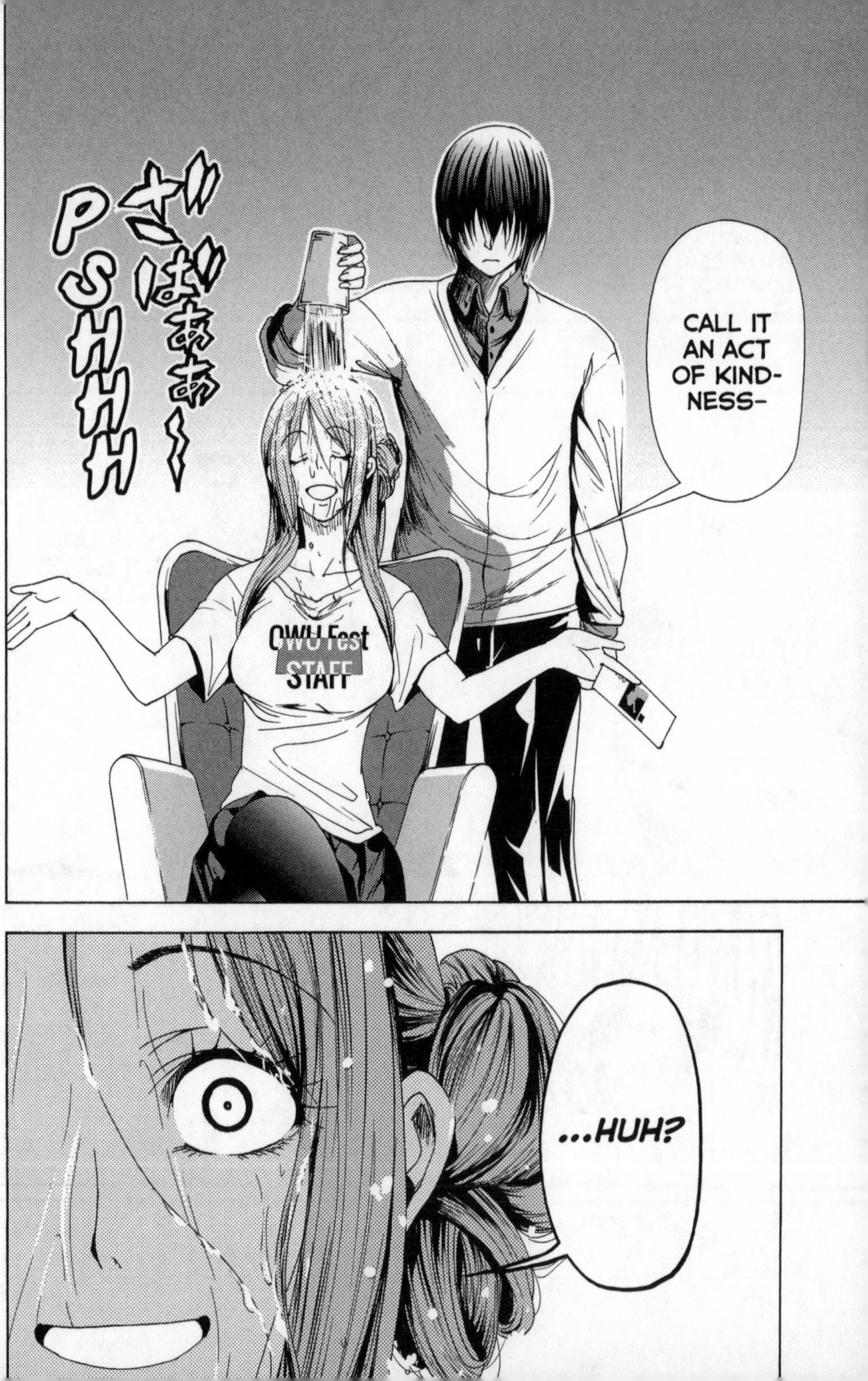
CALL IT AN ACT OF KIND-NESS-
ざばああ～
PSHHHH
OWU Fest STAFF
...HUH?

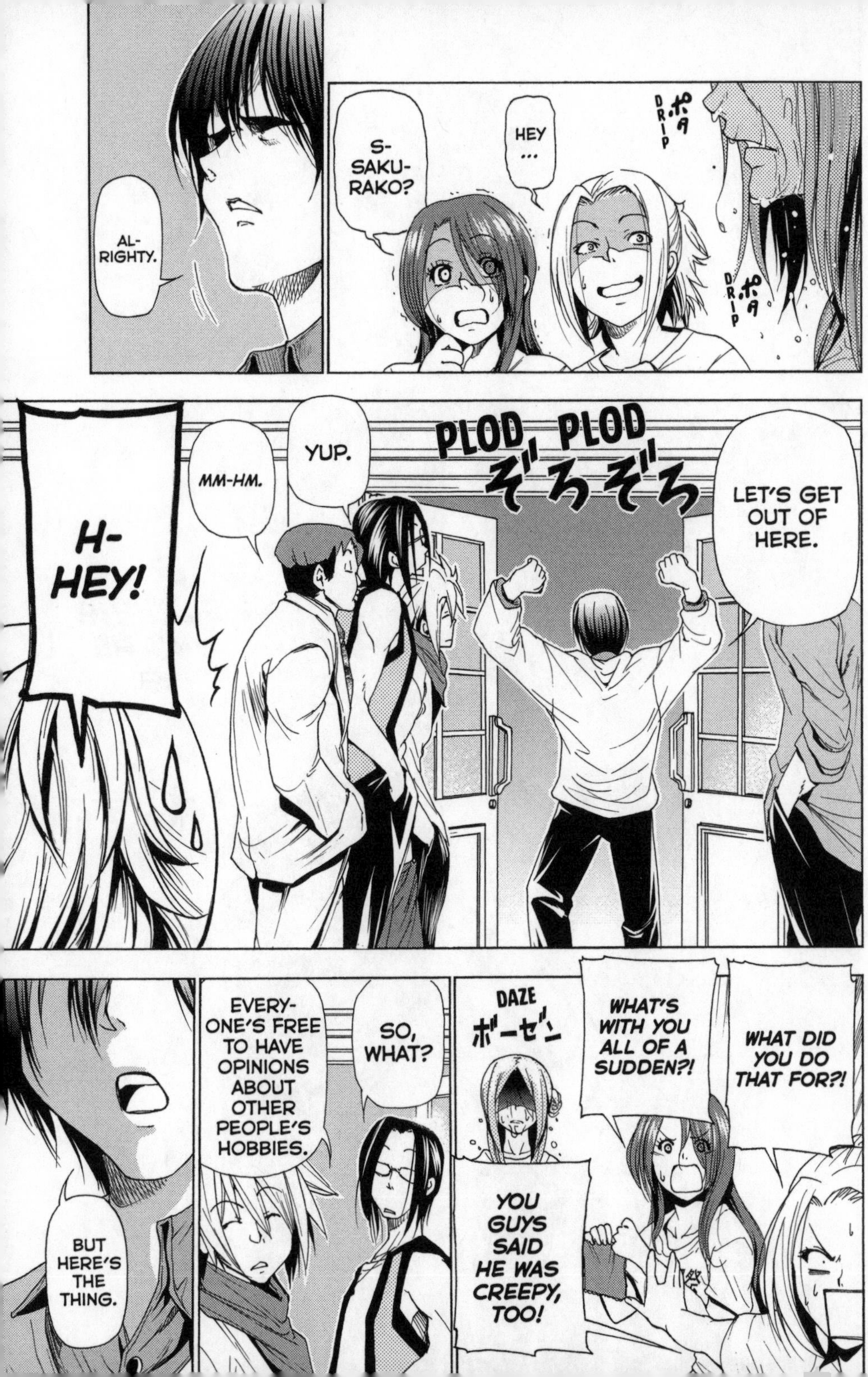
DRIP ポタ
HEY ...
S-SAKURAKO?
DRIP ポタ
ALRIGHTY.
LET'S GET OUT OF HERE.
PLOD PLOD ぞろぞろ
YUP.
MM-HM.
H-HEY!
WHAT DID YOU DO THAT FOR?!
WHAT'S WITH YOU ALL OF A SUDDEN?!
DAZE ボーゼン
YOU GUYS SAID HE WAS CREEPY, TOO!
SO, WHAT?
EVERYONE'S FREE TO HAVE OPINIONS ABOUT OTHER PEOPLE'S HOBBIES.
BUT HERE'S THE THING.

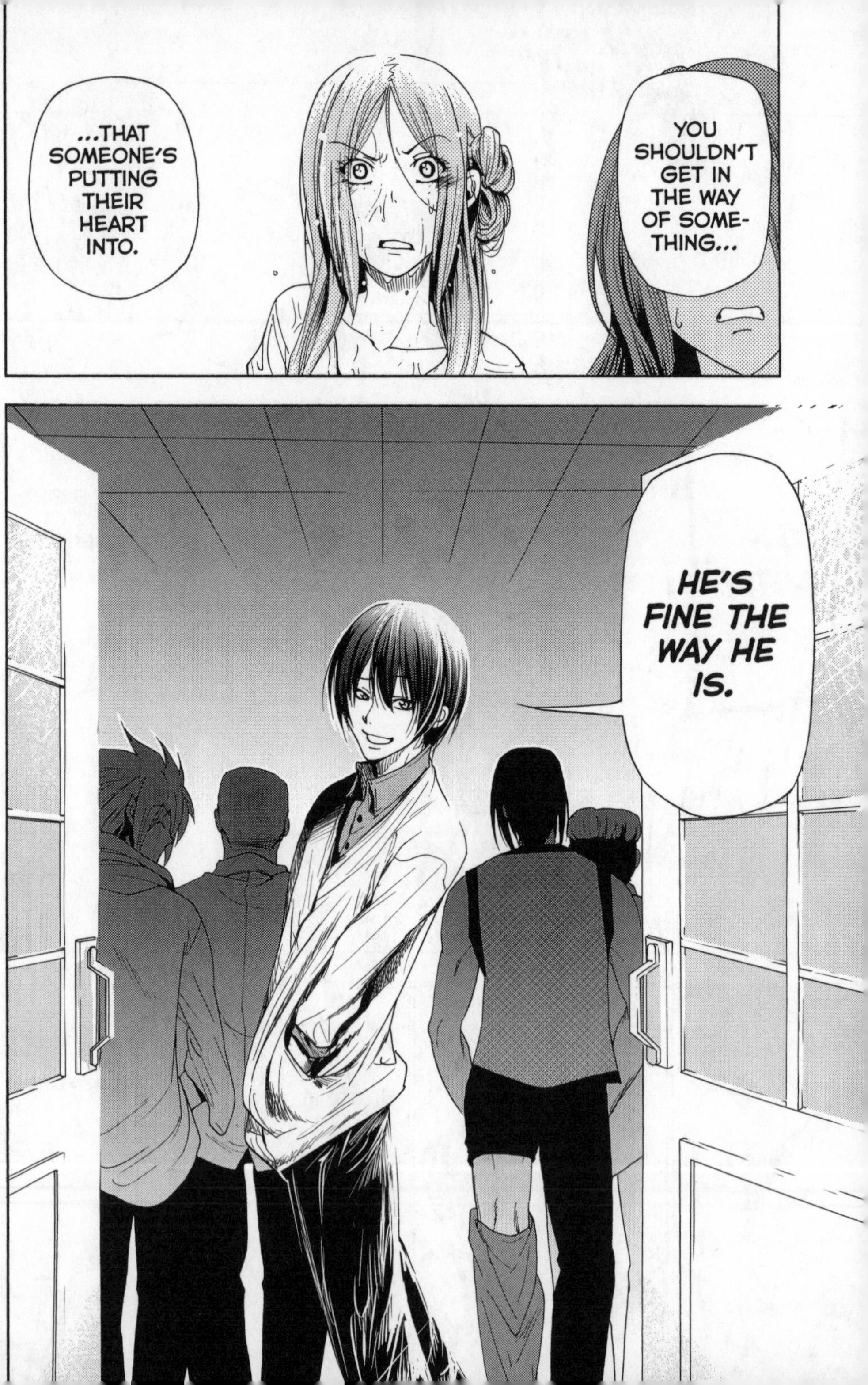
YOU SHOULDN'T GET IN THE WAY OF SOME-THING...
...THAT SOMEONE'S PUTTING THEIR HEART INTO.
HE'S FINE THE WAY HE IS.

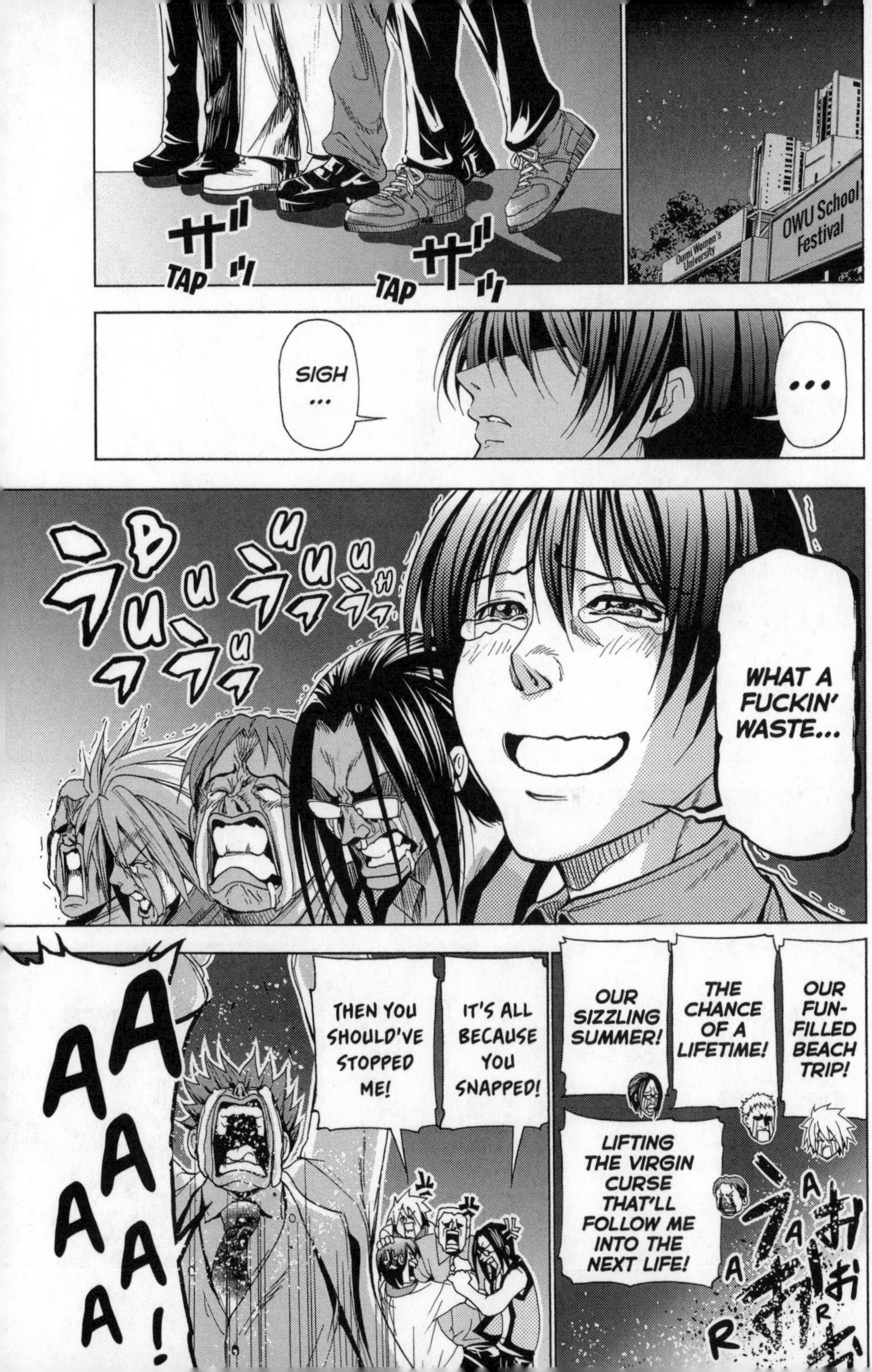
OWU School Festival
Oumi Women's University
ザッ TAP
ザッ TAP
...
SIGH ...
!
WHAT A FUCKIN' WASTE...
BUUUUUUH
OUR FUN-FILLED BEACH TRIP!
THE CHANCE OF A LIFETIME!
OUR SIZZLING SUMMER!
LIFTING THE VIRGIN CURSE THAT'LL FOLLOW ME INTO THE NEXT LIFE!
AAARR
IT'S ALL BECAUSE YOU SNAPPED!
THEN YOU SHOULD'VE STOPPED ME!
AAAAAA!

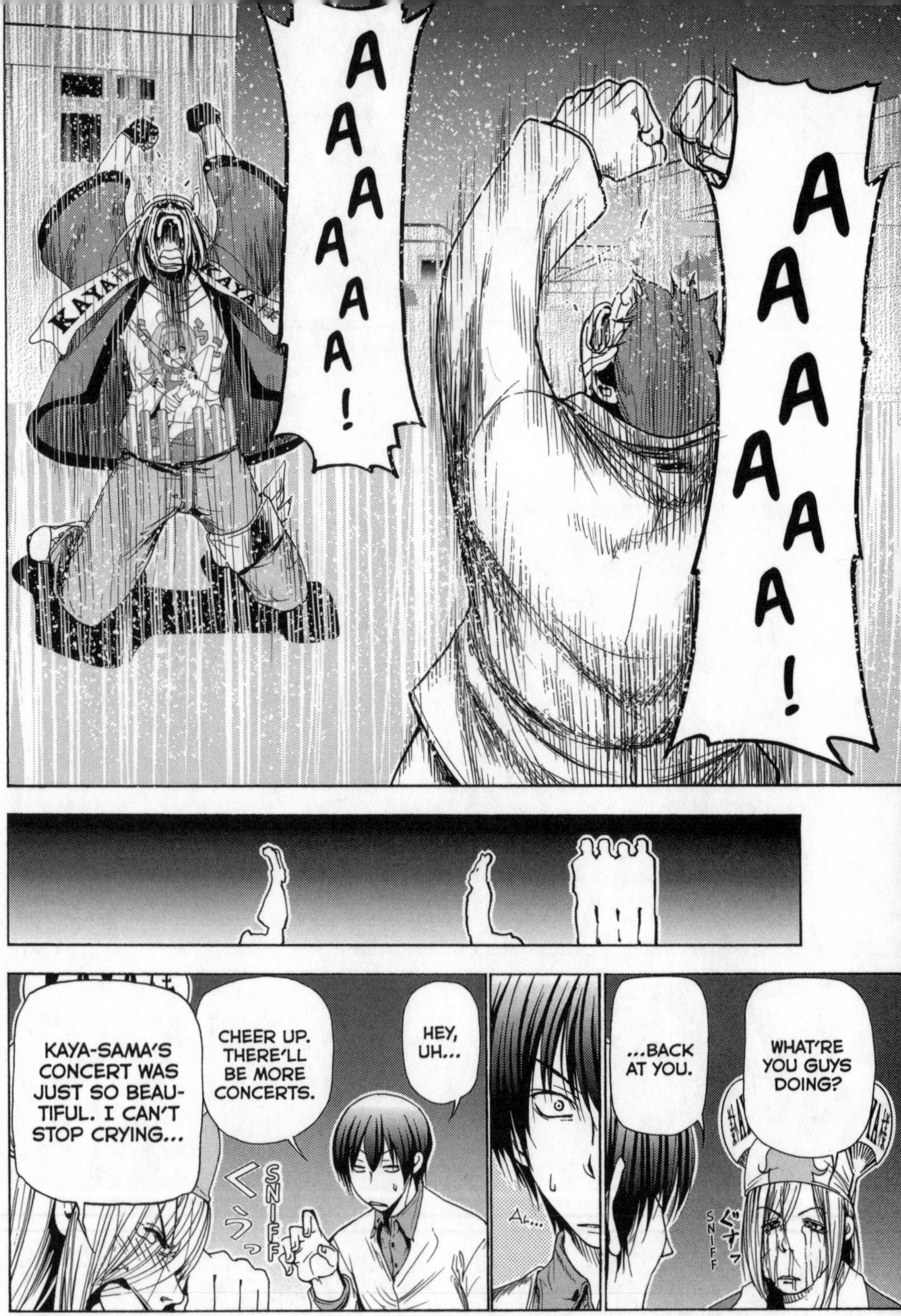
AAAAAA!
AAAAAA!
KAYA
KAYA
WHAT'RE YOU GUYS DOING?
ぐすっ SNIFF
...BACK AT YOU.
Ah...
HEY, UH...
CHEER UP. THERE'LL BE MORE CONCERTS.
KAYA-SAMA'S CONCERT WAS JUST SO BEAU-TIFUL. I CAN'T STOP CRYING...
くうっ SNIFF

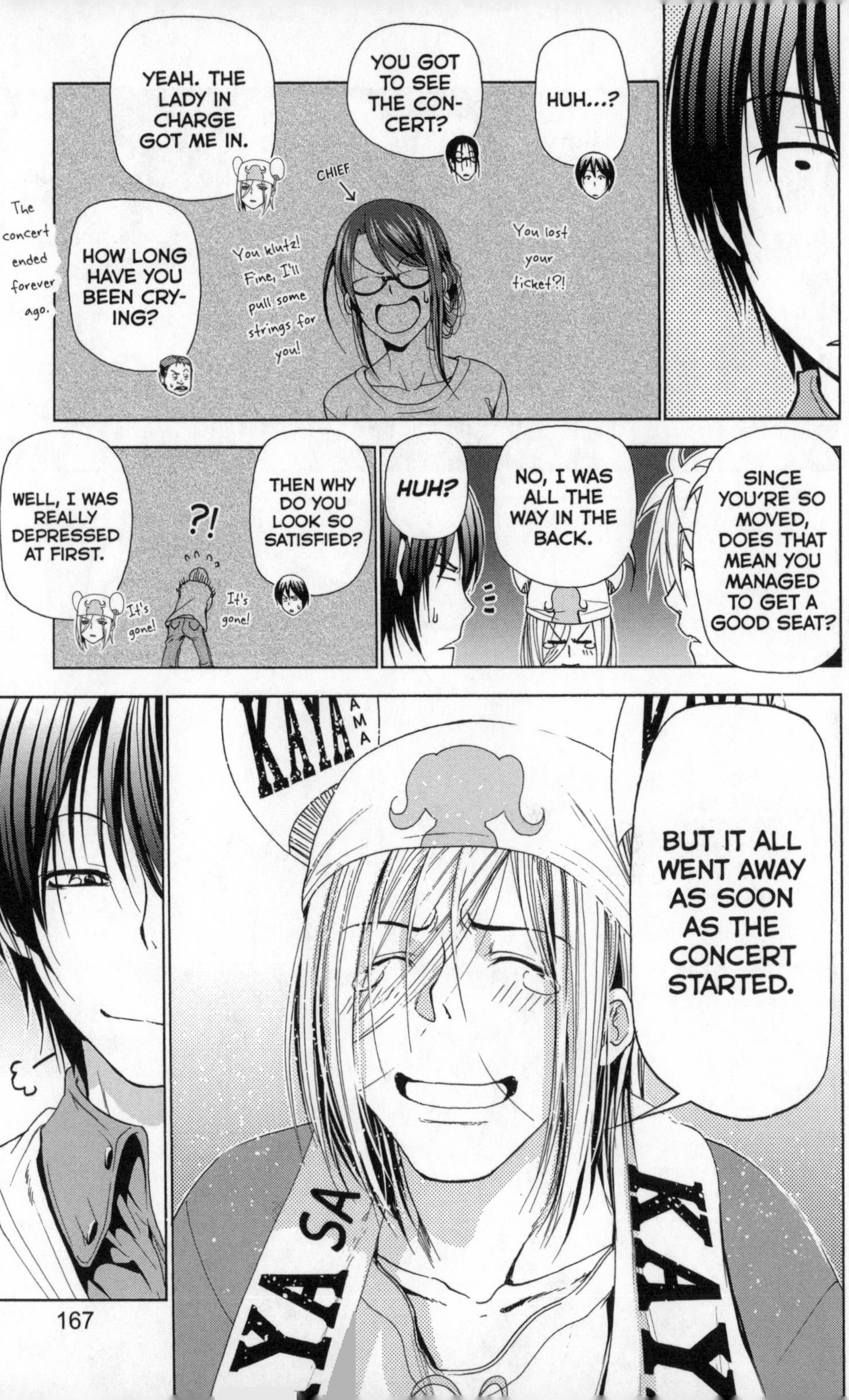
HUH...?
YOU GOT TO SEE THE CONCERT?
YEAH. THE LADY IN CHARGE GOT ME IN.
CHIEF
You lost your ticket?!
You klutz! Fine, I'll pull some strings for you!
HOW LONG HAVE YOU BEEN CRYING?
The concert ended forever ago.
SINCE YOU'RE SO MOVED, DOES THAT MEAN YOU MANAGED TO GET A GOOD SEAT?
NO, I WAS ALL THE WAY IN THE BACK.
HUH?
THEN WHY DO YOU LOOK SO SATISFIED?
?!
It's gone!
It's gone!
WELL, I WAS REALLY DEPRESSED AT FIRST.
BUT IT ALL WENT AWAY AS SOON AS THE CONCERT STARTED.

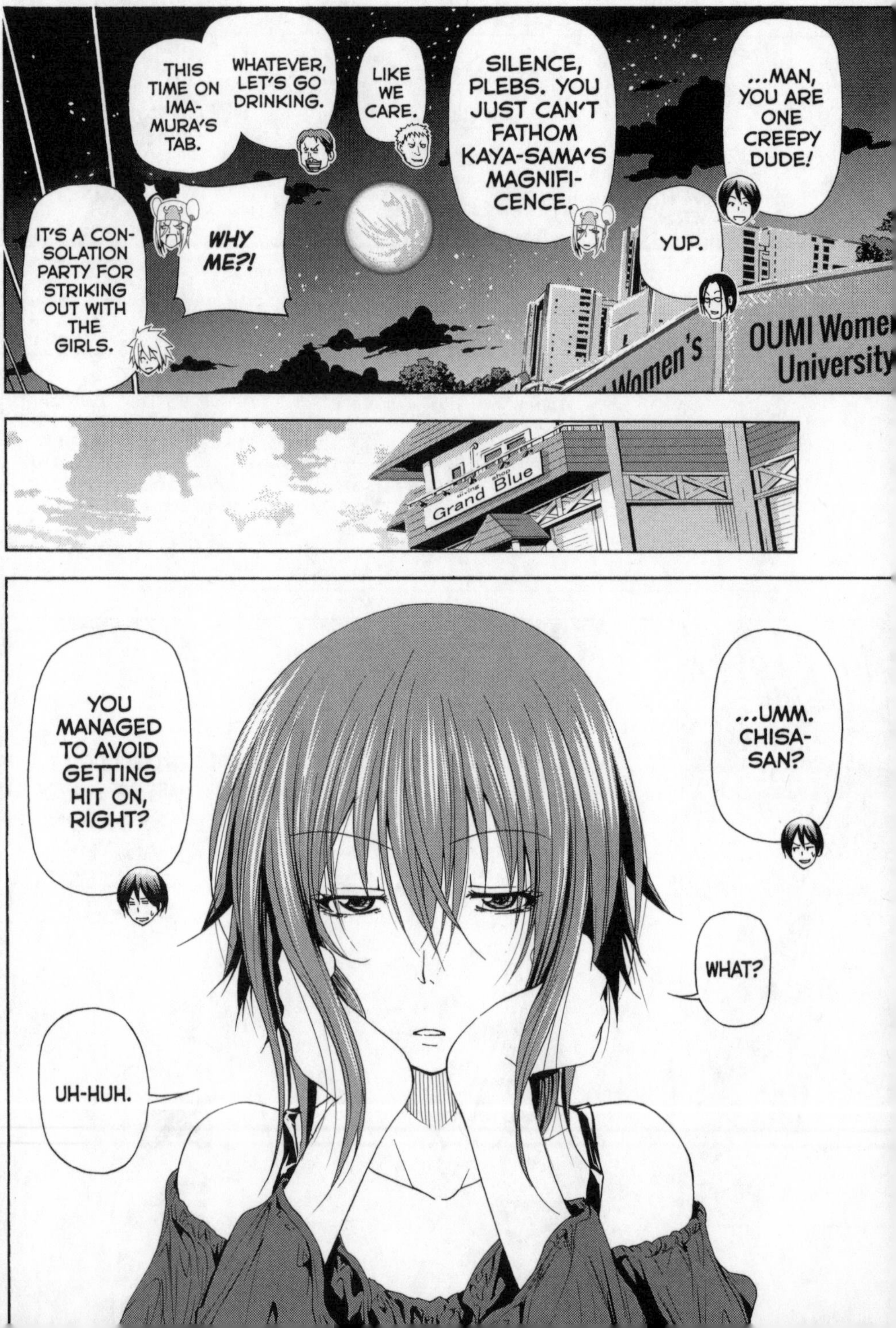
OUMI Women's University
Women's
...MAN, YOU ARE ONE CREEPY DUDE!
YUP.
SILENCE, PLEBS. YOU JUST CAN'T FATHOM KAYA-SAMA'S MAGNIFICENCE.
LIKE WE CARE.
WHATEVER, LET'S GO DRINKING.
THIS TIME ON IMAMURA'S TAB.
WHY ME?!
IT'S A CONSOLATION PARTY FOR STRIKING OUT WITH THE GIRLS.
diving shop
Grand Blue
...UMM. CHISA-SAN?
YOU MANAGED TO AVOID GETTING HIT ON, RIGHT?
WHAT?
UH-HUH.

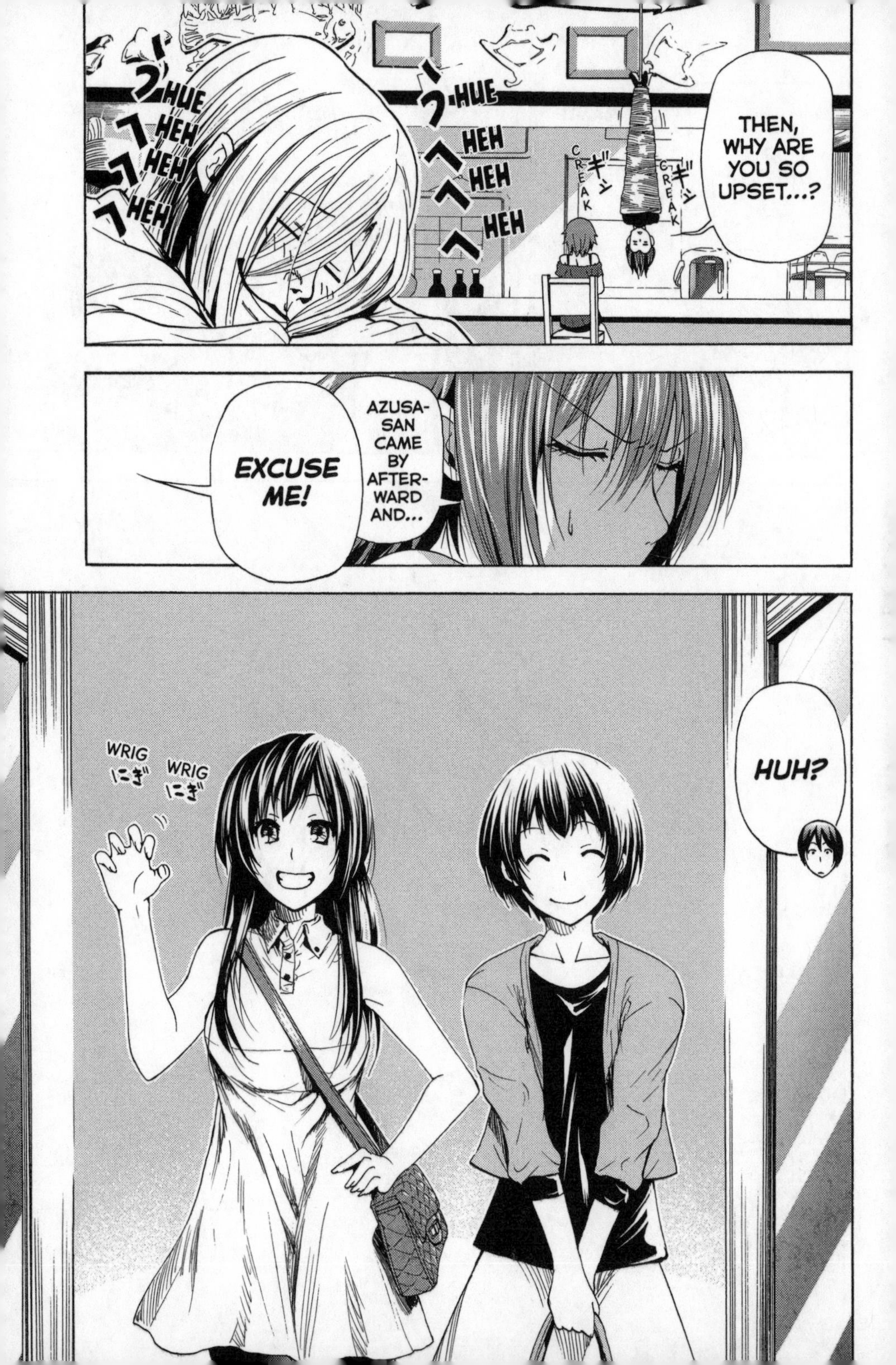
THEN, WHY ARE YOU SO UPSET...?
CREAK CREAK
HUE HEH HEH HEH
HUE HEH HEH HEH
AZUSA-SAN CAME BY AFTER-WARD AND...
EXCUSE ME!
HUH?
WRIG にぎ WRIG にぎ

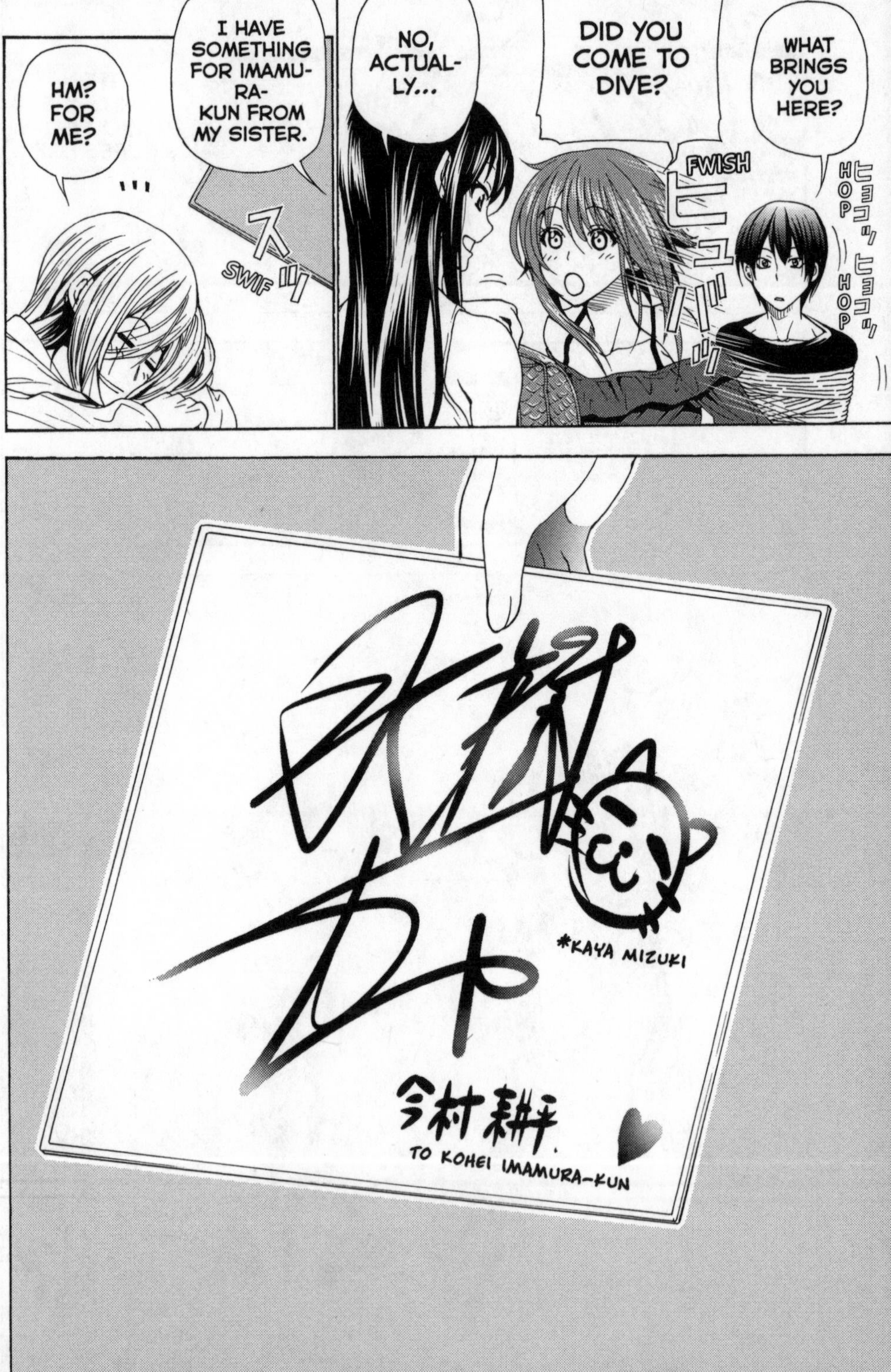
WHAT BRINGS YOU HERE?
ヒョコッ ヒョコッ
HOP HOP
DID YOU COME TO DIVE?
ヒュバッ
FWISH
NO, ACTUAL-LY...
I HAVE SOMETHING FOR IMAMU-RA-KUN FROM MY SISTER.
スッ
SWIF
HM? FOR ME?
...
*KAYA MIZUKI
今村耕平
TO KOHEI IMAMURA-KUN

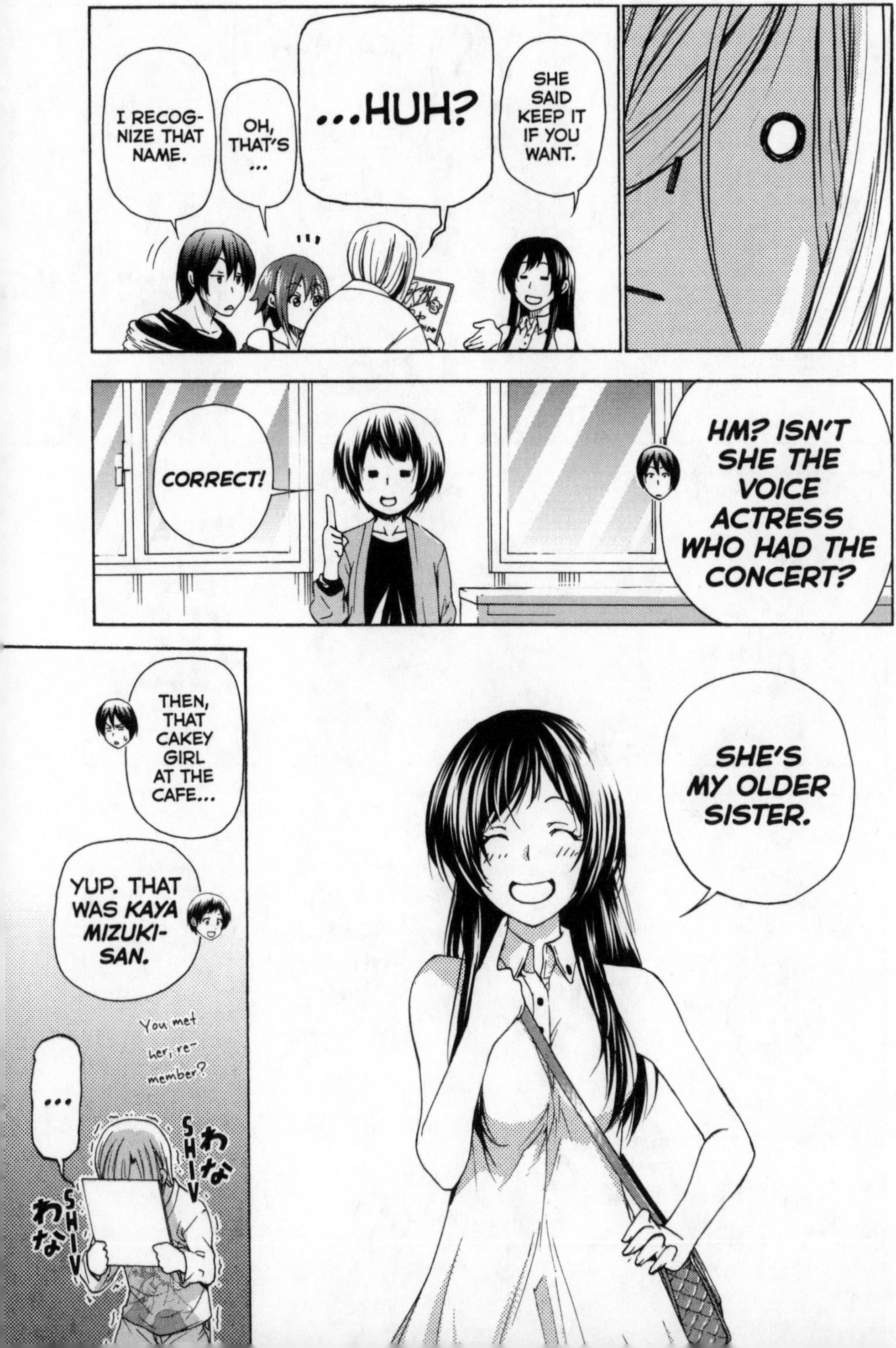
SHE SAID KEEP IT IF YOU WANT.
...HUH?
OH, THAT'S ...
I RECOG-NIZE THAT NAME.
HM? ISN'T SHE THE VOICE ACTRESS WHO HAD THE CONCERT?
CORRECT!
SHE'S MY OLDER SISTER.
THEN, THAT CAKEY GIRL AT THE CAFE...
YUP. THAT WAS *KAYA MIZUKI-SAN.*
You met her, re-member?
...
わな SHIV
わな SHIV

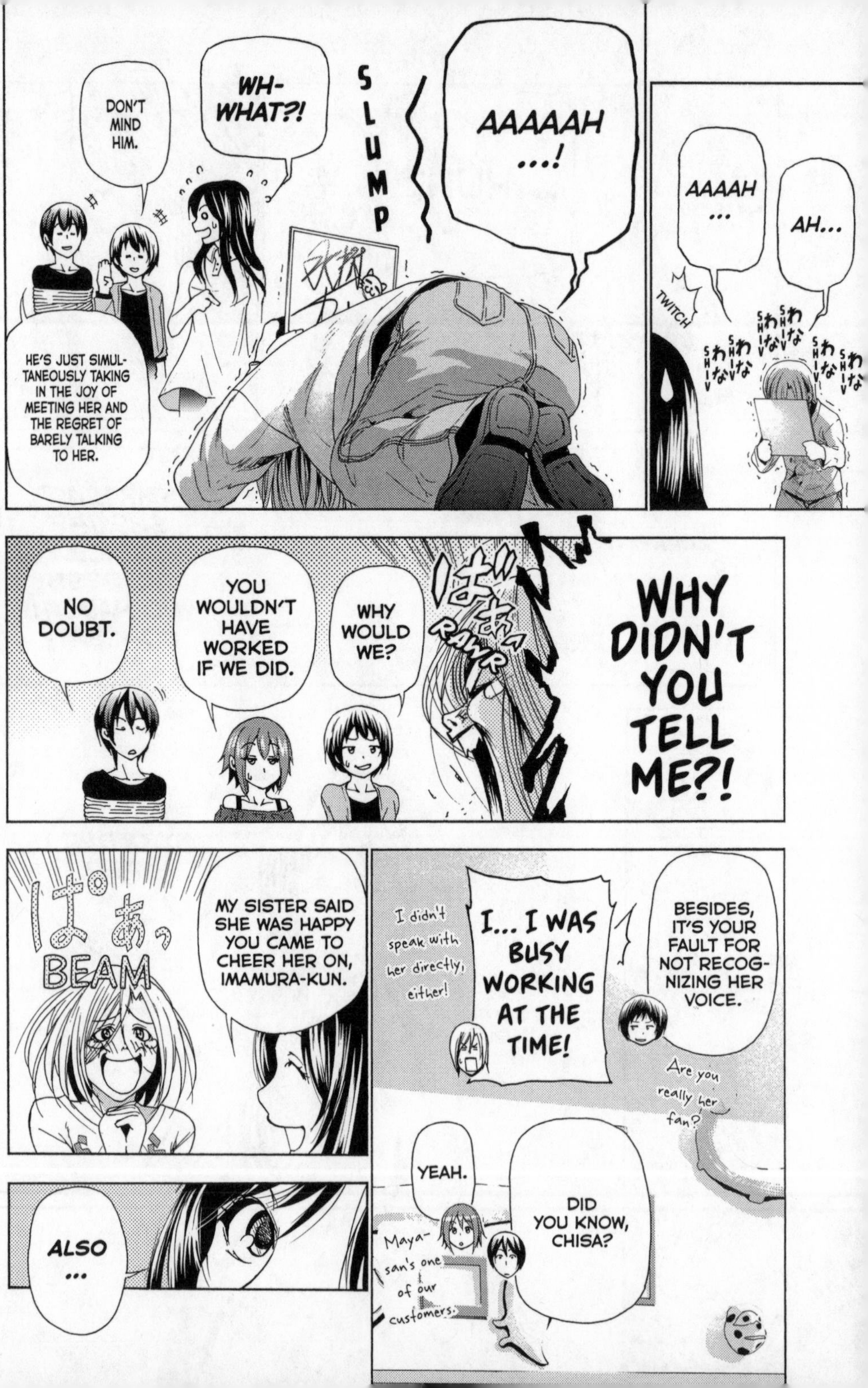
AAAAH ...
AH...
TWITCH
SHIV わな SHIV わな SHIV わな SHIV わな SHIV わな SHIV わな
AAAAAH ...!
SLUMP
WH-WHAT?!
DON'T MIND HIM.
HE'S JUST SIMULTANEOUSLY TAKING IN THE JOY OF MEETING HER AND THE REGRET OF BARELY TALKING TO HER.
WHY DIDN'T YOU TELL ME?!
ばぁ RAWR
WHY WOULD WE?
YOU WOULDN'T HAVE WORKED IF WE DID.
NO DOUBT.
BESIDES, IT'S YOUR FAULT FOR NOT RECOGNIZING HER VOICE.
I... I WAS BUSY WORKING AT THE TIME!
I didn't speak with her directly, either!
Are you really her fan?
DID YOU KNOW, CHISA?
YEAH.
Maya-san's one of our customers.
ぱあっ BEAM
MY SISTER SAID SHE WAS HAPPY YOU CAME TO CHEER HER ON, IMAMURA-KUN.
ALSO ...

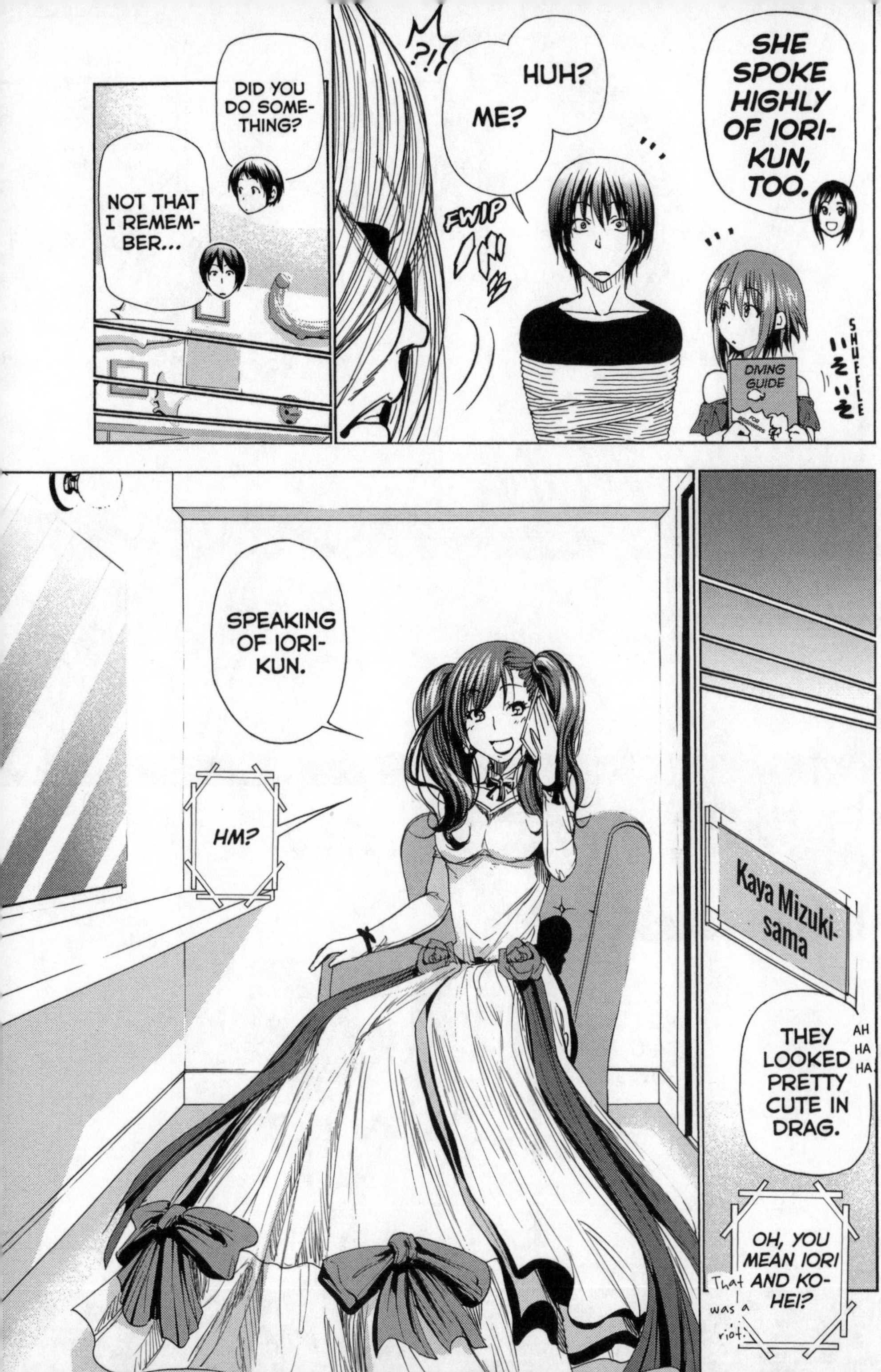
SHE SPOKE HIGHLY OF IORI-KUN, TOO.
...
...
SHUFFLE
いそいそ
?!
HUH? ME?
FWIP
DID YOU DO SOME-THING?
NOT THAT I REMEM-BER...
Kaya Mizuki-sama
THEY LOOKED PRETTY CUTE IN DRAG.
AH HA HA!
OH, YOU MEAN IORI AND KO-HEI?
That was a riot.
SPEAKING OF IORI-KUN.
HM?

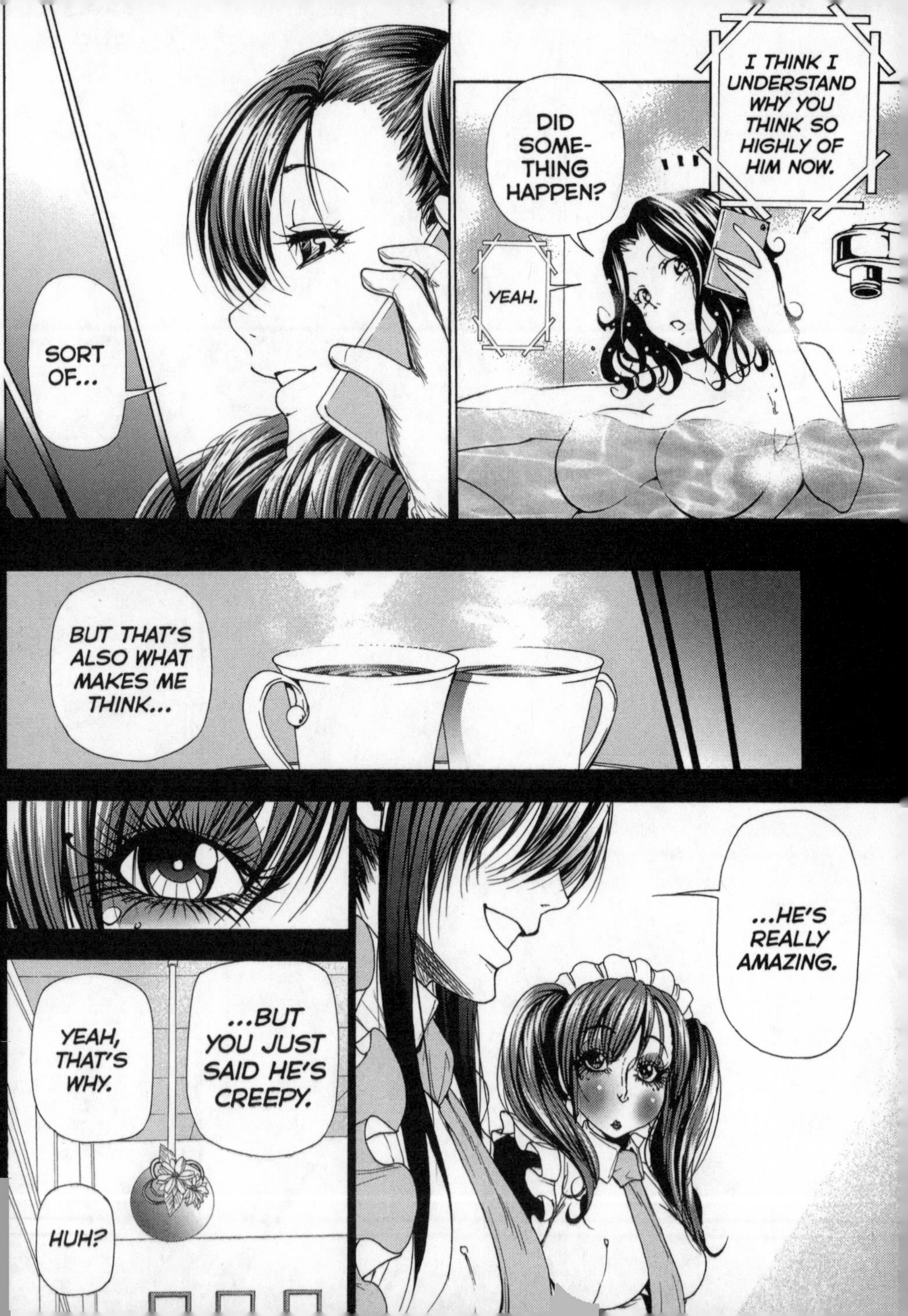
I THINK I UNDERSTAND WHY YOU THINK SO HIGHLY OF HIM NOW.
DID SOME-THING HAPPEN?
YEAH.
SORT OF...
BUT THAT'S ALSO WHAT MAKES ME THINK...
...HE'S REALLY AMAZING.
...BUT YOU JUST SAID HE'S CREEPY.
YEAH, THAT'S WHY.
HUH?

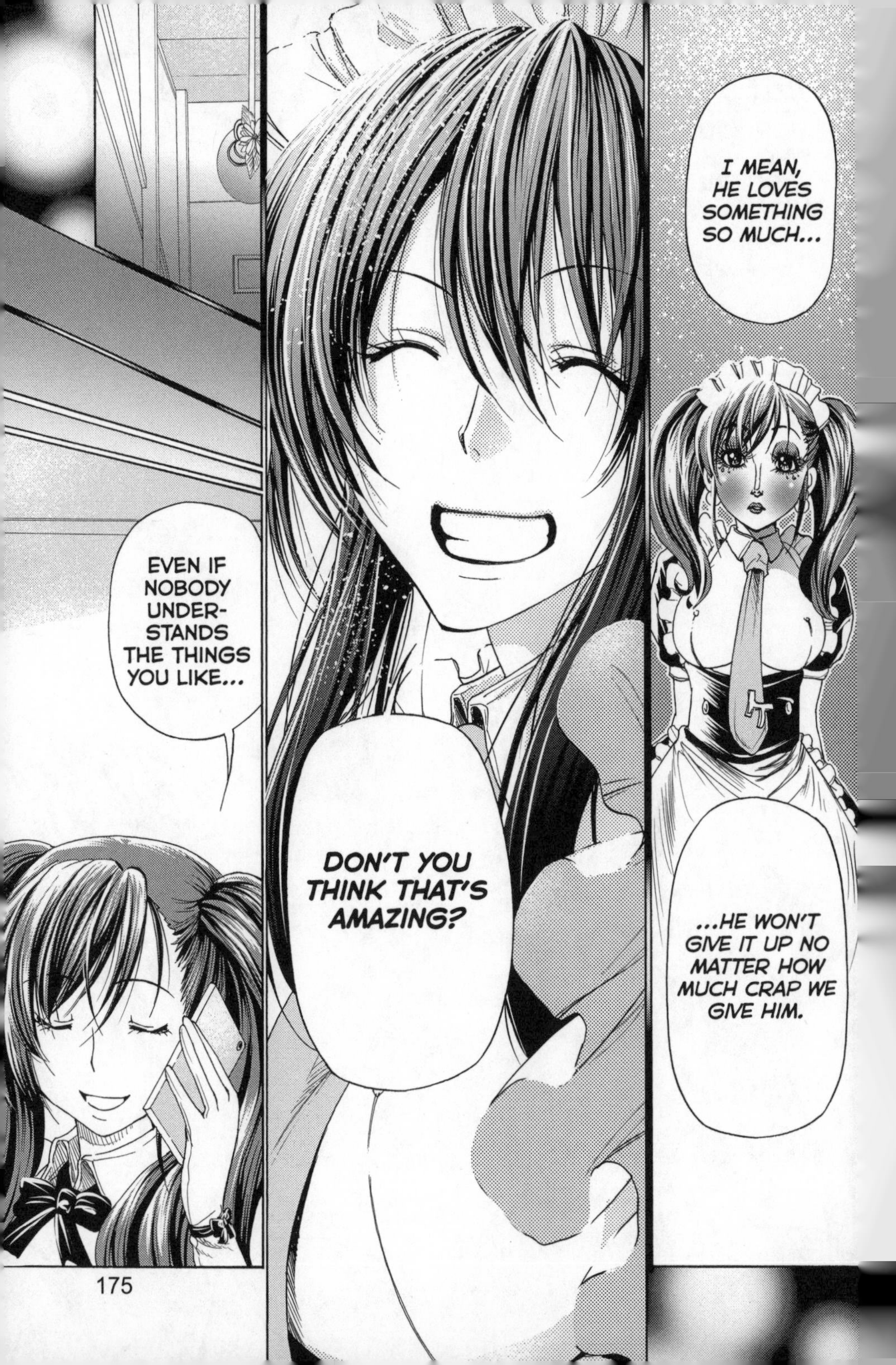
I MEAN, HE LOVES SOMETHING SO MUCH...
...HE WON'T GIVE IT UP NO MATTER HOW MUCH CRAP WE GIVE HIM.
DON'T YOU THINK THAT'S AMAZING?
EVEN IF NOBODY UNDER-STANDS THE THINGS YOU LIKE...

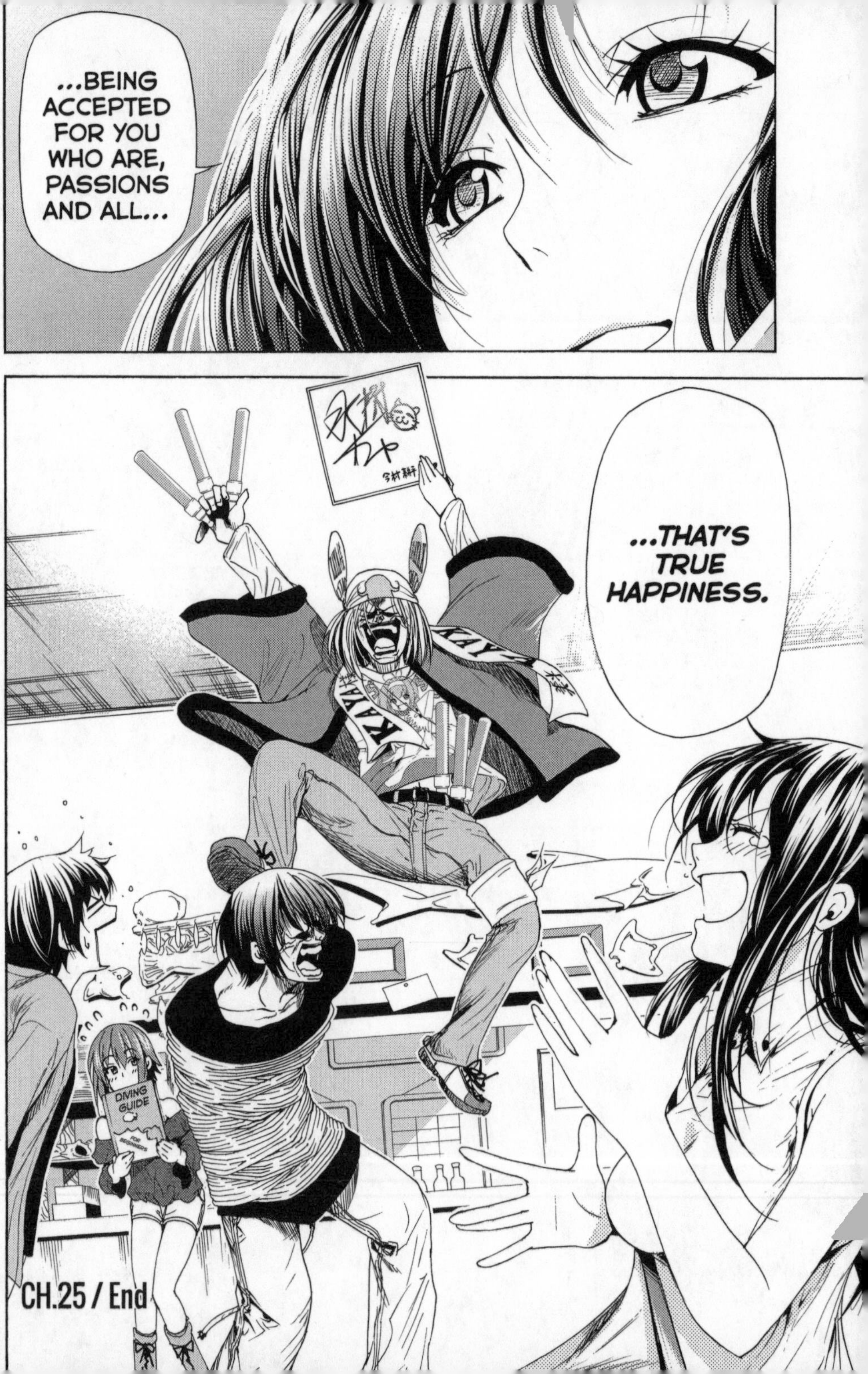
...BEING ACCEPTED FOR YOU WHO ARE, PASSIONS AND ALL...
...THAT'S TRUE HAPPINESS.
KAYA
DIVING GUIDE
CH.25 / End

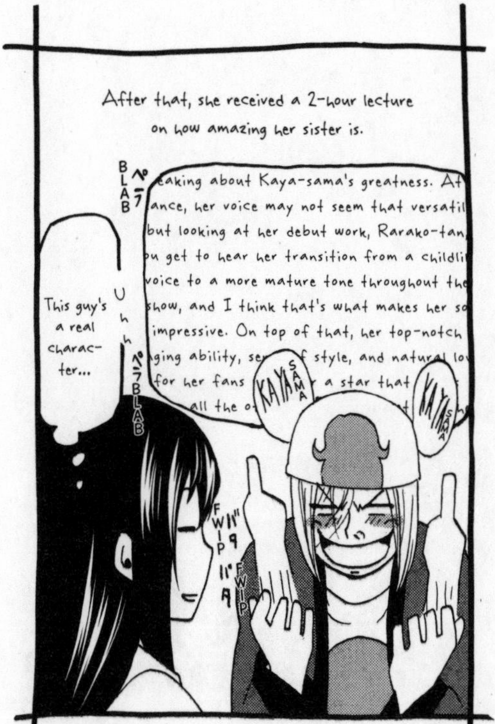
After that, she received a 2-hour lecture on how amazing her sister is.
BLAB
eaking about Kaya-sama's greatness. At ance, her voice may not seem that versatil but looking at her debut work, Rarako-tan, u get to hear her transition from a childli voice to a more mature tone throughout the show, and I think that's what makes her so impressive. On top of that, her top-notch ging ability, se f style, and natural lo for her fans a star that all the o
KAYA SAMA
KAYA SAMA
BLAB
Uhh
This guy's a real charac-ter...
FWIP
FWIP

Grand Blue Dreaming

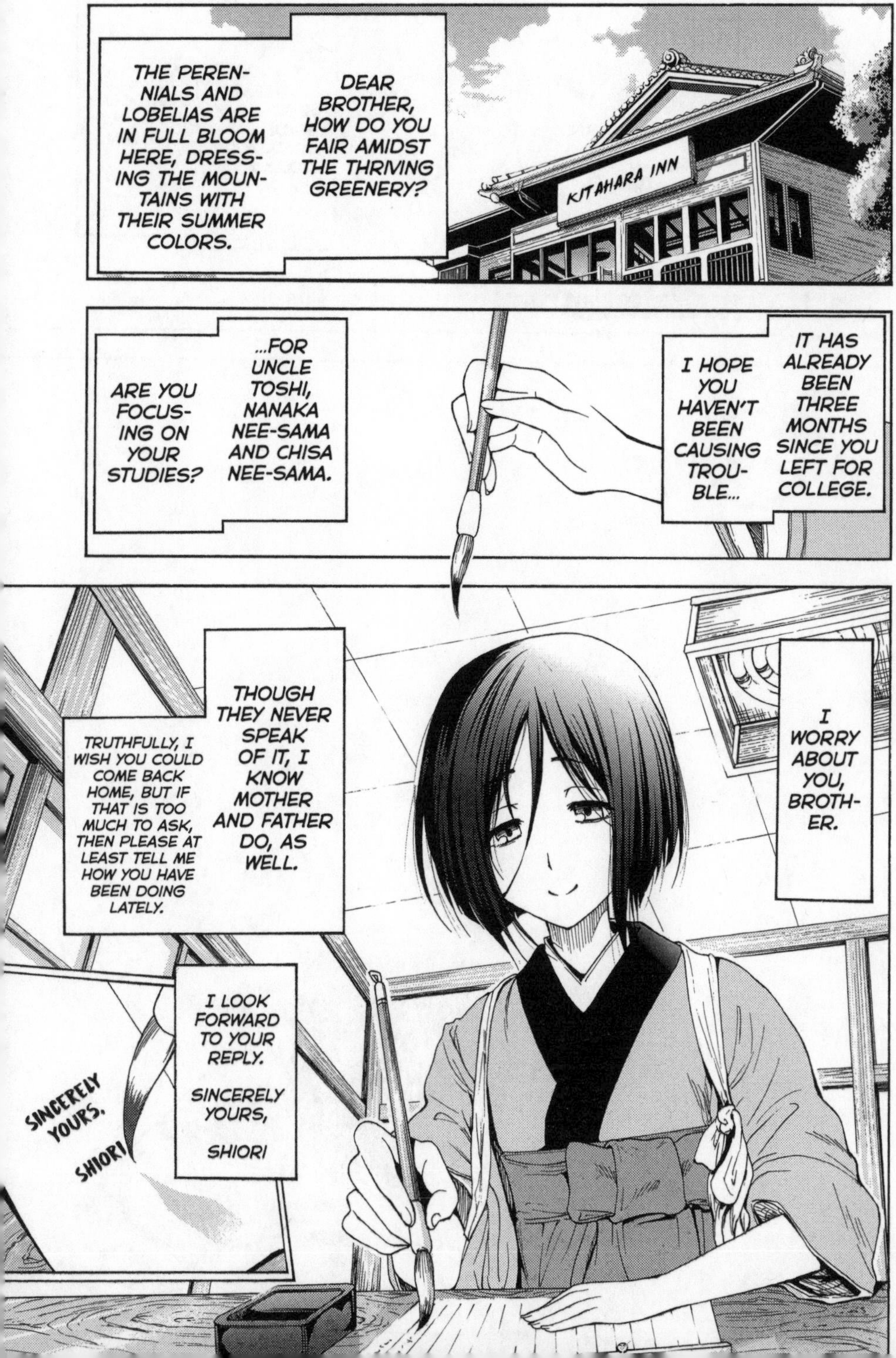
KITAHARA INN
DEAR BROTHER, HOW DO YOU FAIR AMIDST THE THRIVING GREENERY?
THE PEREN-NIALS AND LOBELIAS ARE IN FULL BLOOM HERE, DRESS-ING THE MOUN-TAINS WITH THEIR SUMMER COLORS.
IT HAS ALREADY BEEN THREE MONTHS SINCE YOU LEFT FOR COLLEGE.
I HOPE YOU HAVEN'T BEEN CAUSING TROU-BLE...
...FOR UNCLE TOSHI, NANAKA NEE-SAMA AND CHISA NEE-SAMA.
ARE YOU FOCUS-ING ON YOUR STUDIES?
I WORRY ABOUT YOU, BROTH-ER.
THOUGH THEY NEVER SPEAK OF IT, I KNOW MOTHER AND FATHER DO, AS WELL.
TRUTHFULLY, I WISH YOU COULD COME BACK HOME, BUT IF THAT IS TOO MUCH TO ASK, THEN PLEASE AT LEAST TELL ME HOW YOU HAVE BEEN DOING LATELY.
I LOOK FORWARD TO YOUR REPLY.
SINCERELY YOURS,
SHIORI
SINCERELY YOURS,
SHIORI

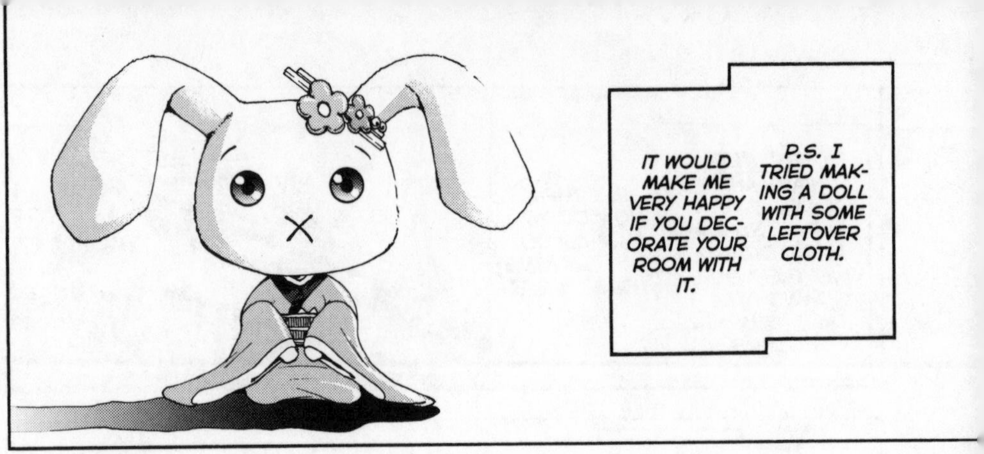
P.S. I TRIED MAKING A DOLL WITH SOME LEFTOVER CLOTH.
IT WOULD MAKE ME VERY HAPPY IF YOU DECORATE YOUR ROOM WITH IT.

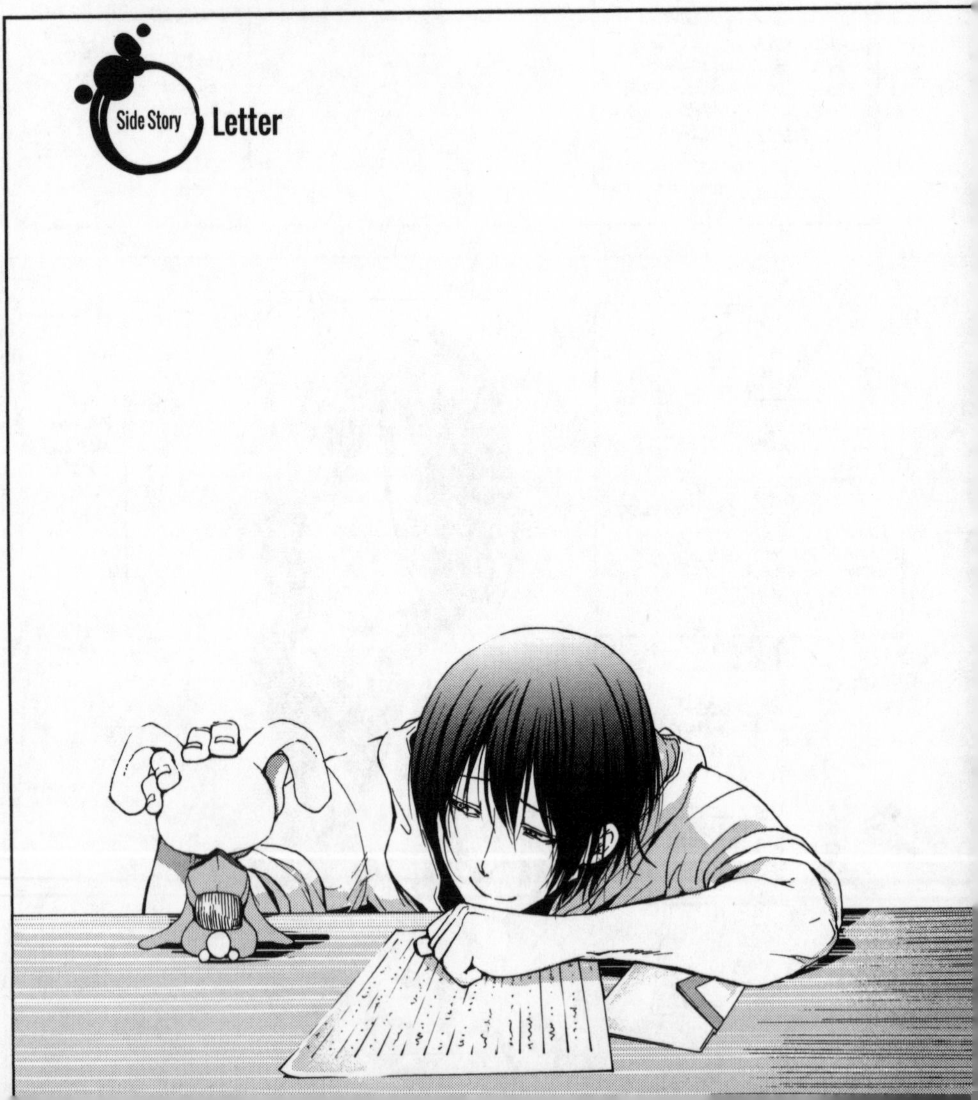
Side Story Letter

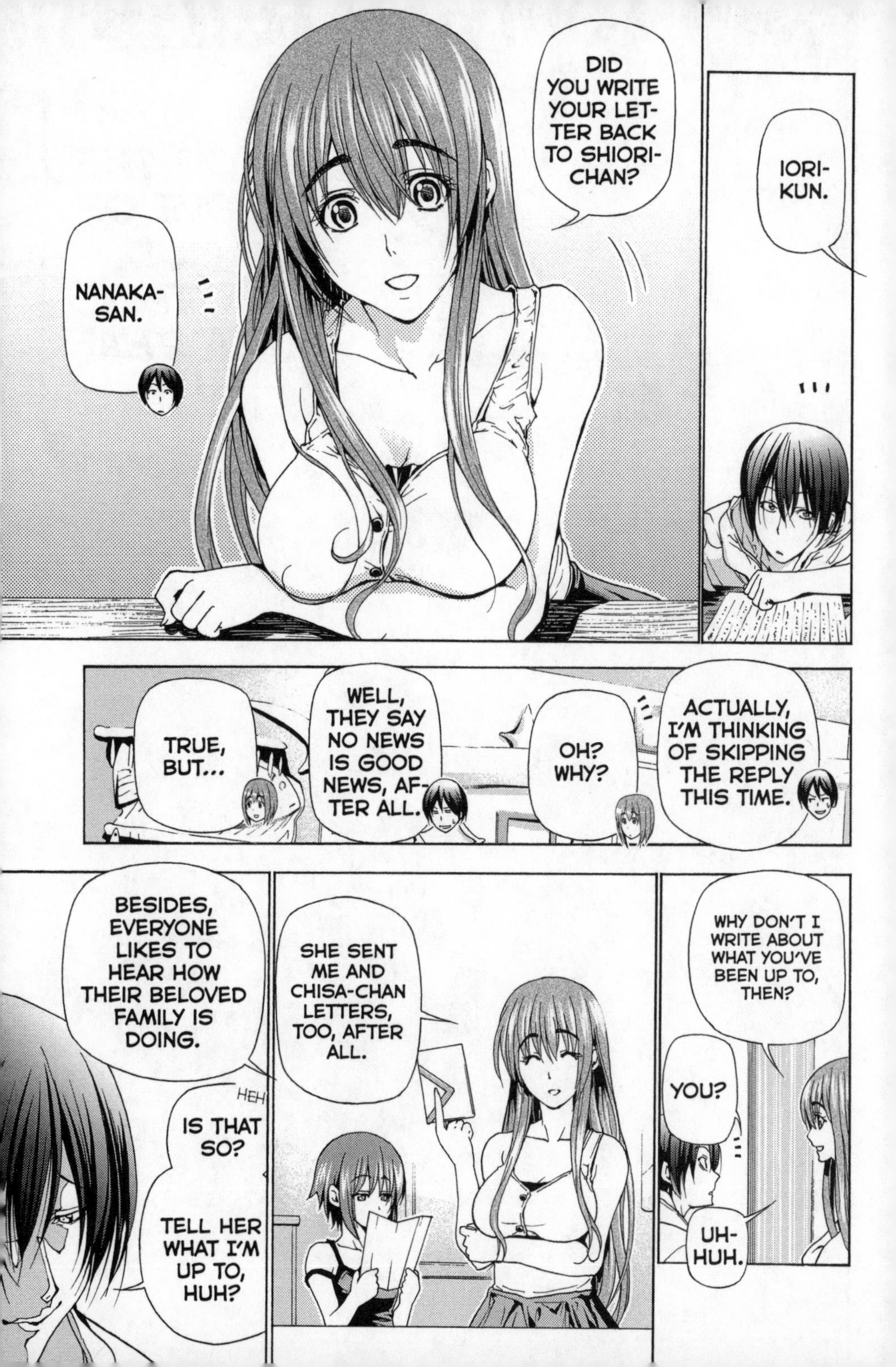
IORI-KUN.
DID YOU WRITE YOUR LETTER BACK TO SHIORI-CHAN?
NANAKA-SAN.
ACTUALLY, I'M THINKING OF SKIPPING THE REPLY THIS TIME.
OH? WHY?
WELL, THEY SAY NO NEWS IS GOOD NEWS, AFTER ALL.
TRUE, BUT...
WHY DON'T I WRITE ABOUT WHAT YOU'VE BEEN UP TO, THEN?
YOU?
UH-HUH.
SHE SENT ME AND CHISA-CHAN LETTERS, TOO, AFTER ALL.
BESIDES, EVERYONE LIKES TO HEAR HOW THEIR BELOVED FAMILY IS DOING.
HEH
IS THAT SO?
TELL HER WHAT I'M UP TO, HUH?

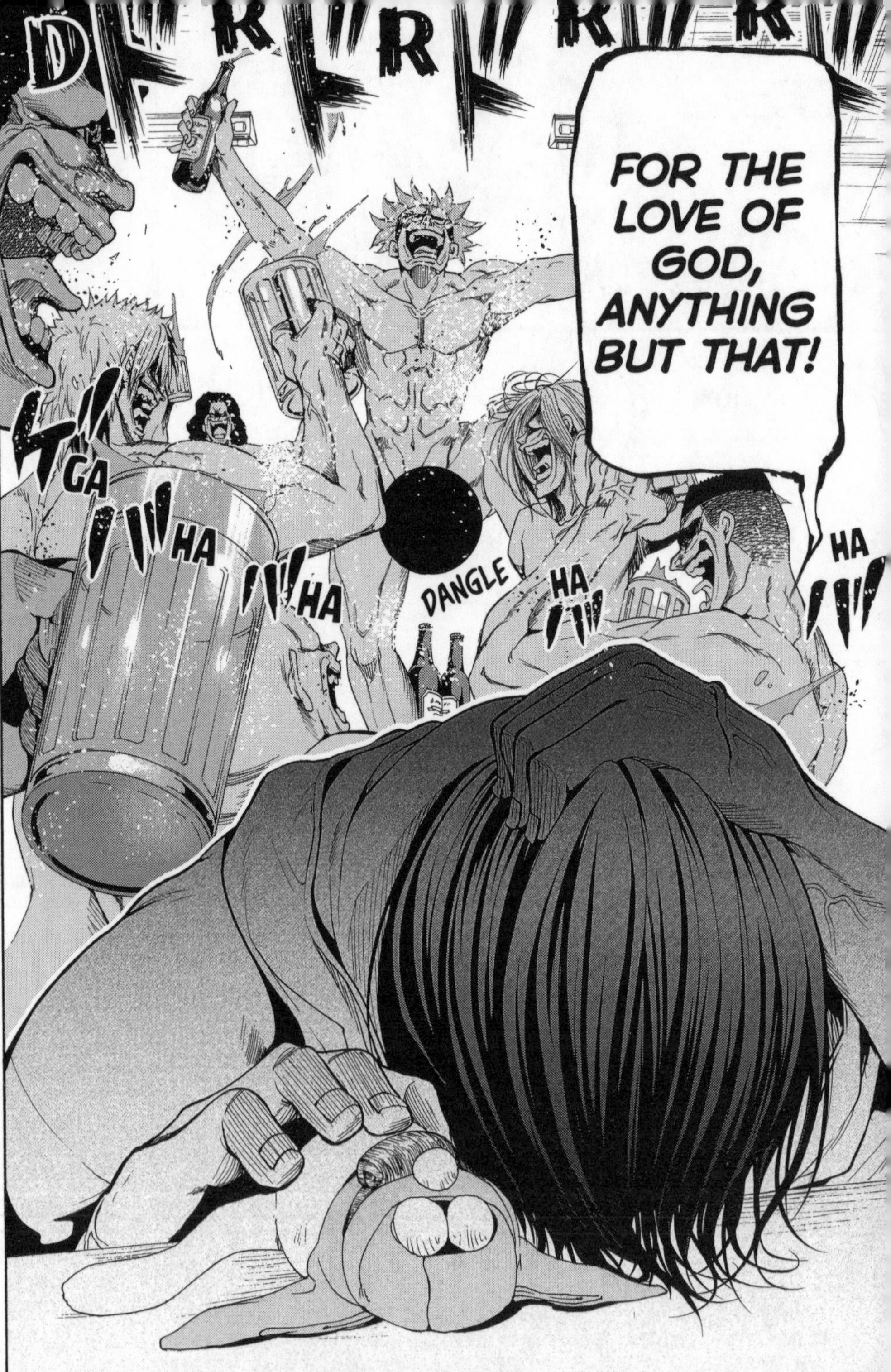
DRRRR
FOR THE LOVE OF GOD, ANYTHING BUT THAT!
HA
HA
DANGLE
GA HA HA

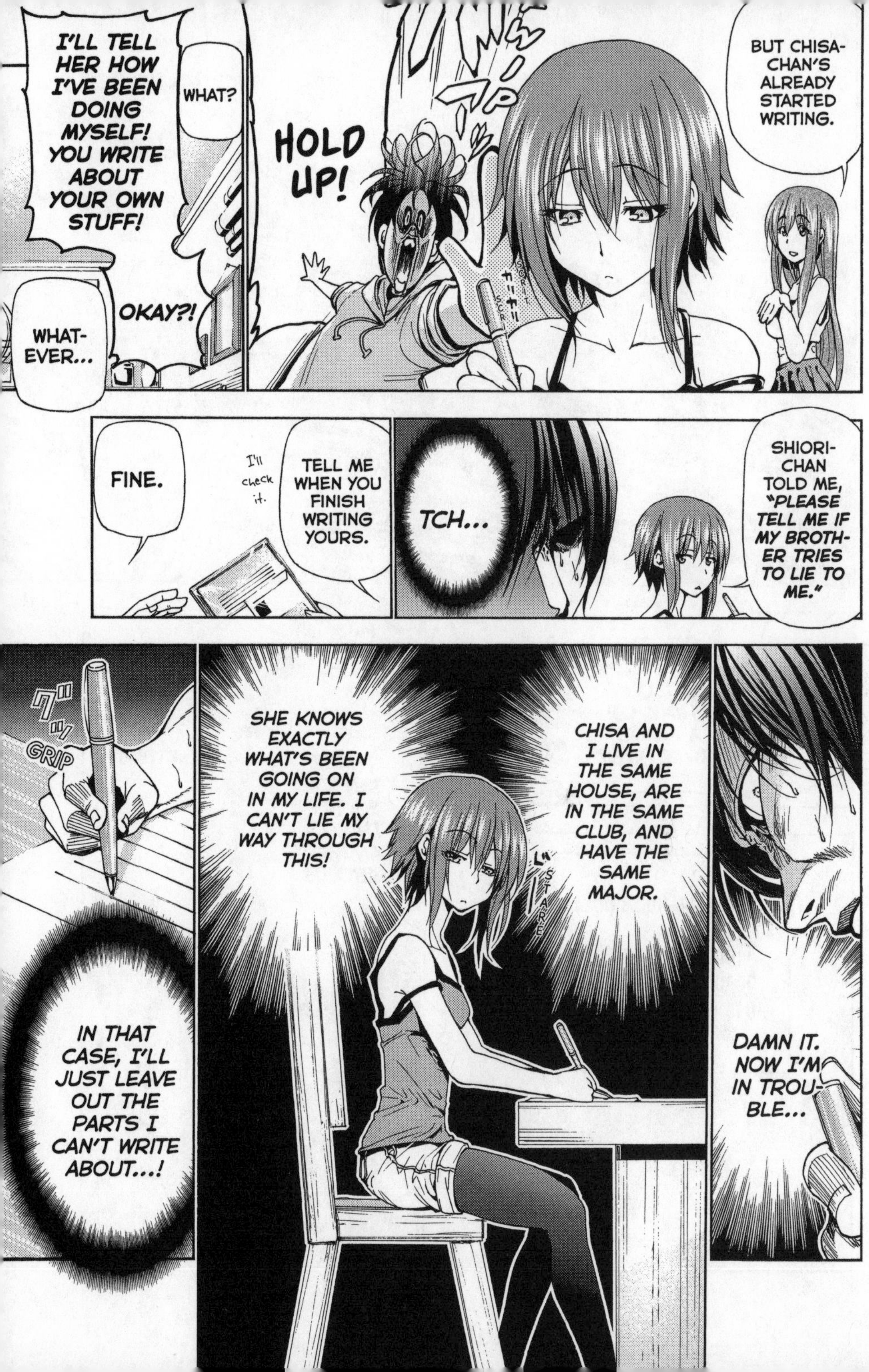
BUT CHISA-CHAN'S ALREADY STARTED WRITING.
SCRIT SCRIT
WHIP
HOLD UP!
I'LL TELL HER HOW I'VE BEEN DOING MYSELF! YOU WRITE ABOUT YOUR OWN STUFF!
WHAT?
OKAY?!
WHAT-EVER...
SHIORI-CHAN TOLD ME, "PLEASE TELL ME IF MY BROTH-ER TRIES TO LIE TO ME."
TCH...
TELL ME WHEN YOU FINISH WRITING YOURS.
I'll check it.
FINE.
DAMN IT. NOW I'M IN TROU-BLE...
CHISA AND I LIVE IN THE SAME HOUSE, ARE IN THE SAME CLUB, AND HAVE THE SAME MAJOR.
STARE
SHE KNOWS EXACTLY WHAT'S BEEN GOING ON IN MY LIFE. I CAN'T LIE MY WAY THROUGH THIS!
GRIP
IN THAT CASE, I'LL JUST LEAVE OUT THE PARTS I CAN'T WRITE ABOUT...!

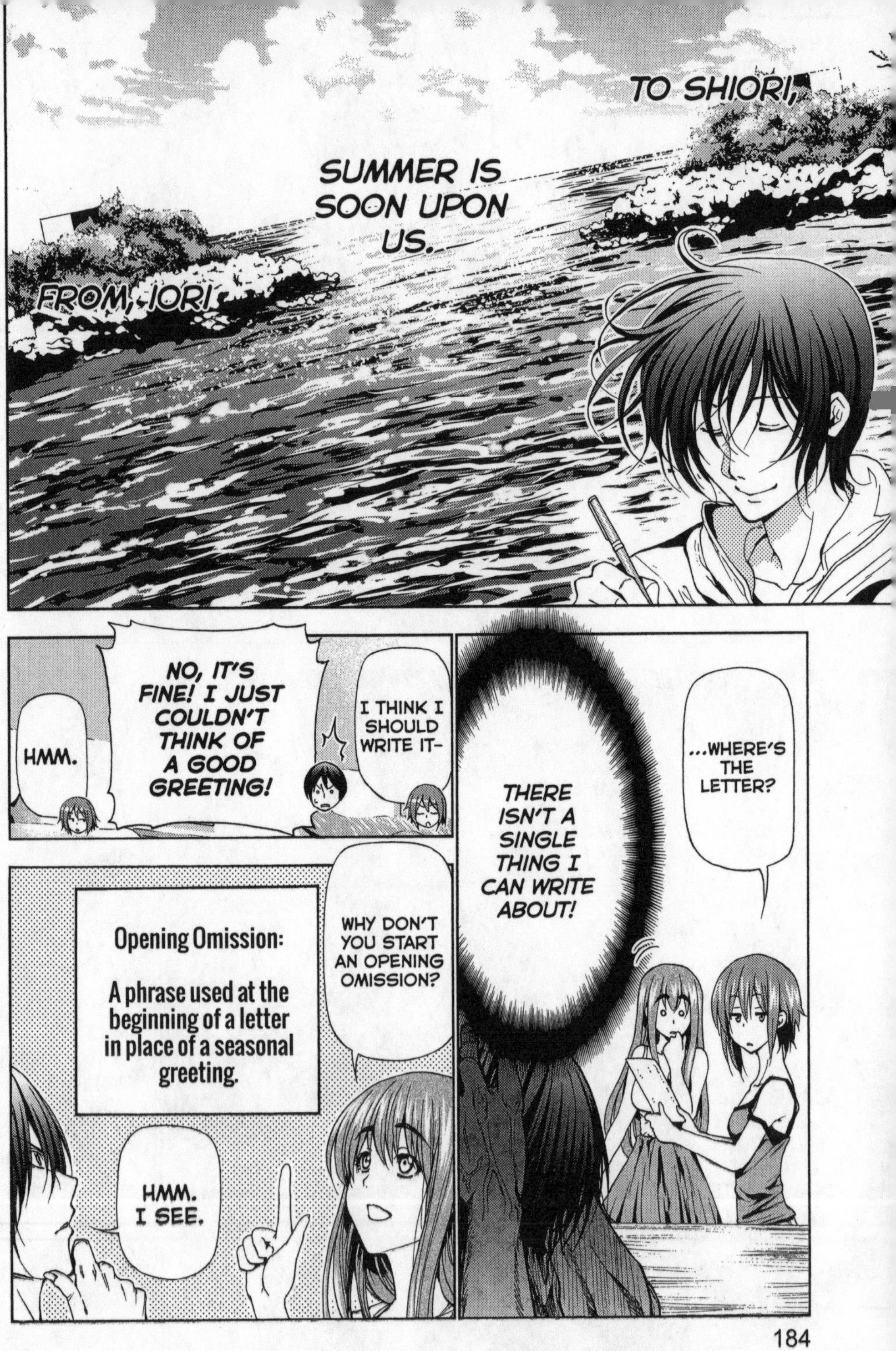
TO SHIORI,
SUMMER IS SOON UPON US.
FROM, IORI
...WHERE'S THE LETTER?
THERE ISN'T A SINGLE THING I CAN WRITE ABOUT!
I THINK I SHOULD WRITE IT-
NO, IT'S FINE! I JUST COULDN'T THINK OF A GOOD GREETING!
HMM.
WHY DON'T YOU START AN OPENING OMISSION?
Opening Omission: A phrase used at the beginning of a letter in place of a seasonal greeting.
HMM. I SEE.

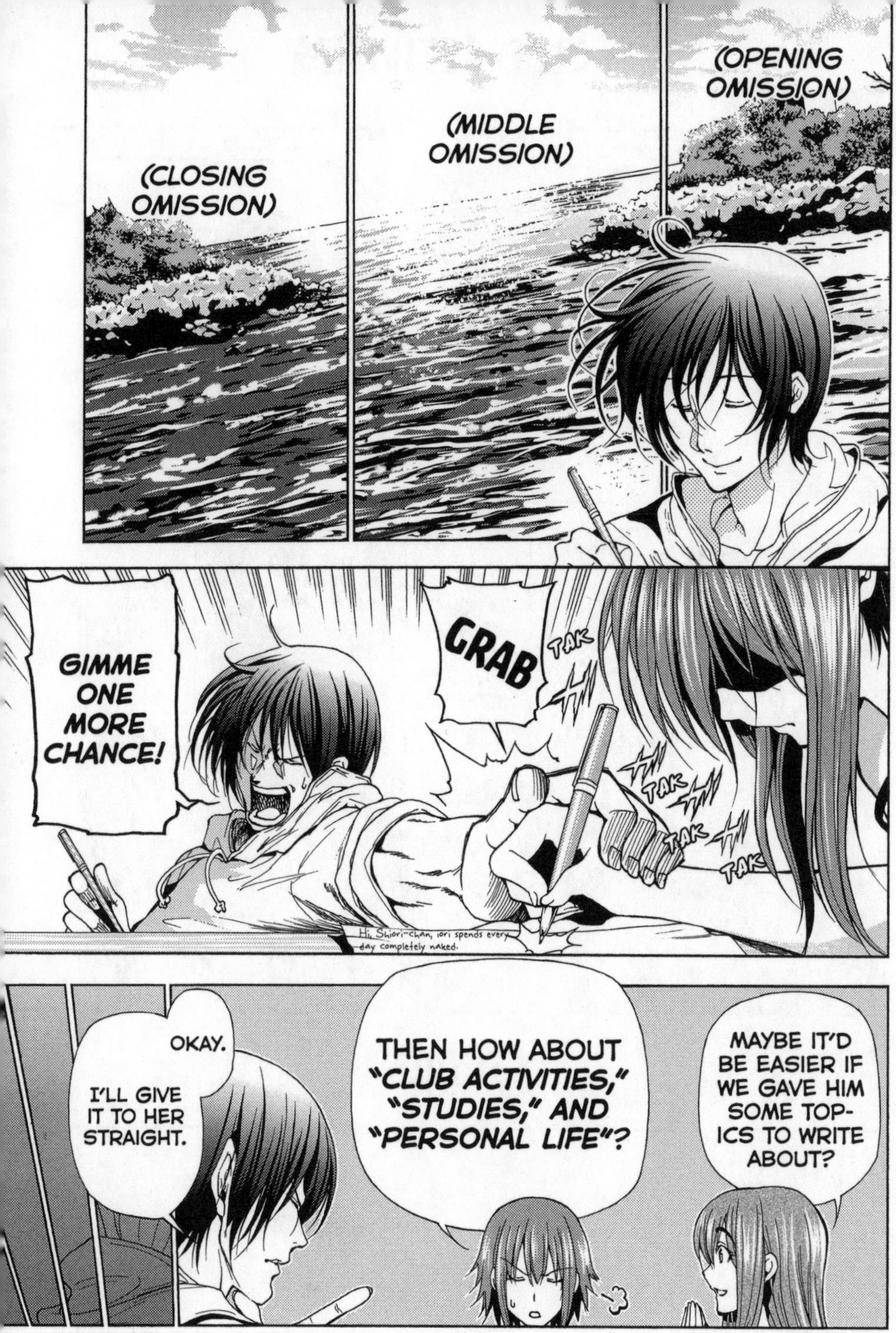
(OPENING OMISSION)
(MIDDLE OMISSION)
(CLOSING OMISSION)
TAK TAK TAK TAK
GRAB
GIMME ONE MORE CHANCE!
Hi, Shiori-chan, Iori spends every day completely naked.
MAYBE IT'D BE EASIER IF WE GAVE HIM SOME TOPICS TO WRITE ABOUT?
THEN HOW ABOUT "CLUB ACTIVITIES," "STUDIES," AND "PERSONAL LIFE"?
OKAY.
I'LL GIVE IT TO HER STRAIGHT.

CLUB ACTIVITIES

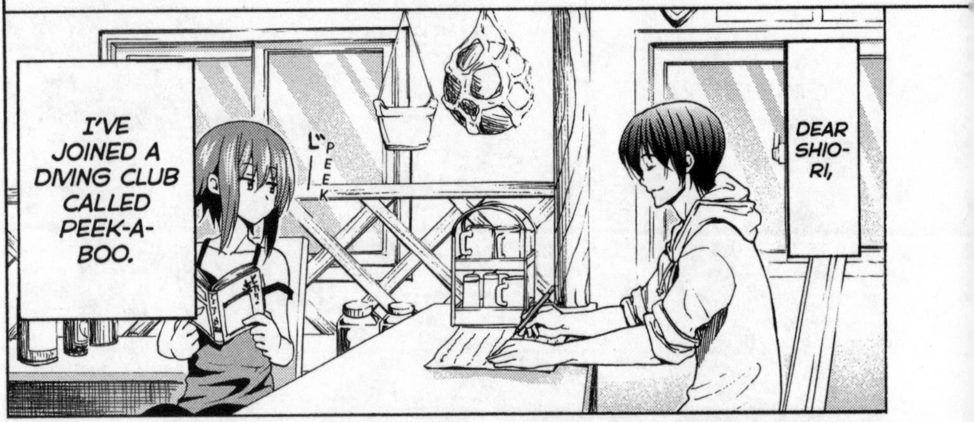
DEAR SHIO-RI,
PEEK
I'VE JOINED A DIVING CLUB CALLED PEEK-A-BOO.

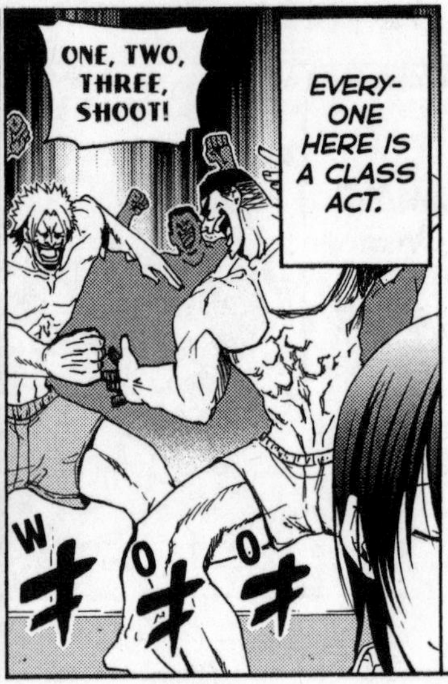
EVERY-ONE HERE IS A CLASS ACT.
ONE, TWO, THREE, SHOOT!
WOO

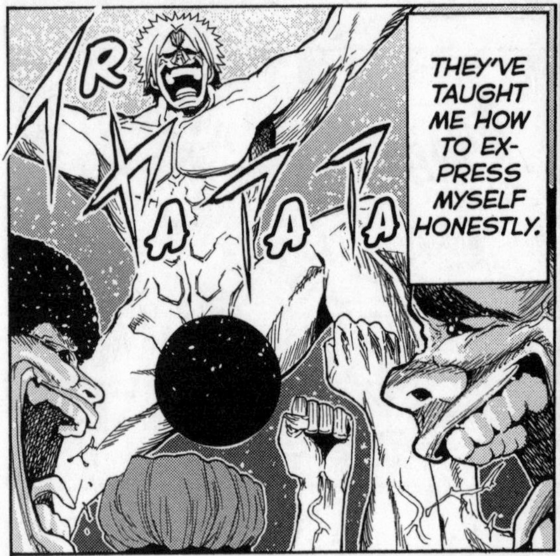
THEY'VE TAUGHT ME HOW TO EX-PRESS MYSELF HONESTLY.
RAAA

STUDIES

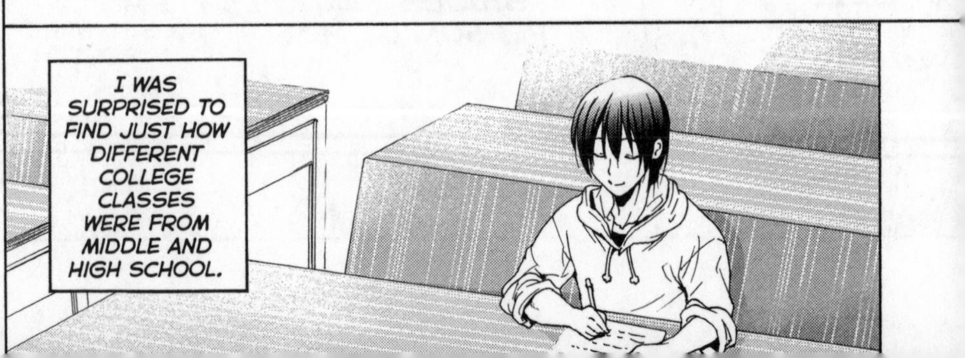
I WAS SURPRISED TO FIND JUST HOW DIFFERENT COLLEGE CLASSES WERE FROM MIDDLE AND HIGH SCHOOL.

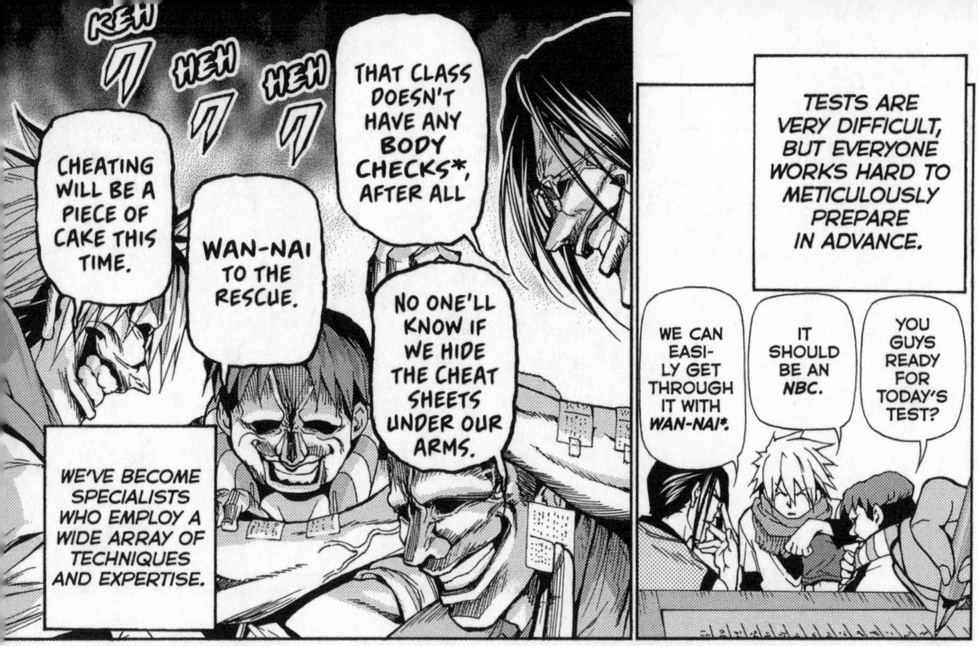
TESTS ARE VERY DIFFICULT, BUT EVERYONE WORKS HARD TO METICULOUSLY PREPARE IN ADVANCE.
YOU GUYS READY FOR TODAY'S TEST?
IT SHOULD BE AN NBC.
WE CAN EASILY GET THROUGH IT WITH WAN-NAI*.
THAT CLASS DOESN'T HAVE ANY BODY CHECKS*, AFTER ALL
KEH
HEH
HEH
CHEATING WILL BE A PIECE OF CAKE THIS TIME.
WAN-NAI TO THE RESCUE.
NO ONE'LL KNOW IF WE HIDE THE CHEAT SHEETS UNDER OUR ARMS.
WE'VE BECOME SPECIALISTS WHO EMPLOY A WIDE ARRAY OF TECHNIQUES AND EXPERTISE.

*Wan-nai: Inner-arm switcheroo

*NBC: No Body Check

PERSONAL LIFE

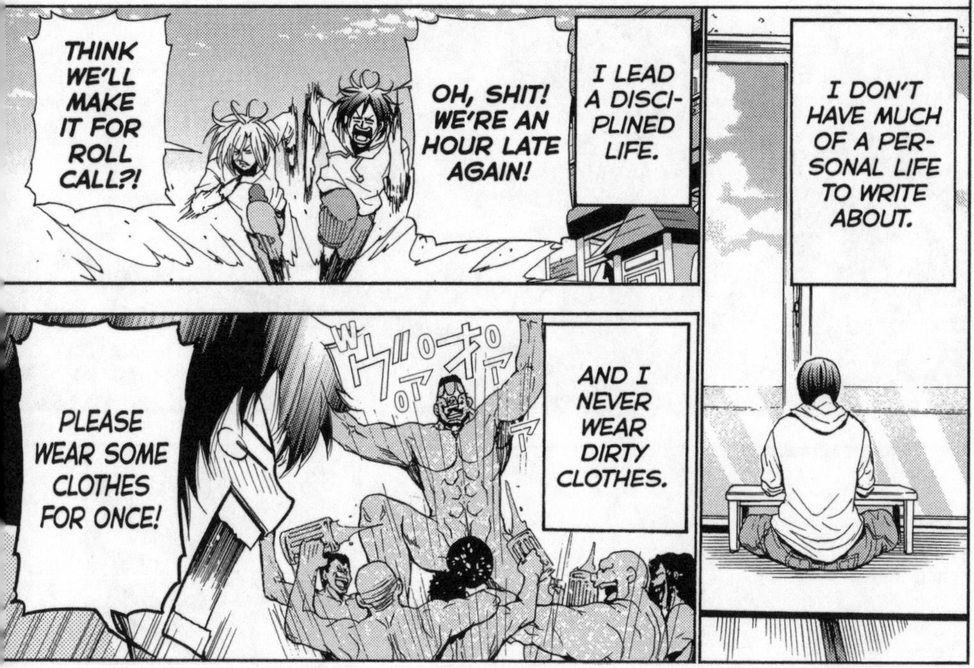
I DON'T HAVE MUCH OF A PERSONAL LIFE TO WRITE ABOUT.
I LEAD A DISCIPLINED LIFE.
OH, SHIT! WE'RE AN HOUR LATE AGAIN!
THINK WE'LL MAKE IT FOR ROLL CALL?!
AND I NEVER WEAR DIRTY CLOTHES.
PLEASE WEAR SOME CLOTHES FOR ONCE!

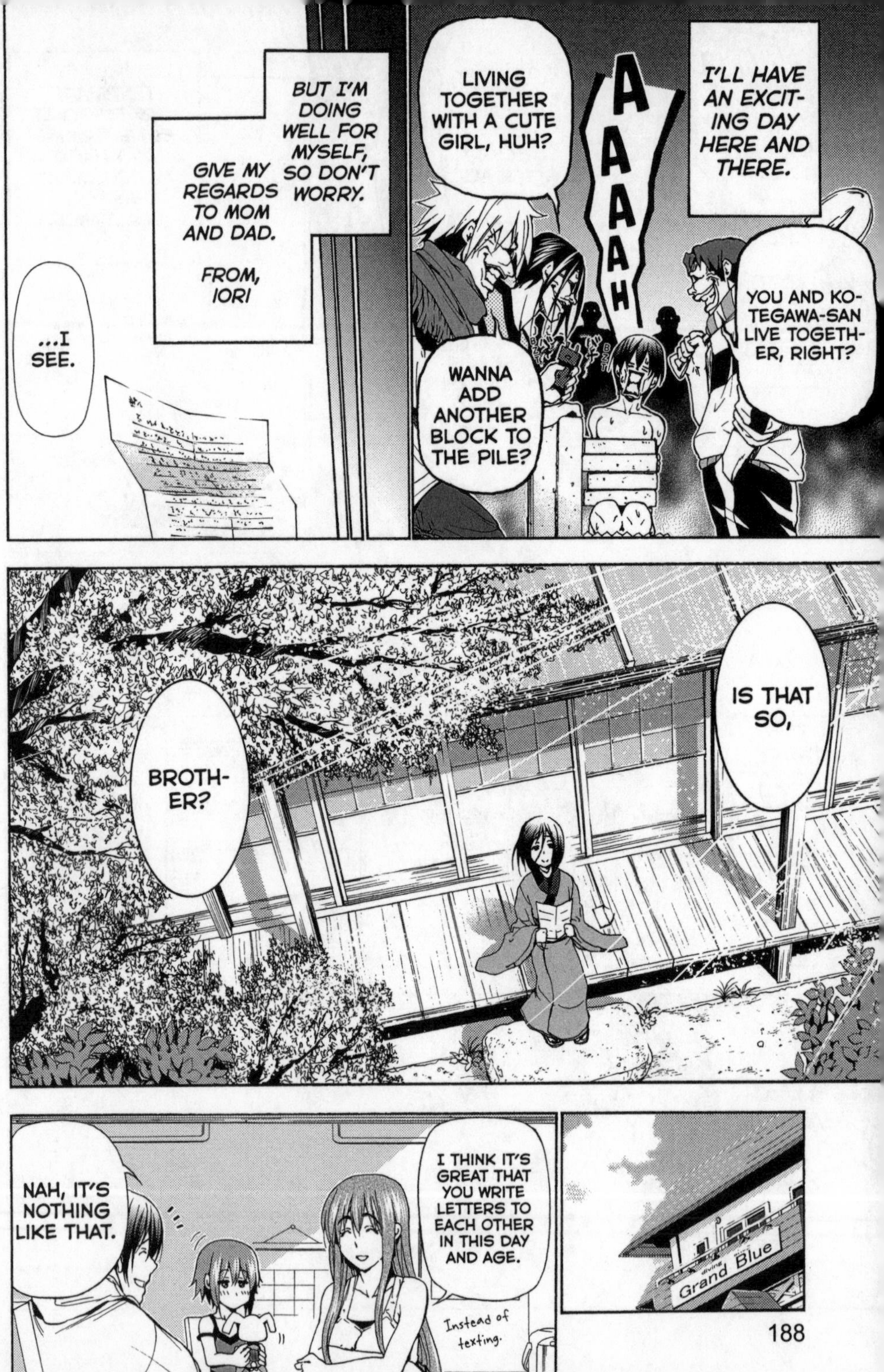
I'LL HAVE AN EXCITING DAY HERE AND THERE.
LIVING TOGETHER WITH A CUTE GIRL, HUH?
AAAAH
YOU AND KOTEGAWA-SAN LIVE TOGETHER, RIGHT?
WANNA ADD ANOTHER BLOCK TO THE PILE?
BZZT
BUT I'M DOING WELL FOR MYSELF, SO DON'T WORRY.
GIVE MY REGARDS TO MOM AND DAD.
FROM, IORI
...I SEE.
IS THAT SO,
BROTHER?
diving Grand Blue
I THINK IT'S GREAT THAT YOU WRITE LETTERS TO EACH OTHER IN THIS DAY AND AGE.
NAH, IT'S NOTHING LIKE THAT.
Instead of texting.

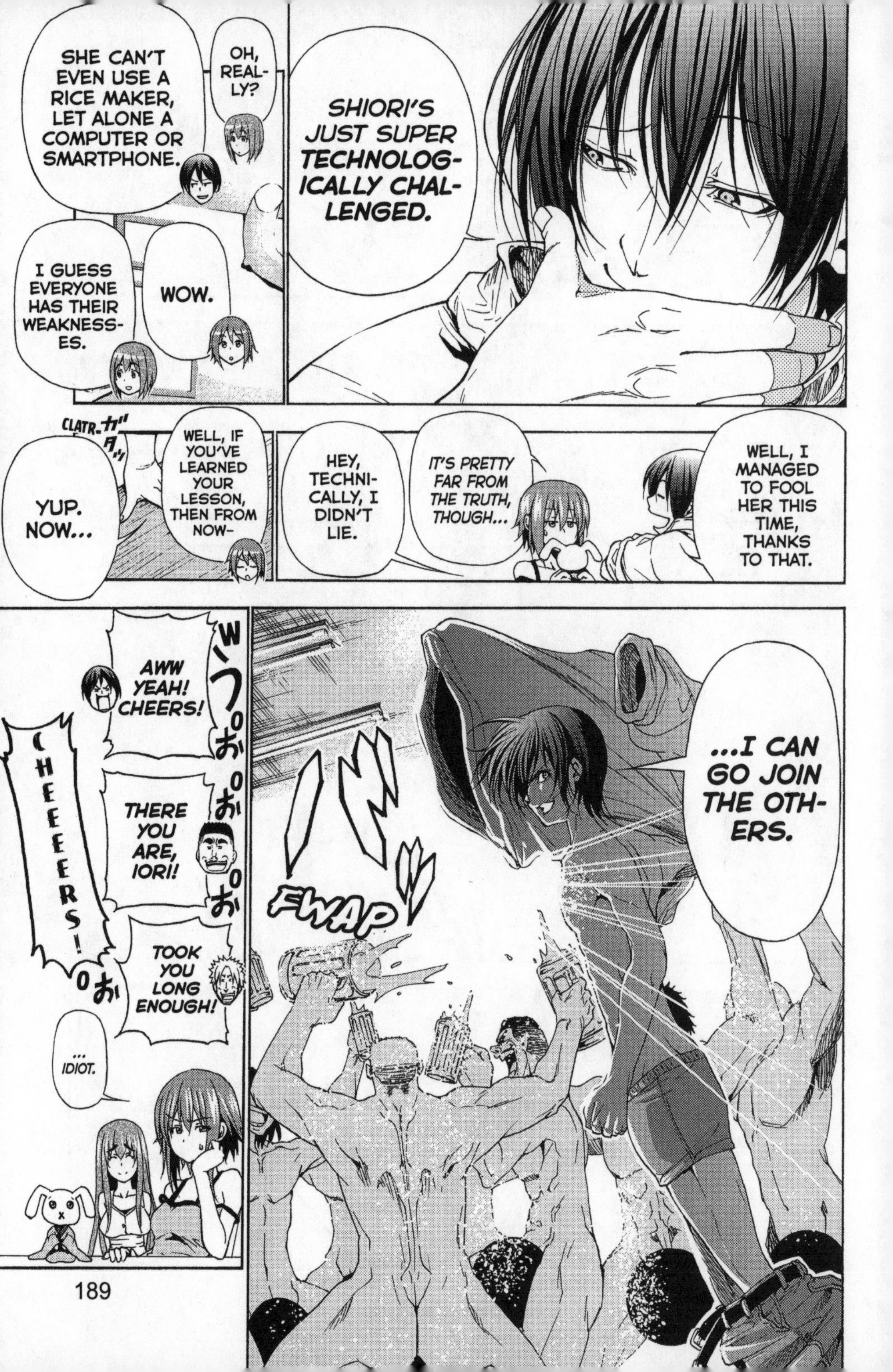
SHIORI'S JUST SUPER TECHNOLOGICALLY CHALLENGED.
SHE CAN'T EVEN USE A RICE MAKER, LET ALONE A COMPUTER OR SMARTPHONE.
OH, REALLY?
WOW.
I GUESS EVERYONE HAS THEIR WEAKNESSES.
WELL, I MANAGED TO FOOL HER THIS TIME, THANKS TO THAT.
IT'S PRETTY FAR FROM THE TRUTH, THOUGH...
HEY, TECHNICALLY, I DIDN'T LIE.
WELL, IF YOU'VE LEARNED YOUR LESSON, THEN FROM NOW-
CLATR- ガタッ
YUP. NOW...
...I CAN GO JOIN THE OTHERS.
FWAP
うぉおぉおぉおぉ
AWW YEAH! CHEERS!
THERE YOU ARE, IORI!
TOOK YOU LONG ENOUGH!
CHEEEERS!
...IDIOT.

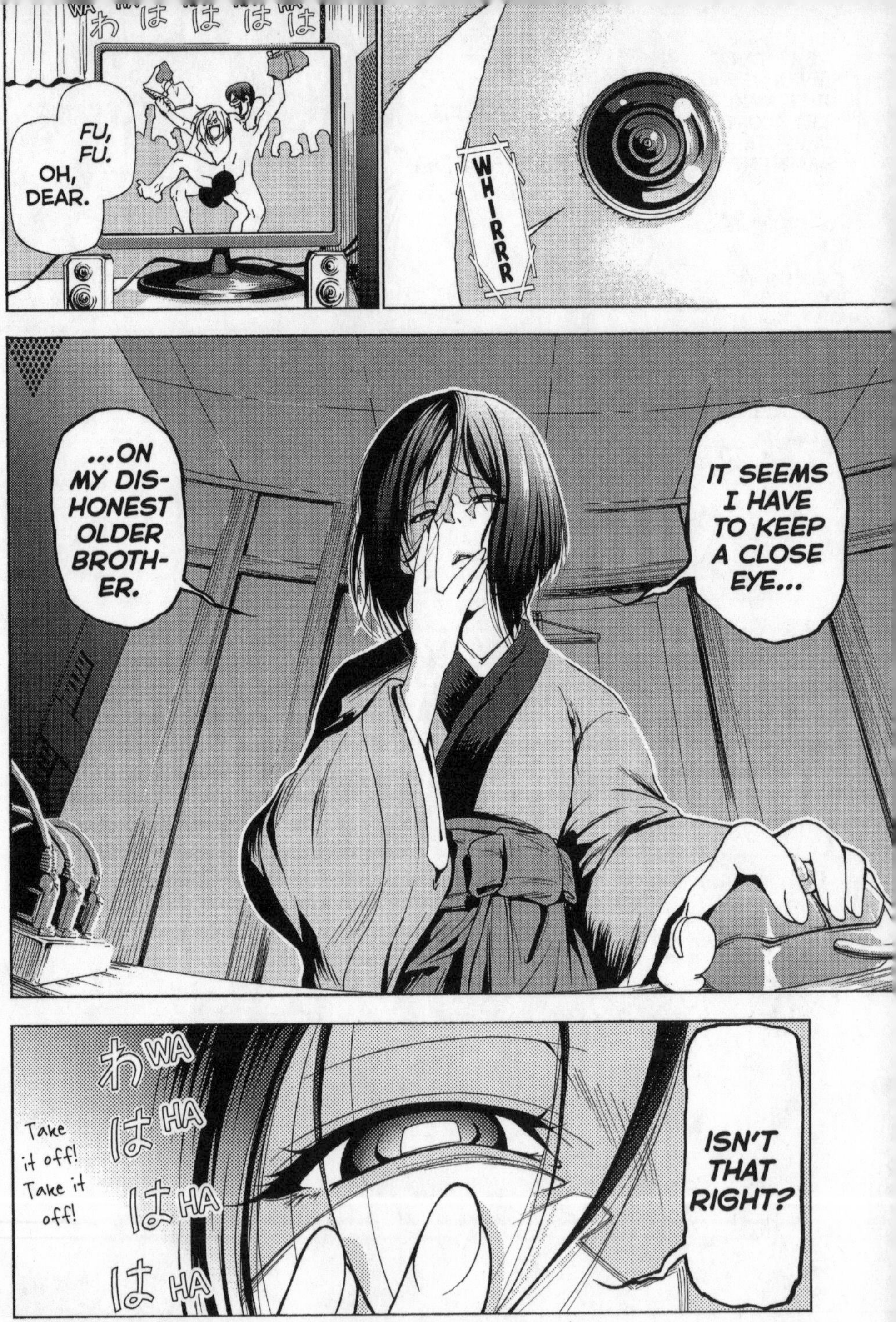
WHIRRR
わははは
FU, FU. OH, DEAR.
IT SEEMS I HAVE TO KEEP A CLOSE EYE...
...ON MY DISHONEST OLDER BROTHER.
ISN'T THAT RIGHT?
わ WA は HA は HA は HA
Take it off! Take it off!

Side Story/ End

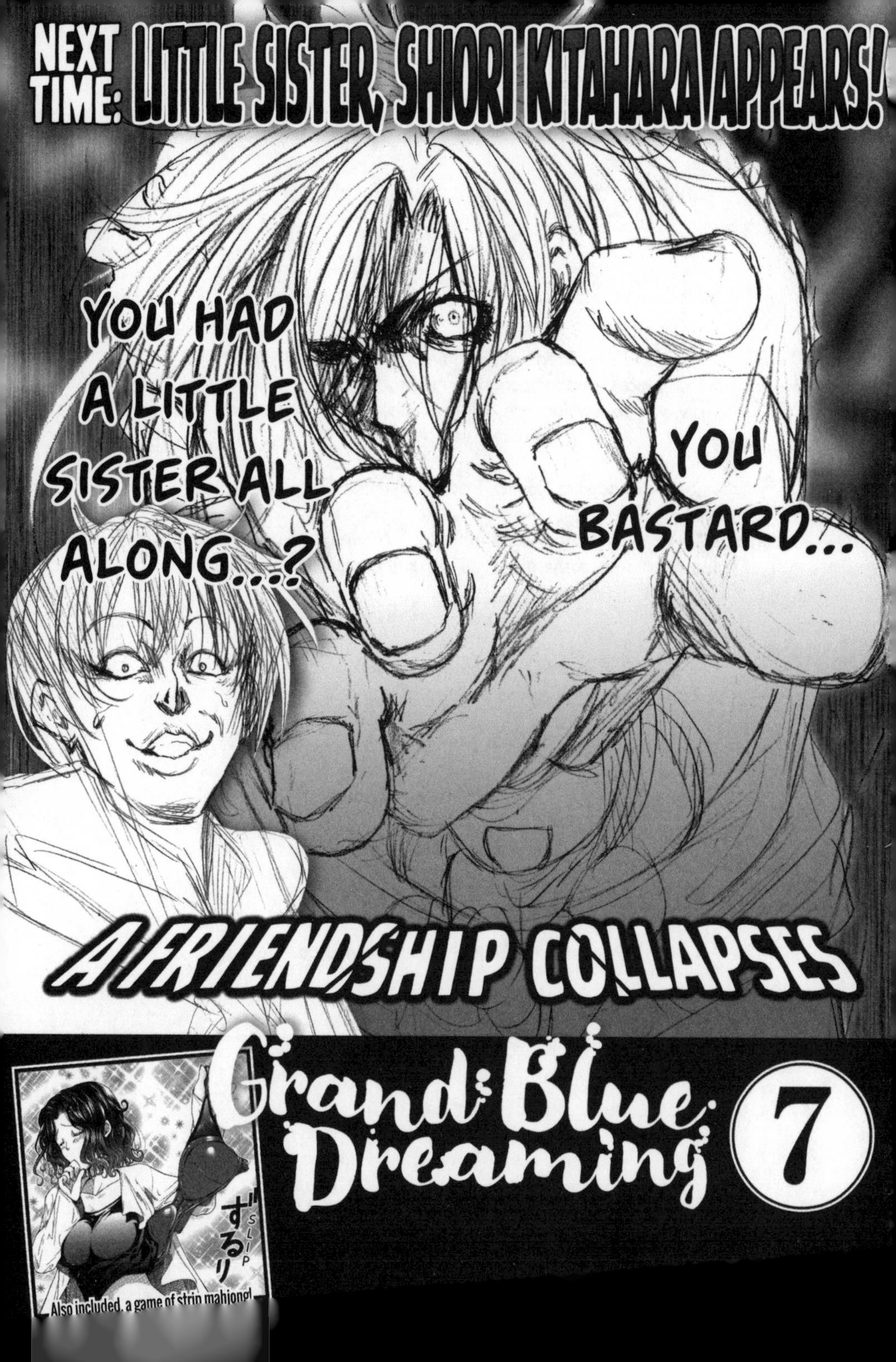
NEXT TIME: LITTLE SISTER, SHIORI KITAHARA APPEARS!
YOU HAD A LITTLE SISTER ALL ALONG...?
YOU BASTARD...
A FRIENDSHIP COLLAPSES
Grand Blue Dreaming 7
ずるり SLIP
Also included, a game of strip mahjong!

A Kodansha Comics Trade Paperback Original.

Published in the United States by Kodansha Comics,
an imprint of Kodansha USA Publishing, LLC, New York.

Publication rights for this English edition arranged through Kodansha Ltd., Tokyo.

First published in Japan in 2016 by Kodansha Ltd., Tokyo.

Cover Design: YUKI YOSHIDA (futaba)

ISBN 978-1-63236-725-9

Printed in the United States of America.

www.kodansha.us

9 8 7 6 5 4 3

Translation: Adam Hirsch
Lettering: Jan Lan Ivan Concepcion
Editing: Sarah Tilson and David Yoo
Editorial Assistance: YKS Services LLC/SKY Japan, INC.
Kodansha Comics Edition Cover Design: Phil Balsman